"BANGKOK! I THRILLED. I HAD BEEN SIX YEARS AT SEA, BUT HAD ONLY SEEN MELBOURNE AND SYDNEY, VERY GOOD PLACES, CHARMING PLACES IN THEIR WAY – BUT BANGKOK!"

JOSEPH CONRAD

Photographs: Chao Phraya River, c. 1890. Wat Arun gate, c. 1890.

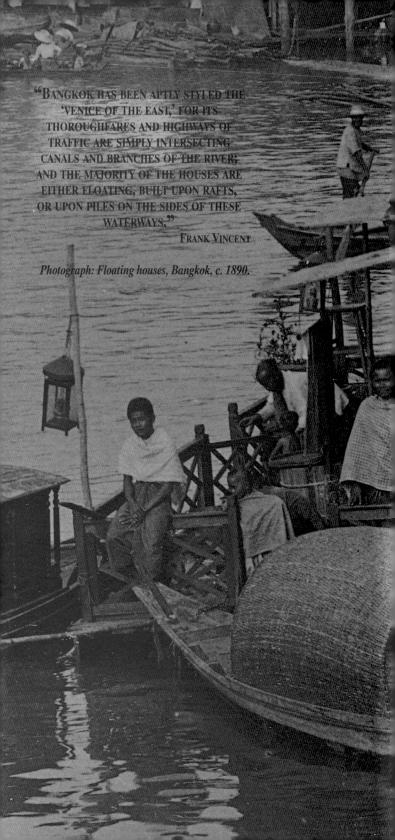

"BANGKOK HAS BEEN APTLY STYLED THE
'VENICE OF THE EAST,' FOR ITS
THOROUGHFARES AND HIGHWAYS OF
TRAFFIC ARE SIMPLY INTERSECTING
CANALS AND BRANCHES OF THE RIVER;
AND THE MAJORITY OF THE HOUSES ARE
EITHER FLOATING, BUILT UPON RAFTS,
OR UPON PILES ON THE SIDES OF THESE
WATERWAYS."

FRANK VINCENT

Photograph: Floating houses, Bangkok, c. 1890.

This is a Borzoi Book
published by Alfred A. Knopf

Completely revised
and updated in 2006

www.aaknopf.com

ISBN 10: 0-375-71107-4
ISBN 13: 978-0-375-71107-7

Originally published in France by Nouveaux
Loisirs, a subsidiary of Editions Gallimard,
Paris, 1993. Copyright © 1993 by Editions
Nouveaux Loisirs

Series editors
Shelley Wanger and Clémence Jacquinet

Translated by
Anthony Roberts

Edited and typeset by
Book Creation Services, London

Printed and bound in Italy by
Editoriale Lloyd

■ **EDITORIAL TEAM**
FOR THE ORIGINAL EDITION
Anne-Valérie Cadoret, Vivien Crump, Harry Tan,
Antoine Vidalin, Gwenhaelle Le Roy (update)
Production: Jeremy Chan
Layout: Jimmy Chan, Tan Tat Ghee
Illustrations: Anuar Bin Abdul Rahim
Picture research: Luca Invernizzi Tettoni
Graphics: Elizabeth Cohat
Nature: Michel Chantraine, Xavier Demangeon,
Kang Nee, David Stone, Manfred Wilkler
History and architecture: Dieter Ande,
Martine Buysschaert, M.L. Triyosudh Devakul,
Christine Hawixbrock
Art and traditions: Luca Invernizzi Tettoni,
William Warren

ITINERARIES IN THAILAND:
Christine Hawixbrock, Christine Lorian,
Luca Invernizzi Tettoni, William Warren
North Hill Tribes: Hansiorg Mayer

PHOTOGRAPHY :
Éric Guillemot, Patrick Léger, and Luca Invernizzi
Tettoni (National Tourist Office of Thailand)

Numerous specialists and academics have
contributed to this guide.
Special thanks to: William Warren,
David Stone and Luca Invernizzi Tettoni.

THAILAND

KNOPF GUIDES

CONTENTS

HOW TO USE THIS GUIDE

The symbols at the top of
each page refer to
the different parts
of the guide.

■ NATURAL ENVIRONMENT

● UNDERSTANDING VENICE

▲ ITINERARIES

◆ PRACTICAL INFORMATION

The itinerary map
shows the main points
of interest along the
way and is intended
to help you find
your bearings.

The mini-map
locates the particular
itinerary within
the wider area
covered by
the guide.

CANNAREGIO

*The gateway to
Venice, after all, is
neither the station
nor the Piazzale,
but the Grand Canal
before its churned
by propellers,
refracted into a
green river as a*

Fernand Braudel, *Venice*

Santa Lucia Station.

Immediately outside the railway station lies Cannaregio, the
first of the six sestieri of Venice. Situated at the north-west
end of the city, this is the second largest sestiere after Castello
▲ 155, covering an area of 150 hectares. Nearly a third of the
population of Venice is concentrated here, amounting to
more than twenty thousand people. There are two theories
about the origin of the name Cannaregio, according to one,
it comes from Canal regio (the Royal Canal), meaning the
broad waterway which once provided convenient access to the
city from the mainland, by draining the lagoon. Canal of San
Secundo (which runs parallel to the Palazzo bridge). The
other hypothesis is that the word derives from the reeds and
canes which used to abound in this area. In any case, a system
of straight, parallel canals, with long fondamenta abutting
southwards and linked by calli, criss-cross this zone of
workmen's houses interspersed with magnificent palaces. To
the south, behind the houses the Strada Nuova was built at the
end of the last century. Now known as the Campo Santi
street runs from the station to the Campo Santi
Apostoli, crossing the section of different names to
other and adopting a number of different names to
it goes. Few people lived in this sestiere until the
11th century, and it seems to have taken form only
gradually, as the process of drawing and
consolidation of the site progressed. From the 15th
century onwards, Cannaregio was a definable quarter, though
it was still peripheral to Venice proper. Before the railway
bridge and the station were built, manufacturing was the
principal industry in the district, despite attempts to create a
new area of growth with the Fondamenta Nuove. A similar
project in the 16th century, the draining of the Sacca della
Misericordia, was also never realized.

THE GATEWAY TO VENICE ★

PONTE DELLA LIBERTA. Built by the Austrians 50 years after
the Treaty of Campo Formio in 1797 ● 34, to link Venice with
Milan. This bridge ended the thousand-year separation from
the mainland and shook the city's economy to its roots as
Venice, already in the throes of the industrial revolution, saw
its dependence on the mainland grow out of all recognition.
SANTA LUCIA STATION. The present station dates from 1955,
but still bears the name of the Renaissance church
demolished in 1861 to make way for it. Opposite is the green
domes of the Church of San Simeone Piccolo.

 ✹ Half a day

BRIDGES TO VENICE
The Austrians
conceived a project
for a bridge between
Mestre and Venice as
early as 1814, but it
was not until 1846
that the construction
of the Ponte
della Liberta was finally
begun. The bridge
boasts an immense
span of
almost 11,800 feet,
and is carried on
222 stone arches. On
April 25, 1933, the
Ponte della Liberta,
then more than
11,800 feet, was
extended by the
engineer Eugenio
Miozzi. Built in the
this bridge was
intended for use by
motor cars.

136

136

● ▲ ■ ◆
The symbols alongside a
title or within the text
itself provide cross-
references to a theme
or place dealt with
elsewhere in the guide.

★ The star symbol
signifies that a particular
site has been singled out
by the publishers for its
special beauty,
atmosphere or cultural
interest.

At the beginning of each
itinerary, the suggested
means of transport to be
used and the time it will
take to cover the area are
indicated:

 🚤 By boat
 ✹ On foot
 🚲 By bicycle
 🕒 Duration

THE GATEWAY TO VENICE ★

PONTE DELLA LIBERTA. Built by the Austrians 50 years after
the Treaty of Campo Formio in 1797 ● *34,* to link Venice with
Milan. The bridge ended the thousand-year separation from
the mainland and shook the city's economy to its roots as
Venice, already in the throes of the industrial revolution, saw

 ✹ Half a day

BRIDGES TO VENICE

Nature

RED RHODODENDRON

Much of Thailand's natural heritage is due to the shape of the country, a stretched ribbon of land over 900 miles long, spanning both seasonally dry zones and habitats where rain falls throughout the year. The present-day Thai landscape has been molded by the actions of various colonists in the past, with farming being the most important influence. About 20,000 square miles of the country are set aside as conservation areas (for example, northeast Thailand national parks ▲ *238–40*), many of which are open to the public, offering visitors an opportunity to encounter a wide range of plants and animals within a natural environment.

Tropical rain forest

Savanna

Monsoon forest

KOUPREY
Once a widely distributed species, the kouprey is today one of the most seriously threatened large mammals in the world.

BARKING DEER
Also called *muntjac*, these solitary animals are found in woodlands, rain forests and monsoon forests with dense vegetation.

MIXED DECIDUOUS FOREST
It supports a great proportion of the country's interesting and varied wildlife.

BANTENG
The banteng is a species of wild ox native to Southeast Asia.

UNDERWATER WORLD

TROPICAL RAIN FOREST
It is one of the richest ecosystems on the planet today.

MANGROVES
Coastal mangrove formations help protect shorelines from erosion and also provide a safe haven and nursery ground for a huge variety of fish species.

RIVERINE GRASSLANDS
Open patches of riverine grassland and savanna are important feeding and browsing areas for many forest herbivores. Many areas of grassland were formerly forested but regular outbreaks of fire prevent woody regeneration of these areas.

MONITOR LIZARD
The monitor lizard is a diurnal species that feeds on insects, eggs, fish, other lizards, snakes, nestling birds and small mammals.

GLORIOSA SUPERBA

HORNBILL
The strong and often ornate beak of the hornbill is perfectly molded for picking and cracking large fruit and seed pods from a wide range of forest plants.

LEAF MONKEY (1) AND GIBBON (2)
These primates dwell in the forest canopy and feed on fruit and leaves. The leaf monkey has a large, especially adapted stomach similar to that of a cow.

ASIAN BLACK BEAR
The Asian black bear is a forest dweller that feeds mainly on nuts and fruit, as well as ants, insect larvae and carrion.

MONTANE EVERGREEN FOREST
This is typified by an open canopy with trees festooned in lichens and epiphytes. Trees are also much shorter and less straight when compared with those of lowland forest.

HILL EVERGREEN RAIN FOREST
Climbing from montane evergreen forests, an unclear transition zone of slightly smaller trees that are widely spaced apart lies at an altitude of 2,300–2,600 feet above sea level.

EVERGREEN RAIN FOREST
True evergreen rain forest exists only in the extreme southern region of peninsular Thailand, near the Malaysian border.

WILD GINGER
One of a large number of economically valuable plants that grow wild in the forests of Thailand, the wild ginger plant is believed to have a number of medicinal healing properties that are now being investigated.

FUNGI
As part of the nutrient recycling scheme of the natural forest, fungi play an essential role in all forests and woodlands.

DRY DECIDUOUS WOODLANDS
Extensive dry deciduous woodlands with some dipterocarp species still occur in the north and east of the country.

BAMBOO FOREST
Bamboo stands are present in monsoon forests and generally thrive in areas previously cleared by man, blocking out most growth beneath their lofty foliage.

GREEN PEAFOWL
The only viable population of green peafowls remaining in Thailand is found in the Huai Kha Khaeng Wildlife Sanctuary where about 300 birds gain refuge.

TROPICAL FORESTS

Tropical forests are like a kaleidoscope of different worlds. They cover a fifth of the earth's land surface and are home to about half of the known species of animal and plant life. The forests ▲ *238–40* are confined to a belt around the equator, where the stable climate, temperature and humidity permit a great diversity of vegetation and wildlife.

162 FEET

EMERGENT LAYER
The few emergent trees above the canopy are home to insectivorous bats and birds such as eagles and hornbills.

122 FEET

CANOPY LAYER
The canopy is a continuous layer of foliage about 22 feet deep that supports a broad variety of animals. Mammals like flying squirrels, gibbons and macaques feed on the rich supply of fruit, leaves, bark and nuts.

FLYING SQUIRREL

PIG-TAILED MACAQUES
These are diurnal primates, living in groups of 15–30 animals, feeding on fruit, small vertebrates and insects. They are mostly found in hill forests.

Constant temperature and high humidity levels favor the growth of lianas, trailing vines, lichens and epiphytes.

FOLIAGE
The leaves of the canopy can change their positions in order to catch the maximum amount of sunlight. Their drip-tips allow the rain to drain away and the waxy coating is a protection against algae and moss.

79 FEET

UNDERSTORY
Mammals like the peculiar binturong, pangolin and civet move freely in the understory between the ground and the upper tree layer in search of morsels and a safe place to rest.

The buttress or stilt-like roots of the trees help support them in the shallow soil.

41 FEET

FOREST FLOOR
At the top of the food chain are predators such as tigers or leopards that stalk their wary prey in the shade of the lower canopy and the forest floor.

TAPIR
A shy forest-dweller, this herbivore is often found near quiet rivers and wallows, feeding on leaves and small trees.

GROUND
The plants, insects and fungi that dwell at ground level are fed upon by mammals and birds.

The dark forest floor is alive with communities of omnivorous insects such as ants and termites.

N   Ph   K   Ca   Mg   C

NUTRIENT STORAGE

While in temperate forests a high proportion of nutrients is held in the soil (left-hand columns, above); in the poorer tropical soil, they are held in the biomass (right-hand columns, above). Because the scarce soil nutrients are found near the surface, the roots of the trees seldom grow deeper than 26 feet.

SILVER-EARED MESIA

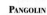

BINTURONG
Resembling a small bear, the binturong has a bushy, prehensile tail that enables it to feed in the trees as well as on the ground.

BLACK-THROATED SUNBIRD

PALM CIVET
The agile small-toothed palm civet is a nocturnal species that searches for insects, fruit and small mammals in the branches of tall secondary forests.

ELEPHANT
The largest land mammal in Thailand, the Asian elephant is now a rare sight, with fewer than 3,000 animals remaining. Most of them are found in the national parks of the northeast.

SLOW LORIS
This is a solitary nocturnal primate with large eyes and a thickly furred body.

TIGER
This is the largest member of the cat family; fewer than 250 now survive in Thailand.

CLOUDED LEOPARD
Living in tall secondary forests, the clouded leopard is a nocturnal predator that feeds on pigs, deer, monkeys and smaller animals.

PANGOLIN
The scaly armor plating of the pangolin allows it to roll into a tight ball when threatened. It feeds exclusively on ants and termites.

NUTRIENTS RECYCLING

Different forms of plants and animals have evolved in harmony on the forest floor to recycle decaying materials such as leaves and tree trunks, returning valuable nutrients back to the soil. In time these are taken up by other plants, sustaining the incredible diversity that exists in the forest and thereby continuing the natural cycle that began millions of years ago. The harmony and natural balance of this network is threatened by deforestation, shifting agriculture and human intrusions.

19

The orchid family is the largest of the flower kingdom, with more than 35,000 wild species and as many hybrids. Thailand's tropical forests ▲ 238–40 and mangroves ■ 22–3 host an amazing diversity of both terrestrial and epiphytic species, presenting a vast array of shapes, sizes, vibrant colors and intoxicating perfumes. Breeders in orchid farms ▲ 290 continually produce new hybrid species using artificial cross-pollination and propagation methods. Their creations are in great demand for the international cut flower market.

VENUS' SLIPPER
This yellow terrestrial orchid is found growing at low altitudes in limestone crevices near the coastal areas of Thailand, southern Burma and Cambodia.

CORYBAS
This terrestrial orchid named after the *Corybas*, the dancing priests of Phrygia, because of its helmet-shaped sepals, lives in the dark undergrowth of the rain forest. It thrives on the abundant supply of moisture and nutrients of the forest soil.

CYMBIDIUM SIAMENSIS
Cymbidium orchids, from the Greek word *kymbion*, which means boat-shaped, were praised by Confucius as the "queen of all flowers." Although such orchids occur all over Asia, this particular ivory species is native to Thailand where it grows at altitudes of between 1,000 and 2,500 feet.

GARDENS IN THE AIR
Falling organic litter lodged between the tree branches forms a rich soil in which epiphytic plants such as bromeliads and orchids grow. Orchids are non-parasitic species. Their elaborate structure allows them to make the most of the supply of rainwater and nutrients without damaging their host plants.

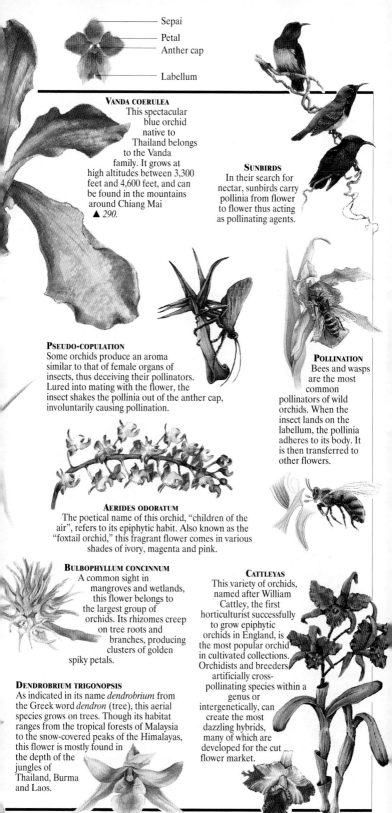

Sepai
Petal
Anther cap

Labellum

VANDA COERULEA
This spectacular blue orchid native to Thailand belongs to the Vanda family. It grows at high altitudes between 3,300 feet and 4,600 feet, and can be found in the mountains around Chiang Mai ▲ *290*.

SUNBIRDS
In their search for nectar, sunbirds carry pollinia from flower to flower thus acting as pollinating agents.

PSEUDO-COPULATION
Some orchids produce an aroma similar to that of female organs of insects, thus deceiving their pollinators. Lured into mating with the flower, the insect shakes the pollinia out of the anther cap, involuntarily causing pollination.

POLLINATION
Bees and wasps are the most common pollinators of wild orchids. When the insect lands on the labellum, the pollinia adheres to its body. It is then transferred to other flowers.

AERIDES ODORATUM
The poetical name of this orchid, "children of the air", refers to its epiphytic habit. Also known as the "foxtail orchid," this fragrant flower comes in various shades of ivory, magenta and pink.

BULBOPHYLLUM CONCINNUM
A common sight in mangroves and wetlands, this flower belongs to the largest group of orchids. Its rhizomes creep on tree roots and branches, producing clusters of golden spiky petals.

CATTLEYAS
This variety of orchids, named after William Cattley, the first horticulturist successfully to grow epiphytic orchids in England, is the most popular orchid in cultivated collections. Orchidists and breeders artificially cross-pollinating species within a genus or intergenetically, can create the most dazzling hybrids, many of which are developed for the cut flower market.

DENDROBRIUM TRIGONOPSIS
As indicated in its name *dendrobrium* from the Greek word *dendron* (tree), this aerial species grows on trees. Though its habitat ranges from the tropical forests of Malaysia to the snow-covered peaks of the Himalayas, this flower is mostly found in the depth of the jungles of Thailand, Burma and Laos.

21

Mangroves and intertidal mudflats are of great conservation value in Thailand, helping sustain valuable inshore fisheries and protecting the coast from erosion. With a constant supply of water, sunlight and nutrients the rate of growth of mangrove trees is very fast. The most extensive and species-rich mangrove ecosystems are found along the west coast of the peninsula ▲ 218–19, 220, 224. There are also several important mangroves and mudflats on the east coast, as well as in the inner gulf, although large areas have been converted to prawn ponds. The total area of mangrove forest is about 2,300 square miles most of which are along the west coast.

The fruit of the Nipa palm is edible. The Nipa borders waterways in the mangrove deltas off the open sea and usually covers much of the swamp area.

Hardy fruits of *Amoora calcullata* and *Xylocarpus gremata*. There are few flowers or fruits in the mangrove forest.

Crab-eating macaques are one of the numerous mammal species living in this environment.

Charcoal making is one of the many threats facing the coastal mangrove forest. Shrimp farming is another.

Free form furniture, made from the roots of the mangrove.

Cross-section of the mangrove coastline. The swamps are criss-crossed by tidal channels, which are often bordered by the Nipa palm. The mangrove's enormous root systems are the dominant feature of the habitat. It extends to the low tide mark, below which the roots cannot obtain enough oxygen for growth. Where the ground rises above high tide mark level away from the open sea, the surroundings gradually assume the character of lowland rain forest.

A mangrove coast in southern Thailand, covering sinking limestone ranges millions of years old. As the sea level changes, the mangrove forest cover advances or retreats.

The Brahmini kite circles above the mangrove.

This large estuarine crocodile is rarely seen. Forest clearance and aquaculture projects are responsible for its dwindling numbers ▲ 191.

The mangrove snake is particularly adapted to this unusual habitat and is found just above the water level.

The collared kingfisher (1), gray heron (2) and little cormorant (3) are bird species common in the coastal swamps and mud flats.

Rhizophora mucronata produces pointed spikes (right) that form effective instant seedlings. Equipped with tiny leaves at the top end, they drop off the parent into the mud below and take root at once. Apart from this unusual mode of propagation, *Rhizophora mucronata* produces conventional seeds as well.

Below the water level, the mud and the roots give shelter to a plethora of marine life, including fish, crabs and molluscs.

RICEFIELDS

CRIMSON HERON

An extraordinary amount of human energy is invested in producing the rice crop throughout the year. Rice plays an important role in the daily lives of the people, providing the staple diet for the Thai population as well as being a major export crop. Many cultural rituals are closely tied to the cultivation of rice and complex calculations are made to predict forthcoming rainfall patterns and the bounty of future crops. Little has changed in the ricefields of Thailand ▲ *246–7* over the centuries and, in addition to providing an important wildlife refuge for a large number of species, they also remain a source of great spiritual and intellectual inspiration.

PAPAYA TREES
All available land is cultivated. Papaya and banana trees are frequently planted on the verges of the ricefields.

BEAST OF BURDEN
Although mechanical means of plowing ricefields are now available, most farmers still prefer traditional means of cultivation involving the use of the water buffalo as a general beast of burden. Known locally as the "Asian tractor", the water buffalo is also an important source of milk and meat for many people. Its hide is used in clothing and its dung is collected as a fertilizer or as a source of fuel for burning.

1. PREPARING THE LAND
The farmer and the water buffalo drag a heavy plow to loosen up the water-logged soil, and their trampling actions also help to redistribute the valuable nutrients stored in the soil. Prior to planting, a heavy log is pulled across the muddy base to prepare a firm bed for the young seedlings.

LIFE AT THE WATER'S EDGE
The ricefield provides an ideal habitat for reptiles, fish and amphibians. Many of the fields are deliberately stocked with carp and catfish, which feed on decaying plants, algae and insect larvae. Frogs also help control the level of harmful insects, thereby eliminating the use of costly and often destructive pesticides.

2. TRANSPLANTING THE SEEDLINGS
Once the ricefield has been flooded and suitably prepared, bunches of bright green seedlings are transplanted from the tiny nursery beds where they were raised. This work is done entirely by hand, people laboring all day to set out row upon row of tender young plants. The softened mud base facilitates the planting process and seedlings quickly take root in this habitat.

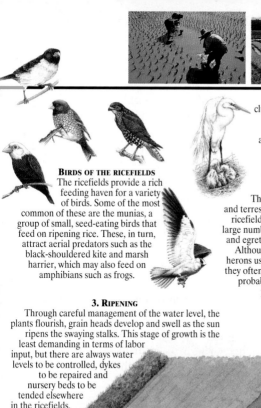

The bright green seedlings clustered in ricefields prior to transplanting and the sun-drenched fields of rice that await harvesting are familiar sights in Thailand.

BIRDS OF THE RICEFIELDS
The ricefields provide a rich feeding haven for a variety of birds. Some of the most common of these are the munias, a group of small, seed-eating birds that feed on ripening rice. These, in turn, attract aerial predators such as the black-shouldered kite and marsh harrier, which may also feed on amphibians such as frogs.

EGRETS AND HERONS
The rich aquatic and terrestrial life of the ricefields attracts large numbers of herons and egrets in all seasons. Although egrets and herons usually feed alone, they often roost together, which probably assists in detecting predators ▲ 208.

3. RIPENING
Through careful management of the water level, the plants flourish, grain heads develop and swell as the sun ripens the swaying stalks. This stage of growth is the least demanding in terms of labor input, but there are always water levels to be controlled, dykes to be repaired and nursery beds to be tended elsewhere in the ricefields.

COMB DUCK
The comb duck is a frequent visitor to ricefields and it nests on the edges of wooded marshland. It flies with broad wing beats.

HARVESTING THE RICE AND THRESHING
The long stalks of ripe corn are harvested and then beaten over a drum to dislodge the grains from the chaff. Winnowing sifts off any remaining waste while the plump rice grains are dried in the sun before being stored.

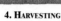

4. HARVESTING
The harvesting of a paddy crop marks the end of a long period of hard labor and no time is lost in cutting the ripened golden stalks lest wild animals or inclement weather threaten to destroy the season's efforts. Rice stalks are harvested using a sharp sickle; the cutter lays the stalks tenderly on the ground in his wake. Later these will be collected and stacked, prior to threshing.

PESTS IN THE RICEFIELDS
The ricefield mouse and rat are common inhabitants of all ricefields and open grasslands, feeding on fallen grain, seeds and insects. The rat may also feed on rice plants and may be a pest in granaries where the dry grain is stored.

25

TRADITIONAL SILK LOOM

Several spectacular species of butterfly are found in the mountain ranges of north and northwest Thailand, near Chiang Rai, Pai, Mae Hong Son, and in the national park northwest of Chiang Mai ▲ 273. In the cultivated zones, ricefields and rubber plantations, few species have survived the process of deforestation. The entire zone from Lampang to Chiang Mai is undergoing reforestation but the plant species being used do not produce a habitat favorable to the reestablishment of butterfly species. Certain "cosmopolitan" species of butterfly can travel for miles across oceans. The first explorers to arrive in Siam found several well-known European, African and North American species.

15–18 d
Ecdysis

10–12 day
Hatching

ATROPHANEURA POLYEUCTES
A jungle butterfly that sometimes ventures into towns and villages.

STICOPHTALMA CAMADEVA
This is the biggest diurnal butterfly in Thailand and South East Asia with a wing span of 5.6 inches.

TROIDES AEACUS
The *Troides aeacus* reigns in the north. Its caterpillar deters birds and insectivorous reptiles by living on a poisonous liana, the *aristoloche,* which protects it against predators. This butterfly has recently been designated an endangered species.

PAPILIO ARCTURUS
The black part of the wings of the *Papilio arcturus* looks as though it is sprinkled with emerald dust. This spectacular butterfly can often be seen along mountain tracks.

ACHERONTIA LACHESIS
The *Acherontia lachesis,* which lives in the northern mountains, is the Thai cousin of the European "death's head hawk moth" (*A. atropos*). It is a nocturnal butterfly and will risk its life to penetrate beehives to gorge itself on the honey.

BHUTANITIS LIDDERDALI
This butterfly is from the northern mountain valleys. At rest, its fore wings are covered by the fore wings, hiding their magnificent colors and allowing the insect to blend with its surroundings.

TERINOS CLARISSA
The *Terinos clarissa* belongs to the *nymphalides* family. This small butterfly is mauve, varying in shade with the angle of vision. It flies discreetly close to the ground in the deep forest and at rest it is camouflaged against the vegetation.

1. Doi Inthanon, highest point in Thailand (8,547 feet), poor soil and cold climate where small mountain butterflies are found.

2. Chedi (6,600–8,250 feet), few cultivated areas and little highland forests. Habitat of small butterflies.

3. Chiang Mai plains, *pierides* and swallow-tail butterflies.

4. Mae Chaem, cultivated valley (1,580 feet) with a wide range of butterflies within the low vegetation.

5. Mae Surin rain forest (330–4,950 feet), privileged home to the most beautiful specimens in Thailand.

6. Khun Yuan (1,650–3,300 feet), a zone where rain forest butterflies live side by side with the small valley species.

LIFE CYCLE OF THE MULBERRY BOMBYX

4–6 days
Silk spinning

4–12 days
Pupation

2 days
igenesis

THE SILK INDUSTRY

The silk industry in Thailand is now located mainly in the northeast of the country. The larvae of the *Mulberry bombyx*, probably the best-known Thai moth, produce silk. This moth does not exist in the wild. Having long been domesticated, it has even lost the ability to fly.

After ecdysis the silkworms are placed on bamboo trays, known as *jo*, where they secrete a fibrous slime that protects them until metamorphosis.

A mural painting from Wat Phumin in Nan Province, showing a Lanna lady selecting spools of yarn while working at a Thai frame loom.

The filaments are spun and eventually skeins are produced. Each cocoon yields about 2,000 feet of usable thread (*mai luad*), although in total a mature cocoon can contain over 1 mile of thread in about 30 layers. Silk made from thread still coated with sericin is called raw silk. Natural silk or *tussah* is the silk produced by undomesticated caterpillars living in trees.

Cocoons are taken from the *jo* and boiled to remove the sticky sericin coating the silk filaments.

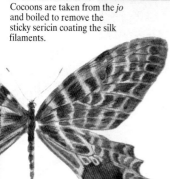

The raw thread is bright yellow. Before weaving it is washed first in a herbal mixture made from the bark and leaves of the banana tree, and then in a *ke* solution made from a thorny vine that is commonly found on hillsides, then dyed. Traditional dyes used include lac, indigo, krajai berries and thalang roots. To the east of Chiang Mai, on the way to Charoen Muang, it is possible to visit a *magnanerie* (silkworm rearing house) and to taste chrysalides which have been grilled after the removal of their silk filaments.

BIRDS' NESTS OF SOUTHERN THAILAND

Thailand is one of the major producers of edible birds' nests, a delicacy in Chinese cuisine dating as far back as the Ming and Qing dynasties of the 17th century. The swiftlets (*nok kin lom*) nest in caves along the southwestern coast and on the offshore islands ▲ *215, 223*. They find their way by echolocation. A series of up to 20 audible clicks per second is emitted and the echoes reflecting off the walls enable the birds to maneuver in the darkness. Already an expensive delicacy, these birds' nests could become more expensive as overcollection threatens the normal cycle of nest building.

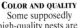

TYPES OF NESTS
The black nest swiftlet (*Aerodramus maximus*) uses its black feathers to build nests, hence the name "black nests." In contrast, the white nest swiftlet (*Aerodramus fuciphagus*) builds its nest wholly with saliva.

GRADES OF BIRDS' NESTS
The price of edible birds' nests varies according to their quality. White nests, wholly made of saliva, are more expensive. The best birds' nests are the first ones built during the breeding season. Thicker and translucent white, they expand to almost 20 times their volume upon soaking. Second and third nests are of lower grade, appearing dirtier and thinner.

COLOR AND QUALITY
Some supposedly high-quality nests are reddish. However, the coloration bears no relation to blood and may have leached into the nest from the substrate.

NEST COLLECTING TOOLS

COLLECTING BIRDS' NESTS
In Thailand this is carried out between February and July. Three collections are made each breeding season. Birds' nests are usually found in the lofty and dark interiors of caves. The nest collector, armed with a small torchlight and rope, stealthily climbs up the bamboo stilt that leads him to the nest ▲ *215*.

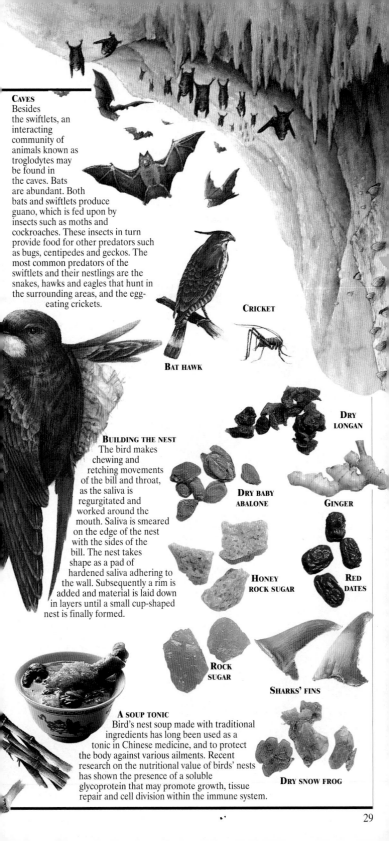

CAVES

Besides the swiftlets, an interacting community of animals known as troglodytes may be found in the caves. Bats are abundant. Both bats and swiftlets produce guano, which is fed upon by insects such as moths and cockroaches. These insects in turn provide food for other predators such as bugs, centipedes and geckos. The most common predators of the swiftlets and their nestlings are the snakes, hawks and eagles that hunt in the surrounding areas, and the egg-eating crickets.

CRICKET

BAT HAWK

DRY LONGAN

BUILDING THE NEST

The bird makes chewing and retching movements of the bill and throat, as the saliva is regurgitated and worked around the mouth. Saliva is smeared on the edge of the nest with the sides of the bill. The nest takes shape as a pad of hardened saliva adhering to the wall. Subsequently a rim is added and material is laid down in layers until a small cup-shaped nest is finally formed.

DRY BABY ABALONE

GINGER

HONEY ROCK SUGAR

RED DATES

ROCK SUGAR

SHARKS' FINS

A SOUP TONIC

Bird's nest soup made with traditional ingredients has long been used as a tonic in Chinese medicine, and to protect the body against various ailments. Recent research on the nutritional value of birds' nests has shown the presence of a soluble glycoprotein that may promote growth, tissue repair and cell division within the immune system.

DRY SNOW FROG

CORAL REEFS

GREEN TURTLE
Green turtles are exploited for their shell, flesh and eggs, and their numbers have been decimated wherever they occur.

The coral reef ecosystem is one of the richest habitats on earth. Coral colonies are composed of countless individuals – polyps – that feed on plankton. Although coral reefs can cover a large area, they grow very slowly: it may take 1,000 years for a reef to grow just 3 feet. When corals die, their skeletons remain and a new generation of polyps can grow on top of them. Each type of coral has its own distinctive shape, adding further to the splendor of the reef ecosystem.

COACHMAN FISH
The name of this fish derives from the long, whip-like appendages that often hang from its dorsal fin.

SURGEON FISH
Originating in the Indo-Pacific region, this species is quite aggressive.

EMPEROR FISH
This fish has one of the largest territories of all coral-reef dwellers.

TRIGGERFISH
Its common name refers to an erect spine in its dorsal fin, which cannot be released until a second spine (the trigger) is withdrawn.

PARROT FISH
Parrot fish have large scales and a typically bird-like beak formed of fused teeth.

CORAL REEFS AND POLYPS
Coral reefs provide an important source of food and income to local Thais. A coral polyp is a soft, almost transparent animal that builds its skeleton outside its body. Polyps feed at night by extending their tentacles, each of which is armed with a series of stinging cells that paralyse any passing prey. The moray eel is a key predator in the reef ecosystem; it hides in crevices, lunging out to seize unsuspecting fish.

TRIPLE BANDIT CLOWN FISH
This fish lives in close association with sea anemones.

History

PEOPLE OF SIAM

DEMOGRAPHY
Thailand has a total population in the order of 63 million with around 35% below the age of 20.

Thailand is a mosaic of peoples and cultures, and yet it has never suffered any serious racial conflict. This may be due to the fact that the central Thai have ruled more by consensus than by force. The widespread practice of Theravada Buddhism has also promoted racial harmony that has benefitted the whole country.

THE THAIS. At the beginning of the first millennium, a people known as the Tai migrated from what is now southern Chinas into the Chao Phraya River valley. When the Tai first

arrived, the region was inhabited by Austro-Asiatic groups speaking Mon and Khmer; the present-day Thais are the product of the assimilation and fusion of these three groups. Many Thais still live in southern China (particularly in Yunnan, Guangdong, and Guangxi). Today four subdivisions of Thais are recognized in the country: the central Thais (from the region between Sukhothai and Phetchaburi), who speak the standard Thai taught in schools; the Pak Isan Thais (a mixture of Thai and Khmer in the northeast), who also speak standard Thai; the Pak Tai Thais (south of Phetchaburi), who have a darker complexion and speak a dialect largely incomprehensible to central Thais; the northern Thais, who speak a different dialect and who are a fusion of Thai immigrants with Karens and Lawas (Austro-Asiatic). Each of these groups had largely independent histories until recent centuries.

LIFE EXPECTANCY
The average life span for Thai men is 69 years, while for women it is 73 years.

BUDDHISTS
Ninety-five percent of its population are Buddhists, making Thailand the largest Theravada Buddhist country in the world.

THE CHINESE. As traders, the Chinese arrived long before the Thais. They settled more permanently, at first in coastal cities in the south and then in other areas. The peak period of Chinese migration was in the 19th and early 20th centuries, and they now form a substantial part of most urban populations. Thanks to extensive assimilation, it is difficult to distinguish them as a separate ethnic group.

THE LAOS. Much of the northeast is inhabited by groups of Lao-speaking people (known in Thailand as the Issan) – Lao Wieng, Yuai, Yo, Lao Kao and Phutai – who migrated (some were forcibly moved) mostly during the last century and are today among the poorest in the country. Like the Thais, they belong to the Sino-Tibetan group. They are renowned for their weaving skills, and some groups were once distinguished by their dress, rather like today's hill tribes; these elaborate costumes can still be seen during village festivals. Though Buddhist, many still practice animistic rituals.

THE KHMERS. Khmer-speaking people are also numerous in some parts of the northeast, particularly in Surin province near the Cambodian border. Most of them migrated during the 19th century when Siam occupied a large part of Cambodia. The recent war in Cambodia has driven millions of Khmer refugees into Thailand but many of them are being gradually repatriated.

LANGUAGE
There are today more Laos in Thailand (18 million) than in Laos itself.

THE SHANS. The Thai Yai (right), called the Ngiaw by the Thais, belong to the Tai linguistic family and migrated from the Shan states of Burma in the 19th century. Today the Shans are scattered throughout the north, especially in Mae Hong Son and Mae Sariang.

Shan women at the start of the 20th century.

THE MUSLIMS. Thailand's largest religious minority, Muslims, are concentrated mainly in the southernmost provinces of Narathiwat, Pattani, Yala and Satun. Most are of Malay descent and speak yawi (ancient Malay) as well as Thai.

Throughout history, they have jealously guarded their independence and their traditions. The violence of the so-called separatist groups, which claimed many victims in 2003 and 2004, has re-opened old wounds.

MUSLIMS
More than 3 million Muslims, most of whom are Sunni, live in Thailand. There are about 2,900 mosques in the country.

THE MONS. These people, who live mostly in Nakhon Pathom, Samut Songkram and Samut Prakan, are not ancestors of the ancient Mon culture that once ruled over portions of central Thailand, but relatively recent Buddhist immigrants from Burma.

HILL TRIBES. The majority of the hill tribes ▲ 284, 294–301 in northern Thailand are relatively recent immigrants to the region. Only the Karens and the Lawas (right) were settled in the country before the arrival of the Thais. The hill tribes form a minority. In 1983, their total population was about 416,000. Apart from the Karens and the Lawas, this group also includes the Miens (Yaos), Lisus, Lahu Shis and the Blue and White Hmongs. While aspects of religions such as Christianity, Buddhism and Islam have been adopted by some hill tribes, animism is still in evidence.

A Karen with traditional pendants.

PREHISTORY

ROCK PAINTINGS
Several caves or rock
faces are decorated
with paintings from
simple handprints to
complete tableaux
showing scenes of
hunting, fishing and
dancing. These could
date back to the 4th
century BC. Some are
easily accessible, like
those at Khao Chiang
Ngam, 124 miles from
Bangkok on the road
to Khorat.

PLEISTOCENE. Evidence of Pleistocene cultures, dating from
600,000–130,000 BC, have been found in various parts of
Thailand, from
Lampang in the north
to Krabi in the south.
The earliest imple-
ments found were
pebble tools, followed
by early flake tools
(300,000–290,000 BC),
then by Proto-
Hoabinhian pebble tools (140,000–13,000 BC)

TRIPOD
(c. 2000 BC)
This pottery
tripod was
found at
Ban Kao,
in the

HOABINHIAN. This term was coined by a
French archeologist in Vietnam in the 1920's
and covers a period from around 120,000
–2000 BC. The earliest Hoabinhian tools in
Thailand were found in caves in Mae
Hong Son and Kanchanaburi. In the
former, the American archeologist
Chester Gorman found tools and seeds
of various cultivated plants including
betel nut, black pepper, bottle gourd
and cucumber. These have been dated
by carbon-14 tests to as far back as
9700–6000 BC, far earlier than
previously suspected. More
sophisticated tools like the polished
adze and the edge-ground knife appeared in
the cave around 6800 BC Pottery has also
been found at the same level.

Kanchanaburi
province. It was
probably copied from
a tin prototype, and is
reminiscent of the
Chinese bronzes of the
Han dynasty.

BAN CHIANG ▲ *229.* The discoveries
of a prehistoric culture at Ban Chiang,
in the northeastern province of Udon
Thani, have aroused considerable
archeological controversy, with some
historians questioning the early dates
originally ascribed to the appearance of
copper and bronze. Most now accept that
the initial dating of 4000 BC is too early but
still maintain that the two metals could
possibly be dated to between 2500 BC and
2000 BC – later than their first appearance in the Middle East
but approximately contemporaneous with copper in China –

3000 BC
*First civilizations in
Mesopotamia.*

2700–2300 BC
*Egyptian pyramids of
Kheops, Khephren
and Mykerinos built.*

1765–1122 BC
Shang Dynasty.

566–486 BC
Buddha.

219 BC
*Hannibal crosses
the Alps.*

and that Thailand had a
true Bronze Age. Painted
pottery found in the burial
sites at Ban Chiang and
elsewhere in the northeast
was produced relatively
late in the culture's
history, between 1000 BC
and 500 BC. The most
recent level of the Ban
Chiang excavation is dated at
around 250 BC.

THE INDIAN INFLUENCE. In the 1st century AD, Indian merchants began arriving in peninsular Thailand in search of new products to trade. They brought with them Indian ideas of art, architecture, religion and government that dominated the south over the next five centuries and later spread to other parts of the country. At first Hindu images were produced, but, from the 5th century onward, Buddhist images appeared in greater numbers, reflecting this new religion, which also came from India.

SRIVIJAYA ▲ *200.* Beginning in the 8th century AD a new, more warlike empire called Srivijaya was established in the southern peninsula, originating from Sumatra. It remained the principal force in the region until the 13th century. Many historians disagree about the exact center of the empire, but one of its important centers was Ligor, or Nakhon Si Thammarat. Wholly Hindu at first, Srivijaya later also practiced Mahayana Buddhism and beautiful images were created for both religions.

DVARAVATI ▲ *158, 160.* What is traditionally called the Dvaravati Period extends from the 7th to 11th centuries AD; a more accurate name might be Mon, for during this period, several Mon kingdoms rose in central Thailand, first at U Thong near the subsequent Thai capital of Ayutthaya, and later at Lopburi and Nakhon Pathom. All three were centers of Theravada Buddhism, the sect eventually adopted throughout the country. The Mons eventually succumbed to the more powerful Khmers.

KHMER EMPIRE. In the 7th century AD the rising Khmer Empire began to extend its power over the northeastern region. By the 11th century it had reached the Chao Phraya River valley. The great period of Khmer monument building commenced with the reign of Suriyavarman I (AD 1002–50) ▲ *230.* The principal religion in the early centuries was Hinduism, which was replaced with Mahayana Buddhism by the late 12th century. Khmer power began to wane in the 13th century.

MIGRATION OF THE THAIS. It is thought that in the 11th century AD Thais migrated in large numbers from Yunnan in southern China, driven by a desire for greater independence and better farmland. They formed two groups of kingdoms, in the north near the Mekong River and further south at the edge of the Chao Phraya River valley.

Votive tablet of the Srivijaya era.

WHEEL OF THE LAW
This wheel dates from the 7th century and is a symbol of the law taught by Buddha.

27 BC–AD 14
Foundation of the Roman Empire.

AD 330
Foundation of Constantinople.

AD 348
Buddhist settlements at Dunhuang.

AD 395
Fall of the Roman Empire.

AD 518–907
Tang Dynasty.

AD 571–632
Mohammed

AD 762
Foundation of Baghdad.

AD 800–14
Reign of Charlemagne, Holy Roman Emperor.

AD 960–1274
Sung Dynasty.

AD 1066
The Norman Conquest in England.

AD 1096–9
The First Crusade.

Soldiers and elephants, in celadon, from the Sukhothai era.

THE SIAMESE KINGDOM

1245
Jean de Plancarpin travels to Karakorum.

1253
Guillaume de Rubrouck travels to Karakorum.

1274
Death of Thomas Aquinas.

1276
Arrival of Marco Polo in China.

1279–1368
Yuan Dynasty.

1338
Beginning of the Hundred Years War between England and France.

1348
Black Death reaches Europe.

1368–1644
Ming Dynasty.

1492
Christopher Columbus discovers the Americas.

1602
Foundation of Dutch East India Company.

1644–1911
Qing Dynasty.

POWER STRUGGLE IN SUKHOTHAI.
In the first half of the 13th century, probably in the 1240's, a Thai chieftain later known as King Intradit joined forces with several other groups, overthrew the Khmer overlord at Sukhothai ▲ 251, 254, and established an independent Thai kingdom of the same name. Sukhothai remained small under its first two rulers; it expanded dramatically, however, during the reign of King Ramkhamhaeng (left), exerting either direct or indirect power over much of present-day Thailand through force and strategic alliances. Ramkhamhaeng is also credited with devising the Thai alphabet as well as a paternalistic system of monarchy that is regarded as ideal even to this day. Aside from its political achievements, Sukhothai is also remembered for its superb Buddhist art and architecture, which were distinctively Thai, and which are still considered the finest ever created in the country. Also notable were the beautiful ceramics produced first at Sukhothai and later at the satellite city of Si Satchanalai. Sukhothai's empire began to fall apart rapidly after Ramkhamhaeng's death and by 1320 it had once more become a small kingdom of little regional significance. By 1378 it had become a vassal state of Ayutthaya.

THE RISE OF AYUTTHAYA. Ayutthaya was founded on the Chao Phraya River by King Ramathibodi in 1350. Over the next four centuries, it grew from a small, fortified city into one of the great capitals of the region, its power reaching far beyond the fertile river valley. The capital fell to the Burmese in 1569, but less than two decades later regained independence under the able leadership of the future King Naresuan, who proceeded to extend its rule over most of the southern peninsula, the north, and both Cambodia and Laos. Relations with Europe began with a treaty between Siam and Portugal in 1516. The Dutch received permission to build a trading station in 1604, followed by the British in 1612. By King Narai's reign in 1656, Ayutthaya already had a cosmopolitan population of nearly a million. The first French Catholic missionary arrived in Ayutthaya in 1662, joined by others two years later. Given land on which to build churches and schools by King Narai, they became an important force in relations between the two countries. The first Thai embassy sent to France was lost at sea in 1681, but a second arrived safely in 1684 and formally requested a French mission to Ayutthaya. The first of these missions arrived in

1685, headed by the Chevalier de Chaumont; a second arrived two years later. A Thai embassy accompanied the first on its return to France, and was received at the court of Louis XIV. Following the death of King Narai in 1688, conservative elements assumed control and expelled many Europeans during the latter part of Ayutthaya's rule ▲ *242–3*.

THE FALL OF AYUTTHAYA. Shortly after King Ekatat assumed the throne in 1758, Ayutthaya was attacked once more by the Burmese under King Alaungpaya. A second invasion led by Alaungpaya's son, Hsinbyushin, succeeded in capturing Ayutthaya, after a siege lasting more than a year. The city was burned and looted by the victors and more than 30,000 of its inhabitants were taken to Burma. Son of a Chinese father and a Thai mother, the future King Taksin was a military officer at the time of Ayutthaya's fall. Within seven months he managed to rally Thai forces, expel the Burmese from the ruins of the city, and establish a new capital at Thonburi, further down the Chao Phraya River.

THE CHAKRI DYNASTY. In March 1782 a revolt broke out against King Taksin ● *39* ▲ *262*, who was thought to have become insane. He was replaced by a prominent military commander who, as King Rama I, founded the Chakri Dynasty and, for strategic reasons, moved the seat of government across the river to a small trading port known as Bangkok. King Rama IV, or King Mongkut (r. 1851–68, left), is best known as the hero of *The King and I*. To the Thais, however, he is remembered as one of the most far-sighted Chakri rulers, who negotiated important treaties with European powers, introduced modern sciences, and set his kingdom on the path to reforms that undoubtedly helped save it from the colonial fate that befell all its immediate neighbors. During his reign from 1868 to 1910, King Rama V (below), or King Chulalongkorn as he is better known, carried his father's reforms further. He abolished slavery, reorganized the governmental system, and built the first railways. The first Thai king to visit European capitals, Rama V also sent most of his sons abroad for further education. Forced by France to concede some of his territory to Cambodia, Rama V also had to relinquish sovereignty over Laos. Thus he was able to preserve his country's independence.

1762–96
Reign of Catherine II of Russia.

1787
American Constitution drafted.

1789
The French Revolution.

1804–14
Napoleon Bonaparte, Emperor.

1868–1912
Meiji Period in Japan.

1869
Suez Canal opened.

RAMA V SURROUNDED BY HIS FAMILY
This portrait was painted by the Italian artist Gelli.

THE LANNA KINGDOM

6TH CENTURY AD
Arab invasions.

571–632
Mohammed.

982
Erik the Red discovers Greenland.

A Bodhi tree at Wat Pong Yang Kok in Lampang Luang.

1099
The First Crusade – Jerusalem taken.

1325
Foundation of Tenochtitlan by the Aztecs.

1453
Constantinople taken by the Turks.

1497
Vasco da Gama discovers sea route to India.

Wat Ched Yod at Chiang Mai, built in 1455.

Northern Thailand, which has a history largely independent from the rest of the country, appears to have been populated by different groups of Thais, who assimilated with local inhabitants and settled in the fertile valleys of the north around the first millennium. Present-day Chiang Saen was the seat of the Ngong Yang kingdom, and was one of the main centers. Chiang Saen ▲ *302* and Payao, another center, were both in contact with India, through Burma, and traded with the Srivijaya empire. The decline of the latter led to the emergence of a trade route to China and ultimately to the birth of a powerful kingdom in the north.

HARIPUNCHAI (LAMPHUN) ▲ *274–5.* Mon immigrants from the Dvaravati kingdom of Lopburi founded the city of Haripunchai in the 7th century, as well as a string of fortified towns around it. Devout Buddhists, the Mons were a key force in the conversion of the Thais in the north and Haripunchai remained an important cultural center for centuries.

KING MENGRAI. Unification of the small northern principalities was achieved by King Mengrai, a Ngong Yang chief of mixed Thai and Lawa blood. Embarking on a grand scheme for conquering the whole region, he founded Chiang Rai ▲ *292*, seized Haripunchai in 1292, annexed Payao and, in 1296, founded his new capital of Chiang Mai. He thus established the powerful Lanna kingdom, which was to last for 600 years before being annexed by Siam. For a considerable period, toward the end of the kingdom, it was in effect under Burmese or Central Thai control ▲ *262, 267.*

THE GOLDEN AGE OF LANNA. The 15th century saw the flowering of the Lanna kingdom, which was powerful enough to host an international Buddhist gathering in 1455. Trade, art and education flourished, despite the occasional feudal battles between vassals and princes. The west bank of the Mekong (today parts of Laos, Burma and Thailand) was also ruled by the King of Lanna.

THE BURMESE INVASION. Quarrels over the possession of

a powerful talisman, an image of the Buddha, led to a Burmese invasion in 1558 and Lanna became a vassal state of the King of Pegu, governed by Burmese-appointed rulers. King Naresuan of Ayutthaya, fighting the Burmese who had invaded Siam, expelled these rulers from Lanna in 1598 and for the next 17 years Ayutthaya remained the dominant power in the north.

THE BURMESE ERA. In 1615, the Burmese King of Ava reestablished control over Lanna, which lasted for more than a century. Actual Burmese presence in the north, however, remained minimal and had very little effect on most of the population. The darkest period in the history of the north began with the rebellion of General Thip, who defeated a Burmese army and proclaimed himself King of Lampang in 1727. His successors eventually ruled in the 19th century, but before that, the King of Ava sent army after army into Lanna and Siam. After the fall of Ayutthaya, Kawila of Lampang and King Taksin of Thonburi joined forces against the Burmese. Having reconquered Chiang Mai in 1776, however, the Thais were forced to abandon the impoverished city. Lanna and Laos were decimated by the endless war; towns such as Chiang Saen, Luang Prabang and Vientiane, previously spared by the Burmese, were destroyed by the Thais to prevent their recapture. The strain, accumulated over many hard-fought battles, took its toll on Taksin and affected his mental health. He became eccentric and cruel toward his subordinates. In 1782, an élite group of officials led by Phya San rebelled, forcing Taksin to abdicate.

THE 19TH CENTURY. Independent but impoverished, 19th-century Lanna was governed by the family of Kawila ▲ 279, nominally a vassal of Thailand, but in fact autonomous. Not until 1874 was a Thai High Commissioner sent to administer the north and during the reign of King Rama V the region was slowly incorporated into the Thai kingdom. Laos, east of the Mekong, annexed by King Rama I during the Burmese War, was ceded to France in 1893, following a show of force by gunboats.

1588
Spanish Armada defeated.

The old walls of Chiang Mai.

1733
John Kay invents flying shuttle.

1769
Richard Arkwright erects spinning mill.

A BURMESE PRINCE
Mural painting at Lampang (left).

1837–1901
Reign of Queen Victoria.

1894
Japan declares war against China.

Chao Kaew Nawarat, last king of Chiang Mai (1911–39).

CONTEMPORARY HISTORY

1910
Annexation of Korea by Japan.

1914
Outbreak of World War One.

1917
Russian Revolution.

1918
End of World War One.

1922
Mussolini's Fascists march on Rome.

1927
Lindbergh makes first solo flight across the Atlantic.

1933
Hitler appointed chancellor.

1936–9
Spanish Civil War.

1939
Outbreak of World War Two.

In 1910, at the time of King Rama V's death, Thailand had become a modern nation recognized by the Western world, its boundaries apparently more or less secure. The following 80 years, however, were to be turbulent and marked by momentous events both inside the country and beyond.

FROM RAMA VI TO MODERN LEADERS. The first Thai ruler to be educated abroad, King Rama VI continued many of the reforms initiated by his father. In 1913, a law was passed requiring Thai citizens to have surnames for the first

time; the first university, Chulalongkorn, was established in 1917; the country entered World War One on the side of the Allies; and unequal treaties with Western powers were renegotiated in Thailand's favor.

END OF THE ABSOLUTE MONARCHY. King Rama VI's successor, Rama VII (above and below), inherited numerous economic and social problems. On June 24, 1932, a small group of foreign-educated military officers and civil servants staged a coup d'état calling for a constitutional monarchy. The king, who had already been thinking along such lines himself, granted their request. Later, he became disillusioned and abdicated in 1935, spending the rest of his life in England. Prince Ananda Mahidol, then a boy of 10, was named his successor and a regency council was appointed until he completed his studies in Switzerland.

POWER STRUGGLES. The two dominant figures in Thai politics during the 1930's were Luang Pibulsonggram, later known as Field Marshal Pibul, and Dr Pridi Panomyong. Both men were educated in France. These two leaders held

different views on many issues and were in frequent conflict. By the end of the decade, Pibul had become the country's Prime Minister and Dr Pridi had held several senior posts, including that of Minister of Foreign Affairs.

THE PACIFIC WAR. In 1940, following the fall of France, skirmishes broke out along the borders of Thailand and Indo-China which resulted in the return of areas in Laos and Cambodia to Thailand the following year. Upon the outbreak of the Pacific War on December 8, 1941, Japan demanded free passage through southern Thailand for its attack against British territories. Unable to resist, Pibul granted permission and, further, issued a declaration of war against Great Britain and the United States in January 1942. A Free Thai underground movement was organized by Pridi during the war, not only bringing him back to power but also enabling Thailand to avoid being treated as an enemy nation following Japan's defeat.

THE NEW KING. On June 9, 1946, the young King Ananda (right) was found shot dead in his room at the Grand Palace during a visit from Switzerland. His younger brother thus came to the throne as King Bhumibol Adulyadej, Rama IX, in circumstances that were both tragic and politically explosive.

TUMULTUOUS TIMES. The next three decades saw a number of coups and counter-coups. Accused of complicity in the death of the king, Pridi was forced into exile by Pibul. Though Pridi attempted two comebacks, in 1949 and 1951, both ended in failure and he retired first to China and finally to France. Pibul remained in power until he, too, was overthrown by Field Marshal Sarit Thanarat in 1957. In October 1973 Thai students staged a series of massive demonstrations that overthrew the military government and sent its leaders into exile. Three years of chaotic democracy ensued, but in 1976, alarmed by the unrest and by the fall of Indo-China to communists, rightist elements returned to power in a violent coup in which several hundred students were killed.

A UNIQUE MONARCHY. One of the outstanding forces in contemporary Thailand is the monarchy that has evolved under King Bhumibol Adulyadej (below) following his official coronation in 1950. Though theoretically operating under constitutional limitations similar to those that apply in England, the king has achieved an imposing moral authority rivaling that of his absolute ancestors, largely through an extensive network of royally initiated programs aimed at rural development. Today the king and other members of the royal family spend much of the year outside Bangkok, overseeing such projects as crop substitution for northern hill tribes to replace their traditional opium poppy and improved water resources in the arid northeast. The great respect earned through these endeavors has enabled the king to act as a decisive mediator in times of severe civil unrest, particularly during the student revolution of 1973 and, even more dramatically, during the recent upheaval of 1992 when he made an unprecedented television appearance to effect a compromise between the opposing groups.

1941
Japanese attack on Pearl Harbor.

1945
Atomic bomb dropped on Hiroshima. End of World War Two.

1947
Indian Independence.

1948
Assassination of Mahatma Gandhi.

1950–3
Korean War.

1953
Edmund Hillary and Sherpa Tenzing reach summit of Everest.

1958
Treaties establishing EEC come into force.

1963
Assassination of John F. Kennedy.

1969
First men land on the moon.

MODERN THAILAND. Thailand's recent history has been marked by further military coups, successful and otherwise, but it has also enjoyed steady economic and social progress, particularly during the eight-year premiership of General Prem Tinsulanonda (1979–88). The local communist insurgency, at its strongest in the 1970's, petered out and disappeared completely, relations with neighboring countries have been improved, and democratic institutions have gained increasing support among the general population. At the same time, Thailand has achieved the status of a "Newly Industrialized Country" and is now one of South-East Asia's giants.

1975
End of Vietnam War.

1979
Phnom Penh, capital of Cambodia, falls to the Vietnamese.

1989
The Berlin Wall is demolished.

1990
Iraq invades Kuwait.

1991
Operation Desert Storm liberates Kuwait.

There was an apparent setback to national development in May 1992, when bloody riots forced the resignation of the non-elected Prime Minister General Suchinda Kraprayoon and damaged the country's international image of stability. The positive outcome of these riots, however, was that the Thai population had demonstrated its refusal to accept traditional military dominance in political affairs.

𝕭𝖆𝖓𝖌𝖐𝖔𝖐 𝕻𝖔𝖘𝖙
Established in 1946

1997
July 1: following the agreement reached between London and Peking, Hong Kong's sovereignty is transferred back to China.

2004
December 26: a tsunami (large wave caused by an earthquake) kills thousands in Thailand and more than 150,000 across southeast Asia.

For many years, Thailand has been one of the most stable and dynamic countries in the region. It is regarded as one of the tiger economies of southeast Asia. The 1990's were marked by a popular desire for greater democracy and a significant increase in the standard of living for the majority of Thais. The financial crash of 1997 and the ensuing economic crisis revealed the lack of governmental control over the country's as yet fragile growth. A rapid succession of governments based on unstable alliances, often headed by unscrupulous politicians, delayed the implementation of the reforms anticipated by the Thai people, especially in the social sector. Today the country is achieving considerable economic growth, though noticeable disparities remain. After the disastrous tsunami of December 2004 which killed thousands, the Thai authorities embarked on a massive program of reconstruction which has erased virtually all traces of the catastrophe.

Arts and traditions

The primary aim of Buddhists is to overcome the suffering of this world by salvation through enlightenment. Mahayana (Greater Vehicle), or northern Buddhism, is found in China, Korea and Japan. Theravada, or southern Buddhism, the only surviving school of the Hinayana (Lesser Vehicle) system, originated in Sri Lanka and incorporates elements of Hinduism and local beliefs. It predominates in Thailand, Burma, Laos and Cambodia.

WHEEL OF THE LAW
Known as *dharmacakra*, the wheel symbolizes the living nature of Buddhist teachings, the perpetual changing of all objects and beings, and the constant quest for salvation. The deer refers to a deer park near Benares, where Buddha preached his first sermon, "setting in motion the Wheel of the Law."

DIVINE KING
This bejeweled image of Buddha shows the identification of Buddhahood with kingship in Cambodia, where under Jayavarman II, Mahayana Buddhism was declared the state religion. This *devaraja* (divine king) cult was introduced by Jayavarman II in the early 9th century and influenced Buddhist iconography in the 11th century when the Central Plains of Siam were under Khmer rule.

A SYMBOLIC ACT
Siddhartha Gautama (563–483 BC), the founder of Buddhism and better known as Sakyamuni or Buddha, was educated as an Indian prince. One day he rode from his palace accompanied by his groom, Chana, while the gods muffled the sound of the hooves with their hands. In the countryside, he cut off his long hair and beard, and donned plain clothes to symbolize his renouncement of the world and decision to become an ascetic.

"MUDRA"
Mudra are the hand gestures found in Buddhist iconography. This 14th-century image of Buddha shows the *bhumisparsa mudra* (touching the earth), made when Sakyamuni called the earth to witness his attainment of Buddhahood.

BODHI TREE
The tree under which the future Buddha obtained full enlightenment was a fig (*Ficus religiosa*). There he sat, vowing not to move until he had gained enlightenment, successfully resisting Mara's assaults. Many temples in Thailand were built around sacred Bodhi trees brought back as cuttings from India by pilgrims.

MERCIFUL BODHISATTVA
Avalokitesvara is one of the most popular Bodhisattvas, who sees all the misery of the world and treats it with compassion, and is often depicted with 11 hands and 1,000 arms, each symbolizing one aspect of the help he can provide.

BODHISATTVAS
In Theravada Buddhism, only a chosen few can ever reach full enlightenment and terminate the chain of rebirths. However, in Mahayana Buddhism, Bodhisattva intercessors and enlightened individuals voluntarily postpone their own nirvana indefinitely in order to devote themselves to the salvation of mankind.

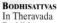

VICTORY OVER MARA
Mara, the god of death, tried to prevent Sakyamuni's salvation, fearing that his own kingdom of deaths and rebirths would be in peril. He vainly attempted to dislodge Sakyamuni from his meditations by sending an army of demons and by tempting him with his beautiful daughters and their voluptuous dancing. But when Sakyamuni performed the earth-touching *mudra*, and the earth trembled, Mara fled.

MEDITATION
It is one of the many ways of reaching enlightenment, a state that can be described in Buddha's own words: "There is a sphere which is neither earth, nor water, nor fire, nor air, which is not the sphere of the infinity of space, nor the sphere of the infinity of consciousness, the sphere of nothingness, the sphere of neither perception nor non-perception, which is neither this world nor the other world, neither sun nor moon. I deny that it is coming or going, enduring, death or birth. It is only the end of suffering."

● BUDDHISM IN THAI LIFE

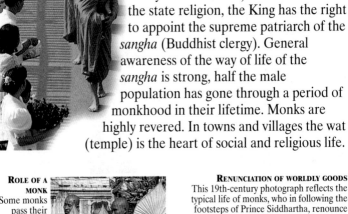

Thailand is one of the most strongly Buddhist countries in the world; 95 percent of the population practice Theravada Buddhism (a branch of Hinayana Buddhism). As Buddhism is the state religion, the King has the right to appoint the supreme patriarch of the *sangha* (Buddhist clergy). General awareness of the way of life of the *sangha* is strong, half the male population has gone through a period of monkhood in their lifetime. Monks are highly revered. In towns and villages the wat (temple) is the heart of social and religious life.

ROLE OF A MONK

Some monks pass their time studying Buddhist scriptures and practicing meditation. Many others, however, perhaps the majority, play an active role in daily life, sometimes as teachers, sometimes as advisors in village disputes. Monks are called on, too, to preside over a wide variety of ceremonial occasions, from funerals to the opening of a new business.

RENUNCIATION OF WORLDLY GOODS

This 19th-century photograph reflects the typical life of monks, who in following the footsteps of Prince Siddhartha, renounce material possessions, pain and passion in pursuit of enlightenment.

ACQUIRING MERIT

Thai Buddhists acquire merit through a number of traditional acts. The most common is offering food to monks in the early morning, while others include presenting robes and other necessities to monasteries, releasing caged birds, and building new temples.

MEDITATION

The purpose of meditation is to cleanse the mind of irrelevant thoughts and enhance concentration on the central aim of achieving nirvana. There are a variety of schools, with different teachers and methods, all with the same ultimate purpose.

BUDDHIST ART

Buddhism has been the greatest source of inspiration in Thai art, producing not only countless images but also temples and their elaborate decorations. The purpose is not to create objects of beauty but to express the piety of the artist and thus gain merit.

MONKS AS TEACHERS

For centuries the only schools in Thailand – necessarily limited to boys – were those in temples, where monks offered instruction in secular as well as religious matters. Despite the growth of state education, senior priests are still regarded as scholarly sources of wisdom; their philosophical books are widely read and they are often consulted in times of crisis.

ORDINATION

At some point in his life, generally just before he marries and starts a family of his own, a young Thai may undergo training as a monk, often for three months during the rainy season. In villages, the entire population takes part in the ordination ceremony, which involves both religious solemnity and enthusiastic celebration ▲288. The *nak buat*, or future novice, has his head shaved and is dressed in

white robes symbolizing purity; carrying an incense stick, a candle and a flower, he is then carried in a gala procession to the temple, where the ordination ceremony is conducted by resident monks.

Short-lived though they may be, traditional Thai flower arrangements qualify as genuine works of art. The object is not to reflect nature but to fashion something that, at first appearance, could hardly be less natural; Thai flower arrangements are often reminiscent of the complex patterns on painted porcelain or intricately set pieces of jewelry. Women of the royal court were celebrated for their skill at producing such creations and the art still continues today in numerous offerings for both religious and secular occasions ▲ *265*.

"BAI-SRI"

Bai-sri are special creations used in a number of Thai ceremonies. These are based on a structure of deftly folded banana leaves, which are then further adorned with such flowers as jasmine and sometimes food. *Bai-sri cham*, for instance, has a central banana-leaf cone filled with cooked rice topped by a hard-boiled egg; surrounding it are other cones decorated with various flowers. This is often given as a token of respect by a student to a teacher or presented as a good-luck offering to infants.

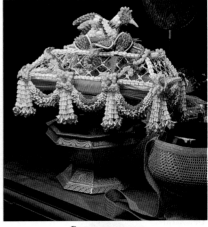

GIFT PRESENTATION

Flowers and garlands are used to embellish gifts. This beautiful flower arrangement covers robes and items presented to monks on special occasions.

"JAD PAAN"

Jad paan, or bowl arrangements, are also called *poom*, because of the traditional rounded pyramidal shape, which resembles a budding lotus. The core, 4 to 8 inches high, is made of moistened earth, sawdust, or styrofoam. The entire core is tightly embedded with flowers which resemble multi-colored pieces of porcelain. Bowl arrangements are often used in wedding ceremonies, when they are placed beneath the hands of the bride and groom, to receive holy water poured by the guests.

"MALAI"

Exquisitely fashioned *malai*, or garlands, play an important part in Thai social and religious life. In the most common kind, fragrant white jasmine buds are threaded thickly together, with accents of color provided by other flowers such as roses, marigolds and orchids. There are also highly complex versions requiring many hours of work. Nearly everyone who visits a shrine brings a *malai* as an offering to the resident spirit. Taxi drivers hang a garland from the dashboard to avoid accidents, and Buddhist altars in Thai homes receive a fresh one daily. You are also likely to be given a *malai* if you move into a new house, get engaged, or depart from or arrive at a party.

BASIC "KRATHONG"

Krathong, the elegant little boats set adrift on waterways during the Loy Krathong festival ● *73*, belong to the *bai-sri* category, the base being composed of banana leaves folded to resemble an open lotus blossom. This is then decorated with flowers, incense sticks and lighted candles and sent out as an offering to the water spirits on the night of the full-moon in the 11th lunar month, usually in late October or early November. In recent years, *krathong* have been made of colorful papers arranged around a base of styrofoam.

ORNATE "KRATHONG"

According to legend, Loy Krathong originated in Sukhothai ▲ *251, 265*, as a palace pastime in which royal ladies competed to see who could produce the most spectacular *krathong*. The same sense of competition remains today, with some creations towering more than 3 feet high in a variety of fantastic shapes. Prizes are awarded to the most imaginative.

49

A wide variety of traditional Thai occasions call for an offering of one kind or another. Some are secular: an auspicious birthday celebration, greeting an honored guest or the opening of a business. By far the greatest number, however, are religious in nature, presented during special merit-acquiring rituals and almost any visit to a Buddhist temple or shrine. The composition of such an offering varies considerably and may range from flowers and symbolic items to food and paper money – all, of course, arranged attractively.

BASIC OFFERINGS
The basic offering made to images of Buddha and on ceremonial occasions consists of incense sticks, candles and flowers, usually lotus buds. The first symbolizes life's fragrance, the second suggests its transitory nature, and the third is a reminder of the impermanence of beauty – all significant concepts in the Buddhist faith.

MONEY TREES
Thod kathin, held at the end of the annual Rains Retreat, are ceremonies in which groups visit temples to present various necessities to the resident monks. Besides new robes and Buddhist literature, offerings may include financial donations, in which case the money is elegantly arranged in the form of a tree that is proudly carried in a gala procession to the monastery. Such trees are often displayed for several days in front of the house of the donor, and anybody can join the merit-acquiring ceremony by adding their own contribution to the tree.

MEALS FOR MONKS
On Buddhist holy days the laity often offers the midday meal to monks at a temple as a means of acquiring. Much care goes into the presentation of the various dishes, which are traditionally displayed on shaped banana leaves and decorated with fresh flowers and delicately carved fruits.

Far older than Buddhism in Thailand is belief in spirits, as well as various gods and demigods. There are spirits who guard individual pieces of land, for instance, and others who watch over villages and capital cities or make their home in trees and caves. The general term for such invisible beings is *phi* ▲ *291*, but special names are given to many who enjoy demigod status. To avoid difficulties and ensure harmony and prosperity, all must be placated, sometimes with a special abode of their own, always with carefully prepared offerings. Such animistic beliefs do not clash with Buddhism; rather they coexist comfortably and often overlap in ways mystifying to outsiders.

DAILY PLACATIONS
To promote harmony and goodwill, the guardian spirit is placated with daily offerings by household members, the most basic being fragrant incense sticks, candles and flowers. Employees and shopkeepers regularly present offerings at the spirit house of their workplace while actors and dancers do so before a performance. Chinese shopkeepers usually have a spirit house for the local spirits and a small shrine painted in red, dedicated to the Taoist gods.

SPIRIT HOUSES
The guardian spirit of a particular compound, whether residential or commercial, is generally provided with a small house on the property; the exact site must be determined by an expert and has nothing to do with esthetic considerations. Elevated on a post, the houses come in a wide variety of forms, some simple wooden replicas of a traditional Thai dwelling, others ornate cement creations that resemble miniature Buddhist temple buildings down to the smallest decorative detail.

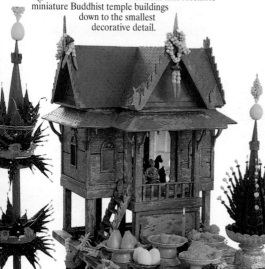

ELABORATE OFFERINGS
Spiritual abodes in wealthier compounds are lavishly supplied with a variety of elaborate offerings. In addition to small dolls to symbolize attendants, these may include floral displays, fresh fruits, and culinary delicacies ranging from sweets to full meals, carefully arranged on plates.

51

The elephant, which once roamed wild in large numbers in Thai forests, has played an important cultural and economic role since the early days of the kingdom ▲ 229. "White elephants" were revered as symbols of royalty; the Thai national flag used to show a white elephant on a red background, until the adoption of the present striped flag in 1917. The kings and princes of Ayutthaya rode into battle on war elephants, and King Rama IV of Bangkok in a letter offered a supply of the animals to US President Buchanan. In the past and to some degree at present, elephants, valued for their skill and their might, provided the main work force in the teak forests of the north.

ELEPHANT TUSKS
While their collection is deplored by environmentalists today, elephant tusks were treasured possessions in the past; some, like the ones shown above, were carved with Buddhist motifs, while others were mounted for display in palaces.

SOUTHERN ROUNDUP
In southern Thailand, as elsewhere, wild elephants were captured by driving them with drums, trumpets and gunfire into stockades, where they were tamed and trained.

TRAINING MANUALS
As far back as 2,000 years ago, Sanskrit manuals outlined precise procedures for capturing and, most importantly, training wild elephants. The manuscript book shown above, written during the reign of King Rama II, undoubtedly drew on these ancient sources, as well as on the practical experience of Thai trainers. While force was sometimes required, the most important part was winning the animal's confidence and affection.

ELEPHANTS IN WAR

Their value in war may well have been a major catalyst in the taming of elephants. About 22,000 supposedly took part in ancient Indian battles, leading the charge, and a 16th-century Burmese invasion force against Ayutthaya consisted of 300,000 men, 3,000 horses and 700 elephants. One of the most celebrated encounters in Thai history was an elephant-back duel between the Ayutthayan King Naresuan and a Burmese Crown Prince in 1592, resulting in victory for Naresuan.

ELEPHANTS IN HUNTING

Kings and royal princes often rode on elephants while hunting, as seen in this illustration from an ancient manuscript.

MYTHICAL ELEPHANTS

Elephants figure not only in Buddhism but also in Hindu mythology. The three-headed Erawan, for example, is the mount of the god Indra, while the *gajasingha* was a lion with the head of an elephant and Ganesha was the elephant-headed son of Shiva and Parvati, regarded as the god of arts or knowledge.

HOWDAHS

Howdahs, or elephant chairs, came in a wide variety of forms. Some were relatively simple wooden seats secured to the animal's back with leather straps, while those for royalty could be ornate, comfortably appointed palanquins. Palaces had special platforms for mounting and descending.

THE WHITE ELEPHANT

White elephants – actually a silvery gray – were revered as auspicious symbols by rulers in the past. Even today, when one of these rare animals is discovered in Thailand, it is presented to the king and kept in a special enclosure at Chitralada Palace, the royal residence. Ten have been found so far during the reign of King Rama IX.

An aspect of Ayutthaya noted by almost every early European visitor was the spectacle of the ornately carved and gilded royal barges, sometimes hundreds of them rowed by chanting oarsmen in elaborate costume. The custom was continued in Bangkok, where new barges were built by King Rama I and used to deliver offerings to monasteries along the river. After a long period of disuse following the end of the absolute monarchy in 1932, the elegant craft have been restored or entirely rebuilt during the present reign and processions have been held on several occasions, most notably during the Bangkok bicentennial celebrations in 1982.

EKACHAI BARGE
There are two Ekachai barges in the procession, used to carry religious items. The prows are stylized horns of *hera*, or horned dragons, the bodies of which are painted in gold-and-black lacquer.

SUPHANAHONGSA
The most important of the barges is the Suphana-hongsa or Golden Hansa – the mythical, swan-like mount of Brahma – in which the king rides ▲ *174*. The present one, built by King Rama VI in 1911, is made from a single teakwood trunk, 150 feet long and over 10 feet wide at the beam; a full crew consists of fifty oarsmen, two steersmen, two officers fore and aft, one standard-bearer, one signalman, one chanter and seven royal insignia bearers.

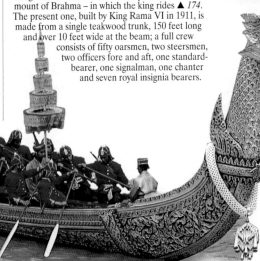

ADORNMENT
Intricately woven floral wreaths, resembling thick bejeweled necklaces, adorn the prows of the barges during a procession.

CLASSIC FORMATIONS

The royal barge procession held in 1982 was based on the formation shown in a 19th-century manuscript, probably a copy of a much earlier one. The procession extended for 3,220 feet and involved a total of 51 principal barges, all richly decorated, and 2,192 men. In addition, there were numerous smaller craft, known as *rua dang* and *rua saeng*, which acted as outer escorts and attendants; most of these were plain, with slightly raised stem and stern pieces, though a few performed special duties and were decorated with gold leaf. The crews consisted of officers and men of the Royal Thai Navy, who were carefully trained in traditional ways of propelling the long boats.

GUNBOATS

In early times, the barges were used in fighting. They were manned by crews of 60 to 70 oarsmen, or *rua chai*. Later they were armed with cannons protruding through the prow, which subsequently began to be decorated with figureheads from mythology, partly, perhaps, for identification but also to bring good fortune in battle.

EARLY IMPRESSIONS

The first visual impressions of the royal barges, in the 17th century, came in the form of sometimes fanciful engravings that accompanied books written by members of the two French embassies that came to the court of King Narai.

BOAT SONGS

"It was a breathtaking sight," wrote Father Guy Tachard, a Jesuit priest who witnessed a royal barge procession in late 17th-century Ayutthaya. "The sound of traditional chanting reverberated along both banks of the river which were crowded with people waiting to see the spectacular event." The rhythmic barge songs still survive, varying in pace to match the different speeds and strokes of the oarsmen.

"They wear few clothes," wrote Simon de la Loubère of the ordinary Thais he saw in 17th-century Ayutthaya, "not so much by reason of the heat as by the simplicity of their manners." In everyday traditional life, the only apparel for both men and women was a length of homespun cotton that could be worn as skirt or trousers. Silk was reserved for royalty ▲ 228. Despite the growing popularity of Western fashions, many people in the countryside still regard the old-style dress as being more suited to their ways of life.

"JONGKRABANE"
The *jongkrabane*
● 105, a length of cloth was wrapped around the waist then pulled through the legs and secured at the back, was popular with women in the past. A similar fashion worn by men was called a *pannung*.

ADORNMENT
Elegant jewelry – gem-studded brooches, buckles, pendants, tiaras, heavy gold belts and body chains – has been worn in Thailand since the Dvaravati period. An innovation of the Ayutthaya period was the wearing of particular colors on different days of the week: red for Sunday, yellow for Monday, pink for Tuesday, green for Wednesday, orange for Thursday, blue for Friday, and purple for Saturday.

MENSWEAR
Traditionally, Thai men wore only a sarong, sometimes pulled between the legs to form pantaloons. This fashion survives today in the all-purpose length of cotton called a *phakoma* ▲ 271, which can also be used as a head-covering, a wash cloth, or an impromptu tent for a siesta in the ricefields.

PRINTED FABRICS

In the late Ayutthaya and early Bangkok periods, some pieces of cloth used by the aristocracy, both silk and cotton, were printed in India, using Thai motifs (above) that denoted various degrees of rank. The most popular of these was called *pha lai-yang,* or "designed cloth," and had to meet stringent esthetic requirements; less prized varieties were called *pha lai-nok-yang,* "cloth not according to design," and *pha liang-yang,* "copied design."

"MOR HOM"

A basic item of attire for most Thai farmers is the loose cotton shirt called *mor hom,* traditionally fastened with string at the front. These are dyed dark blue with indigo and worn by both men and women, often with a broad-brimmed hat of woven palm leaf to ward off the sun.

HAIRSTYLES

In former times, Thai men and women cut off almost all their hair except for a growth on the crown, as shown in the above detail from an early 19th-century mural; the remaining hair was compared to a lotus flower. Sometimes after childbirth or on the death of a close relative, women shaved their heads as completely as men did when entering the monkhood. Even today, older countrywomen often wear their hair closely cropped like a man's.

NORTHERN "PASIN"

In northern Thailand *pasin,* as women's sarongs are called, have horizontal stripes and richly decorated areas at the bottom; on silk *pasin* the decorations are often in gold brocade, a craft for which the region is noted. Certain bright color combinations are deemed appropriate only for young, unmarried girls, while older women wear more subdued hues like dark blue and purple. Extending almost to the ankles, *pasin* are worn tightly tucked around the waist and often further secured with a belt.

NORTHEASTERN ELEGANCE

In northeastern Thailand, where a sizeable part of the population is ethnically Lao, numerous striking costumes can be seen, particularly during festivals, when the best clothing is brought out. Lao embroidery is a notable skill of the region and is used to adorn sarongs as well as *sabai;* the latter are long pieces of cloth about a foot wide that are draped diagonally over the shoulder and fall to the waist.

TATTOOS

Tattoos are worn by Thai men less for esthetic purposes than to ward off a variety of dangers and bring good fortune; on some men of the far north elaborate designs of auspicious animals once covered large areas of the body, almost like a suit of clothing. The practice has declined in modern times, but still it has its adherents and master tattooists command great respect from believers.

Thai royal attire was designed to impress, particularly on ceremonial occasions when the king, sitting high on his throne, wore so many ornaments and jewel-encrusted robes that he resembled a statue more than a living man. Royal children wore similarly elaborate clothing on important occasions, such as the top-knot cutting ceremony when they came of age. The costumes of court officials – including the patterns of the silk they wore and the accessories they carried – usually varied according to their rank. Each costume was strictly prescribed by royal order.

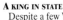

A KING IN STATE
Despite a few Western innovations, full ceremonial dress for royalty has changed remarkably little from the ancient past, as demonstrated in this photograph (left) of King Rama VI (1910–25). Prominent among its features are the tiered Great Crown of Victory with wing-like appendages on either side, a tight-fitting, high-necked tunic and trousers of gold-brocaded silk, special slippers and a richly embroidered and bejeweled robe. Some of the same features can be seen on images of the Buddha in royal attire made in the late Ayutthaya and early Rattanakosin periods.

DRESSED FOR THE OCCASION
At important ceremonies, princes would wear clothing and jewelry similar to that of their elders.

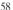

> "His costume consisted of a pair of trousers, a short brown jacket of some thin material, and slippers; on his head he wore a little copper helmet… and at his side, a rich sabre."
>
> Henri Mouhot

TONSURE CEREMONY
In the past, both boys and girls had shaven heads except for a tuft of hair on the crown. The cutting of this top-knot marked their official coming of age and, especially in the palace, was accompanied by elaborate ceremonies that extended over several days.

A ROYAL PRINCE
Royal princes of the mid-19th century wore rich gowns and sarongs of silk, the patterns of which were forbidden to those of lesser rank. Imported cloth from China and Japan was highly esteemed because of its comparative rarity, but Cambodian and Laotian silks were also prized. The gilded, broad-brimmed hat came into fashion during the Ayutthaya period, probably as a result of foreign influence.

A KING AND QUEEN
It was during the reign of King Rama IV, shown here with one of his queens, that Western fashions first appeared in royal circles. When British photographer John Thompson was invited to take some royal photographs in 1865, the King posed for one in "a sort of French Field Marshal's uniform" as well as others in more traditional dress.

WESTERN INFLUENCE
Western dress became widespread under King Rama V, shown on the right, the first Thai ruler to travel abroad and experience European culture at first hand. Men of the court adopted European suits and uniforms so enthusiastically that within a short time the old Thai costumes had virtually disappeared in palace circles.

ROYAL REGALIA
The royal regalia, received by each king on his coronation, include a number of swords, jeweled slippers, a fan and a staff, among other items, most dating back to the first Chakri ruler.

ROYAL WOMEN
The women of King Rama V's court were inspired by the fashions of England's Queen Alexandra, particularly her blouses with puffed sleeves. Sometimes these were worn with cumbersome Victorian skirts, sometimes with more graceful Thai *pasin*, or sarongs.

As well as the clothing already described as being worn by royalty and ordinary people, both past and present, there is another category in Thailand: that of special attire, real and imagined. The real includes the saffron robes prescribed for monks, a familiar sight in and out of Thailand's numerous temples, as well as certain military uniforms and costumes for special ceremonies. The imaginary takes in most of the early Western views of Thailand and its people, some recorded on the scene but many executed later by artists more influenced by fantasy than by a desire to portray reality.

A MONK'S ROBES

After ordination, a monk discards the clothing of the outside world and adopts priestly robes made of saffron-colored cotton cloth. These consist of three pieces of cloth, one worn sarong-like around the waist, another as a shoulder sash, and a third long enough to envelop the entire body. Only the first two are worn inside the monastery. New priests are instructed in the prescribed way of tying the robes. Vegetable dyes were traditionally used, but today most cloth is dyed with chemicals.

A MONK IN FULL ROBES

This old engraving shows a monk wearing the full set of three robes and standing near one of the gilded, tiered parasols seen in Buddhist temples.

SOLDIERS

Military uniforms have changed considerably over the years, becoming more Westernized. The soldier shown above is wearing one favored in late Ayutthaya and early Bangkok.

CEREMONIAL COSTUME

The figure on the right is dressed in one of the ornate costumes worn during the plowing ceremony, an ancient Brahminic ritual that originated in Ayutthaya to mark the beginning of the rice-planting season. It is similar to a court costume, consisting of a tall hat, richly brocaded tunic and pantaloons, and a semi-transparent gown trimmed with gold brocade. The ceremony was revived by the present king and is held annually in Bangkok during May at Sanam Luang, across from the Grand Palace.

THE AMBASSADOR'S HAT

In 17th-century French engravings of Ayutthaya, Thais are often shown wearing what some called the "ambassador's hat," known thus because it was worn by the three ambassadors who were received at Versailles. In reality, such a costume was never worn by commoners.

THE ORIGINAL HAT

An original specimen of the ambassador's hat is preserved at Lopburi National Museum.

Habit of an Ambassador of Siam to the Grand Seignior.

A MANDARIN

The figure, from Simon de la Loubère's account of his visit to 17th-century Ayutthaya, is labeled "A Siamese Mandarin" and shows a silk *pannung* tucked between the legs, a blouse and an ambassador's hat.

AMBASSADOR'S ATTIRE

One of the ambassadors who were received by Louis XIV in Paris is shown above.

THAI AMBASSADORS AT VERSAILLES

The three Thai ambassadors who were received by Louis XIV in 1686 at Versailles caused a sensation, because of the lavish gifts they brought and also because of their exotic dress. Thai motifs appeared on French textiles and tapestries and their fancy costumes became the subject of endless engravings and calendars.

The earliest Thai musical instruments were given names that reflected the sounds they made, such as *krong, chap, ching, so* and *khong*. Later more complex instruments were created, many adapted from foreign cultures like Indian and Khmer. During the Ayutthaya period, an instrumental ensemble was composed of four to eight musicians; this was expanded to twelve in the early Bangkok reign of King Rama II. There are now about fifty different types of Thai musical instruments, including many regional variations. Music accompanies most traditional Thai occasions, from the classical dance festivals to folk theater and boxing matches.

XYLOPHONE

Closely akin to the Western xylophone is the instrument called *ranad*, one of the six basic components of most musical groups that accompany classical dancing and many ceremonies. The *ranad* comes in a number of types, some slightly curved and others flat, producing different tones. Its musical purpose is usually to produce variations on the principal melody and the rhythm. The keys are made of bamboo or seasoned wood mounted on a wooden frame.

AN EVOLVING ART

Music dates back to the earliest days of the kingdom, as suggested by the stucco frieze below showing a group of musicians in the Dvaravati period (7th–11th century). Dvaravati instruments, the result of Indian influence, were adopted by the Thais, who went on to produce a number of new instruments. These are mentioned in the *Tribhumikatha*, one of the first books written in Thai, as well as on a stone inscription attributed to King Ramkhamhaeng of Sukhothai.

THE LONG DRUMS
The beat of a drum is essential to Thai music, providing a rhythmic excitement that rises and falls. In small ensembles, the most common type is the relatively small, double-ended *klong tad thapon*, but in the north huge drums called *klawng yao*, often several yards long and requiring several men to carry them, are frequently heard at festivals.

GONG
Large gongs ▲ *274* are often elaborately mounted, like the one above, which is suspended between a pair of elephant tusks. Smaller versions are used in most ensembles, along with xylophones, drums, the oboe-like *pinai*, the circular *khong wong yai*, and a set of small cymbals called *ching lek*. In addition to the role they play in music, gongs were traditionally struck to announce important events.

"KHONG WONG"
Known as *khong wong lek* (small) or *khong wong yai* (large) depending on their size, these consist of a circular series of small gongs suspended on a rattan frame and provide the melody in a Thai musical performance. There is no doubling in parts, so if two are involved only one plays the melody while the other plays variations.

ENSEMBLE
A typical small musical ensemble is called a *phipat* band. The majority of the instruments are percussive but there is always at least one reed, the *pinai*, which sounds somewhat like a bagpipe. In the illustration above, the man on the right is using a flute-like instrument composed of varying lengths of hollow bamboo; this is most often heard in the northeast and is of Lao origin.

STRINGED INSTRUMENTS
The *chakhay* is a thick-necked guitar-like instrument requiring great skill, it is heard only in larger orchestras and played on a low table, almost always by a woman. Another popular traditional Thai stringed instrument is the *saw sam sai*, a fiddle composed of a triangular coconut shell, an ivory neck, and three silk strings; King Rama II was a noted *saw sam sai* performer, so enthusiastic that he exempted from taxation all plantations that grew the triangular coconuts needed for its manufacture.

The classic Thai theater is the *khon*, a masked drama performed in dance and gesture at the royal court; it probably originated in Indian temple rituals and came to Thailand by way of Indonesia. The story lines are drawn from the *Ramakien*, the Thai version of the Indian *Ramayana*. During the Ayutthaya period, men played both male and female roles because the movements were thought too strenuous for women to perform, though by the early 19th-century Bangkok period both men and women were appearing on the stage together. All records of the story were lost with the destruction of Ayutthaya in 1767; King Rama I of Bangkok, together with literary members of his court, wrote a new version in 1798 and later additions were made by King Rama II.

"KHON" TROUPES
Khon performers are trained from early childhood in the dance steps and gestures which require considerable physical strength and agility. A royal troupe was part of the palace retinue in both Ayutthaya and early Bangkok; later, a number of high-ranking princes had troupes of their own.

NARRATION
Narrative verses accompany *khon* performances. The verses are recited or sung either by a chorus or by a

THE "RAMAKIEN"
The *Ramakien* ▲ *151,* on which the *khon* is based, is an epic account in lyrical verse of the triumph of good over evil. The hero is Phra Ram, a king of Ayutthaya and also a reincarnation of the god Vishnu. His consort, Nang Sida, is abducted by the wicked King Thotsakan of Longka (Sri Lanka) and the lengthy drama recounts the ultimately successful efforts of the King and his brother Phra Lak, assisted by the clever monkey-god Hanuman, to rescue her. Performances were often staged on two consecutive nights for a total of more than 20 hours; a *khon* staging of the entire *Ramakien* would require 311 characters and take more than a month of continuous performance.

single narrator sitting with a musical ensemble consisting of woodwinds, gongs, drums and other traditional instruments.

MASKS

Khon masks are creations made of lacquered papier mâché, decorated with gold and jewels, reflecting the personalities of the characters being portrayed.

THEATERS

Traditional *khon* performances were presented by torchlight in palace halls and courtyards with no complicated scenery to distract from the characterizations. Gradually, however, they moved outside the palaces in the early Bangkok period and could be seen in public theaters especially erected for the purpose during festivals and ceremonies. The shorter version of the *Ramakien* written by King Rama II is the most popular, and only selected episodes are offered to contemporary audiences. Even these are comparatively rare, however; the average visitor sees only brief excerpts performed between courses at Thai restaurants catering for tourists.

GESTURES

The familiar story is told through stylized postures and gestures, which express action, thought and feeling. Anger is shown by stamping a foot. Raising the upper lip with a pinch of the fingers conveys a smile and, thus, pleasure. Stiffening of the body with a certain arm motion suggests ambition, while supporting the brow bending and with one hand expresses sorrow. Discriminating audiences decipher the most subtle gestures and evaluate a performance on the basis of them.

COSTUMES

Khon costumes are made of heavy brocades decorated with costume jewelry and closely resemble the dress of royalty and celestial beings in classical Thai mural paintings. The major characters are identifiable by the color of their dress; Phra Ram, the hero, wears deep green, while his brother Phra Lak wears gold and the monkey-god Hanuman wears white. Phra Ram, Phra Lak and Nang Sida usually do not wear masks; Thotsakan, the villain, has a green mask on which small faces are painted to indicate that he is a 10-headed demon and Hanuman, a white simian one with a mischievous expression. Green masks denote high rank and purple and blue masks are for minor characters.

When the *khon* moved outside the limited confines of the royal palace and became part of the popular culture, it did so in a form known as *lakhon*. This is less formal and the movements are less angular, more graceful and sensual. The stories are drawn not only from the *Ramakien* but also from a collection of morality tales called the *Jataka* and from a Javanese historical romance known in Thai as *Inao*. *Lakhon* is subdivided into several variations, the three major ones being *lakhon chatri*, *lakhon nok* and *lakhon nai*; another form of popular theater, relying more on social satire and pantomime than on pure dance, is the *likay*.

ACTORS

Unlike *khon*, skilled *lakhon* and *likay* performers are able to earn a living from their talents outside places mainly limited to tourists. There are resident troupes of female *lakhon* dancers at nearly every major shrine, for example, and their services are often called upon by people wishing to thank the resident deity for answered prayers; *lakhon* dancing is also often a feature of festivals and private entertainments. Similarly, *likay* troupes tour the country presenting their shows at fairs held in towns and villages, some of the performers becoming major stars among rural audiences.

"MANORA"

One of the principal sources of *lakhon chatri* is a Javanese romance called *Manora*, in which the heroine is half-human and half-bird. Long, curving metal extensions (below) amplify her graceful fingers. Simpler performances of *lakhon chatri* can be seen regularly at popular shrines in Bangkok such as the *lak muang* (the city's foundation stone) and the one near the Erawan Grand Hyatt Hotel, where supplicants whose wishes have been granted pay resident troupes of dancers to perform.

> "The greater part of the performance consisted of merely twisting the fingers and hands and arms in such positions as to make them appear out of joint."

Carl Bock

GRACEFUL FINGERS
In *lakhon* performances, especially those by women, the hands are particularly expressive, assuming gestures that

are only possible after years of training. The use of long metal nails, which originated in southern Thailand with the *Inao*, can now be seen in other parts of the country; one of the best-known variations is the romantic *fawn lep*, or "nail dance," a mainstay of northern celebrations.

THEATER TRAINING
Training for the Thai dance begins at an early age, with boys and girls at first learning to move their heads, bodies, limbs and fingers to music. Only later do they begin to practice the sixty-eight separate movements that comprise the more intricate alphabet of the dance, each movement having a picturesque name such as "the bee caressing the flower" or "the stag walking in the forest."

"LIKAY"
Likay performances can be seen at most Thai temple fairs. This combines a burlesque of *lakhon* with low comedy; the plots vaguely follow classical lines, with traditional characters, but much of the humor is spontaneous, involving double meanings and puns as well as allusions to local scandals and prominent figures.

67

● THAI PUPPETS

Puppets were once an important part
of traditional Thai theater. Predating
both the *khon* and the *lakhon* was the
shadow play, subdivided into *nang yai* and
nang talung. Introduced from the
Sumatran empire of Srivijaya, this was a
form of entertainment in 17th-century Ayutthaya. Also seen
were *hun* marionettes, little carved figures that enacted classical
stories in the royal court. A popular
version was *hun krabok* ("rod
puppets").

"HUN KRABOK"
A variety of *hun* marionette, *hun krabok*
have detailed wooden heads and
costumes that conceal a central rod;
there are no arms or legs, only hands
operated by two sticks hidden within the
robe. Chakraphand Posayakrit, a
contemporary artist, has fashioned a
beautiful new set, which can be seen in
occasional performances.

PUPPET DRAMA
Puppets were often dressed in the same
costumes and masks found in *khon* dances,
though some were used to perform Chinese
dramas and were appropriately attired;
considerable skill was required to paint the

miniature faces and create the accessories.
Puppet theater was a palace diversion and
because of its slow pace never became widely
popular outside.

"NANG YAI"

In *nang yai*, or "big nang," the cowhide shadow-play figures are huge, up to 6 feet tall and intricately designed, depicting characters from the *Ramakien* and other classical romances. Each is mounted on two sticks and held behind a brilliantly backlit white screen by bearers who dance their parts to the accompaniment of music and choral singing. Some scholars believe the movements of the bearers later evolved into a stylized dance and eventually led to the *khon* masked drama.

A DECLINING ART

A common form of night-time entertainment in the royal court of Ayutthaya, *nang yai*'s appeal gradually declined, because of the popularity of the *khon*.

"NANG TALUNG"

Nang talung is a more popular version of the shadow-play found at festivals in southern Thailand. The figures are smaller and have one or more moveable parts such as a chin or an arm. Concealed behind the screen along with the manipulators are singers and comedians whose witty contributions to the performance probably account for the continuing popularity of the form.

SHADOW-PLAY FIGURES

Shadow-play figures are carved from the hides of water buffaloes or cows that have been soaked, dried and scraped, then darkened with charcoal or tinted with herbs and berries.

"HUN LEK"

Hun lek, small *hun* marionettes, date from the reign of King Rama V; they were modeled either on characters from the *khon* or from Chinese dramas and manipulated by concealed threads pulled from below rather than from above. These puppets have almost vanished from Thailand's art scene, though one superb set can be viewed at Bangkok's National Museum.

Sanuk, a Thai term usually translated as "fun," is a much-valued pursuit and covers a wide range of activities. Prominent among them are various traditional sports that, despite such innovations as Western football and bowling, have never lost their appeal to the vast majority of Thais, especially in rural areas. During leisure time, almost any open field or festival offers a display of some kind, from the balletic ferocity of Thai-style boxing to more esoteric amusements such as a struggle between two giant horned beetles or multicolored Siamese fighting fish.

"TAKRAW"
In its traditional form, the game of *takraw*, which is also popular in neighboring countries such as Malaysia, involves keeping a hollow rattan ball aloft as long as possible. The circle of players can use their feet, knees, elbows and head but not their hands. Groups of young men start a casual *takraw* game almost anywhere during a break from work or school, demonstrating remarkable grace and footwork.

PROFESSIONAL "TAKRAW"
Over the years, more professional forms of *takraw* have evolved, using nets to separate opposing teams or high baskets through which the ball must be sent, along with strict rules of play. *Takraw* competitions of this kind are often held in Bangkok at Sanam Luang and also at the Asian Games. The sport has been an Olympic event since the Atlanta Games.

BEETLE BATTLES
The large male horned beetle, commonly found in the Thai countryside, becomes aggressive when confronted by another member of his sex in the presence of a female. The ensuing battle, which ends when one of the contestants is overturned, is a popular spectator sport in villages, with wagers on the outcome.

"CHULA" KITES

The detail above, from an old mural painting, shows a *chula*, or "male", kite caught on a temple roof. On breezy afternoons during the hot season, kites of all kinds can be seen in the sky above Sanam Luang, the great oval field across from the gold spires of the Grand Palace.

KITE-FIGHTING

Kite-fights in Thailand are actually a symbolic battle of the sexes. The "female" is a small diamond-shaped kite called a *pukpao*, while the "male", called a *chula*, is a huge star-shaped creation that requires teams of up to seventy men to send it aloft and maneuver it. The object is for one of the *chula* to snare a *pukpao* with a bamboo hook and bring it down in "male" territory; alternatively, the more agile *pukpao* often succeed in looping their lines around a *chula* and bring it crashing to earth on their side of the field.

THAI BOXING

In modern Thai-style boxing, gloves are used but in most other ways it is similar to the sport of the past. Any part of the body, except the head, can be used as an offensive weapon. Some professional matches give rise to a fair amount of betting. This very popular sport is now practiced all over the world.

THE MARTIAL ARTS

As this old illustrated manuscript shows, boxing was an important part of self-defense. In the old days, no gloves were used and both hands and feet were bound in cloth that often contained bits of ground glass for added effect. Several Ayutthaya kings were famed for their skill in this graceful yet lethal art.

Festivals are liberally sprinkled throughout the Thai year: religious and secular, national and local, high-spirited and gravely reverent. This has been true since the earliest days of the kingdom; a Sukhothai stone inscription, describing an annual merit-acquiring event, says, "They join together in striking up the sound of musical instruments, chanting and singing. Whoever wants to make merry, does so; whoever wants to laugh, does so." Today Thais seize almost any occasion for a chance to don their best clothes and celebrate, whether it be one of the several milestones in the Buddhist calendar or merely some notable village event.

ROYAL HOLIDAYS
Many of Thailand's annual events celebrate the monarchy and involve lavish public decorations as well as festivities. These include the birthdays of the King (December 5) and the Queen (August 12), the date of the founding of the present Chakri Dynasty (April 6), Coronation Day (May 5), and Chulalongkorn Day (October 23), which honors the dynasty's beloved fifth ruler.

PLOWING CEREMONY
The royal plowing ceremony, an ancient Brahminic ritual marking the start of the rice-planting season, had been allowed to lapse for many years when it was revived by the present king in 1960. Held every May at Sanam Luang, across from the Grand Palace, it is a colorful event that climaxes with a prediction of the coming harvest for Thailand's farmers.

ROCKET FESTIVAL
Known as *bun bang fai*, northeastern rocket festivals combine Brahminic, Buddhist and animist elements and are basically concerned with bringing rain through the firing of homemade skyrockets and high-spirited village merrymaking that go on for two days.

CANDLE FESTIVAL
The beginning of Buddhist Lent, or Phansa, during July, is observed in the northeastern city of Ubon Ratchathani with the Candle Festival, when hundreds of beautifully carved candles, some several feet tall, are carried in gala parades before being presented to local temples.

SONGKRAN
Officially, Thailand begins the new year on January 1; at the same time, however, the old solar New Year, called Songkran, continues to be a major two-day celebration in mid-April. This is a typically Thai blend of solemn ritual and riotous festival. Offerings are brought to various temples, where both the abbot and the principal Buddha images are anointed with lustral water, while homes are given a thorough cleaning and homage paid to senior family members. Outside, pleasure reigns in the form of lavishly decorated parades, beauty contests, and buckets of water cheerfully thrown at anyone passing in the streets ▲ 265, 268.

LOY KRATHONG
Perhaps the loveliest of Thai festivals, Loy Krathong honors the water spirits through the launching of little candlelit boats, or *krathong*, in ponds and waterways all over the country. This occurs on the night of the full moon in the 11th lunar month, usually November, when the rivers and canals are at their highest ● 49 ▲ 251, 268, 288.

BUDDHIST OBSERVANCES
This detail from a mural painting shows the making of miniature sand chedis ● 98, or chedi *sai*, in temple compounds during the celebration of Songkran, the traditional New Year; the act reflects the origins of the oldest form of Buddhist monument. The importance of Buddhism can be discerned in many festivals.

73

Of all traditional Thai crafts,
none plays a more significant
and continuing role than baskets
▲ 273. Made from a variety of easily
obtainable materials – bamboo is the most common but certain
reeds, grasses, palms and even ferns are also used – they were
born of rural necessity and serve a wide range of needs: catching
and keeping fish, carrying rice, storing household goods and
steaming food, to mention only a few. Such baskets are basically
utilitarian; at the same time, however, many of them display an
undeniable elegance of form and delicacy of workmanship that
raises them to the level of
genuine folk art.

WATER BASKET
This ingenious device (called
mah or *timah*), made with
palm leaves and fitted with a
wooden handle, is found in the
south. Water can be scooped
from a pond or, with the aid of
a rope, drawn from a well.

SEED CONTAINER
Made of lacquered basketry to
make it waterproof and also
deter insect pests, this seed
container is also decorated with
stylized motifs and an outside
frame of bamboo slivers. It is
used in the north for storing
seeds that will be sown during
the next planting
season.

RICE BASKET
Known as a
krabung, this sort of
basket is found in all
regions of the country.
It is neatly woven with
bamboo supports up to
its widest part and is
used for measuring and
carrying rice; four loops
on the sides enable it to
be strung on a carrying
pole. *Krabung* may vary in
shape from area to area.

"SAI" (FISH TRAP)

This bomb-shaped trap, called a *sai*, is found in all regions and is used for trapping prawns or small fish, which swim into the opening and are prevented from escaping by bamboo slivers around the inside of the mouth. The average length is around 3 feet. Such traps are placed in ponds or rivers, and are usually fastened to stilts for locating purposes.

GLUTINOUS RICE BASKETS

Baskets like these are common in northern and northeastern Thailand, where they are used by farmers as a kind of lunch pail to carry glutinous rice with them when they go to work in the fields. The wooden foot keeps the basket raised from the ground, while the cord makes it easy to transport; the contrasting weaves add an esthetic touch.

DUCK-SHAPED CONTAINER

All over Thailand, one can spot narrow-necked baskets like the one shown below, cleverly designed to keep a trapped fish alive while preventing it from escaping. The loose string attached at the neck makes it easy to carry.

"SARB" (FISH TRAP)

This kind of fish trap is normally found in the northeast and is about 3 feet long. It is placed in streams and irrigation systems supplying the ricefields ▲ *24–5*, where it is left to trap any fish that might pass when the ricefields are flooded.

Thai food, like Thai culture, is the product of various influences, blended to form one distinctive cuisine. Ordinary fare in Sukhothai and early Ayutthaya was simple: mainly fish, fresh or dried, mixed with rice, vegetables, a few spices, and a salty sauce made from fermented fish or shrimp. Other ingredients and flavors came through increased contact with foreign cultures, China and India in particular, and also Europe. Today it covers a wide range of dishes, many of them regional specialties; those of the northeast, for instance, are generally regarded as the spiciest; in the south seafood is plentiful and Muslim specialties appear on the menu.

CHILLIES

Chillies, known in Thai collectively as *prik*, were introduced to Asia by the Portuguese from South America in the 16th century and quickly spread so widely that their searing flavor is now basic to numerous cuisines. Thai cooking employs over forty varieties of chilli, ranging from large and mild to tiny bombshells called *prik-kee-nu*, which translates as "mouse-dropping pepper," on account of their shape.

FISH SAUCE

Nam pla is a pungent sauce made from fermented fish, served as a salt substitute in early Thai cooking and still an essential condiment on any table. A number of brands are available on the market, each with its devoted adherents, and several coastal towns on the Gulf of Thailand are famous for the production of the sauce.

ROYAL CUISINE

Thai food that is prepared and served with enhanced elegance is often referred to as "royal cuisine" since it is supposed to have been inspired by palace chefs. Fruit and vegetables are carved into exquisite shapes, with colors and textures carefully matched, turning each dish into edible art.

STICKY RICE

A glutinous variety of rice, or *khao niaow*, is the staple in north and northeastern Thailand, largely due to the influence of neighboring Laos. Traditionally, this is rolled into small balls with the right hand and then dipped into the various liquid dishes. Special woven bamboo baskets are used to serve the rice at tables and to carry it into the fields by working farmers.

A THAI MEAL

A Thai meal, even in rather grand households, is an informal affair. Steamed rice forms the centerpiece – loose-grained in most parts of the country, glutinous in the north and northeast – and the other dishes are placed around it, to be eaten in any order a diner prefers. There may be many or few of these, depending on economic status, but there is usually some kind of curry, a soup and a spiced salad, along with fish sauce, chopped chillies and other condiments, and fresh fruit as a dessert.

NOODLES

Originally introduced from China, noodles often take the place of rice in quick meals supplied by vendors and sidewalk food shops. They come in numerous sizes, the most common being made from rice, flour or mung beans.

FRESH SEASONINGS

Besides chillies, a number of fresh herbs and roots are regularly used in Thai cooking. Coriander leaves and lemon grass are two of the most popular, while others include root ginger, basil, galangal, garlic and the kaffir lime (both leaves and fruit).

DRY SPICES

Black pepper, used as a hot spice before the introduction of chillies, is still a popular dry ingredient. Among the others are crushed coriander seeds, turmeric, cinnamon, cloves and sesame seeds.

Thailand is blessed not only with a wide selection of delectable fruits but also with some of the best varieties to be found in Southeast Asia. There are more than two dozen kinds of bananas, including a small, finger-sized species noted for its sweetness, as well as mango, durian, pineapple, jackfruit, rambutan, mangosteen, melons, lychee, papaya, guava, fresh coconuts and countless others. Fruit frequently serves as the dessert course, but there are also other choices, including a variety of confections that are eaten as snacks between meals.

STREET SWEETS
Khanom is the general Thai word for "sweet," and many street vendors specialize in one kind or another to tempt passers-by. The woman shown above is preparing a popular delicacy known as *khanom krok*, in which a mixture of thick coconut milk, rice flour, eggs, and sugar is cooked on the spot in a special clay mold.

FRUIT AND VEGETABLE CARVINGS
The art of fruit and vegetable carving was a renowned skill among women of the royal palace and even today many otherwise ordinary dishes in restaurants are enhanced by a radish or spring onion transformed into an unexpected flower. In the hands of a true expert almost any firm-fleshed fruit becomes an object of extraordinary beauty.

PORTUGUESE INFLUENCES
The Portuguese were the first Europeans to open trade relations with Ayutthaya, in the 16th century. Among their cultural influences that still survive are a number of delicate sweets based on egg yolks and sugar, sometimes spun into a mass of thin threads through a special device made for the purpose.

ORNAMENTAL FRUITS

On special occasions, miniature fruits called *look choop* are made from a mixture of mung-bean paste and sugar, then flavored with fragrant essences and realistically colored with food dyes. The creation of these requires considerable skill, and, like fruit and vegetable carving, was once associated with the women of royal and aristocratic households. Decorative baskets of the little fruits are often presented as gifts on birthdays and other celebrations.

COCONUT MILK

A number of Thai desserts consist of various ingredients in sweetened coconut milk. Thin glass noodles may be served in this way, as well as tapioca, rice-flour dumplings that resemble lotus seeds, and sweet blackened jelly cubes. These are often colored with shocking pink and green food dyes and served with ice.

SWEET SELECTION

Presentation is an important part of the appeal of Thai sweets. Coconut custards and jellies are often wrapped individually in banana leaves, which imparts a subtle flavor as well as serving as a useful container, while egg-yolk confections are rolled into golden balls and cakes are cut into varied shapes. Other popular ingredients include glutinous rice, sweet potatoes, pumpkin, palm sugar, slivers of fresh young coconut and mung-bean paste.

DURIAN

A controversial fruit among Westerners because of its distinct smell ("like rotten onions and stale cheese," one writer described it), the durian is highly prized by Thais, fetching high prices during its short fruiting season. The creamy flesh is usually eaten together with sweet sticky rice. Numerous hybrids have been produced by Thai growers, bearing such imaginative names as "Golden Pillow," "Frog" and "Transvestite," the last so called because its seeds will not germinate.

FRUIT AND FRUIT VENDORS

Few Thai street scenes would be complete without a fresh-fruit vendor; his moveable shop dispenses a selection of succulent pineapple, green mango, crisp guava (often dipped into a mixture of dried chillies and salt), banana fritters, prickly rambutans, ruby-red mangosteens, and juicy slices of chilled watermelon.

● KAENG PHED PED YANG

This spicy dish from central Thailand is typical of Thai cuisine with its use of *nam pla*, chillies and other spices and herbs such as coriander. *Kaeng* is a common type of dish meaning "with spicy gravy" and there are many variations on its basic theme. This particular dish can be made with chicken, pork or beef, and is always served with rice and sometimes with salted hard-boiled eggs.

INGREDIENTS
FOR KAENG PHED PED YANG
1 roast duck, boned and cut into small pieces
3 cups of coconut milk
½ cup water
2-3 tablespoons red chilli paste (see "Ingredients for Chilli Paste," opposite)
2 stalks lemon grass
5 small tomatoes
3 tablespoons *nam pla* (fish sauce)
½ cup peas
4 green or red chillies
10 leaves of Asian basil

RECIPE FOR CHILLI PASTE
Fry the cumin and coriander seeds for 1–2 minutes until golden brown. Chop the dried peppers, shallots, garlic and galangal finely. Pound all the paste ingredients, including the fried cumin and coriander, until a smooth paste is obtained. Set the chilli paste aside.

RECIPE FOR KAENG PHED PED YANG

1. Cut the chillies and soak them in water for 10 minutes. Cut the tomatoes into halves. Leave the chillies and tomatoes to one side.

2. In a pan, add two thirds of the coconut milk to the water and bring it to the boil. Leave to simmer.

3. Add the chilli paste and stir well. Cook for a few minutes.

4. Add the pieces of duck to the warmed coconut milk and paste mixture. Turn up the heat and cook for 10 minutes.

80

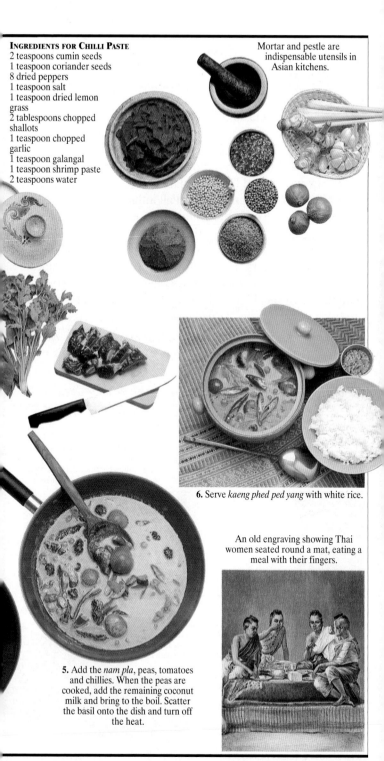

Ingredients for Chilli Paste

2 teaspoons cumin seeds
1 teaspoon coriander seeds
8 dried peppers
1 teaspoon salt
1 teaspoon dried lemon grass
2 tablespoons chopped shallots
1 teaspoon chopped garlic
1 teaspoon galangal
1 teaspoon shrimp paste
2 teaspoons water

Mortar and pestle are indispensable utensils in Asian kitchens.

6. Serve *kaeng phed ped yang* with white rice.

An old engraving showing Thai women seated round a mat, eating a meal with their fingers.

5. Add the *nam pla*, peas, tomatoes and chillies. When the peas are cooked, add the remaining coconut milk and bring to the boil. Scatter the basil onto the dish and turn off the heat.

81

Thai is a pentatonal language belonging to the so-called group of Ka-Tai languages that includes Shan and Khun in Burma, Thô in Vietnam, Buyi and Zhuang in Yunnan and Guizhou provinces of China, and long-extinct languages such as Ahom in Assam. Most of the words are monosyllabic. There are five main dialects in Thailand.

Literature is mostly written in the central dialect spoken in and around Bangkok. Due to the early importance of Buddhism, a strong Sanskrit and Pali influence can be felt in the vocabulary as well as in the syntax. One of the main difficulties in learning Thai lies in the various conversational styles. There are several speech levels in spoken Thai, which depend on age, sex and social factors. The first-person pronoun, for instance, can be rendered in numerous ways ranging from the very humble, when speaking to the king, to the most dismissive.

THAI ALPHABET

Ko Khò Khó Khò Khoo Khoo-ngo ||Cho chó chò Sò choo yo || do to thó thò

thoo no ||bo po ppó fo ||ppò fo ||ppo mo yo ro lo ro|| So Só

According to tradition, the first Thai alphabet was created in 1283 by King Ramkhamhaeng, Rama the Powerful of Sukhothai, who based it on Mon and Khmer versions of an old South Indian script. All these scripts are organized around a horizontal line that runs throughout the words. The script of modern Thai, written from left to right, follows very strict phonological rules. It consists of 44 consonants and 32 basic vowels that cannot be used alone and are written in close relationship to the consonants in order to create syllables.

MANUSCRIPTS

Old Thai manuscripts were written on two kinds of material: *khoi* paper, made from the bark of a local tree, and palm leaf. To make the latter, the leaves of palm fronds were dried and trimmed to form flat sheets; the calligraphy was etched with a sharp needle and the surface rubbed with ink to fill in the engraved areas. Palm leaf books were used only for religious texts and were rarely illustrated. *Khoi* books consisted of sheets folded concertina-fashion into a series of panels. These were often illustrated and dealt not only with religious subjects but also, especially in early Bangkok, with such secular matters as anatomy, warfare, the martial arts and auspicious elephants.

Architecture

1. TEMPLE
2. SCHOOL
3. MARKET AND
   SHOPHOUSES

4. HOUSES ON STILTS
5. VEGETABLE FARM

The typical Thai village is built along a waterway; these form the principal artery of communication in the countryside. Each village is self-contained, comprising a Buddhist temple, a school and a market. Usually, a cluster of Chinese shophouses make up the village market. To stay above floodwaters, many of the houses in the village are built on stilts.

The basic Thai house of the past, rarely seen today, was a simple structure of bamboo and thatch, raised off the ground for protection against floods and wild animals. Most family life took place on a veranda-like platform outside the one or two rooms that served as sleeping quarters. In time, this model evolved into more complex structures of wood, varying in both form and decoration to suit conditions in different regions but always retaining their essential simplicity.

FLOATING HOUSES
Early Bangkok had many floating shophouses, where the family lived and traded. The floorboards in such structures are loosely fitted to allow for movement as the water rises and falls.
▲ 141.

CENTRAL PLAINS HOUSES
The best-known traditional house style is found in the Central Plains. Elevated on stout round posts, it has steep roofs with curved bargeboards and paneled walls leaning slightly inward; the various components are prefabricated to enable easy dismantling and reassembly. The simplest house consists of a single unit with an outside veranda, while those accommodating larger families might have several separate units arranged around a central platform
▲ 246.

ROOF GABLE ("NGAO")
A distinctive feature of the Central Plains house is the elegant curved decoration at the ends of the peaked bargeboards surrounding the gables. Known as *ngao*, it evolved from Khmer architecture and appears in elaborate forms on religious buildings and palaces. A stylized version can also be seen in domestic houses.

PANELING
Paneled walls are a relatively recent addition to the Thai house.

GATE
Houses belonging to more prosperous families usually have a gate, often sheltered by a Thai-style roof that opens on to the central platform. A jar of water is placed at the bottom of the steps so that visitors and residents can wash their feet before ascending.

ROYAL HOUSES

Royal houses were similar in design to those of commoners except that they were generally closer to the ground and had more decorative features.

A famous example that survives from early Bangkok is the Tamnak Daeng, or "Red House," ▲ *157* now in the compound of the National Museum. Built by King Rama I as a residence for one of his queens, it was originally in Ayutthaya style but acquired more Rattanakosin elements during several moves. King Rama V presented the house to the museum as a reminder of an architectural style then becoming rare.

"SALA"

Sala, or pavilions, are open structures with characteristic Thai roofs where people relax and watch the world go by. They can still be seen in many parts of the country: near the entrance to temples, along roadsides and canals, and in several private compounds.

THE NORTHERN HOUSE

The northern Thai house differs significantly from its counterpart in the Central Plains. The walls lean outward, giving it a sturdier look, and windows are often smaller. A notable decorative feature, especially in the Chiang Mai area, are the V-shaped designs at the ends of the roof, called *kalae.* Some authorities believe they represent a pair of buffalo horns.

NORTHERN RICE BARN

A rice barn is a component of most traditional compounds in the northern region. Raised on pillars and with a ladder for access, it is a solid structure with few windows, used to store grain.

THAI TEMPLE

1. "Bot"
The bot, or ubosot, where new monks are ordained, is the most important building in the wat compound, though it may not be the largest or most impressive. It is always surrounded by eight boundary stones (*bai sema*) demarcating the consecrated area, which is outside the authority of any governing body.

The Thai temple, or wat, is actually a complex of buildings and religious monuments within a single compound, often varying in both age and artistic value, designed to serve a number of practical purposes in the surrounding community. One section houses the resident monks, for instance, while elsewhere there are structures for worship, for meetings, for education, for cremations, for enshrining relics and ashes of the deceased.

The focal point of village life, a wat is erected as an act of merit by the community as a whole or by a private patron and is best appreciated through an understanding of its different functions.

"VIHARN"
(NOT FEATURED)
The viharn is an assembly hall used by monks and the laity who come to hear sermons. The compound shown here is without a viharn; other compounds may have several. Viharns and bots are similar architecturally, only distinguishable by the presence of the *bai sema*.

2. "CHEDI"
A chedi, or stupa, is a reliquary monument where relics of the Buddha or the ashes of important people are enshrined. The chedi is often the main reason behind the construction of the wat compound.

3. BELL TOWER
Most wat compounds contain a bell tower. The bell is rung to summon resident monks to prayers in the late afternoon.

4. MONKS' QUARTERS
The monks' quarters in a wat consist of individual houses where the resident monks live, the largest unit being reserved for the abbot.

5. & 6. "HO TRAI"
Ho trai, or libraries, are usually built in the middle of a pond (5) or on a raised platform (6) to keep the manuscripts away from termites and other domestic pests.

7. "SALA KANPRIEN"
The *sala kanprien* usually serves as a meeting hall.

8. "SALA"
Other *sala* in the compound are used by visitors and pilgrims.

9. CREMATORIUM
Cremations are held in a tall, tower-like structure with steps leading to the area where the body is consigned to flames.

Thai architecture evolved from various cultural influences, adapted and subtly transformed into something distinctly different. The process began at Sukhothai, where the first models were stone-roofed Khmer temples and Mon structures. The Thais introduced wooden roofs and more ornamental features, such as colored tiles and ceramic adornments. Other architectural forms came from India, China and Sri Lanka. During the Ayutthaya period, Thai architecture achieved its own unique style.

SUKHOTHAI VIHARN
No Sukhothai-period viharns exist today in their original form, but as shown by this model displayed at the Sukhothai Archeological Park, they were rectangular, open-sided structures with sloping wood roofs in two sections, the lower part supported by pillars with lotus capitals. Ceramic decorations were liberally used ▲ 253, 254.

SUKHOTHAI MONDOP
Mondop, like this one at Wat Si Chum in Sukhothai, were cube-like structures, adapted from Sri Lanka through the Mons. The buildings, which had thick brick walls, were used to house an object of worship, such as a Buddha image or a sacred footprint. The name comes from the Sanskrit word *mandapa*, though in India the structure is designed either as an open hall or as a pavilion ▲ 253.

AYUTTHAYA TEMPLE BUILDINGS
Ayutthaya-style religious structures ▲ 245 were designed to impress with their size and splendor.

A characteristic of the viharns and bots of the period was a concave curve of the base called *thong sampao*. Interiors tended to be dark, to emphasize the mystery and royalty of the Buddha, while elaborate decorations were used on the outside. The example shown above is Wat Na Phra Meru, built in the 15th century and restored by King Rama III of Bangkok.

AYUTTHAYA-PERIOD LIBRARY WINDOW
This window of gilded wood, adorned with inlaid mosaic, is in an Ayutthaya-period *ho trai*, or library; the late 17th-century structure was moved from the old capital to Bangkok.

AYUTTHAYA-PERIOD DOORS
Shown here are doors at Wat Yai Suwannaram in Phetchaburi, which date from the Ayutthaya period. Beautifully carved and gilded, they are particularly fine examples of the graceful curves that characterize Ayutthaya style.

AYUTTHAYA-PERIOD SLIT WINDOWS
Windows with narrow openings, like the one shown here from Wat Na Phra Meru in Ayutthaya, were of Khmer origin and contributed to the darkness of the interior.

THRONE HALL
Though the original has vanished, Ayutthaya's splendid Sampet Prasat Throne Hall at the ancient city has been reconstructed from its remains and from the evidence of records. It clearly shows the ship-hull shape – a prominent feature then – that may have symbolized a ship carrying Buddhist pilgrims to salvation.

LOTUS CAPITAL
Columns surmounted by water-lily or lotus-bud decorations were common on structures dating from the Sukhothai to Ayutthaya periods; in Bangkok, the lotus capital was replaced entirely by the water-lily motif. This example is from the Viharn Daeng in Ayutthaya Province.

● RATTANAKOSIN ARCHITECTURE

At the beginning of the Rattanakosin, or Bangkok, period, a conscious attempt was made to recreate the splendor of Ayutthaya. Some of the first buildings were replicas of former ones, with careful attention paid to every detail. Later Rattanakosin decorations became even more elaborate than those of Ayutthaya, influenced by Chinese motifs and love of color. Western influences became predominant under King Rama V, when foreign architects were brought in to design palace buildings and even temples reflected the new styles.

WAT PO BELL TOWER
Covered with glazed tiles and adorned with pointed finials and ornate decorations, the bell tower at Bangkok's Wat Po ▲ *154* exemplifies all the best qualities of Rattanakosin art. The temple was a favorite with early Chakri rulers, particularly King Rama III.

WAT SUTHAT BOT
Built by King Rama I, founder of Bangkok, the finely proportioned bot of Wat Suthat is 264 feet long and stands on two terraces, adding to its imposing appearance. A colonnade surrounds the structure and bears the weight of the massive four-tier roofs. The interior is decorated with well-preserved mural paintings.

WAT SUTHAT VIHARN
Wat Suthat viharn, one of the finest surviving structures of early Bangkok, has a double-layered roof and eight doors preceded by porticoes. The gables have magnificently carved decorations of various religious symbols, while the interior is divided into three sections by two rows of columns.

CHINESE INFLUENCE
Chinese architectural styles and decorations were popular during the reign of King Rama III, as can be seen in the viharn of Wat Tepidaram.

GATE OF WAT TEPIDARAM
Both Chinese and Western influences are revealed in the external walls of Wat Tepidaram, which are made of whitewashed brick and decorated with Chinese tiles and statues.

WAT SUTHAT DOOR
Leading to the bot enclosure, this door in Wat Suthat is framed with marble and displays the graceful curving lines typical of Rattanakosin.

WAT PHRA KEO WINDOW
Wat Phra Keo, enshrining the sacred Emerald Buddha and serving as the royal chapel, is the most splendid of all Rattanakosin temples, constituting a virtual textbook of classical architecture and decoration. The window shown above reflects the richness and intricate detail of its adornment.

WAT RAJABOPIT WINDOW
Wat Rajabopit, built by King Rama V, displays both traditional and Western styles. Windows like the one above are decorated with mosaics and carvings, and walls and pillars in the temple are covered with colored porcelain tiles.

WAT PHRA KEO MONDOP
The *mondop* at Wat Phra Keo, dating from the reign of King Rama I, is regarded as the most beautiful example of Rattanakosin architecture. Square-shaped and surmounted by a slender spire, it is supported outside by tall elegant columns and is covered with an incredible profusion of lavish decorations.

WAT BENCHAMABOPIT (MARBLE TEMPLE)
Popularly known as the Marble Temple, Wat Benchamabopit ▲ *179, 258* was built toward the end of King Rama V's reign and displays an eclectic blend of cultural influences. The walls are covered with marble brought from Carrara, Italy, while the yellow roof tiles are Chinese. The bot has stained-glass windows as well as massive marble Khmer-style *singha* (guardian lions), flanking the doors.

93

Religious architecture in the northern Lanna kingdom developed independently from that of Ayutthaya in the Central Plains and is linked more with the Thai people of Yunnan, the Shan states and Laos. Thanks to the surrounding teak forests, wood was used extensively in construction and also in decorative carvings to adorn temples. Old Lanna viharns were open, like those of Sukhothai, and the columns supporting the roof were often low.

VIHARN OF WAT CHIENG KHONG
Originally located in Chiang Rai, this example of early Lanna style ▲ *190* was dismantled and brought to the ancient city outside Bangkok to be reassembled. Except for a brick base, the viharn is built entirely of wood, including wooden tiles, and is open on all four sides; low columns support the huge tiered roof.

VIHARN LAIKAM OF WAT PHRA SINGH
This early 19th-century viharn at Wat Phra Singh is possibly the finest example of late Lanna style surviving in Chiang Mai. It is a closed structure with brick walls and a wooden façade; guardian serpents stand on the entrance stairs ▲ *266*.

LIBRARY OF WAT PHRA SINGH
Wat Phra Singh's library is a small wooden building, raised on a high brick base, decorated with stucco deities. The library itself is adorned with intricate inlaid decorations and reflects pure Lanna style at its best ▲ *266*.

KU OF WAT PHRA THAT LAMPANG LUANG
A unique feature of Lanna architecture is the *ku*, a brick structure used to house the Buddha image. Similar to a chedi, it is gilded and placed inside a temple. The *ku* above is in Lampang province ▲ *276, 281*.

WAT PHUMIN

Wat Phumin in Nan province ▲ *285* was established in 1596 by a local ruler and restored in 1865 and 1873. Its main building, serving as both bot and viharn, is a unique structure built on a perfect cruciform plan, with four axial porches leading to four Buddha images placed in the center. On the interior walls are lively murals depicting the Jataka stories and painted about a hundred years ago. The stairways of two opposite entrances are flanked by *naga* with the tail at one doorway and the head at the other. The chapel has a five-tier roof, decorated with *naga* symbolizing the water flowing down from Mount Meru.

MONDOP OF WAT PONGSANUK TAI

This graceful *mondop* at Wat Pongsanuk Tai in Lampang ▲ *279* is a typical example of old Lanna style. Completely open on all sides, it has a tiered roof with false upper stories and a cage enclosing four Buddha images flanking a Bodhi tree. The decorations display a wit and ingenuity lacking in many modern temples of the region, which have been influenced by Bangkok tastes.

CEREMONIAL GATE, WAT SUAN DOK

Monumental gates, like this one at Wat Suan Dok in Chiang Mai, are typical of the north and were also a feature of now-vanished palaces. Wat Suan Dok was once a *wiang,* or fortified monastery, built on the site of a royal garden ▲ *269, 279*.

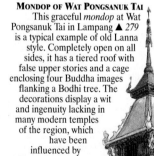

RELIQUARY CHEDI
A reminder of the original significance of the chedi is this example, made of limestone and standing 19 inches high; dating from the 7th and 8th centuries, it was found in Saraburi Province and is now in the National Museum.

It is traditionally claimed that, as the Buddha was dying, one of his disciples asked how they could remember him and his doctrines. He replied that they could make a mound of earth in which a relic of his body could be placed after his cremation. Thus began what has become known as a chedi, a monument that over the years became taller, narrower, and often of considerable size, used to enshrine relics of the Buddha or the ashes of important people, religious and royal. Chedis are found in every wat, often along with prangs, an older type of monument adapted from Hindu architecture, and introduced to Thailand by the Khmers.

SRIVIJAYA CHEDI
Chedis of the Srivijaya period, which lasted in the southern peninsula from the 7th to the 13th centuries, were built of brick and stucco and had strongly Javanese characteristics. The only surviving example in good condition is the one shown on the right, which stands on a square foundation and has four square tiers ascending in decreasing size; located at Wat Phra Boromathat in Chaiya ▲ 201, it dates from the 8th century but has been restored several times, most recently in 1901 and 1930.

SUKHOTHAI LOTUS-BUD CHEDI
The monument after which Wat Chedi Chet Thaew is named was built during Sukhothai's classic period, in the mid-14th century, at the satellite city of Si Satchanalai. An almost identical copy of one at Wat Mahathat in Sukhothai, it has a lotus-bud finial, a feature unique to Sukhothai religious architecture and found on other Sukhothai monuments throughout the kingdom ▲ 256.

AYUTTHAYA PRANG
The prang as a form came to Thailand with the Khmers, who had acquired it from India. In Hindu mythology, it represents the 33 levels of heaven, which in Buddhism became the 33 stages of perfection. It was revived in Ayutthaya to emphasize the concept of divine kingship, as seen here in the prang of Wat Raja Burana ▲ 243, built of stuccoed brick and laterite in 1424. A rare collection of gold objects was found in 1957 in a large crypt beneath the prang.

BELL-SHAPED CHEDI
The bell-shaped chedi originated in Sri Lanka and first appeared in Thai religious architecture during the Sukhothai period; it has been used since throughout Thai history up to the present. The one shown above, at Wat Yai Chai Mongkol in Ayutthaya, is 238 feet high, composed of brick and stucco, and was built by King Rama-thibodi in 1358 ▲ 245.

PHRA PATHOM CHEDI
The orange-tiled, bell-shaped Phra Pathom Chedi at Nakhon Pathom is reputed to be the tallest in the world, 352 feet high and 315 feet in diameter. It was built in the 19th century during the reigns of King Rama IV and Rama V, and encases a much earlier 132-foot monument dating from the Dvaravati period. Several monuments are similarly built around one or more older structures ▲ 186.

WAT ARUN
Wat Arun, or the Temple of Dawn, is one of Bangkok's major riverside landmarks ▲ 170. The central prang, 221 feet high, stands on a 122-foot base; originally only 50 feet high, it was raised to its present height during the reigns of King Rama II and Rama III. Stairways lead up at the four cardinal points, and there are smaller prangs at each of the four corners. All are decorated with multicolored ceramic.

Early Lanna chedis display a number of Sinhalese features and are similar to those of Sukhothai. The region had extensive religious contacts with the outside world; in 1455, during the reign of King Tilokaraja, Chiang Mai was the site of an international Buddhist gathering. Later, in the 19th century, Burmese influences ▲269, 280, altered both temple buildings and monuments. Generally, Lanna chedis are smaller than those in the Central Plains, with the notable exception of Wat Chedi Luang in Chiang Mai, which was raised to 300 feet before its destruction by an earthquake in 1545.

CHEDI AT WAT PHRA SINGH
This chedi at Chiang Mai's Wat Phra Singh consists of a square block topped with a tiered spire, an ancient Lanna form that is related to some in Sukhothai ▲ 266.

CHEDI AT WAT LAI HIN
This chedi at Wat Lai Hin, in the Kokha district of Lampang Province, dates from the late 18th century. Its proportions are modest but the form attests to the grace and elegance of Lanna style ▲ 281.

CHEDI AT WAT CHIANG MAN
Wat Chiang Man, founded in 1296 and restored in the 19th century, was probably the first temple built in Chiang Mai by King Mengrai. The chedi, possibly a 15th-century reconstruction of the original, displays the characteristic motif of the square block but here in huge proportions. The base is decorated with rows of buttresses shaped like elephants, a Sinhalese inspiration that can also be found at several temples built during the Sukhothai period, among them Wat Chang Rop and Wat Chang Lom. The bell-shaped upper part is covered with brass sheets ▲ 267.

CHEDI AT WAT PONGSANUK TAI
The chedi at Wat Pongsanuk Tai ▲ 279 in Lampang is bell-shaped and very elongated, entirely encased in copper sheets; it is surrounded by a low brick wall, which is typical of Lanna monuments. Monks of the monastery walk around the chedi while meditating. A similar but larger chedi can be seen at Wat Phra That Haripunchai in Lamphun ▲ 274.

Thailand as seen by painters

"We went for a walk outside the town. I paused frequently
to admire the strong great city, seated upon an island round
which flowed a river three times the width of the Seine."

Abbé de Choisy

The first Western impressions of Siam are found in early atlases and accounts of voyages and explorations. There are many interesting engravings that accompany the publications of the travels of French Jesuits and the two French embassies to Ayutthaya in 1685 and 1687. The flurry of diplomatic activities and the arrival in Paris of Siamese ambassadors increased the interest in this newly discovered exotic land. One of the most popular subjects was the grand parade of royal barges carrying the Chevalier de Chaumont and his retinue to the king's palace. While the original theme was engraved in the book by Father Guy Tachard, the subject was elaborated and developed in countless prints such as that

shown left (1). Royal elephants and their rich caparisons were another favorite subject (2). This image comes from La Loubère's works. Prints were rarely drawn first-hand and were produced from descriptions and sketches by missionaries. The Cabinet des Estampes in Paris preserves a collection of 33 watercolors that cover most of the themes depicted in the engravings. Reproduced here are a map of Ayutthaya (3) and two views (4 and 5) of the observatory that was constructed by King Narai and given to the Jesuits to pursue their astrological studies.

1		3
		4
2		5

ARUNOTHAI:
LIFE IN THE HAREM

The languid tempera ladies who appear on these pages are the work of Arunothai Somsakul, a contemporary Thai artist. He is inspired by his affection for the elegance of turn-of-the-century court life in Bangkok, which he portrays in a decadent, almost Symbolist manner. A large portion of Arunothai's output is manifestly erotic, and even his more decorous works are suffused with an air of almost palpable sensuality. The oblique looks and whispered conversations of the palace ladies suggest either intrigues or assignations, the imminence of scandal. Even the figures carved in relief on the walls seem privy to many an exciting secret. The concupiscent atmosphere is sometimes reinforced by the presence of small erotic embellishments hidden within the composition that go unnoticed at first – or even second – glance.

The figures conspire in detailed settings that accurately portray the objects of court life at the time. Specific situations are often recognizable: the Vimarn Mek Palace seen through the window behind the gossiping ladies, for example.

The paintings are, as is usual with Arunothai, set during the fifth reign, when Western fashions, often somewhat modified, were already being adopted by Bangkok society.

A record of the colorful mosaic of races and cultures of northern Thailand is preserved in the murals at Wat Phra Singh, Chiang Mai. The surviving Lanna murals are engaging portraits of life in the north, before the irresistible influence of the culture of Bangkok overwhelmed the more delicate Lanna traditions. The murals were probably painted by a local artist named Jek Seng, who completed them during the late 19th century. The changing fashions and growing cosmopolitanism of the period are depicted in a detail from a mural (1), where the man watching the buffaloes wears a Bangkok-style *pannung* ● *56*, evidence that the culture of the capital was already spreading northward at this time. On the same mural, the lofty personages asking for directions are Shan, as is evident from the turbans and striped shawls they wear (2). Their Lue guide is heavily tattooed about the legs and loins and is armed with a red umbrella. The ladies of the market are more conservatively attired; their classic striped sarongs, bare bosoms and thin shoulder-cloths are typically Lanna (3). Life in a typical northern Thai house is also clearly shown (4).

1	3
2	4

The lush green countryside of Thailand did not appear in Thai paintings until relatively late. The religious nature of the works and the flat two-dimensional style confined naturalistic elements to the role of embellishments, with which Thai artists filled up small empty corners of their compositions. The influence of Chinese landscape painting was first felt in the 19th century, gradually filtering into the work of Thai muralists and causing larger areas of their paintings to be treated as landscape. Even so, it was not until the advent of the artist-monk from Phetchaburi, Khrua In Khong ▲ 196, that the landscape per se became a subject in Thai art. An intimate of King Rama IV, Khrua In Khong found inspiration in the traditions of Western painting, which he discovered in the form of reproductions brought to Thailand by ambassadors and missionaries. Khrua In Khong introduced the concept of perspective to Thai painting; he also showed affection for the American neo-classical style of architecture, which made its earliest appearance in Thailand during the 19th century. Khrua In Khong added new colors to the Thai painter's palette, showing a clear preference for darker tones. The two images here of a river scene (1) and town life (2) were finished at Wat Bowornivet, Bangkok, around 1860, and are intended as figurative depictions of religious teachings. The metaphorical landscapes depicted are recognizably Thai; the abundance of water and rolling limestone hills in the background are almost certainly a remembrance of his native Phetchaburi. Khrua In Khong's stormy skies, however, are not particularly Thai; the treatment of clouds and sunlight effects owe a visible debt to the *Tempesta* of Giorgione, a work that was fresh in Khrua In Khong's mind at the time. The geometric perspective of some of the buildings is inspired by the *Flagellazione* of Piero della Francesca.

1

2

"There it was…the oriental capital which had as yet suffered no white conqueror; an expanse of brown houses of bamboo…sprung out of the brown soils on the banks of the muddy river."

Joseph Conrad

Following the expulsion of the French from Ayutthaya in 1688, a century of isolationism followed. During this time few foreigners visited Siam. As a result most of the atlases and books printed contained illustrations adapted from those of La Loubère and Father Guy Tachard. Normal relations with Western countries were resumed during King Rama IV's reign (1851–68) and Siam once again received the attention of writers and publishers, though still very few artists traveled in the country. One of the few artists to visit Siam was Eduard Hildebrandt (1818–69), who produced a series of watercolors of Bangkok and had them published as chromolithographs in his book, *Drei Reise um die Erde* (London, 1867). The two reproduced here show the banks of the Chao Phraya, which at that time was the main thoroughfare of the city. In the first painting, beyond the floating houses, Wat Arun, a famous landmark, can clearly be seen (1). The second provides a glimpse into one of the many floating shophouses that lined both banks (2). The Chinese temple behind would have been one of the few edifices at the time to be built of brick.

1

2

> "I will leave! Steamship with swaying masts, weigh anchor toward exotic nature."
>
> Stephane Mallarmé

By the turn of the century, in that period of revolutionary ideas that was to transform the art scene in the West, many artists felt a special fascination for the Orient and its exotic themes. However, only a few were able to experience at first hand the colors and atmosphere of the East. One artist who did was Galileo Chini (1873–1956). He was summoned to Bangkok in 1911 to decorate the ceiling of the new throne all there, which had recently been completed by Annibale Rigotti. Chini spent two and a half years in Siam, painting the vaulted ceiling of the throne room with friezes in the Secessionist style and large frescoes depicting the glory of the Chakri Dynasty. The artist's long, prolific career subsumed many crucial phases in the development of

modern art: the Pre-Raphaelite movement, Secessionism, Symbolism and Divisionism. Underlying these explorations was a solid Florentine mastery of his craft. The friezes in Bangkok are among the most charming of Chini's paintings. However, the work he completed during the Siam years ranks among his finest in that period. The mood suggested in *Mesu the*

Performer (1), a study of a Thai dancer against a stark black background, is almost erotic, with a touch of the Symbolist manner. Another of Chini's masterpieces is undoubtedly the *Chinese New Year Festival in Bangkok* (2), its phantasmagoric quality achieved through strength of color and diffused light from an apparent multiplicity of sources. A vague hint of the Futurist work of Boccioni is

visible here. *Nostalgia by the River* (3), painted in 1913 in the Divisionist style, creates a suggestive mood around what has long been one of the most popular Thai themes among artists: the river with its decadent, sensual atmosphere.

Chini was fascinated by the elaborate costumes of the Siamese court and pursued his studies with a series of large temperas of figures which are almost scenographic cartoons rather than paintings. The Brahmins shown in the picture above are an exemplary study on white with the translucent and transparent nuances of their immaculate clothes rendered with luminous precision.

Thailand as seen by writers

● THE KINGDOM OF SIAM

EARLY ACCOUNTS OF SIAM

AN IMPORTANT DOCUMENT

The kingdom of Siam had hardly any contact with the West until the 16th century; at least, no notable account of it is found in Western chronicles. Nicolò de' Conti (1395–1469) mentioned the kingdom of Siam, but never visited Ayutthaya, although he crossed the Tenasserim in 1420–30. The first travelers to give a full description of Siam and its inhabitants are the Portuguese. In 1511 Afonso de Albuquerque conquered Malacca, made it a Portuguese stronghold in the Far East, and at once set out to establish relations with all the neighboring peoples. The following is an extract from the instructions given by Afonso de Albuquerque to the ambassador Antonio Miranda de Azevedo in early January 1512, and is the first Western document to recognize the importance of Siam.

❝You shall tell the King of Siam that I am sure that he will rejoice with the destruction of the King of Malacca, with whom he has always been at war. Tell him that the King of Portugal will be very pleased that the Siamese ships and people will trade again with Malacca and that this was the main reason for which I took the city. And tell the King of Siam that if he needs the support of our fleet and our men to preserve his nation, I, as captain-general of the King of Portugal, will serve him in everything he will command.❞

BRAS DE ALBUQUERQUE, *COMENTARIOS DO GRANDE AFONSO DE ALBUQUERQUE* COIMBRA, 1923, PART III, CHAPTER XXXVI

THE KINGDOM OF SIAM

The following, written between 1513 and 1515, is from "A Suma Oriental" by Tomes Pires (1468–1522), who worked as a clerk in the Portuguese trading house in Malacca for over two years; while there is no evidence that he actually visited Siam, he talked with many who did and based this account on their reports. Pires was sent on important missions in India and China and following a series of misunderstandings was eventually imprisoned and killed by the Chinese at Canton. The memoirs of the first part of his adventurous life were first published in Italian by the Venetian scholar Ramusio, in the second half of the 16th century.

❝The kingdom of Siam is heathen. The people, and almost the language, are like those of Pegu. They are considered to be prudent folk counsel. The merchants know a great deal about merchandise…The kingdom is justly ruled. The king is always in residence in the city of Odia (Ayutthaya). He is a hunter. He is very ceremonious with strangers; he moves freely and easily with the natives. He has many wives, upwards of five hundred. On the death of the king a person of the royal blood, usually a nephew, the son of a sister, if he is suitable, and if not there are sometimes agreements and assemblies to decide who will be the best. Secrets are closely kept among them. They are very reserved. They speak with well-taught modesty…❞

TOMES PIRES, *A SUMA ORIENTAL* TRANSLATED BY ARMANDO CORTESAO, LONDON 1944

VENICE OF THE EAST

Soldier, merchant and traveler, Fernão Mendez Pinto (1510–83) lived for many years in the East, writing a record of his pilgrimage in what is perhaps the most original work of this period of Portuguese expansion. A literary masterpiece, the "Peregrinação" was first published in Lisbon in 1614 and has been translated into Spanish, French and English. Fernão Mendez Pinto was in Siam twice in the mid-16th century. The following is extracted from a letter he wrote to the Fathers and Brothers of the Society of Jesus.

"…In the Kingdom of Sornau which is called Siam where I was on two occasions I went to the city of Ayutthaya where the court of the King can be found, and I can state that it is the greatest affair that I saw in all those parts. This city is like Venice because one travels more by water than one does by land. I heard it be said by many that there were over two hundred thousand boats but I did not see a league's length of waterway which was so full that one could not pass; for many fairs are held on the rivers round the city and these are like the feasts of the idols. And to each one of these fairs come five hundred boats and at times over one thousand. The King is called Precaocale, which I have been told means the second person of God. No foreigners have been allowed to see his palaces except for the Ambassadors or those who are to become his vassals. On the outside the palaces are covered with metal and on the inside there is a great deal of gold. The King comes out two times in each year in order that all should see him and is accompanied by two hundred elephants on which are mounted many lords and captains, and he is accompanied by between five and six thousand guardsmen…He is carried on an elephant, sitting on a very ornate chair and one of his pages sits on the elephant's head carrying a gold rope in his hand. On his right hangs a bag full of coins which he distributes as alms."

Transcribed in *Fernão Mendez Pinto, Subsidios Para A Sua Biografia*,
by Cristovão Aires, Lisbon 1904

DUBIOUS MORALS

Little is known of Thomas Herbert, an English adventurer who traveled around the world in the first half of the 17th century. The strange habits mentioned in the following extract, however, are not entirely fictional, and they are often mentioned by other contemporary authors.

"[The Siamese] have beene (in foregoing times) wicked Sodomites, a sinne so hateful to nature itselfe, that it aborres it; and to deterre these calamites, a late Queen commanded that all male children should have a Bell of gold (in it an Adders tongue dried) put through the prepuse, which in small time not only became not contemptible, but in way of ornament and for musick sake few now are without three or foure; so that when they have a mind to marry, he has his choice of what maid he likes, but beds her not, till the Midwife present a sleepie ophiated potion, during which the Bell is loosed from the flesh, and fastened to the fore-skin, which hinders not but titulates; the unguent is applied, and the cure is perfected. But to see a Virgin here, at virgins yeeres, is as a black Swan, in regards, in green yeeres they give the too forward maids a virulent drink; whose vertue (vyce rather) is by a strange efficacy to distend their mullebria so capaciously that Bells and rope ring too easily: and which is worst (dull memory compels us to write it) the women here are not ashamed (the better to allure men from Sodomitry) to go naked to the middle, where with a fine transparent cobweb-lawn they are so covered, that by a base device is made to open as they go; so that any impure ayre gives all to mens immodest viewes, denudating those parts which every modest eye most scorns…"

Thomas Herbert, *Some Years Travels
into Diverse Parts of Asia and Afrique*,
London 1638

SUKHOTHAI

TEMPLES OF SUKHOTHAI

One of the greatest figures of the Portuguese Renaissance, João de Barros (1496–1570) was Factor of the House of India, 1533–67, and, as such, had access to sources and information about the overseas expansion of Portugal. He wrote the four "Decadas da Asia" ('Asian Decades"), first published in Lisbon between 1552 and 1615. Because of his impeccable style and the availability of abundant material, João de Barros is sometimes called the Portuguese Titus Livius. Sukhothai had lost its political importance when João de Barros wrote his "Decadas", but the fame of the city was obviously still alive, and the great temples were then still standing in all their magnificence.

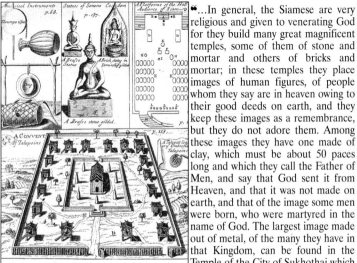

❝...In general, the Siamese are very religious and given to venerating God for they build many great magnificent temples, some of them of stone and mortar and others of bricks and mortar; in these temples they place images of human figures, of people whom they say are in heaven owing to their good deeds on earth, and they keep these images as a remembrance, but they do not adore them. Among these images they have one made of clay, which must be about 50 paces long and which they call the Father of Men, and say that God sent it from Heaven, and that it was not made on earth, and that of the image some men were born, who were martyred in the name of God. The largest image made out of metal, of the many they have in that Kingdom, can be found in the Temple of the City of Sukhothai which they say is the oldest city in the Kingdom. This idol measures 80 palmos and there are a great number of smaller figures, down to human size. The Temples are large and sumptuous and the Kings spend much money on them and every King, as inheritor of the Kingdom, at once starts building a Temple in praise of God, and then builds two or three more, to which they bequeath great revenues.❞

JOÃO DE BARROS, *DECADAS DA ASIA*,
LISBON 1777

PATTANI

THE QUEEN OF PATTANI

Pattani, a Malay kingdom on the coast of the Gulf of Siam, was from early times a vassal of Siam. The kingdom is often mentioned in ancient chronicles because of its importance as a trading post between Siam, China and the Indonesian archipelago. The Portuguese and the Dutch had their trade factories there. The following extract, based on reports of contemporary travelers, is found in the "Pilgrimage" of Rev. Samuel Purchas, a British erudite who compiled a geographical description of the world in the early 17th century.

❝Patane is a City Southwards from Siam, chiefe of that Kingdome, whereto it giveth name, in the height of seven degrees. The buildings are of Wood and Reede, but artificially wrought. The Mesquit (for many of them are Mahumetanes) is of Bricke. The Chinois are more then the native inhabitants. Adulterie is here a capital offence, the father of the malefactor being the Executioner, or his next kinsman, if he be dead; yet is this vice common (notwithstanding this rigor) by reason of the womens unbrideled lust. The Kingdome hath bin governed many yeares by a Queene, who...keepes her selfe close at home among her women; of which some may not marry (but yet may doe worse) others may, having first obtained the Queen's licence. It is seldome that she is seene; yet sometimes she rideth on an Elephant in Progresse, for her recreation. And her Elephants, they have a device to take them in this sort. Some ride into the woods on a tame Elephant, and when they espice a wilde one, they provoke him to fight. Whiles these are fastened in the encounter by the teeth or tuskes, each striving to overthrow the other, some come behinde the wilde Elephant, and fasten his hinder feet, and so either kill him for his teeth, or by famine tame him.**"**

SAMUEL PURCHAS, *PILGRIMAGE, OR RELATIONS OF THE WORLD AND THE RELIGIONS OBSERVED IN ALL AGES AND PLACES DISCOVERED FROM THE CREATION UNTO THE PRESENT*, LONDON 1617

THE END OF A WEALTHY KINGDOM

Pattani was eventually ravaged and destroyed by the Siamese and incorporated into the kingdom; its inhabitants were brought to Bangkok as slaves. This is what George Windsor Earl saw, two hundred years after Purchas' description.

"During many years the Siamese have been making annual excursions into the Malay Peninsula, apparently for no other purpose than to procure slaves. They lately took Queda, a town nearly opposite to Penang, the aggression being connived at, indeed materially assisted by the English, in consideration of some commercial advantages to be granted by the King of Siam.

Two junks, bringing the remainder of the inhabitants of Patani, arrived in the river during my stay. The decks of the junks could not contain these miserable captives, and platforms were erected on the outsides of the vessles for the purpose of affording greater space. These unfortunate creatures were tied hand and foot during the voyage, in order to prevent them from throwing themselves overboard, which many would have done had they been at liberty....Many of the men were wounded, but no consideration was shewn them on that account, not even a bit of cloth being given to bind up their wounds. During the few days of their detention in the factory, numbers of them, particularly of the young children, died from want of food, and from the horrible state of disease which prevailed in consequence of the miseries which they had endured on the voyage. Those who survived were assigned away as slaves to the nobles, and were selected for removal with the utmost disregard to natural ties.**"**

GEORGE WINDSOR EARL, *THE EASTERN SEAS*, LONDON 1837, REPRINTED SINGAPORE 1971

AYUTTHAYA

THE PRESENTATION OF THE LETTER

Faced with a rebellious nobility and a growing Dutch naval presence in Asia, King Narai (1656–88) turned to the French. A 1684 embassy from Siam to the court of Louis XIV stirred up great interest in Paris and its court society, and led to a flurry of diplomatic activity. Ambassadors and members of the retinue published memoirs of their visits to Narai's great capital Ayutthaya, for a European audience that had only now discovered Siam. The first French embassy of the Chevalier de Chaumont in 1685 included Father Guy Tachard (1651–1712), a Jesuit priest whose book relates the diplomatic maneuvering that attended this contact between Europe and Asia.

"It was a Surprise to the Ambassador, when he entered the Hall, to see the King so high above him, and he seemed somewhat troubled that he had not been told of it. When his Complement was made, the next thing he was to do in course, was to advance and present his Master's Letter to the King of Siam. It was agreed upon with the Lord Constance, that to show greater respect to the King's Letter, the Ambassador should take it from the Abbott de Choisi, who for that end should stand by his side during his speech, and hold the Letter in a golden Cup with a very long Foot. But the Ambassador perceiving the King to be so high above him, that to reach up to him he must have taken the Cup by the lower part of the Foot, and raised his Arm very high, thought that that Distance suited not with his Dignity, and that he ought to present the Letter nearer hand. Having a little considered, he thought it was his best Course to hold the Cup by the Boul, and to stretch his Arm but half out. The King perceiving the reason why he acted so, rose up smiling, and stooping with his Body over the Throne, met him half way to receive the Letter: He then put it upon his Head which was a Mark of extraordinary Honour and Esteem that he was willing to shew to the great that sent it.**"**

FATHER GUY TACHARD, *A RELATION OF THE VOYAGE TO SIAM*, LONDON 1688

A VIEW OF AYUTTHAYA

After a somewhat scandalous youth, mostly spent as a transvestite in high Parisian social circles, the Abbé François de Choisy (1644–1724) became a Jesuit priest and went to Siam with the first French embassy in 1685 as assistant to its head, the Chevalier de Chaumont. The following view of Ayutthaya is from a memoir he published in the form of letters.

"We went for a walk outside the town. I paused frequently to admire the great city, seated upon an island round which flowed a river three times the width of the Seine. There rode ships from France, England, Holland, China and Japan, while innumerable boats and gilded barges rowed by 60 men plied to and fro. No less extraordinary were the camps and villages outside the walls inhabited by the different nations who came trading there, with all the wooden houses standing on

Mᴿˢ LES AMBASSADEURS
DU ROY DE SIAM, ENVOYÉ
AU ROY LOUIS LE GRAND
EMPEREUR DES FRANÇOIS
EN 1686.
A Paris rue St Jacques, a l'Image St Francois.

posts over the water, the bulls, cows, and pigs on dry land. The streets, stretching out of sight, are alleys of clear running water. Under the great green trees and in the little houses crowd the people. Beyond these camps of the nations are the wide rice fields. The horizon is tall trees, above which are visible the sparkling towers and pyramids of the pagodas. I do not know whether I have conveyed to you the impression of a beautiful view, but certainly I myself have never seen a lovelier one.**

ABBÉ DE CHOISY, *JOURNAL DU VOYAGE DE SIAM*, LONDON/PARIS 1687

ESTHETICS OF TEETH IN SIAM

"The Natural and Political History of the Kingdom of Siam", from which the following extract comes, was written by Nicolas Gervaise (1662–1729), a French priest who came as a missionary to Ayutthaya in 1683 and remained for four years; published in 1688, the book was used as a source by the better-known Simon de la Loubère.

One thing that the Siamese ladies cannot endure about us is the whiteness of our teeth, because they believe that the devil has white teeth, and that it is shameful for a human being to have teeth like a beast's. Therefore, as soon as the boys and girls reach the age of fourteen or fifteen, they start trying to make their teeth black and shiny. They do this in the following manner: the person whom they have chosen to render them this service makes them lie down on their back and keeps them in this position for the three days that the operation lasts. First, he cleans the teeth with lemon juice and then having rubbed them with a certain fluid which makes them red, he adds a layer of burnt coconut, which blackens them. The teeth are so weakened by the application of these drugs that they could be extracted painlessly and would even fall out if the patient risked eating any solids, so for these three days he subsists on cold soups, which are fed to him gently so that they flow down the throat without touching the teeth. The least wind could spoil the effect of this operation and that is why the patient stays in bed and makes sure that he is well covered until he feels that it is successfully accomplished...

NICOLAS GERVAISE, *THE NATURAL AND POLITICAL HISTORY
OF THE KINGDOM OF SIAM*, LONDON 1688

A SIAMESE FESTIVAL

"A New Historical Relation of the Kingdom of Siam" by Simon de la Loubère, who led the second French embassy to Ayutthaya in 1687, is one of the most comprehensive sources of information about Siamese life and culture in the 17th century.

**When the Waters begin to retreat, the People return them Thanks for several Nights together with a great Illumination; not only for that they are retired, but for the Fertility which they render to the Lands. The whole River is then seen covered with floating Lanterns, which pass with it. They are of different Sizes, according to the devotion of every particular Person; the
variously painted Paper, whereof they are made, augments the agreeable effect of so many Lights. Moreover, to thank the Earth for the Harvest they do on the first days of their Year make another magnificent Illumination. The first time we arrived at Louvo [Lopburi today] was in the Night, and at the time of this Illumination; and we saw the Walls of the City adorned with lighten Lanterns at equal distances...**

SIMON DE LA LOUBÈRE, *A NEW HISTORICAL RELATION OF THE KINGDOM OF SIAM*,
LONDON/PARIS 1691

THE KINGDOM OF LANNA

THE CITY OF CHIANG MAI

Toward the end of the 19th century, Holt S. Hallett made an extensive trip through northern Thailand in search of a route for a British railway that would go from Burma, through upper Thailand, and eventually to China. The railway was never built but Hallett's account of his journey, entitled "A Thousand Miles on an Elephant in the Shan States", offers a rare view of a region visited by relatively few foreigners at the time. Here is an excerpt from his stay in Chiang Mai in 1876.

"It is a pretty sight in the early morning to watch the women and girls from the neighbouring villages streaming over the bridge on their way to the market, passing along in single file, with their baskets dangling from each end of a shoulder-bamboo, or accurately poised on their heads. The younger women move like youthful Dianas, with a quick, firm and elastic tread, and in symmetry of form resemble the ideal models of Grecian art...The ordinary costume of these graceful maidens consists of flowers in their hair, which shines like a raven's wing, and is combed back and arranged in a neat and beautiful knot; a petticoat or skirt frequently embroidered near the bottom with silk, worsted, cotton, or gold and silver thread; and at times a pretty silk or gauze scarf cast carelessly over their bosom and one shoulder. Of late years, moreover, the missionaries have persuaded their female converts and the girls in their schools to wear a neat white jacket, and the custom is gradually spreading through the city and into the neighbouring villages...

After passing through the gates of the outer city we entered the market which extends for more than half a mile to the gates of the inner city, and beyond them for some distance towards the palace. On either side of the main road little covered booths or stalls are set up; but most of the women spread a mat on the ground to sit upon, and placing their baskets by their side, expose their provisions upon wicker-work trays or freshly cut plantain-leaves...Passing from the outer into the inner town, we continued along the main road until we came to the enclosure wall of the palace grounds. The gate of the palace lies 1140 yards from the entrance of the inner town, and leads into an extensive court containing several buildings. The palace faces the gate, and is a substantial one-storied building slightly Chinese in aspect, with brick walls, plastered over with an excellent cement and a tiled roof. Ascending a flight of steps, paved with black tiles, we entered the audience-hall, which occupied the whole front of the building. The floor of the hall is inlaid with various woods, several chandeliers hung from the ceiling and the walls were papered like an English drawing-room, and adorned with long narrow gilt framed mirrors. The remainder of the furniture consisted of a lounge, an easy-chair, a dozen drawing-room chairs, upholstered in green rep, and a small tea-table. Through the doors leading into the private apartments some elegantly designed carved lattice-work partitions were seen, which served as screens in the interior of the palace."

HOLT S. HALLETT, *A THOUSAND MILES ON AN ELEPHANT IN THE SHAN STATES*
LONDON 1891
REPRINTED BANGKOK 1988

STOICAL INDIFFERENCE

Carl Alfred Bock (1849–1932), a Norwegian naturalist of the positivist school, was an enthusiastic explorer and a prominent adventurer. Having acquired fame for his Borneo expeditions and published a book "The Head-Hunters of Borneo", Bock set out to explore northern Thailand at a time when the region was impoverished by continuous wars and misrule. Ever in search of the exotic and the sensational, Bock was often known to cast negative remarks on the natives, his judgment usually tainted by the desire to make his "adventures" seem a great deal more treacherous than they actually were.

"If a man's face is an index to his feelings, then the Laosians must be bereft of all capacity to appreciate any variety of mental emotions. It is the rarest phenomenon to see any change in their countenance or deportment, except – there is always one exception to every rule – when they are aroused to anger. This statement is more particularly true of the men, but even the women – demonstrative as the sex usually are – are seldom moved to either laughter or tears. Whatever news a Laosian may receive, whether of disaster or of joy, he hears it with a philosophic indifference depicted on his calm stoical countenance that a European diplomatist would give a fortune to be able to imitate. But when any sudden feeling of anger or any latent resentment is aroused, then the passion begins to display itself, if not in any great change of facial expression, at any rate in general demeanor, and in quick restless movements of impatience and irritation.

This natural stoical indifference to their surroundings is fostered by the influence of their religious belief, and by the general state of ignorance in which the people are kept, as well as by their isolation from the rest of the world. They are naturally lazy, and, with a fertile soil which provides them with all the necessaries of life without any appreciable effort on their part, their indolence is encouraged."

CARL A. BOCK, *TEMPLES AND ELEPHANTS, TRAVELS IN SIAM IN 1881–82*,
LONDON 1883

THE GOLDEN TRIANGLE

AN ASIAN ARCADY

THE LAND AND PEOPLES OF NORTHERN SIAM

Reginald Le May served for a time in the early years of this century with the British legation in Bangkok and later as Vice-Consul in the north; still later, he worked as an advisor to the Royal Siamese Government. "An Asian Arcady", from which the following comes, is an account of northern Thailand and of a 700-mile trip he took by elephant in 1914.

"Below my feet the river bank went sheer down for nearly fifty feet; the river itself was a mighty expanse of water flowing swift and clear, with just the top of an island showing, and far away on the other side the bank rose fully as high again, lined with row upon row of tall palms, looking like small shrubs in the distance. On the left, the river took a wide bend to the west, and on the right, another sweeping bend to the east, and in front the great gaunt hills rolled down to meet the river at either bend. This was the very apex of Siam. North lay British territory, the southern Shan states, and to the East, across the blue expanse, were the Lao states, which are now French soil. What a magnificent boundary to have for one's country! In full flood it must be a still more thrilling sight, but it is only in September or October, when the rains are nearly over and the northern rivers are beginning to rise, that one can see the river at its height. Once in about twenty years, the Mekhong overflows its banks, and when one thinks of their height and of the breadth of the river, the volume of water must be prodigious.... Chieng Sen is a mysterious old city, surrounded by a high, thick, strong wall with palisades on top of the brick, and deep trenches dug outside. How far the wall extends, and what area it embraces, it is difficult to say. The whole city is now so overgrown with plantations of teak, and thick secondary growth, that one cannot see more than twenty yards ahead, except on the main grassy track; but it must be of wide extent, for the District Officer told me that there are actually now tiger and other game living within the walls, and that he had recently fired several shots at a rhinoceros...

It is sad to contemplate a great city, which once contained seventy-five temple deserted by all, and even its ruins lost in the jungle; but old Chieng Sen has littl hopes of recovery now, for it lies off the main road and the cost of clearing th plantations and undergrowths of brushwood which now choke the city would be to great to repay the undertaking. How are the mighty fallen and the weapons of wa perished! So the old city sleeps, a prey to the wild beast of the jungle and thos craftier two-legged animals, who come to seek what they can find among the ruin which lie to hand.**

REGINALD LE MAY, *AN ASIAN ARCADY*, CAMBRIDGE 1926
REPRINTED BANGKOK 198

BANGKOK

AN AUDIENCE WITH THE KING OF SIAM

After the assassination of Phaulkon and the expulsion of the French from Ayutthaya, Siam remained in almost complete isolation for nearly 150 years. Among the many unsuccessful delegations from the West was tha of John Crawfurd, an Englishman. He came to the court of King Rama II in 1822. The following is an extract from Crawfurd's account of hi first audience with the king.

The curtain placed before the throne was drawn aside as we entered. The whole multitude present lay prostrate on the earth, their mouths almost touching the ground: not a body or limb was observed to move; not an eye was directed towards us; not a whisper agitated the solemn and still air....Raised about twelve feet above the floor, and about two yards behind the curtain alluded to, there was an arched niche, on which an obscure light was cast, of sufficient size to display the human body to effect, in the sitting posture. In this niche was placed the throne, projecting from the wall a few feet. Here, on our entrance, the King sat immovable as a statue his eyes directed forwards. He resembled, in every respect, an image of Buddha placed upon his throne; while the solemnity of the scene, and the attitude of devotion observed by the multitude, left little room to doubt that the temple had been the source from which the monarch of Siam had borrowed the display of regal pomp.

JOHN CRAWFURD, *JOURNAL OF AN EMBASSY FROM THE GOVERNOR GENERAL OF INDIA
TO THE COURTS OF SIAM AND COCHIN-CHINA*, LONDON 1828
REPRINTED SINGAPORE 197

THE FLOATING CITY

Mrs Anna Leonowens, an English widow, arrived in Bangkok in 1862 engaged to teach English to some of King Rama IV's wives and children She wrote two books about her experiences, "The English Governess at the Siamese Court" and "The Romance of the Harem", which later formed the basis of the popular musical "The King and I". Although her books, written in the style of the serial melodrama, are largely inaccurate, her description of Bangkok is quite realistic.

**The situation of the city is unique and picturesque. When Ayutthaya was 'extinguished,' and the capital established at Bangkok, the houses were at first built on the banks of the river. But so frequent were the invasions of cholera, that one of the kings happily commanded the people to build on the river itself, that they might have greater cleanliness and better ventilation. The result quickly proved the wisdom of the measure. The privilege of building on the banks is now confined to members of the royal family, the nobility and residents of acknowledged influence, political or commercial...At night the city is hung with thousands of covered lights, that illuminate the wide river from shore to shore. Lamps and lanterns of all imaginable shapes, colours, and sizes combine to form a fairy spectacle of enchanting brilliancy and beauty. The floating tenements and shops, the masts of vessels, the tall, fantastic pagodas and minarets, and, crowning all, the walls and towers of the Grand Palace, flash with countless charming tricks of light, and compose a scene of more than magic novelty and beauty. So oriental fancy and profusion deal with things of use, and make a wonder of a commonplace...

A double, and in some parts a triple, row of floating houses extends for miles along the banks of the river. These are wooden structures, tastefully designed and painted, raised on substantial rafts of bamboo linked together with chains, which, in turn, are made fast to great piles planted in the bed of the stream. The Meinam itself forms the main avenue, and the floating shops on either side constitute the great bazaar of the city, where all imaginable and unimaginable articles from India, China, Malacca, Burma, Paris, Liverpool and New York are displayed in stalls...

Naturally, boats and canoes are indispensable appendages to such houses; the nobility possess a fleet of them, and to every little water-cottage a canoe is tethered, for errands and visits. At all hours of the day and night processions of boats pass to and from the palace, and everywhere bustling traders and agents ply their dingy little craft, and proclaim their several callings in a Babel of cries.❞

ANNA LEONOWENS, *THE ENGLISH GOVERNESS AT THE SIAMESE COURT*,
LONDON 1870

THE WOMEN'S BURDEN

George Windsor Earl (1805–65) was a British officer in the Far East and Australia. Linguist, antiquarian and author, he wrote several books. His first work, and probably his best, "The Eastern Seas", recounts his travels in the Far East. The book stands out among contemporary literature for its acute judgment and sense of observation.

❝The Siamese empire is apparently on the decline, a circumstance which may be attributed to the ruinous wars in which it is continually engaged, and to the enormous church establishment. Every man is obliged to serve as a soldier when called for, and to bring with him provisions for his own subsistence sufficient for his supply for several months. Wars, therefore, entail little expense on the government which may account for the readiness with which they are undertaken. The men who are engaged in their usually inglorious campaigns, acquire habits of idleness which are never afterwards corrected, and consequently the support of these drones, and of the enormous mass of priesthood, falls entirely on the women. The body of Talapoins or priests is enormously disproportioned to the rest of the inhabitants. In Bangkok alone, their numbers exceed thirty thousand. Like lilies of the valley 'they toil not, neither do they spin,' but are idle consumers of the produce of the soil. They do not even cook their own provisions, not being permitted to do so by their creed, but the younger members of the community go from house to house to collect the viands which are bountifully supplied by the people. The Talapoins received a great accession to their ranks during a late period of scarcity, indeed it must be a matter of surprise that all the males do not become members of the priesthood, since among the privileges of their order may be reckoned exemption from labour, taxation, and military service, while they are at liberty to retire from the office whenever they please; the mode of life, however, led by these lazy vagabonds is found to be so agreeable, that they rarely take advantage of the latter privilege. The males affect to consider the women in the light of an inferior order of beings, but these lordly personages seldom enter upon any undertaking of moment without first consulting their wives. The women indeed, may be said to compose the most important portion of the community. They transact the greater part of the mercantile business, and are the principal cultivators of the soil, cheerfully undertaking the most laborious employments in the support of their families."

GEORGE WINDSOR EARL, *THE EASTERN SEAS*, LONDON, 1837,
REPRINTED SINGAPORE, 1971

CONRAD ARRIVES IN BANGKOK

The future author Joseph Conrad (1857–1924) came to Bangkok in 1888 as a seaman named Josef Teodor Konrad Korzeniowski, to take his first command as captain of a ship called the "Otago". In "The Shadow-Line", he describes his arrival in the city.

"One morning, early, we crossed the bar, and while the sun was rising splendidly over the flat spaces of land we steamed up the innumerable bends, passed under the shadow of the great gilt pagoda, and reached the outskirts of the town…There it was, spread largely on both banks, the Oriental capital which had yet suffered no white conqueror; an expanse of brown houses of bamboo, of mats, of leaves, of a vegetable-matter style of architecture, sprung out of the brown soil on the banks of the muddy river. It was amazing to think that in those miles of human habitations there was not probably half a dozen pounds of nails…

Some of those houses of sticks and grass, like the nests of an aquatic race, clung to the shores, others seemed to grow out of the water; others again floated in long anchored rows in the very middle of the stream. Here and there in the distance, above the crowded mob of low, brown roof ridges, towered great piles of masonry, king's palace, temples, gorgeous and dilapidated, crumbling under the vertical sunlight, tremendous, overpowering, almost palpable, which seemed to enter one's breast with the breath of one's nostrils and soak into one's limbs through every pore of the skin."

JOSEPH CONRAD, *THE SHADOW-LINE*,
LONDON 1986

MAUGHAM ON THAI TEMPLES

Somerset Maugham (1874–1965) was a doctor before he gained fame as a novelist and short-story writer. He served as a British agent in the two world wars. Maugham came to Thailand overland through Burma in 1923. The following extract from one of his travel books, "The Gentlemen in the Parlour", records his vivid impressions of Bangkok's famous Buddhist temples.

"They are unlike anything in the world, so that you are taken aback, and you cannot fit them into the scheme of the things you know. It makes you laugh with delight to think that anything so fantastic could exist on this sombre earth. They are gorgeous; they glitter with gold and whitewash, yet are not garish; against that vivid sky, in that dazzling sunlight, they hold their own, defying the brilliancy of nature and supplementing it with the ingenuity and the bold playfulness of man. The artists who developed them step by step from the buildings of the ancient Khmers had the courage to pursue their fantasy to the limit; I fancy that art meant little to them, they desired to express a symbol; they knew no reticence, they cared nothing for good taste; and if they achieved art it is as men achieve happiness, not by pursuing it, but by doing with all their heart whatever in the day's work needs doing. I do not know that in fact they achieved art; I do not know that these Siamese wats have beauty, which they say is reserved and aloof and very refined; all I know is that they are strange and gay and odd, their lines are infinitely distinguished, like the lines of a proposition in a schoolboy's Euclid, their colours are flaunting and crude, like the colours of vegetables in the greengrocer's stall at an open-air market, and, like a place where seven ways meet, they open roads down which the imagination can make many a careless and unexpected journey.**

A WELCOME FROM MISS PRETTY GIRL

A calling card was given to Somerset Maugham by a street tout during his visit to Thailand in 1923. Reproduced here is its message, which was recorded in the same book. The gentleman, incidentally, refused the invitation.

"Oh, gentleman, sir, Miss Pretty Girl welcome you Sultan Turkish Bath, gentle polite massage, put you in dreamland with perfume soap. Latest gramophone music. Oh, such service. You come now! Miss Pretty Girl want you, massage you from tippy-toe to head-top, nice, clean, to enter Gates of Heaven."

SOMERSET MAUGHAM, *THE GENTLEMEN IN THE PARLOUR*,
LONDON 1930

THE TEMPLE OF DAWN

"The Temple of Dawn" was one of a cycle of four novels by the Japanese author Yukio Mishima (1925–70), the last of which was completed just before his ritual suicide in 1970. Much of the novel takes place in Bangkok, shortly before and during World War Two; in this passage the young hero visits Wat Arun, the Temple of Dawn, in the early morning:

"It was still darkish, and only the very tip of the pagoda caught the first rays of the rising sun. The Thonburi jungle beyond was filled with the piercing cries of birds...The repetitiveness and the sumptuousness of the pagoda were almost suffocating. The tower with its color and brilliance, adorned in many layers and graduated toward the peak, gave one the impression of so many strata of dream sequences hovering overhead. The plinths of the extremely steep stairs were also heavily festooned and each tier was supported by a bas-relief of birds with human faces. They formed a multicolored pagoda whose every level was crushed with layers of dreams, expectations, prayers, each being further weighted down with still other stories, pyramid-like, progressing skyward...With the first rays of dawn over the Menam River,...thousands of porcelain fragments turned into so many tiny mirrors that captured the light. A great structure of mother-of-pearl sparkling riotously...The pagoda had long served as a morning bell tolled by its rich hues, resonant colors responding to the dawn. They were created...to evoke a beauty, a power, an explosiveness like the dawn itself."

YUKIO MISHIMA, *THE TEMPLE OF DAWN*,
NEW YORK 1973

A HUMORIST IN BANGKOK

S.J. Perelman, a leading American humorist, was a regular contributor to the "New Yorker" magazine as well as a playwright and the author of early film scripts for the Marx brothers. Shortly after World War Two he made a trip through Asia, which under the title of "Westward Ha!" became a bestseller; the following extract gives his impressions of Bangkok at a time when it was relatively untouched by mass tourism.

❝From the very beginning I was charmed by Bangkok, and I propose to be aggressively syrupy about it in the most buckeye travelogue manner. I liked its polite, gentle, handsome people, its temples, flowers, and canals, the relaxed and peaceful rhythm of life there. Apart from its shrill and tumultuous central thoroughfare swarming with Chinese and Indian bazaars, it struck me as the most soothing metropolis I had thus far seen in the East. Its character is complex and inconsistent; it seems at once to combine the Hannibal, Missouri of Mark Twain's boyhood with Beverly Hills, the Low Countries, and Chinatown. You pass from populous, glaring streets laden with traffic into quiet country lanes paralleled by canals out of a Dutch painting; a tree-shaded avenue of pretentious mansions set in wide lawns becomes a bustling row of shops and stalls, then melts into a sunny village of thatched huts among which water-buffalo graze. The effect is indescribably pleasing; your eye constantly discovers new vistas, isolated little communities around every corner tempting you to explore them.❞

S.J. PERELMAN, *THE MOST OF S.J. PERELMAN*
NEW YORK, 1978

THE COUNTRYSIDE AND THE CITY

Minfong Ho is a Singaporean, but she spent most of her childhood in Thailand, and was for many years a teacher at the University of Chiang Mai. Her first novel, "Rice without Rain", was based on her experiences in northern Thailand during the 1976 student uprising, and it describes the politicization of an impoverished northern Thai village by a group of idealistic young students. The novel opens with a scene from the ricefields.

❝Heat the colour of fire, sky as heavy as mud, and under both the soil – hard, dry unyielding. It was a silent harvest. Across the valley, yellow ricefields stretched stopped and dry. The sun glazed the afternoon with a heat so fierce that the distant mountains shimmered in it. The dust in the sky, the cracked earth, the shrivelled leaves fluttering on brittle branches – everything was scorched. Fanning out in a jagged line across the fields were the harvesters, their sickles flashing in the sun. Nobody spoke. Nobody laughed. Nobody sang. The only noise was wave after wave of sullen hisses as the rice stalks were slashed and flung to the ground. A single lark flew by, casting a swift shadow on the stubbled fields. From under the brim of her hat, Jinda saw it wing its way west. It flew to a tamarind tree at the foot of the mountain, circled it three times, and flew away. A good sign...❞

The 1976 student movement was put down by the army, with considerable violence. Many of the student leaders fled to the jungle to take up arms with the Communist Party of Thailand (CPT). But most soon found themselves at odds with the CPT's hierarchy. Through a skillful policy of coercion and reconciliation, the Thai government was able to diffuse the Communist threat, and bring the guerillas out of the hills. Today, members of the 1976 movement are among the professional middle classes of Bangkok, and it was this group's willingness to take risks that led to the eventual victory of the pro-democracy forces, after a bloody confrontation in Bangkok's Sanam Luang square in 1992.

MINFONG HO
RICE WITHOUT RAIN

from the author of
SING TO THE DAWN

❝ 'I am Jinda, daughter of Inthorn Sriboonrueng,' she began. To her surprise she found that her voice was steady. It reverberated from all corners of the square, and even from the wall of the temple. She felt awed that her voice could reach so far. She had practised the speech so many times that it had become automatic, and it flowed effortless from her now, separate and yet a part of herself. Like a kite with a lovely long tail, tugging its way upwards as she held the string, her words flew up. It was an exhilarating feeling, and Jinda's voice grew stronger with it. 'My father has farmed all his life,' she said, 'and yet he has never had enough to eat. Why?' She paused, and in that brief silence she felt that maybe, just maybe, she could help change a bit of Thailand after all. 'Because he has had to pay half of his harvest to the landlord, year after year. Flood or drought.'

'Commie bitch!' A shrill voice pierced the air.

Startled, Jinda stopped. Who had shouted that? Why?

Suddenly, a heavy object sailed towards her, landing where the shoe-shine boy had been. There was a loud explosion, and bits of dirt and glass shattered out. In the rolls of smoke which poured forth, people screamed, and started to run.

Ned grabbed the microphone from Jinda, and urged the crowd to be calm. 'Nothing serious has happened,' he announced. 'A small homemade bomb has just been tossed at us. This has happened in previous rallies. It hasn't hurt anyone. Do not panic, I repeat, do not panic. The speech will continue.'

But something was happening on the far side of the square. The soldiers in their olive green fatigues had fanned out in front of the ambulances, and were advancing towards the centre, pushing the crowd forward.

There was another explosion. It landed further away, but the bomb was deafening and devastating. As the smoke cleared, Jinda stared, stunned. At least five students sprawled motionless on the grass...that was when the distant gunfire started. At first Jinda did not know what it was, this sharp staccato rattle. Then she saw students dropping to their knees, in crumpled heaps, and she understood.❞

MINFONG HO, RICE WITHOUT RAIN,
SINGAPORE 1986

BANGKOK NIGHTLIFE

Born in England, Pico Iyer wrote for "TIME" magazine. He has also written for the "Partisan Review", "The Village Voice" and the "Times Literary Supplement". He came to Thailand in the 1980's while gathering material for a travel book later published as "Video Night in Kathmandu", from which the following excerpt is taken.

❝In seedy and improvident Manila, the bars were the fast-buck stuff of a puritan's nightmare; while in high-tech and prosperous Bangkok, they were quicksilver riddles, less alarming for their sleaze than for their cunning refinement, embellished by the country's exquisite sense of design, softened by the ease of Buddhism, invigorated by the culture of *sanuk* (a good time). In Manila girls tried to sell themselves out of sheer desperation; in Bangkok, the crystal palaces of sex were only extra adornments in a bejeweled city that already glittered with ambiguities...In Bangkok, moreover, the ambivalence of the girls only intensified the ambiguity of the bars...no gaze was direct, and no smile clear-cut in the city of mirrors. And the mirrors were everywhere: one-way mirrors walling the massage parlors, mirrors lining the ceilings of the 'curtain hotels,' mirrors shimmering in the bars, pocket mirrors in which each girl converted herself into a reflection of her admirer's wishes. Look into a bar girl's eyes, and you'd see nothing but the image of your own needs; ask her what she wanted, and she'd flash back a transparent 'up to you.' Everything here was in the eye of the beholder; everything was just a trick of the light.❞

PICO IYER, VIDEO NIGHT IN KATHMANDU,
NEW YORK 1988

NAKHON PATHOM

THE WORLD'S BIGGEST PAGODA

Sunthorn Phu (1786–1856) is generally regarded as Thailand's greatest poet, the first to bring realism into Thai verse. Born shortly after the establishment of Bangkok as the capital, he was a particular favorite of King Rama II, during whose reign he wrote perhaps the most famous of his works, "Khun Chang and Khun Phan". Sunthorn Phu is also noted for his works in a Thai genre called the "nirat", a sort of travel poem that blends descriptions of actual places with meditations on life and love by the poet. The following is from his "Nirat Phra Pathom", about a journey to the famous chedi in what is today called Nakhon Pathom.

❝At last, we arrive at the Pagoda of the Sleeping Buddha's Temple.
It stands alone and high on a hill;
Colossally solid like a parapet,
Mounted on a manmade promontory.
It was constructed with sharp corners, showing the front gable,
Covered with a thin sheet of tin up to the top,
Stretching staunch and seamless in brick-and-stucco walls,
Wrought with time-honored and meticulous workmanship.
We walk around the Pagoda at the base,
Seeing deer's traces and hearing wild cocks crowing.
The spot is overgrown with wild creepers,
Winding and sticking in a thick green cluster.
We see secluded cubicles built for monks
Who may take shelter in their pilgrimages.
We are moved by their ardent faith.
At the stairs, we gaze up the slope:
It's so steep that our faces remain upturned.
That must be the way to heaven when we die.
We make an effort to help one another upward.
Once reaching the upper level, we are high spirited.
Pity my sons who also come up.
They are not so tired as us adults, though.
We hold candles in reverential attitude
And walk clockwise around the Pagoda
Three times, according to ceremonious practice.
Then we sit down and pay respects.
We offer incense sticks, candles, and flowers,
Also the candles entrusted to us by many others.
The owners had already made their wishes.
May they keep their beauty to the end.
May they be happy, every one of them,
Until they become enlightened by faith.
I've brought these candles with a desire
To be related to them in every life to come.
May our mutual love materialize now
And, in the future, may it be complete;
I salute the Pagoda of the Holy Relics;
May the true religious live forever.
I make merit, so the Buddha helps me
Increase my power to attain enlightenment.
And I'd like my words, my book,
To preserve, till the end of time and heaven,
Sunthorn the scribe who belongs
To the King of the White Elephant.❞

SUNTHORN PHU, *NIRAT PHRA PATHOM*,
TRANSLATED BY MONTRI UMAVIJANI,
BANGKOK 1986

Itineraries

▲ Bangkok.

▲ Wat Phra Keo and Royal Palace, Bangkok.   ▼ Lumpini Park and modern Bangkok.

▲ ▼ The banks of the Chao Phraya River.

▼ Wat Thong Thammachat, Thonburi, in Bangkok.

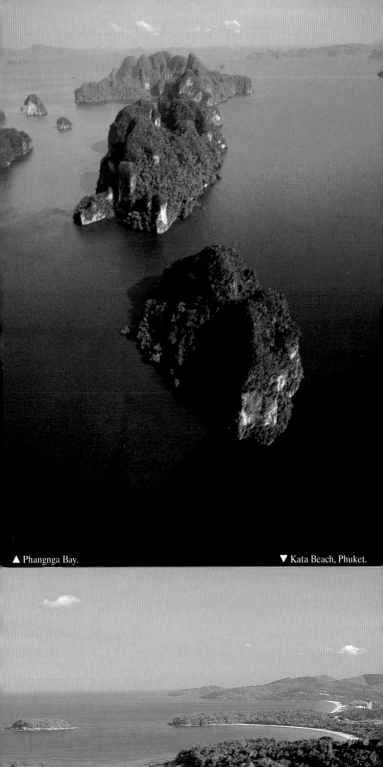

▲ Phangnga Bay.

▼ Kata Beach, Phuket.

▲ Koh Phi Phi Le.

▼ Kata Yai Beach, Phuket.

▲ Wat Phra Si Sanphet, Ayutthaya.

▲ Wat Mahathat, Sukhothai.   ▼ Life on the river, Ayutthaya.

▲ Monks collecting alms in Chiang Mai. ▼ Duck farm, Singhburi.

▼ Floating market, Damnern Saduak.

Bangkok

KLONG BANG LAM PHU

WAT BOWORNIVET

RATCHADAMNOEN ROAD

DEMOCRACY MONUMENT

WAT RATANADDA

WAT SAKET (GOLDEN M...

NATIONAL THEATER

NATIONAL MUSEUM

THAMMASAT UNIVERSITY

WAT MAHATHAT

SANAM LUANG

LAK MUANG

MINISTRY OF DEFENSE

WAT PHRA KEO

GIANT SWING

WAT SUTHAT

WAT RAJABOPIT

RAILWAY STATION

MEMORIAL BRIDGE

WAT ARUN

WAT RAJAPRADIT

ROYAL PALACE

WAT PO

An early view of Bangkok from the murals of Wat Rajapradit, painted in 1864. Behind the roofs of the Royal Palace runs the Chao Phraya, lined with floating houses on its banks. Chinese shophouses and Western-style homes stand among Thai temples and orchards.

Both literally and metaphorically, all roads in Thailand lead to Bangkok (derived from *bang makok*, which means "Village of the Wild Plum"), the center of almost everything: of power both temporal and spiritual, of the ancient monarchy, of commerce and communications, of higher education and the arts, of that indispensable part of life the Thais call *sanuk*, or "fun." It has a dynamic modern façade, sprawling and often confusing to the newcomer, best comprehended perhaps by looking back to the city's early days.

THE FOUNDING OF BANGKOK

Following the 1767 destruction of Ayutthaya, after 400 years of rule from there, the Thai capital was moved first to Thonburi on the west bank of the lower Chao Phraya River and then, in 1782, to a small trading port called Bangkok on the opposite bank. King Rama I, who decreed the move, felt the position of the new capital was more defensible and that it offered the space for a capital worthy of the Chakri Dynasty, which

140

> "The general appearance of Bangkok is that of a large, primitive village, situated in and mostly concealed by a virgin forest of almost impenetrable density."

Frank Vincent, 1871

he had founded. He gave it a lengthy official title, which the Thais have shortened to Krung Thep, "City of Angels," while foreigners continue to use the old name; the period of Thai history thus inaugurated is called Rattanakosin. As a matter of interest, Krung Thep is adapted from its actual name (listed in the *Guinness Book of Records* as the world's longest place name):

Krungthep Mahanakhon Bovorn Rattanakosin Mahintharayutthaya Mahadilokpop Noparatratchathani Burirom Udomratchaniveymahasathan Amornpiman Avatansathit Sakkathattiya-avisnukarmprasit.

RATTANAKOSIN ISLAND

The Grand Palace and its adjacent royal chapel, the Temple of the Emerald Buddha – both replicas of Ayutthayan structures – were built first on an artificial island created by digging a canal where the river curved sharply, a strategy that had been used at Ayutthaya. Walled and fortified, the island was the political and cultural heart of the capital for more than a century. A group of Chinese traders who had occupied the site were moved outside the walls, where they formed the nucleus of a flourishing community of narrow streets, wharfs and warehouses that still exists. Spurred by increasing trade with the outside world, relative political stability and immigration (mainly Chinese), the city of Bangkok expanded rapidly. Two new canals were excavated and rows of floating houses ● 86 appeared on both banks of the Chao Phraya, and ships began arriving from Europe as well as neighboring countries. The floating houses served as both shops and residences for most of the population. Not until the 1820's did non-royal homes begin to appear on land, the majority on the Thonburi side of the river. By the mid-19th century, Bangkok had a population of 300,000 and was well on its way to becoming a major metropolis.

THE FOUNDER OF BANGKOK
King Rama I was a former military commander who succeeded King Taksin of Thonburi as ruler in 1782; he also began the Chakri Dynasty, of which the present king is the ninth monarch. The original buildings of the Grand Palace, as well as numerous temples, date from his seventeen-year reign.

FLOATING HOUSES
Thousands of floating houses, anchored to stout posts, lined the river and canals of early Bangkok.

BANGKOK'S FIRST RICKSHAW

A wealthy Chinaman presented the first rickshaw to King Rama V in 1871; within a generation there were so many on the streets of Bangkok that, in 1901, a law was passed limiting their number. Automobiles arrived the following year. By 1908, there were over 300 cars; the invasion of this modern form of transportation spelled doom for the city's once numerous canals.

EARLY TIMES

Early Bangkok was a water-oriented city, with the river and an intricate system of canals, or klongs, serving as the means of communication. The first proper street appeared in 1862, during the reign of King Rama IV, and ran parallel to the river for a considerable distance. Along it were most of the embassies, trading companies and shophouses selling the latest imported goods. Soon roads began to radiate from the Chao Phraya, through former orchards and across ricefields, accommodating ever-growing numbers of rickshaws, carriages, trams and, in 1902, automobiles. King Rama V, inspired by his visits abroad, attempted to create an orderly, European-style city in the Dusit district, with broad, tree-lined avenues and parks. But Bangkok resisted any such systematic planning; by World War Two it was sprawling in all directions from the original walled island. A building boom that started in the 1950's and continues to this day has transformed the capital almost beyond recognition to older Thais.

MODERN-DAY BANGKOK

Present-day Bangkok covers an area of over 1,500 square kilometres, on both sides of the river –forty-five times larger than its nearest provincial rival – and is home to an estimated seven million people. (The exact population would be impossible to calculate; many are part-time laborers who come to work between farming chores, while others are still registered as residents of their hometowns despite years in the capital.) They live and work in a variety of centers, often commuting for several hours each day by bus, presently the city's only form of public transport. (Bangkok's public bus system, incidentally, is reputedly the largest in the world.) Government offices are concentrated mainly in the area around the Grand Palace and Ratchadamnoen Road, while Yaowarat Road and its environs are largely devoted to Chinese business firms and the powerful military has its headquarters behind high walls in the Dusit district. Silom Road has emerged as the financial district, with Patpong as a major attraction after nightfall; a number of leading hotels are also in this area. Though the streets off Sukhumwit Road comprise the prime residential district popular with foreigners, new suburban housing estates can be found all around the city with shopping and recreational facilities constantly rising to meet the demands of the growing population.

RECENT DEVELOPMENTS

The past decade or so has seen the contruction of impressive and often luxury appartment buildings in the city center especially along the Chao Phraya for affluent Thais seeking a location more convenient to their offices. Nearly all of the country's major domestic and foreign businesses are located in Bangkok, along with the official residence of the royal family, government ministries, the most prestigious universities and preparatory schools, and the leading sports and cultural facilities. Thanks to this concentration of wealth and power, 90 percent of all the motor vehicles in the country are registered in the city, creating traffic congestion that the authorities are attempting to solve by the construction of an exstensive network of overpasses and expressways, and the metro. Though government policy encourages decentralization of industry into provincial areas, most of the modern factories are located in or near Bangkok, which is still the focus of the aviation, railway and communications systems, not to mention the extremely busy port of Klong Toey on the river, through which almost half of the country's imports and exports pass.

THAI TRAMS
Horse-drawn trams appeared on the streets of Bangkok in 1888; by the end of the century, the trams ran on electricity and continued to operate in decreasing numbers along New Road until the 1960's. The above painting, by contemporary artist Arunothai ● *102*, shows fashionably dressed tram passengers in the past.

CHINATOWN IN THE 1950'S
Yaowarat Road ▲ *176* is pictured in Chinatown during the 1950's, when trams were no longer the only public transport as buses were growing in popularity.

143

LATER PALACE BUILDINGS

The first Western-style buildings appeared in the palace enclosure during the reign of King Rama IV. These included a suite of rooms in the Siwalai Gardens, behind the Phra Maha Monthien, where the king lived and kept his collection of scientific instruments, and a tall structure with clocks on four sides. None of these remain today; they were torn down during the next reign, which saw the most extensive additions since the palace was built. King Rama V, the first Thai ruler to travel to Europe, ordered the construction of a new throne hall and royal residence. They were completed in time for the celebration of Bangkok's centenary in 1882.

CHAKRI MAHA PRASAT. Designed in neoclassical style by an English architect, the Chakri Maha Prasat was originally planned as a domed building, wholly Western in appearance; before completion, however, the dome was replaced with the older structures around it. The king and his principal queen moved to quarters on the upper floors of this structure and used the lower levels for state entertainment; a grand stairway reserved only for the king led down to the women's quarters behind the throne hall.

AUDIENCE HALL
Thai kings since Rama V have traditionally received foreign ambassadors in the Central Audience Hall of the Chakri Maha Prasat, standing before a splendid wooden throne plated with silver and gold niello. On the walls are several large, European-style paintings of celebrated meetings between Thai ambassadors and King Louis XIV at Versailles.

SIWALAI GARDENS. Also added most of the present buildings in now contains the Royal Boromphiman Mansion in the by a German architect as a Prince, and a few Western-style residences for queens and consorts in the Inner Palace. The gardens were used for receptions as well as a recreation area for the royal women and their children. Toward the end of his reign, King Rama V moved out of the Grand Palace to new during the fifth reign were the outer area, one of which Household Bureau, the Siwalai Gardens, designed residence for the Crown

> "How can I describe the barbaric grandeur, the parade, the show, the glitter, the real magnificence, the profuse decorations of today's royal audience!"
>
> Sir John Bowring

quarters in the Dusit district but continued to use the older buildings for royal ceremonies, a tradition that was continued by subsequent rulers of the dynasty.

THE INNER PALACE. This was a secret world that much intrigued European visitors to Thailand in the 19th and early 20th centuries. According to Dr Malcolm Smith, an English physician who attended to King Rama V's principal queen and other royal patients, it "was a town complete in itself, a congested network of houses and narrow streets with gardens, lawns, artificial lakes and shops. It had its own government, its own institutions, its own laws and law courts. It was a town of women, one controlled by women. Men on special construction or repair work were admitted, and the doctors when they came to visit the sick. The king's sons could live there until they reached the age of puberty; after that they were sent to live with relations, or with the governors in the provinces. But the only man who lived within its walls was the king." At its peak, in King Rama V's reign toward the end of the 19th century, about 3,000 women lived in this part of the palace, most of them servants or daughters of noble families who were sent here to learn various refined skills such as cooking, embroidery, and making floral wreaths. With the advent of royal monogamy in the next reign, the number steadily decreased as wives and princesses were allowed to move outside. A few stayed on, however, and the last resident died in the 1970's.

MUSEUMS IN THE PALACE COMPOUND

Just beyond the entrance is the Coins and Royal Decorations Museum. Early Thai coins and other items used as money are displayed here, in addition to medals and other decorations presented by Chakri kings for outstanding service, many of them set with precious stones. On the ground level of the Chakri Maha Prasat is a display of ancient weapons while near the Dusit Maha Prasat another museum contains stone inscriptions and palace decorations replaced during various renovations.

THE REGENT QUEEN Queen Sowabha Phongsri, the principal queen of King Rama V, was the first of the royal wives to take up residence with the king outside the Inner Palace. She also served as regent during his trips abroad, and founded the first Thai girls' school and the Thai Red Cross, and, in general, was an important force in the liberation of Thai women from male domination.

THE TONSURE CEREMONY One of the grandest rituals held in the Grand Palace was the Tonsure Ceremony, which marked the coming-of-age of children in the Inner Palace. After the tuft of hair was cut by Brahmin priests, the climax of a celebration that lasted several days, male children had to move out of the women's quarter to an outside residence.

145

The mythical half-bird, half-human *garuda* (above right) – legendary steed of the Hindu god Vishnu – is part of the royal insignia and appears among the decorations on many buildings within the palace compound.

As residence of the Lord of Life, as Thai kings are known, the royal palace has been the center of every capital in the country's history. The Grand Palace, surrounded by a high wall, covers nearly a square mile and, in its original form, was a conscious evocation of the one in Ayutthaya, divided into an outer part for government offices, a central portion containing the king's living quarters and audience halls, and an inner area for female members of the royal family and their attendants. Buildings were added to the palace compound by each of the first five Chakri rulers, particularly King Rama V, during whose reign Westernization was rapid.

The Dusit Maha Prasat depicted in a mid-19th-century engraving.

EARLY BUILDINGS

DUSIT MAHA PRASAT. Among the original palace buildings that still remain, though modified by later kings, is the Dusit Maha Prasat throne hall. Covered with four-tier tiled roofs and surmounted by a seven-tier gilded spire, it contains a blackwood throne inlaid with mother-of-pearl dating from the reign of King Rama I. The remains of kings, queens and royal family members are placed in the Dusit Maha Prasat prior to cremation. The building is open to the public.

THE PHRA THINANG APHONPHIMOK PRASAT. King Rama IV introduced Western architecture to the palace and was also responsible for one of its most beautiful traditional structures:

King Rama V alighting at the Phra Thinang Aphonphimok Prasat pavilion at the turn of the century. The pavilion is a major attraction today.

the Phra Thinang Aphonphimok Prasat (right). This pavilion on the east wall surrounding the Dusit Maha Prasat was where the king changed his robes before descending a flight of steps to mount a palanquin. The structure displays graceful elegance and a distinctive blend of simple with sumptuous decoration epitomizes classic Thai architecture. It was reproduced at the Brussels Exposition in 1958.

THE GRAND RESIDENCE GROUP. Also from the earliest period of the palace is a group of connecting buildings known as Phra Maha Monthien, "the Grand Residence." The first three kings of the dynasty lived in one of these, the Phra Thinang Chakraphat Phiman – Phra Thinang is a title bestowed on any structure (building, pavilion, throne and so on) used by a king. It contains the royal bedchamber and it is still traditional for new monarchs to spend a night here upon assuming the throne, symbolizing their assumption of residence in the palace of their ancestors. In front and connected by a flight of stairs is the Phra Thinang Phaisan Taksin, where coronation ceremonies are held. It also houses two historic thrones, the Royal Regalia, and a small, much venerated image called Phra Siam Thewathirat, regarded as the tutelary deity of the Thai nation. The first Chakri king is supposed to have made regular use of this hall and, when old, to have held private audiences from one of its windows with people in the courtyard below. From the Octagonal Throne on the east side, new kings formally receive the invitation to rule over the kingdom, while from the Phattrabit Throne on the west, they receive the Royal Regalia, consisting of the crown, a sword, a royal staff, a fan, a whisk made of yak's tail, bejeweled slippers, and the Great White Umbrella of State. In the northern wall of the Phaisan Taksin is a gate known as Thewarat Mahesuan, through which only the king, the queen, and the royal children may walk. This leads to the Phra Thinang Amarin Winitchai, originally the principal audience hall of the Middle Palace where officials of state and foreign ambassadors were received. Dominating this hall – the only one in the group now open to the public – is the Phra Thinang Busbok Mala, an open-pillar construction of ornately carved wood with a tiered roof, made during the reign of King Rama I; to the left and right of the base are lateral extensions that make the structure appear to be floating in the air. The whole rests on a gilded masonry dais that dates from the reign of King Rama III. Curtains were drawn to conceal the king when he entered from the Phaisan Taksin; when it was time for the audience a fanfare sounded, the curtains dramatically parted, and the ruler was revealed in all the magnificence of his Royal Regalia. The Phra Thinang Busbok Mala throne (above right) is reserved for kings and objects of veneration. It holds the urns containing the ashes of previous Chakri kings. From his place on the throne, the reigning Chakri king receives offerings and presides over the prayers of the royal family. Another throne in the building from the first reign, known as the Phra Thaen Sawetachat, is still used by the King for some of the investiture ceremonies as well as for the annual birthday audience.

View of the palace walls and roofs of Wat Phra Keo (above).

The Phra Thinang Busbok Mala throne, which contains funerary urns of the Chakri kings (below).

A large collection of ancient topiary – shrubbery trimmed into fancy shapes – adorns the front courtyard of the palace, a decorative technique that was probably inspired by plants in Chinese gardens.

147

WAT PHRA KEO

Wat Phra Keo, the Temple of the Emerald
Buddha, serves as the royal chapel and as such
is located in one corner of the Grand Palace
compound; unlike other Buddhist temples,
it has no resident monks.

THE EMERALD BUDDHA ▲ *170.* The fabled
statue – the Phra Keo – was discovered when
lightning struck an ancient stupa in northern
Thailand in the early 15th century. Over the next
five centuries, legends accumulated around the
small seated image – 26 inches high and 19
inches wide at the lap span, actually carved from
a semiprecious form of jade. It was enshrined in
a number of northern cities and also, for more
than 250 years, in Laos; the future King Rama I
brought it back to Thailand after having
destroyed Vientiane to take possession of it, and
later made it the principal Buddha image of his
new capital at Bangkok. The image is the most
venerated of all the thousands in the country.

PALLADIA
The Emerald
Buddha is the most
eminent example of
the Palladia, images
reputed to be
endowed with
supernatural powers
and considered
protectors of a town,
a king, or a dynasty.

Today the Emerald
Buddha sits high atop
an ornate throne of
gilded wood in the
bot of Wat Phra Keo,

constructed by King Rama I but extensively refurbished and added to by later kings. The carved gable boards of the building show the god Vishnu astride a *garuda* ▲ 146, while the outer walls are richly decorated with gilded stucco and glass mosaics. Three times a year, at the beginning of each season – cool, hot and rainy – the robes of the image are changed in an elaborate ceremony presided over by the king. Countless ordinary Thais also come regularly to make offerings at the temple and pray for various wishes to be granted.

OTHER BUILDINGS. On the side of the bot, also aligned on an east-west axis, are three elaborate buildings set very close to each other: the Prasat Phra Thep Bidom, reconstructed by Rama V, and converted by Rama VI into the royal pantheon; a library in the shape of a square *mondop* ● 90, a replica of the Temple of the Buddha's Footprint in Saraburi; and a gilded chedi built with a design similar to those of Wat Phra Keo in Ayutthaya, with the explicit intention of recreating the splendor of the ancient capital and the magical powers of its landmark buildings. Khmer-style prang are positioned at every corner of the cloister, a clear political statement by the early Chakri kings repeating the imperialist attitude of the Khmer rulers.

THE ROYAL PANTHEON The reconstructed Prasat Phra Thep Bidom contains statues of previous Chakri kings. Usually closed, it is open to the public only on special occasions. According to temple caretakers, the reason for its closure is that the bare-chested images of the first three sovereigns are now deemed an embarrassing sight not quite befitting royalty.

1. BOT
2. PRASAT PHRA THEP BIDOM (ROYAL PANTHEON)
3. LIBRARY
4. CHEDI
5. MONDOP

MYTHOLOGICAL CREATURES
Many of the divinities whose statues adorn the compound of Wat Phra Keo are of Hindu origin, further evidence of the blending of Buddhism with other religions. Some are fabulous animals that inhabited an imaginary forest in the Himalayas called the Himavat (the Himaphan in Thai). These include the *tantima* bird, a strange creature with a cock's comb and a parrot-like beak; the more graceful, swan-like *hong,* often at the top of a pole with a bell in its beak; and the elegant bird-humans, the *kinnon* (male) and *kinnari* (female). Also present is the *garuda,* traditional mount of the god Vishnu; Siva's steed, the sacred bull called *nandi;* and *ganesha,* the elephant-headed son of Siva and his consort Parvati.

ARCHITECTURAL DECORATIONS. The various structures at Wat Phra Keo display a virtual textbook of classic Thai decorative techniques and mythological statuary. Entire walls are transformed into shimmering, jewel-like expanses through the use of glass mosaics or carefully fitted pieces of multicolored porcelain; wooden gables and roof supports are richly carved and gilded, and doors and windows are adorned either with intricate mother-of-pearl inlay designs or gold-and-black lacquer paintings. All of them were restored for the 1982 Bangkok bicentennial celebrations, having fallen into a state of disrepair. The multitiered roofs are covered with colored tiles, chedis and stupas with layers of glittering gold leaf, while the interiors of most buildings are decorated with complex mural paintings. The gates leading into the courtyard are flanked by huge statues of *yaksa,* or demons, supposed to ward off evil spirits. They are brightly painted and covered with glass mosaic decorations. Several bronze statues scattered around the buildings represent mythical animals of the Hindu and Buddhist pantheon. Around the basement

> "This sacerdotal Disneyland is entered
> through a gate set in cloisters whose inner walls
> carry murals depicting the 'ramakien'."
>
> Alistair Shearer

THE "RAMAKIEN"
The *Ramakien,* the
Thai version of the
Ramayana, appears in
mural paintings, as in
the galleries of Wat
Phra Keo, in bas-
relief carvings, like
those at Wat Po, and
also in illustrated
manuscript books. It
provides the stories
for the *khon* (classi-
cal masked dance)
● 64–5. Though all
the manuscripts
recounting the legend
from the Ayutthaya
period were
destroyed when the
capital fell to the
Burmese in 1767, the
story was already an
established part of
Thai cultural
tradition. King Rama
I himself rewrote it
after the founding of
Bangkok, and the
second king of the
Chakri dynasty also
produced a version
for the dance.

**REPLICA OF
ANGKOR WAT**
A model of Angkor
Wat, the famous
center of Khmer
culture, was placed in
the temple compound
by King Rama IV, as a
reminder of the time
when Cambodia was
a vassal state of Thai-
land. The territory
was lost in the late
19th century when the
French exerted
pressure on
King Rama V and
redefined the borders
of Indo-China.

where the chedi, the *mondop* and the pantheon are built,
here are a number of small Chinese gardens embellished by
Qing statues of animals and heavenly guards.

MURAL PAINTINGS OF THE "RAMAKIEN". On the walls of the
galleries surrounding Wat Phra Keo are a series of panoramic
mural paintings that depict the story of the *Ramakien*, the
Thai version of the *Ramayana*, an Indian epic dealing with the
triumph of good over evil. The tale is told in 178 panels, each
occupying the area between two pillars of the many that
support the gallery; poems about the action, composed in the
reign of King Rama V, are inscribed on marble slabs set into
the relevant pillar. Though originally painted by order of King
Rama I when the temple was built,
the murals have been restored many
times, most recently for the 1982
Bangkok bicentennial celebrations.
These works are almost identical to
the original 1930 compositions
executed under the direction of
Phra Thewapinimmit, and reflect
the style of that era with Western
perspective, the use of shadows, and
naturalistic rendering of the landscape, and with characters drawn in
a conventional Thai manner.

STONE BALLASTS
Literally hundreds of
Chinese stone figures
– animals both
realistic and whim-
sical, humans both
small and fearsomely
huge – are scattered
throughout Wat Po;
similar ones can be
seen in other major
Bangkok palaces and
temples. Most came
to Thailand in the
early 19th century as
ballast on ships
returning empty from
the lucrative rice
trade and were placed
in the temple during
King Rama III's
reign, a period that
also saw an increase
in Chinese influence
on architecture and
decorative motifs.
Prominent among the
statues are the tower-
ing door guardians, or
protective demons,
that stand beside each
of the sixteen
monumental gates
leading into the
temple and beside
those that divide the
various compounds.
The latter represent
Europeans, as shown
by their tall, brimmed
hats that the sculp-
tors had perhaps
observed in Chinese
port cities and
assumed all
foreigners
wore.

The oldest and largest temple in Thailand, Wat Phra
Chetuphon, popularly known as Wat Po – derived from its
original name of Wat Bodharam – was founded in the 16th
century during the Ayutthaya period. It was a particular
favorite with the early Chakri kings, most of whom restored

or added buildings to its huge compound. Chetuphon Road,
along which King Rama I supposedly rode on his way to
Thonburi when he was crowned in 1782, separates the
monastic buildings housing some 300 priests from the
enclosure containing the
structures used for religious
ceremonies. In its heyday, this
was the home of more than
500 monks and 750 novices, and
the monks' quarters are still a
veritable city within the city.
Most of the buildings were
reconstructed during the
fifth reign, replacing older
wooden houses, and the
mansions of the most
reverend monks are
often embellished with
precious gilded stucco.

Wat Po's greatest benefactor was King Rama III
(1824–51), who was responsible not only for most of
the buildings the visitor sees today but also for turning
the temple into a kind of open university, filled with
displays of educational material. Twenty small hills
scattered around the compound, for example, contain
geological specimens from all parts of Thailand; a
collection of stone Rishi, or hermits, demonstrates

various yoga positions; and inscriptions and mural paintings deal with such diverse subjects as warfare, medicine, astrology, botany and history. Anyone who was interested in either religious or secular knowledge could study the wealth of information compiled from ancient textbooks and presented to the public in this most democratic way. It was an unprecedented move in a society where knowledge had always been the privilege of the few. King Rama I, who was the founder of Bangkok and the first restorer of Wat Po, is credited with salvaging 1,200 statues from the ruins of Ayutthaya. The collection contains 689 of the rescued statues. Many others were added to it by later kings. The temple is a veritable gallery of Thai art, practically covering every historical period. Most of the images are displayed along the cloisters and serve to top the chedis containing ashes of the illustrious deceased. In an attempt to preserve these rows of statues, renovation work has since been carried out, and they are now encased in glass.

SCHOOL FOR TRADITIONAL MEDICINE. One aspect of Wat Po's old educational function that remains very much alive today is the School for Traditional Medicine, in the eastern part of the temple compound. Besides offering courses of instruction in herbal medicines and Thai-style massage, authorized members of the profession offer treatment to the public in the late afternoons; marble engravings on the walls, placed there in the reign of King Rama III, give various rules regarding the subject. Foreigners can take a fifteen-day course in traditional massage, with classes held for two hours daily, while skilled masseurs are usually available at around 120 baht per hour. Within the monks' quarters on the other side of Chetuphon Road, expert chiropractors attend to local patients using ancient techniques under the watchful eyes of monks who sanction the operation by spitting holy water on the ailing part, while assistants beat furiously on the drums.

TEMPLE ASTROLOGERS. This temple, very popular with local and foreign visitors, also attracts a large number of street vendors, snake charmers, astrologers, palmists and other entertainers to its premises. It is well known for its colony of resident astrologers.

RISHI FIGURES
The stone Rishi, or hermits, in the outer courtyard of Wat Po, were formerly located in a series of sixteen pavilions and moved to their present site during the reign of King Rama V. They demonstrate yoga positions to relieve physical and mental complaints and promote meditative contemplation, a reminder of the time when the temple was a leading center of public education.

TREATISE ON MASSAGE
Small buildings around the cloister that encircles the chedis of the Four Kings display a series of murals, showing the techniques of Thai massage. The subject is further illustrated by statues of hermits in various yoga stances and self-massage techniques.

153

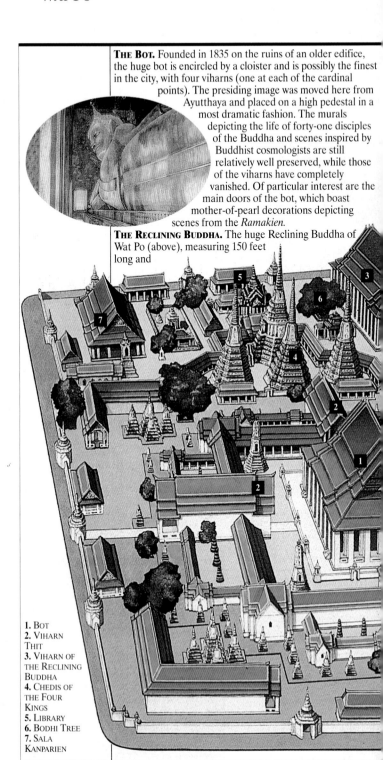

THE BOT. Founded in 1835 on the ruins of an older edifice, the huge bot is encircled by a cloister and is possibly the finest in the city, with four viharns (one at each of the cardinal points). The presiding image was moved here from Ayutthaya and placed on a high pedestal in a most dramatic fashion. The murals depicting the life of forty-one disciples of the Buddha and scenes inspired by Buddhist cosmologists are still relatively well preserved, while those of the viharns have completely vanished. Of particular interest are the main doors of the bot, which boast mother-of-pearl decorations depicting scenes from the *Ramakien*.

THE RECLINING BUDDHA. The huge Reclining Buddha of Wat Po (above), measuring 150 feet long and

1. BOT
2. VIHARN THIT
3. VIHARN OF THE RECLINING BUDDHA
4. CHEDIS OF THE FOUR KINGS
5. LIBRARY
6. BODHI TREE
7. SALA KANPARIEN

> "Oh! Wat Po is the monastery built by a king; it is never neglected and it is resplendent like heaven…"
>
> Sunthorn Phu

50 feet high, and covered with layers of gold leaf, represents the dying Buddha at the moment he entered Nirvana. Its most impressive artistic feature is the inlaid mother-of-pearl designs that adorn the soles of its feet, depicting the legendary signs by which the true Buddha can be recognized. Only the upper parts remain of the once superb mural paintings that adorned the interior walls of the building housing the image, constructed during the reign of King Rama III.

CHEDIS OF THE FOUR KINGS. Not far from the bot, in a low-walled enclosure, stand four tall chedis, or stupas, decorated with porcelain and dedicated to the first four Chakri kings: the green one, containing a standing Buddha from Ayutthaya, to Rama I; the white one to Rama II; the yellow one to Rama III; and the blue one to Rama IV.

THE LIBRARY. Founded by Rama I but restored in the third reign, the library is one of the most graceful edifices in Bangkok. The central chamber is topped by an elaborate crown-like cupola and spire; four extended porticoes create a Greek-cross plan. The building is decorated with glazed tiles and polychrome ceramic pieces. John Crawfurd, who led a British embassy to the court of King Rama II in 1822, noted the gardens surrounding the building, one of which had a pond with crocodiles. Today, the library is set in an elegant Chinese-style garden.

THE BODHI TREE. Next to the library stands an ancient Bodhi tree, whose imposing presence is enhanced by two Chinese pavilions, where a statue of Guan Yin (also known as the Goddess of Mercy), is the object of devotion. The area is called the "Garden of the Transplanted Tree," referring to the tree that grew from a cutting of the original Bodhi tree in Anuradhapura.

"RAMAKIEN" PANELS Around the base of the bot are a series of 152 marble panels engraved with scenes from the *Ramakien,* the Thai version of the *Ramayana.* The panels show one of the main episodes, the abduction of Sida and her eventual recovery after several battles. The incompleteness of the episode and its abrupt ending suggest that they may have been salvaged from other temples – perhaps in Ayutthaya – and subsequently moved to Bangkok. There is, however, no record of their origin. The marble panels were once used to make stone rubbings for sale to tourists; similar rubbings are now made from copies of the carvings ▲ 151.

THE SECOND KING
The office of the Second King, who served as vice-ruler, was a peculiarly Thai institution that began in the Ayutthaya period. The position was abolished in the reign of King Rama V, when the heir apparent became known as the Crown Prince.

SANAM LUANG

The large oval field across from the Grand Palace is popularly known as Sanam Luang, "the Royal Field." More formally, it is called the Pramane Ground, the place where royal cremations are held, the last having been that of the mother of King Rama IX, in 1995. The Plowing

Ceremony to forecast the coming agricultural crop is held here in April, while on the King's Birthday and at New Year Sanam Luang becomes a giant festival, with movies and other amusements. On the eastern side are government ministries, while on the west are Silpakorn University, Wat Mahathat, Thammasat University and the National Museum.

NATIONAL MUSEUM

Bangkok's National Museum – which has over thirty branches throughout the country – is housed partly in the palace of the Second King (a sort of vice-ruler), originally built during the reign of King Rama I. The collection was moved there from the Grand Palace by King Rama V in 1887, and under King Rama VII (1925–34) it was expanded and placed under the Royal Institute of Literature, Archeology and Fine Arts, later the Fine Arts Department. Two modern buildings were constructed on either

A watercolor sketch of Sanam Luang at the turn of the century, when rickshaws were still in existence.

side of the old palace in 1967, while a new gallery on Thai history was opened during Bangkok's bicentennial celebrations (1982).

BUDDHAISAWAN CHAPEL. The Buddhaisawan Chapel was built in 1787 to enshrine an important northern Buddha image called the Phra Buddha Si Hing, and is now within the grounds of the museum. The interior walls are painted with exceptionally fine murals showing scenes from the life of the Buddha, while the building itself is an outstanding example of early Bangkok religious architecture.

TAMNAK DAENG. Tamnak Daeng, or "Red House," was the residence of an elder sister of King Rama I. It was moved from Thonburi by King Rama II to the Grand Palace compound and later, in the fourth reign, to its present location in the museum grounds. Furniture and other items of the early Bangkok period are displayed inside ● 87.

THE MUSEUM COLLECTION. The National Museum's collection covers the whole range of art found in the country, religious and secular, fine and decorative, Thai and otherwise. The Prehistoric Gallery, for instance, includes Neolithic tools and pottery dating as far back as 10,000 BC, in addition to superb painted pots and bronze objects unearthed at various excavations in the northeast. Numerous creations of the pre-Thai Srivijaya, Dvaravati and Khmer kingdoms are also displayed, as well as those of the early Thai settlements of the far north. Thai Buddhist art encompasses images in stone, bronze and terracotta from the Sukhothai, Ayutthaya and Rattanakosin (Bangkok) periods, together with such religious items as illustrated scripture books, manuscript cabinets and votive plaques. Open daily except Mondays and Tuesdays, the museum also contains a large selection of miscellaneous arts, among them Thai and Chinese ceramics, theatrical costumes, textiles, furniture, funeral chariots, palanquins, elephant howdahs, weapons, puppets and assorted objects used in royal households. Guided tours in English are also offered to visitors on certain days of the week by the National Museum Volunteer Group.

PRIZED AMULETS
Amulets, usually in the form of a clay votive plaque bearing the image of the Buddha or of a particularly revered monk, are highly prized by most Thais. Mounted in gold or silver, they are worn on chains around the neck to avert misfortune. Many are sold on the sidewalks near Sanam Luang, particularly around Wat Mahathat.

157

The earliest reminder of Buddha's teachings was a mound of earth, which eventually evolved into the stupa. Later, feeling the need for a more concrete symbol, adherents to the faith began to make images. Various schools of thought arose concerning the exact features and *mudra*, or gestures, of such images, eventually resulting in a wide range of choices as revealed in the different periods of Thai art. This evolution of the image of Buddha can be seen in those displayed in the National Museum.

DVARAVATI
Dvaravati images (7th–11th century), mostly in stone, stucco, or terracotta, are heavy-featured and realistic in appearance, with prominent curls.

LOPBURI
Strongly influenced by Khmer images, those of Lopburi (7th–14th century) have stylized faces with broad mouths that seem to be faintly smiling; later ones are often in royal attire.

SUKHOTHAI SEATED IMAGE
Bronze was the medium preferred by sculptors of 13th–15th-century Sukhothai and the one in which they produced their greatest work. Most images are seated with the hand in the gesture called *bhumisparsa mudra*, or "touching the earth."

CASTING BUDDHA IMAGES

Bronze Buddha images are cast by the "lost wax" process, which involves a clay core in the rough form desired, a covering of wax carved into the shape of the image, and an outer mold of clay. The wax is then melted and drained off and molten bronze poured in to replace it. Casting often takes place in a temple compound, accompanied by a variety of ceremonies. The mural shown on the right, in Wat Bowornivet ▲ *165*, Bangkok, depicts the castings of three famous images, namely the Phra Buddha Chinaraj, Phitsanulok, and two large images now in Wat Bowornivet. The event took place in the late Sukhothai period.

AYUTTHAYA

Ayutthaya images (14th–18th century) display a variety of styles; the most characteristic is richly attired and adorned, reflecting the Ayutthaya association of kingship and religion.

LANNA

The typical northern 13th–20th-century Lanna image has a round face, large curls, a prominent chin, and a thick, solid body; it is often seated on a lotus-blossom base.

RATTANAKOSIN

Rattanakosin or 18th–20th-century Bangkok images are frequently standing and heavily ornamented, the faces narrow and somewhat characterless, and the postures and *mudra* often unfamiliar; after the mid-19th century they display an increased sense of realism.

SUKHOTHAI WALKING IMAGE

The outstanding Sukhothai image is considered by scholars to be the walking Buddha, with exaggerated physical characteristics yet possessing a fluid grace and a powerful spiritual sense.

RATTANAKOSIN

A beautiful ivory image of Buddha, late 19th century.

The stone
Bodhisattva
Avalokitesvara
(left) stands
just over 3 feet
tall and exhibits
Indian influence,
which was very
important throughout the
early to middle centuries
of the first millennium.
This statue, originally
from Chaiya ● 96 ▲ 190,
dates from the 6th–7th
century.

A fine example
of Sukhothai
ceramics, this
glazed stoneware figure of a
horseman dates from the
14th–15th century.

The stone Vishnu from
Takua Pa (left), 7 feet
tall, dates from the
8th–9th century and is
among the large display
of early Hindu statues
that make up one of the
most interesting sections
of the museum's
collection.

There are many bronzes
of Hindu gods dating
from the Sukhothai
period. These were once
worshiped at the
Brahmin temple of
Bangkok, having been
moved there from the
ruins of Sukhothai by
King Rama I. Depicted
here (left) is a 10-foot-
tall image of Shiva.

The art of the early Mon kingdom
of Dvaravati can be seen in the
large collection of terracottas and
stuccos ▲ 187. Above is a stucco
yaksa dating from the 9th century
and found in Nakhon Pathom. The
head (right), dating from slightly
earlier, was found at Ku Bua.

Thepanom Sukhothai glazed stone figure, 14th–15th century.

A pair of Sukhothai-period praying deities in terracotta.

The Buddhaisawan Chapel, within the grounds of the National Museum, contains some of the best mural paintings of the Bangkok School, executed during the reign of Rama I. On the right is a detail from a mural showing the descent of Buddha from heaven on a ladder made of *naga* and jewels. On his left is a golden ladder for Indra and on his right a silver ladder for Brahma. These two gods accompanied him back to earth after he preached to his mother and the gods for three months. A gold-lacquered screen from the early 19th century displays a scene from the *Ramakien* (left) ▲ *151*.

The Lanna bronze elephant (right) dates from AD 1575 and was originally used as a support for presenting offerings. The duck-shaped water vessel (below) dates from the 14th–15th century.

▲ BANGKOK RATTANAKOSIN ISLAND

OTHER SIGHTS IN SANAM LUANG

WAT MAHATHAT. This temple dates from before the founding of Bangkok, but was extensively restored during the reign of King Rama I and became one of the city's most important monasteries. The future King Rama IV served as one of its abbots. Today, Wat Mahathat (above) houses a college for Buddhist priests and offers meditation classes for foreigners. On weekends, the temple is usually filled with peddlers who display and sell amulets to visitors.

"LAK MUANG." Standing outside the walls of Wat Phra Keo, the *lak muang* (the city's foundation stone pillar) is in the form of a *lingam (*below right) that serves as the abode of Bangkok's guardian spirit and as the spot from which distances in the city are measured. First erected by King Rama I in 1782, it is now sheltered by an ornate pavilion and is visited by large numbers of supplicants who come to ask for almost anything, from matrimonial harmony to a winning ticket in the national lottery. In addition to making offerings of flowers and incense, many also pay for dancers to perform the *likay* ● 66 in traditional costumes.

SILPAKORN UNIVERSITY. Silpakorn (Fine Arts) University is housed partly in an old palace of the first reign. It owes its

A VENERATED PIG
Overlooking a canal ► near Saranrom Palace is a large statue of a pig, covered with layers of gold leaf offered by supplicants. This was erected in honor of Queen Sowabha Phongsri, the principal Queen of King Rama V, who was born in the year of that animal. It has become an important shrine for people of the area, who believe it has the power to grant various wishes.

> "Entertain not thy thoughts with worldly things.
> do no work but the work of charity and truth."
>
> Buddhist precepts

existence largely to Corrado Ferroci, an Italian sculptor. Ferroci began working for the Thai government in 1924, founded the School of Fine Arts in 1933, and lived in the country under the Thai name of Silpa Bhirasri until his death in 1962. The building fronting Sanam Luang is decorated with a frieze in Art Nouveau style painted by Italian artists.

NATIONAL THEATER. The huge National Theater was erected in the early 1970's. It became the hub of cultural and musical activities: dance troupes and foreign orchestras once performed here. It plays a less important role today, though classical drama performances are still staged occasionally at the theater. Attached to the National Theater is a dance school where young students practice the art of Thai classical dance. On its premises is a temple that was formerly part of the palace of the Second King. It provides an elegant backdrop to the rehearsals put on by the students.

Wat Rajapradit.

MURALS OF 1864
The bot of Wat Rajapradit is decorated with an unusual set of murals painted in 1864, during the reign of King Rama IV. These depict various royal ceremonies held during the twelve months of the year and constitute a rare historical record of early Bangkok since many of those ceremonies are no longer performed ▲ *140*.

WAT RAJAPRADIT ★

A small, serene temple built during King Rama IV's reign, Wat Rajapradit (above right) is located in a compound adjacent to the garden of the former Saranrom Palace, where King Rama IV often said he wished to retire. The main building is sheathed in gray marble from China and raised on a high stone platform, while on both sides of the building are Khmer-style prangs; on the terrace behind the temple is a stupa also covered with gray marble. The doors are adorned with gold-and-black lacquer paintings and the gables and eaves are decorated with fine carvings. Wat Rajapradit has a restful atmosphere not very often found in larger temple compounds, but as the doors are often locked, tourists may only visit the temple on the 1st and the 15th of each lunar month, when the local folk come to pray and present alms to the monks.

A RESTING PLACE
Wat Saket appears in most 19th-century accounts of Bangkok not only because of its Golden Mount but also because it was a resting place for the dead during cholera epidemics. Too numerous for conventional cremation, the bodies were laid out at the temple for vultures to devour. Anna Leonowens, the Englishwoman who was hired by King Rama IV to teach some of his wives and children, wrote: "None but the initiated will approach these grounds after sunset, so universal and profound is the horror the place inspires – a place the most frightful and offensive known to mortal eyes." Paupers and unidentified dead bodies were also brought to Wat Saket for more conventional cremation.

WAT SAKET AND THE GOLDEN MOUNT

"Just outside the city wall is the Golden Mount, a bell-shaped mound faced with brick, but so overgrown by trees that it has the appearance of a natural hillock…From here we look down upon a forest of palms and plane-trees, through which break the red roofs of the houses. Everywhere rising above the trees are graceful spires and the manifold roofs of temples, with their tiles of rich orange or deep purple, great splashes of color against the clear blue sky…" That was a description by P.A. Thomson in 1910 of the view from the Golden Mount. Today a visitor to the mount enjoys a different view altogether. Phu Khao Thong, the Golden Mount, is an artificial hill topped by a large gilded stupa that has long been the highest elevation in Bangkok and one of the city's most celebrated landmarks. The stupa measures 260 feet from its base to the tip of its spire. A replica of a similar hill in Ayutthaya, this was a major feat of 19th-century engineering, begun by King Rama V but not completed until the following reign. The stupa, reached by a flight of 300 steps, contains relics of the Buddha presented to King Rama V by Lord Curzon, Viceroy of India, in 1897. The Golden Mount lies within the compound of Wat Saket. Built by King Rama I, Wat Saket is one of the oldest temples in Bangkok, though it has often been restored and few of the original mural paintings and other decorations remain. One of its sanctuaries has a large standing Buddha image brought from Sukhothai by the first Chakri king. The temple contains an interesting pavilion that was once a temple library and that was moved to its present location from Ayutthaya. It dates from the late 17th century and features gilded panels with Chinese-style motifs and classic lacquered windows. Some of the windows were exhibited in Paris on the occasion of the third centenary of Thai-French diplomatic relations.

The window panels of the library of Wat Saket portray a series of foreigners – merchants, traders and ambassadors – who used to frequent cosmopolitan Ayutthaya in its heyday.

CITY WALLS

Like Ayutthaya, Rattanakosin Island was once surrounded by a high wall, studded at intervals with watchtowers. Much of the wall has been pulled down in the city's expansion, though a restored turret remains opposite Wat Rajanadda.

The city walls fronting Wat Saket at the turn of the century.

WAT BOWORNIVET

Built by King Rama III for his brother, who spent the better part of his life as a monk before ascending the throne as King Rama IV, this monastery is renowned for the murals of the *ubosot*, painted for the first time in Thai history in Western perspective by the monk artist Khrua In Khong ● *106–7*. The temple houses three important large Sukhothai images ▲ *161* and a Buddha from Borobudur donated by the Dutch government to King Rama V.

The Lohaprasad in the compound of Wat Rajanadda.

WAT RAJANADDA

With the removal of a movie theater that long concealed it, the architectural beauties of Wat Rajanadda are now visible to passers-by. Its most interesting feature is the Lohaprasad, started by King Rama III but only completed a decade ago by the Fine Arts Department. It has six levels, each housing small ornamental pavilions, is 110 feet high and overlooks Ratchadamnoen Klong Avenue. A new pavilion outside the temple serves as a reception area for important foreign visitors to Bangkok.

BAMRUNG MUANG ROAD
This road, which leads to the square with the Giant Swing, is almost entirely devoted to shops selling various Buddhist items – images of all sizes, mostly bronze, as well as robes, fans and alms bowls for monks, carved altar tables, little gilded Bodhi trees, ceremonial umbrellas, candles and incense sticks and countless other items used in temple adornment. These are presented by laymen to the temples on a variety of religious occasions.

WAT SUTHAT

Wat Suthat is one of the most important temples in Bangkok. Work on the temple started during the reign of King Rama I, was continued by his successor, and finally completed under King Rama III. The temple's principal attractions are two unusually large buildings, the bot and the viharn, both of which exhibit outstanding classic Thai religious art and architecture.

THE VIHARN ● *89.* Noted for its graceful proportions, the viharn is raised on a double platform, at the corners of which are pavilions enshrining Buddha images in various positions. The 18-foot-high gables are richly adorned with mythological animals and religious symbols, and the huge doors, carved in three layers, are attributed to King Rama II, who was noted for his artistry. The interior walls and the two rows of supporting columns are covered with fine mural paintings of the early Bangkok period. The principal Buddha image, Phra Buddha Chakyamuni, was moved to Bangkok from Wat Mahathat in Sukhothai and dates from

the 14th century. It was cast together with another much revered image called the Prabu Chinaraj, which is now housed in Phitsanulok.

THE BOT ● *88.* Constructed between 1839 and 1843 by King Rama III, the bot contains an image known as Phra Trai Lok Chet, in front of which is a group of disciple figures. Well-preserved murals also cover the interior walls of this structure. The door of the low brick wall that surrounds the bot are guarded by statues imported from China, all representing Western sailors and soldiers and reflecting the low opinion both the Thai and the Chinese had of Westerners in those days.

The statues of the Westerners, they were fully convinced, were monstrous enough to ward off the evil spirits lurking outside their houses.

BRAHMIN TEMPLE. Overlooking the square containing the Giant Swing is the Brahmin temple. While of little interest architecturally, it is a reminder of the powerful influence white-robed Brahmin priests once exerted in Thailand, particularly in the royal court. Even today Brahmin rituals play an important part in many ceremonies.

THE GIANT SWING. Across Wat Suthat is the Giant Swing, or

Sao Chin Cha, the Giant Swing.

Sao Chin Cha, once the focus of a colorful Brahmin ceremony honoring the god Siva, when teams of young men swung to great heights in an effort to snatch sacks of money with their teeth, the highest sack being on a 76-foot pole. The ceremonial practice was abolished during the reign of King Rama VII.

WAT RAJABOPIT

Located on a road of the same name, Wat Rajabopit was built in 1870, shortly after King Rama V ascended to the throne, and displays the eclectic approach to architecture that was characteristic of the fifth reign. Its central feature is a graceful gilded stupa, modeled after the famous one in Nakhon Pathom, with a courtyard surrounded by a circular cloister with marble columns and two-tiered roofs, interrupted by the bot and three viharns; the exterior walls of the bot, the lower part of the stupa, and the cloister are covered with glazed Chinese tiles in a subtle blending of colors, while the doors and windows of the bot are decorated with mother-of-pearl inlays depicting the five royal orders. The interior of the bot has a vaulted roof that suggests a Gothic cathedral, and its color scheme of pale blue and gold also has a European flavor that contrasts with the classic Thai surroundings.

MINI CEMETERY
To the west of Wat Rajabopit is an atmospheric little cemetery crowded with tombs in assorted styles of architecture, including Gothic and Khmer. These mostly enshrine members of King Rama V's extensive family, evidence of the high regard in which he held the temple.

WAT ARUN
WAT RAKHANG KOSITHARAM
SIRIRAT HOSPITAL
WAT PO
NATIONAL THEATER
NATIONAL MUSEUM
WAT MAHATHAT
CHAKRABONGSE HOUSE
RACHINI SCHOOL
PAK KLONG TAL

WAT KALAYANIMIT
SANTA CRUZ CHURCH
WAT PHRA KEO
WAT PRAYOONWONG
MEMORIAL BRIDGE

Half a day

The Chao Phraya River ● 108–9

A COUP ON THE RIVER
In May 1950, elements of the navy staged a coup on a landing near the Grand Palace. The prime minister of the time was taken at gunpoint to a battle-ship anchored in the middle of the river and held hostage overnight. In the morning, planes from the air force bombed and sank the ship. However, the premier was not aboard: his captors had gallantly told him to swim for it when the bombs began to fall. He reached the shore, rallied his forces and within 36 hours was back in full command of the situation.

Beginning with the confluence of three northern streams snaking 219 miles down to the gulf, the Chao Phraya River ● 108–9 has played a decisive role throughout much of Thailand's history. It waters the broad Central Plains, creating one of the world's most fertile rice-growing areas; at the same time, it provides access to the outside world, making possible the trade that has nurtured three capital cities on its banks – first Ayutthaya, then Thonburi, and last Bangkok – over more than six centuries. The river was the focal point of Bangkok, not only in its early years but also well into the present century. The double and triple rows of floating houses that once lined its banks have vanished, and bridges – nine in the

DEMOCRACY MONUMENT

HOLY ROSARY CHURCH
ROYAL ORCHID SHERATON HOTEL
PORTUGUESE EMBASSY
OLD CUSTOMS HOUSE
FRENCH EMBASSY
ORIENTAL HOTEL
EAST ASIATIC COMPANY
ASSUMPTION CATHEDRAL
SHANGRI-LA HOTEL

WANG LEE HOUSE
SALA RIM NAM
SATHORN BRIDGE
WAT YANNAWA

metropolitan area – make communication with Thonburi easier than the old network of canals. Nevertheless, even today, a relatively short cruise along the Chao Phraya reveals a succession of major landmarks, both cultural and commercial: the Grand Palace enclosure and countless important Buddhist temples, the oldest foreign embassies, Catholic churches, the wharfs and godowns of trading companies, wholesale markets for agricultural produce brought to the capital by boat, spacious palaces and houses of old, where the city's élite once resided (and, in some cases, still do). The same trip will also show evidence of a residential revival along the Chao Phraya in the form of new hotels and towering condominiums rising on both sides amid those nostalgic sights; thanks to the increasingly congested traffic and the difficulty of commuting to distant suburbs, residents are now returning to Bangkok's timeless traditional heart.

CHAO PHRAYA EXPRESS
These ferries operate along the Chao Phraya between 6am and 6pm, with stops on both banks.

CROSS-RIVER FERRIES
Operated by the Chao Phraya Express Boat Company, these run between the two riverbanks during the day and until midnight.

This 1920's guidebook to Wat Arun shows that the temple has been a popular tourist attraction for many years.

WAT ARUN

With the possible exception of the Grand Palace, no Chao Phraya attraction is as celebrated as the soaring 343-foot central prang of Wat Arun ● 97, the Temple of Dawn, on the Thonburi bank. Dating from the Ayutthaya period and considerably restored, the temple served as the royal chapel during the Thonburi reign of King Taksin. The Emerald Buddha ▲ 148 was enshrined here before being brought to its present home at Wat Phra Keo. King Rama II of Bangkok first conceived the idea of raising the great Khmer-style prang, but due to engineering problems, it was

not completed until the following reign. This, as well as the four smaller ones that flank it, are adorned with ceramic tiles and fragments of multicolored porcelain, creating a jewel-like effect in the sunlight. A platform halfway up the tower offers a panoramic view of the river and Bangkok. Traditionally, at the end of the rainy season, the king visits Wat Arun and presents robes to the resident monks in a ceremony, a trip that in the past was made from the Grand Palace using a fleet of carved and gilded royal barges.

OTHER TEMPLES ALONG THE RIVERSIDE

THE MEMORIAL BRIDGE
Just before the towering spire of Wat Prayoonwong, the Memorial Bridge was the first to link Bangkok with Thonburi. It was opened by King Rama VII at precisely 8.16 in the morning – the auspicious time chosen by royal astrologers – on April 6, 1932, which was also the 150th anniversary of the capital's founding.

WAT KALAYANIMIT ★. This imposing edifice, standing where Klong Bangkok Yai enters the Chao Phraya, was built during the reign of Rama III. The *ubosot* shelters a huge bronze Buddha image especially popular with Thai Chinese, who honor the image as Sam Poh Kong in memory of the famous Ming eunuch admiral. The temple grounds contain an impressive collection of Chinese statues brought as ballast by the rice-trade junks. A stone polygonal chedi was also manufactured in China and assembled behind the ubosot. The murals are very well preserved and give a glimpse of life during that period. Next to the monastery a small alleyway leads to a charming little Chinese temple.

WAT PRAYOONWONG. Built during King Rama III's reign, Wat Prayoonwong boasts fine lacquered doors decorated with mother-of-pearl. The temple is also known for its artificial hill surrounded by a pond of turtles that are fed by Buddhist visitors to acquire merit.

> "The river is by no means a silent highway."
>
> Carl Bock, 1883

WAT RAKHANG KOSITHARAM. Across the river from the Grand Palace landing, this wat was built in the reign of King Rama I. "Rakhang" in Thai means "bell," and part of the name is derived from the numerous bells rung in the temple in the morning and evening. The main building is a particularly beautiful example of early Rattanakosin architecture ● *92–3*, with fine Ayutthaya-style stucco decorations around the doors and windows, while the *ho trai* ● *89*, a library on a raised platform, contains some well-preserved murals depicting the *Ramakien* epic and the Buddhist cosmology. Of special interest are three traditional Thai-style houses that were occupied by King Rama I before he became the ruler and later moved to the temple compound. The houses, as well as their gold-and-black lacquered windows and ornate entrance-way, were restored during the celebration of Bangkok's bicentennial in 1982.

HO PHRA TRAI PIDOK
When King Rama I donated his former residence to Wat Rakhang to be converted into a library, the buildings were re-arranged, and murals were added. In the early 1980's, these were restored with the help of a well-known Thai painter, Fua Haripitak.

PAK KLONG TALAAD

The sprawling collection of buildings known as Pak Klong Talaad is Bangkok's main wholesale market, which for over a century has served as a central exchange for vegetables, fruit, cut flowers, and other produce brought by boat (right) from the gardens and orchards of Thonburi, as well as others further upriver. The boats come mostly late at night or early in the morning, when the buildings are a hive of colorful activity as traders assemble from all over the city to select produce. In recent years, there has been talk of moving the market because of the increasing use of motor vehicles to bring goods and the consequent traffic jams on land.

THE WANG LEE HOUSE

In between rows of godowns on the Thonburi side of the river, the Wang Lee House is one of the best preserved of the numerous Chinese-style residences that were common in 19th-century Bangkok. Like the others, it was built by a Chinese immigrant who came to profit from the city's growing rice trade and remained to found several other still-thriving businesses. Most of these houses have fallen into disrepair, but the Wang Lee family has maintained its ancestral home in good condition and still uses it for various ceremonies.

THE PICKLED MURDERER
An unusual feature of Sirirat Hospital, on the bank of the river next to the Phra Pink Lao Bridge, is the ten museums that it contains. The most famous is the Museum of the Department of Forensic Medicine, where the focus is on crime. The most celebrated exhibit here is the preserved body of Si-Oui, a Chinese immigrant who murdered seven children before he was captured and executed in the 1950's. Si-Oui suffocated his victims, then ate their internal organs in the belief that it would promote longevity – a theory best disproved by his own fate.

View of the Chao
Phraya at the end of
the 19th century

COLONIAL INFLUENCE
Overlooking the
river, both the
French Embassy
and the Oriental
Hotel date from the
second half of the
19th century and
originally had the
louvered shutters and
spacious verandas
typical of European
buildings of the time.

THE OLD COLONIAL QUARTER

FOREIGN EMBASSIES. All the early foreign embassies – or legations, as they were then called – were located by the river. The earliest was built by the Portuguese, who had also been the first to establish relations with Ayutthaya, and who were granted permission to erect a trading post and consulate in 1820, during the reign of King Rama II; part of the trading office still remains at the back of the property, while the embassy residence, facing the river, was built later. The British came later, on the site now occupied by the General Post Office, followed by the Americans nearby, the French (next to the Oriental Hotel) and others, all with landings from which the diplomats traveled upriver to the Grand Palace on official business. Today, only the Portuguese and French remain at their respective original sites.

ORIENTAL HOTEL. This building started as a small guest house in 1865, calling itself the Oriental and overlooking the river. The guest house burned down that year, and was replaced

with a more substantial establishment, which in turn was acquired by H.N. Andersen, founder of the nearby East Asiatic Company, in 1884. Feeling that Bangkok was ready for a really luxurious hotel, he built a new one, designed by an Italian architect, which opened its "forty commodious and well furnished" rooms in 1887. The Oriental quickly established itself as the place to stay in the Thai capital and accommodated countless distinguished visitors, among them royalty, movie stars and traveling writers such as Somerset Maugham and Noël Coward. Today, the only part of the original structure that remains is the Author's Wing, graced by a pediment that displays a golden rising sun facing the river by which most of its early guests arrived.

> "Every curve of the river is beautiful with an unexpectedness of its own."
>
> Anna Leonowens

EAST ASIATIC COMPANY. Now one of the world's largest trading conglomerates, the East Asiatic Company evolved from a firm founded by H.N. Andersen in 1884, in a group of wooden buildings next to the Oriental Hotel. The present building dates from 1901. Andersen later returned to his native Denmark, where he served as the Thai Consul-General until his death in 1938.

OLD CUSTOMS HOUSE. Built in the 1880's, during the reign of King Rama V, this finely proportioned structure served as the main customs house for Bangkok until the development of the port facilities at Klong Toey, down river. The building has now been taken over by the fire brigade, but will soon be retrofitted and converted to a shopping center. Just behind the building, a narrow lane leads to a small Muslim settlement and cemetery.

CATHOLIC CHURCHES Catholic missionaries began work in Thailand during the Ayutthaya period and one of the buildings of the Church of the Immaculate Conception, near the Krung Thon Bridge, dates from this early time, when visitors stopped off at Bangkok on their way to the capital. Bishop Jean-Baptiste Pallegoix, who taught the future King Rama IV Latin and French, later resided here. Another river landmark is Santa Cruz Church, near the Memorial Bridge, originally built by Portuguese residents after the fall of Ayutthaya and reconstructed by Bishop Pallegoix in 1834; the present cathedral dates from 1913. Also erected by Portuguese Catholics around the same time was the first Holy Rosary Church, beside the Royal Orchid Sheraton Hotel. The present building, though, is of later vintage. The imposing Assumption Cathedral, standing by the Oriental Hotel, is one of Bangkok's largest, and was built in 1910 to replace an older church on the site.

WAT YANNAWA

Built in the early 19th century, Wat Yannawa was particularly popular with Chinese residents who began to settle in that part of Bangkok as the city expanded. Though of no great artistic interest, it contains a notable feature – a building designed in the shape of a Chinese junk, complete with huge eyes to ward off evil spirits and surmounted by two chedis.

This was added to the compound by order of King Rama III, who had observed the increasing number of steam-powered ships calling at the capital and wanted his subjects to remember the older kind of vessel to which they owed so much of their prosperity.

"HUNG HUNTRAA" Robert Hunter, an English businessman, was granted royal permission to build the first Western-style house on the river in the reign of King Rama II. Known as "Hung Huntraa," it continued to be used as a guest house for notable visitors even after Hunter's departure.

SIAMESE TWINS Crossing the Chao Praya in 1824, Hunter noticed a strange creature swimming near his boat. It proved to be the famous Siamese twins, Chang and Eng, who, partly with Hunter's support, went on to become celebrated attractions abroad. They eventually settled in America, where they died in 1874.

THE LONG TAIL

The *hong yao*, or "long-tail," boat (below) is perhaps the most often seen (and heard) conveyance along the Thonburi klongs. Reportedly developed in Thailand, it has a propeller on a long pole that can be raised to navigate shallow waterways.

"The procession of the royal barges, borne along the bosom of the great mother Menam, with all the accessories of splendour that Bangkok could produce, afforded a sight the beauty of which is hardly to be equalled in any part of the gorgeous East."

Carl Bock

Most of the once-numerous klongs, or canals, of Bangkok have vanished, filled in to widen narrow roads or to create new ones. In Thonburi, however, development has come more slowly, due largely to the lack of bridges across the Chao Phraya until fairly recently, and the klongs retain much of their old atmosphere.

ROYAL BARGE MUSEUM

The Royal Barge Museum, on Klong Bangkok Noi near the point where it enters the river, displays but a few of the spectacular craft that were once used for royal processions along the Chao Phraya. Such processions began in Ayutthaya when, according to one foreign observer, as many as 200 barges were involved, propelled by chanting, uniformed oarsmen "all rowing in synchronized movement and rhythm." The most impressive of the contemporary barges is the gilded Suphanahongsa ● 54 in which the king rides, over 150 feet long and requiring a crew of sixty-four, with a prow in the shape of a mythical, swan-like

> "The broad deep klongs are the great streets of the cities and the highways of the plains."

> Ernest Young

bird. Another, 149 feet long, is adorned with a many-headed *naga,* or sacred serpent, while other figureheads include horned dragons, *garuda,* and characters from the *Ramakien.* Royal barge processions today are rare, the most recent having been held on the occasion of the King's 60th birthday in 1988.

LIFE ALONG THE KLONG ★

"To unaccustomed eyes it is surprising to see a decent old woman with a mop of grey hair deftly maneuvering her canoe amid the traffic as she goes methodically about her day's shopping...On houseboats, people lounge about idly; men mostly half-naked wash themselves or their children, and here and there half-a-dozen urchins scramble about in the water." This description, written by Somerset Maugham in 1923, is still remarkably close to what one sees today on a cruise through the Thonburi klongs. Weathered old wooden houses, some in the steep-roofed traditional style, still crowd the banks; families still bathe

from their doorsteps in the late afternoon, the women preserving their modesty with a well-tied sarong; and vendors in straw hats still paddle small craft laden with various goods.

Thonburi has long been famous for its mangoes and durians, and, while some of the orchards have been turned into building sites, many remain along the waterways. Among the most popular klongs are Bangkok Yai and Bangkok Noi, though smaller ones lead off in all directions and offer glimpses of a fast-disappearing way of life.

WAT SUWANNARAM ★

Wat Suwannaram, located on the southern bank of Klong Bangkok Noi not far from where it joins the river, is a well-proportioned temple built on the foundations of an Ayutthaya-period temple by King Rama I and renovated by King Rama III. In addition to being a good example of transitional architecture of the Ayutthaya and Rattanakosin periods, it is noted for the beautiful mural paintings in its sanctuary; these works of art are attributed to Luang Vichit Chetsada and Krua Khonpae, two prominent painters of the third reign, and have been restored using modern techniques. On the south wall, behind the principal Buddha image, are vivid scenes from the three worlds of Buddhist cosmology. The entrance wall is covered with a huge mural depicting the victory of Buddha over Mara while the side walls are decorated with several rows of praying figures facing the altar and scenes of the last ten Jataka tales of the Buddha's previous lives.

KLONG VENDOR
Selling by water is still as much a part of klong life as it was in the distant past. Vendors in small boats offer almost everything needed by waterside residents. Ernest Young in his book *The Kingdom of the Yellow Robe* observed, "There is a water market, but unlike the land market which remains open all day, this one opens and closes before the sun has risen very high. Scores of boats are massed together in one compact crowd. Each boat is sunk to the gunwale with piles of fruit or fish. The occupants barter and bargain with the same incessant deafening noise of shouting, laughing, and swearing that is characteristic of all markets the world over. The women wear flat-topped hats made of leaves, which slope outwards from the crown, and are stuck on their heads by a circular frame-work of cane placed inside."

"The Chinese here are a model of peaceful intrusion. The several thousands who immigrated into Siam have monopolised trade. Whatever is related to labour in the kingdom is stimulated, organised and soon thriving in their hands. While the Siamese represents sheer idleness, his bustling sycophant counterpart from the Celestial empire is a paragon of greediness and painstaking toil."
The Marquis de Beauvoir

Occupying the site selected by King Rama I for his royal palace in 1782 was a community of Chinese traders. They moved to a new location, just outside the city walls, where they created a teeming district that became Bangkok's Chinatown, long the center of commercial life in the capital.

LION CARICATURE
The painting above reflects the traditional lion dance, regarded as an essential part of the ceremonies that accompany the official opening of many buildings and also suggesting the importance of Chinese customs in Thai life.

SAMPHENG LANE

Beginning at Wat Pathum Khongka – an old temple also known as Wat Sampheng, built a century before Bangkok became the capital – and running for seven blocks parallel to Yaowarat Road, Sampheng Lane is a noisy covered alleyway lined with shops selling goods of all kinds: wedding mementoes, buttons, imported textiles, kitchenware, gold chains, beads, toys and clothing, to mention only a few. The road eventually emerges at Pahurat, just across from Klong Ong Ang, a market famous for its numerous shops and stalls selling textiles at prices substantially lower than anywhere else in the city.

YAOWARAT ROAD

Yaowarat ▲ *143* is the main street of Chinatown. The thoroughfare is congested and the air heavily polluted but it is nevertheless full of life and fascinating discoveries, especially down the narrow lanes leading off each side. It once boasted a large number of opium dens, gambling houses, burlesque shows, and brothels (proclaimed by green lanterns hanging outside); these have mostly disappeared, at least on the surface, but the area still retains a raffish, faintly mysterious ambience at night. Paul

> "Half of the population of the Menam delta is Chinese
> and very few people are without some trace of
> the Chinese blood in them."
>
> Holt S. Hallett, 1890

Morand, writing at the turn of the century, captured the atmosphere of the area in *Rien que la Terre*: "With the noise of the street, the fanfare of gramophones, the clattering of mahjong, like hail on a tin roof, one is reminded of China, but it is the pawnshops which give the impression reality. Gamblers come to pawn their jewels, their silken robes, their pipes. The more the pipes have been smoked and filled with opium, the more they gain for them. Lotteries, cockfights, fish fights, betting on Shanghai races, ten days' journey from here; all are played. Bets are even placed on the number of pips in a melon! It is reported that naval officers, under arrest and confined to their boats, continue to play at sea, by signal!"

Near the end of Yaowarat Road is an area called Nakorn Kasem, once known as the "Thieves' Market" because of the existence of its many shops selling antiques and secondhand goods.

CHINATOWN TEMPLES

Chinatown contains a number of temples both large and small, some for Mahayana Buddhists, some for Taoists, and still others for followers of Theravada Buddhism. The leading Mahayana Buddhist temple is Wat Mangkon Kamalawat, on Charoen Krung Road, where enormous candles decorated with Chinese figures are among the altar offerings. Off Plabplachai Road is Wat Kanikaphon, founded by a former brothel owner, where elaborate paper models of luxury items such as automobiles, planes, computers and houses are burned in honor of deceased relatives. This temple is better known as Wat Mae Lao Fang after the brothel owner. Li Thi Miew, a Taoist temple on Plabplachai, has interesting Chinese paintings on the interior walls. Wat Traimit is located close to where Yaowarat Road meets Charoen Krung Road. It contains the Golden Buddha that was found during construction work at a temple near the river in the 1950's. Originally covered in stucco, the gold Buddha was revealed when it was accidentally dropped during moving, shattering the stucco. The solid gold Buddha weighs over 5 tons.

FORTUNE SEEKER
A client eagerly awaits the verdict as a Chinatown fortune-teller consults his almanac. They are consulted on everything from health to the most auspicious dates for marriage or opening a new business.

Vegetarian food offerings at Wat Mangkon Kamalawat.

ITALIAN ARTISTS
While in Europe, King Rama V made contact with many artists and posed in their studios. He later commissioned several Italian artists to work in Bangkok; Cesare Ferro was the first to become a Siamese court painter in 1904. Besides various portraits of the king, Ferro's works also included the wall decorations of the Amphornsathan Throne Hall in the palace. Prince Naris, who was in charge of the public works department, was also keen to promote innovative ideas such as Siamese subjects and Western techniques. He worked closely with a team of craftsmen and painters, notably Carlo Rigoli, on various projects such as Wat Rajathiwat and the Borom-phiman Mansion. All the Italian artists gave art lessons to Thai painters and influenced the local art scene. However, the one who left a lasting impression was Corrado Ferroci, who came to Thailand in 1923 and lived there until his death. Ferroci produced a number of royal statues and eventually became a teacher. He founded the institute now known as Silpakorn University, which trains hundreds of young artists.

King Rama V was the first Thai ruler to travel to Europe. The result of such trips was a determination to transform Bangkok into a Western-style capital. The main focus of his effort was the Dusit district, which he linked with the traditional center by Ratchadamnoen (Royal Progress) Avenue and where he proceeded to build a new throne hall and palace, residences for members of the royal family (among them Chitralada Palace, where the present king and queen live), and numerous tree-lined avenues suitable for carriage rides. His successor Rama VI followed up his plans on an even larger scale. Since most of Bangkok's expansion has taken place elsewhere, largely to the east, this district still retains much of its early 19th-century flavor, with many of the old buildings occupied by the military and government offices

ANANDA SAMAKHOM THRONE HALL. The center of Rama V's Dusit district was the elaborate, Western-style throne hall. Construction began in 1907, directed by a group of Italian architects and engineers, notably Annibale Rigotti, Carlo Allegri, E.G. Gollo and M. Tamagno, and was completed five years later, after the death of the king. Galileo Chini, whose work the king had admired at the Venice Biennale, was commissioned in 1911–13 to decorate the vault with huge frescoes of notable events in Thai history. For a time following the end of the absolute monarchy the building served as the National Parliament. The square in front of the Ananda Samakhom is decorated with a large equestrian statue of Rama V, modeled by Georges Saulo when the king visited Paris. The statue was cast in parts and assembled in

Bangkok, and was unveiled on November 11, 1908, the 40th anniversary of his coronation. Every year, on October 23, the anniversary of King Rama V's death, many people visit the statue and pay homage to his memory.

VIMARN MEK PALACE. This palace is an 81-room structure of golden teak and was originally intended to serve as a residence of King Rama V on the island of Si Chang in the Gulf of Thailand. Due to conflicts with the French over Cambodia, however, he decided to move the structure to Bangkok, and to use it as a residence during the construction of the nearby Dusit Palace. Long neglected after King Rama V's death, it was beautifully restored and furnished with fifth-reign royal treasures by Queen Sirikit as part of the 1982 Bangkok bicentennial celebrations. Queen Sirikit selected the furnishings, which include such curiosities as Thailand's first shower bath as well as historic photographs of the late 19th century.

VIMARN MEK PALACE
This was the first Siamese house to have electricity.

"BIRTHDAY BRIDGES". During the latter part of his reign, King Rama V started an annual tradition of opening a new bridge on the occasion of his birthday. A number of these "birthday bridges" have been lost in the name of progress, but several remain in all their ornate beauty.

WAT BENCHAMABOPIT. Popularly known as the Marble Temple, this wat was built at the turn of the century by King Rama V ● *93*. It was designed by his brother, Prince Naris, with the help of Italian architect Hercules Manfredi. The temple is a blend of architectural styles and decoration: gray marble from Italy, for example, was imported to sheathe the bot and pave the surrounding cloisters, while inside there are stained-glass windows as well as a replica of the famous Phra Buddha Chinaraj image. Around the cloister are fifty-three bronze Buddha showing every style of Thai religious art and some from neighboring cultures. Also in the compound is a building in which King Rama VI lived as a monk, the interior decorated with murals showing major events of his reign, and an ancient Bodhi tree.

PHYA THAI PALACE
Following King Rama V's death in 1910, Phya Thai Palace served as the residence of Queen Sowabha Phongsri, having previously been occupied by Crown Prince Vajiravudh. The Victorian-style buildings were later a luxury hotel then became the Phra Mongkut Military Hospital.

The three-wheeled vehicle known as a tuk-tuk (right) is a cheap and popular form of transportation in the city.

BANGKOK TRAFFIC In Bangkok, road expansion has failed to keep pace with the increasing number of vehicles, leading to an escalation of traffic congestion. Fortunately, Bangkok now has three metro lines and the government plans to construct another 56 miles of track by the year 2010. However, the present network doesn't link the more heavily populated suburbs with the city's central office district. Thus, although traffic congestion has decreased, it still continues to pose problems.

No complete map exists of modern Bangkok – not surprising, really, in view of the speed with which new suburban developments spring up and the rapid changes even in older districts. The city's present skyline of towering condominiums, hotels and shopping complexes is only a decade or so old, and middle-aged residents can recall a time when now-crowded areas were serene ricefields and "downtown" meant the shops along New Road and Lower Surawong. Today, one's work, place of residence or particular interests are more likely to determine what one regards as the "center" of Bangkok. Sometimes such places overlap. More often they involve long trips through congested traffic; thus

quite a number of residents have never even seen such older landmarks as Wat Po and the National Museum. If some visitors enjoy strolling about at random, savoring the animated street life that can be found almost anywhere, the majority, for whom time is limited, will probably prefer to plan each day's activities based on the area where their hotel is located.

SILOM ROAD, COMMERCIAL HUB

Silom Road, extending from Rama IV Road to New Road, has become an important commercial area. Many leading banks, advertising agencies, airline offices and handicraft shops are located along its length, as well as several large hotels and popular centers of nightlife such as Patpong and Thaniya Road. Lower Silom is a center of the booming Thai gems and jewelry industry, with numerous shops and wholesale outlets. Day and night the sidewalks near the Rama IV Road end are also crowded with vendors offering locally made copies of brand-name clothing and accessories, watches, CDs and DVDs.

NIGHTLIFE IN PATPONG. Despite official disapproval, frequent feminist protest, and the looming shadow of AIDS, Bangkok's anything-goes nightlife remains a major attraction for many visitors. The center of activity is Patpong Road, between Silom and Surawong, and several smaller side streets in the area; Thaniya Road, further up Silom,

> "In Asia, a silver key can open any lock."
>
> Carl Bock, 1883

a particular favorite with Japanese. The attractions range from small bars with go-go dancers, sex shows and massage parlors to discos, which are as popular with younger members of Thai society as with tourists. A smaller but similar concentration can be found on Soi Cowboy, off Sukhumvit Soi 23. Though the reputation of Patpong is mainly due to the development of mass sex tourism, one should keep in mind that traditionally in Thailand sex education for males starts with a visit to a brothel. Despite the natural shyness and puritanism of the Thais, prostitution remains an accepted part of life.

"As Calcutta smells of death and Bombay of money, Bangkok smells of sex, but this sexual aroma is mingled with the sharper whiffs of death and money."
Paul Theroux

LUMPINI PARK

Across from the Dusit Thani Hotel, Lumpini (right) is the only park in central Bangkok. It was presented to the city by King Rama VI in the 1920's. Vehicular traffic is banned in the park, thus enhancing its appeal to joggers and others who come to exercise in the early morning and late after-noon. Many elderly Chinese who are early risers use the park as a venue for their *tai chi* exercises and folk-dance sessions.

Paddle boats await customers at the lake in Lumpini Park.

ERAWAN SHRINE

During the construction of the Erawan Hotel in the 1950's, work was plagued by a series of mysterious accidents that included the death of several laborers. The Erawan Shrine, containing an image of Brahma, was erected near the site in an effort to stop these mishaps. Large crowds now visit the shrine and present wooden elephants, garlands and other offerings in the hope of having their wishes granted; many successful supplicants hire resident dancers to perform in the courtyard as a way of showing their gratitude.

The ever-busy Erawan Shrine receives various forms of offerings from devotees throughout the day until late evening.

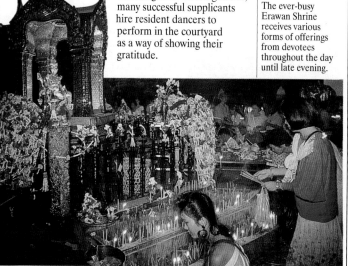

MISSING JIM
The disappearance of Jim Thompson, "the Silk King of Thailand," is one of the enduring mysteries of modern Asia. In March 1967, shortly after his 61st birthday, he went with friends for a holiday in the Cameron Highlands, a resort in northern Malaysia. There he went for a walk alone on Easter Sunday afternoon and never returned. Despite an exhaustive search by soldiers and local volunteers – not to mention advice offered by numerous experts in the supernatural – no trace of him was found, nor have any real leads turned up in the more than twenty-five years since. There are plenty of theories, however, ranging from a kidnap that somehow went wrong to any of a variety of misadventures in the surrounding jungle. Interest in the case has been maintained through factual account, several novels, and hundreds of newspaper and magazine articles.

JIM THOMPSON'S HOUSE. Located on Soi Kasemsan 2, off Rama I Road, is the Thai-style house built by Jim Thompson, an American who came to Thailand at the end of World War Two and stayed to revive the Thai silk industry. He disappeared mysteriously while on holiday in Malaysia in 1967. Actually the house is a group of old teak structures brought from several places and reassembled on the bank of a klong. Thompson filled them with his large collection of art from Thailand and other Asian countries, including paintings, porcelain, statuary and antique furniture. The house is now a museum open to the public daily except Saturdays and Sundays.
SUAN PAKKARD PALACE. The former home of Prince and Princess Chumbhot, Suan Pakkard Palace stands in a large, beautifully landscaped tropical garden on Si Ayutthaya Road. It consists of five traditional Thai houses assembled on the property in the

> "Not only do you have beautiful things, but what is rare you have arranged them with faultless taste."
>
> Somerset Maugham, in a letter to Jim Thompson

COLLECTOR'S HOUSE

The components of Jim Thompson's house came from various sources. The largest of the structures came from a village across the canal that runs behind the property; others were found near Ayutthaya. Produced in pre-fabricated sections, they were brought to the site by river barges. Carpenters skilled in traditional methods rebuilt the house and completed it in 1959.

SIAM SOCIETY

The Siam Society was founded by a group of Thais and foreign residents in 1904 for research and investigation in matters appertaining to Siam. Placed under royal patronage during the reign of King Rama VI, it moved to its present location in 1933. The Society has an extensive library of books and other publications on Thailand and the rest of Asia. It issues a journal for members, and organizes frequent lectures and exhibitions.

1950's as well as the Lacquer Pavilion, an elegant structure found in Ayutthaya and probably dating from the early Bangkok period. The interior walls of the pavilion are covered with fine gold-and-black lacquer paintings. The art collection displayed in the houses covers a wide range, from prehistoric bronze jewelry and pottery found in the northeast to furniture and other items that belonged to Prince Chumbhot's family. The palace is open daily except Sundays.

THE KAMTHIENG HOUSE.

Bangkok's only real ethnological collection – fish traps, traditional stoves and cooking pots, implements used by Thai farmers – is displayed in and around the Kamthieng House, in the compound of the Siam Society on Sukhumwit Road Soi 21. The classic, northern-style teak house, over 200 years old, came from Chiang Mai and was brought to Bangkok in sections. Also in the society's compound is a fine example of a Central Plains house ● *86–7*, thus offering visitors an opportunity to compare the architectural differences between the two styles. Both are open daily except Sundays and Mondays.

GEMS AND JEWELRY
Export of gems and jewelry now ranks as Thailand's fifth-largest earner of foreign exchange. Gems such as sapphires, rubies, zircons, garnets and cat's-eyes are brought into the country from all over the world to be cut and polished by a growing force of skilled workers. This activity is mainly centered around the Charoen Krung district, between the Silom Road and the Chao Phraya river.

THE WEEKEND MARKET

From Saturday morning until Sunday evening, one of the busiest places in Bangkok is the great near Chatuchak Park, which can now be reached by the elevated metro line (alight at Mo-Chit station). Almost everything the country produces is on sale somewhere in this huge network of several thousand stalls: fruit trees, garden plants, clothing, antiques, handicrafts, fresh and preserved foods, fruit, furniture, contemporary porcelains, army surplus goods and pets of all kinds. Most of the prices are negotiable, as they are at all Thai markets, and for visitors who mind the heat the early morning hours are the best time to go.

PERMANENT PLANT MARKET. Between the end of the Kamphaengphet Road and the Weekend Market is another market which is open daily and is entirely devoted to plants. A true garden-lover should devote at least a few hours to strolling along the long row of shops displaying the full range of ornamental trees, shrubs and creepers available to local enthusiasts, in addition to pots and gardening tools. The shops and sidewalk vendors offer dazzling displays of flowering orchids at prices that will seem ridiculously low to visitors from more temperate countries.

PRATUNAM MARKET

Pratunam, literally translated, means "water gate," and the market by that name is located near the locks of Klong Saen Sap, at the intersection of Phetchaburi and Rajadamri roads. The nearby 'World Trade Center' is a shopping mall selling all kinds of fabric and off-the-peg clothing, either singly or semi-wholesale. Low prices and an almost limitless choice make this a highly popular place, particularly on weekends, so be prepared for crowds and some shrewd bargaining.

SIDEWALK VENDORS. Just about every Bangkok governor, at some point in his term of office, has made a determined effort to clear the city's streets of sidewalk vendors. None has succeeded, since this informal sector supports a significant proportion of the population and is as integral part of the urban landscape and traditions. Sidewalk shopping is a city-wide affair, but certain areas are more crowded than others. Upper Silom Road, for instance, caters more to tourist tastes, and so does the stretch of Sukhumwit Road extending from Soi 11 to Plernchit, no doubt because both areas are convenient to numerous hotels; a street-long bazaar springs up on Patpong after dark. Rajadamri Road from the Rajprasong intersection to Pratunam is another popular gathering place for vendors to sell goods, as is the lane leading from New Road to the Oriental Hotel.

SHOPPING CENTERS

Modern shopping centers are a relatively new phenomenon in Bangkok, but the city has more than made up for lost time in the past two decades. The Plernchit branch of the locally owned Central Department Store is the largest in Southeast Asia. The goods are of high quality and, surprisingly, quite reasonably priced in view of the luxurious surroundings and compared with other countries. Popular department stores include Sogo, Isetan and Thai Daimaru, opened by the Japanese, who are the main investors in Thailand. Shopping centers are equally ubiquitous and most contain fashion boutiques, restaurants and fast-food outlets, movie theatres and other recreational facilities on several levels in one building. Among those shopping areas most frequented by visitors are Central Plaza, Emporium, Robinson, Mahboon Krong and Siam Center. In recent years, huge shopping complexes have opened on the outskirts of Bangkok, such as Seacon Square, the largest in Asia, on Srinakarin Road.

THAI SILK
Probably the most sought-after product is Thai silk. The material is believed to have originated from the village folk of northeastern Thailand, who weaved it using primitive handlooms. The silk remained popular until its decline at the end of the 19th century, when Chinese and Japanese silk imports flooded the local market. The silk industry was revived by entrepreneur Jim Thompson after World War Two. The pioneer company he established remains one of the best and biggest silk producers in the country today. The main shop, open 12 hours daily to accommodate the endless flow of customers, is located at the intersection of Surawong and Rama IV roads. There are silk clothes and scarfs as well as the material itself, which can be bought by the yard.

THE FLOATING MARKET

Floating markets, consisting of hundreds of vendors congregating by boat, usually in the early morning, at some point on a river or canal, have long fascinated visitors to Bangkok and other parts of Thailand. A few decades ago, the most popular place to view this colorful phenomenon was the canal outside Wat Sai in Thonburi; eventually however this market became overcrowded with tourists.

DAMNERN SADUAK. Today the best of such markets convenient to Bangkok is on Klong Damnern Saduak in Ratchaburi province, a trip most itineraries combine with a visit to Nakhon Pathom. The floating market here takes place somewhat later than at other places – between 8am and 10am – and offers a busy, photogenic scene of boats laden with fruit, vegetables, cooked foods and other produce, sold principally by women wearing the broad straw hats and dressed in the blue cotton clothing favored by rural Thai people. For food lovers there are also many restaurants lined along the banks.

RATCHABURI'S WATER JARS

Ratchaburi province is noted for its production of huge, glazed water jars, often decorated with swirling Chinese dragons and floral motifs, which are sent to many parts of Thailand. A recent industry using similar skills is producing fine reproductions of Chinese blue-and-white porcelains.

NAKHON PATHOM

One of the oldest cultural centers in Thailand, Nakhon Pathom (*nakhon* means "town" and *pathom* "first") is believed to be the first Mon capital, dating from several centuries before the Christian era. It was deserted at various times in its history,

and the present town dates from the middle of the 19th century, when King Rama IV ordered restoration work to be done on its chedi.

PHRA PATHOM CHEDI. Dominating the town of Nakhon Pathom, and visible from many miles away, is the impressive Phra Pathom Chedi, which, at 352 feet, is the tallest Buddhist monument in the world and the oldest in Thailand ● 97. It was originally built about a thousand years ago but had fallen into a pile of rubble by the middle of the 19th

RIVER RITUAL
One of the most memorable sights along the canals of Ratchaburi and other provinces is that of Buddhist monks collecting their early-morning alms by boat from waterside houses. Strict rules apply not only to the type of boat used for this ritual but also the seemingly effortless manner in which it is paddled.

> "That must be the way to heaven when we die."
>
> Sunthorn Phu

DVARAVATI STUCCOES
Nakhon Pathom was an important town of the Dvaravati Mon kingdom (6th–10th century). Excavations at the Chedi Chula Pathom, on the outskirts of the modern town, have led to the discovery of an interesting series of bas-reliefs in stucco. Other terracottas were found at Ku Bua and U Thong. These are now displayed in the museums of Nakhon Pathom, U Thong and Bangkok ▲ *158*. They throw light on the ancient Mon aristocratic life of the elegantly dressed court ladies. Mon society was evidently refined and cosmopolitan, in touch with India, Indonesia and perhaps the Mediterranean.

century, when the future King Rama IV, then a Buddhist monk, came on a pilgrimage. Restoration work, which involved covering the old ruins with an entirely new chedi, began in 1853 but – due to numerous technical difficulties – was not completed until the reign of King Rama V. The base

of the chedi is surrounded by a circular cloister, with chapels containing Buddha images from various periods situated at the four cardinal points. A museum houses numerous early religious objects that have been found in the area, among them the Wheel of the Law and terracotta bas-reliefs of the Dvaravati period (7th–11th century). A popular festival is held in the temple grounds each November, when the great chedi is beautifully illuminated.

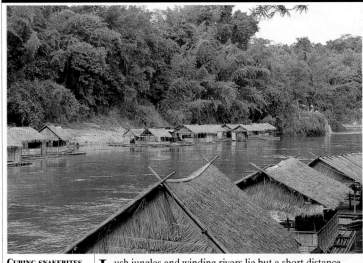

CURING SNAKEBITES
Here is Ernest Young's recipe, from his book, *The Kingdom of the Yellow Robe*, for a mixture that could help cure snakebites in the event of an encounter with poisonous reptiles in the parks or rivers:
a piece of the jaw of a wild hog;
a piece of the jaw of a tame hog;
a piece of the bone of a goose;
a piece of the bone of a peacock;
the tail of a fish; and
the head of a venomous snake.

L ush jungles and winding rivers lie but a short distance away from the modern town of Kanchanaburi, which is also haunted by a modern epic of heroism and tragedy.

RIVER RESORTS

In recent years, the Kanchanaburi area – particularly the Kwai Noi and Kwai Yai rivers – has become a popular vacation spot for Bangkok residents in search of lush natural scenery. By boat along one of the rivers, and also by road, you can travel to a number of rural resorts, some built on floating rafts and some substantial structures with all modern conveniences. The Kwai Yai leads to a large, scenic lake formed by the Srinakharin Dam, while the Kwai Noi, the more developed of the two in terms of resorts, winds through Saiyok National Park to another beautiful expanse of water created by the Khao Laem Dam.

ERAWAN NATIONAL PARK

Established in 1975, the 220-square-mile Erawan National Park is protected on the west by Saiyok National Park, on the south by Salak Phra Wildlife Sanctuary, on the east by the Kwai Yai River, and on the north by the Srinakharin National Park.

Its most celebrated feature is the spectacular Erawan Waterfalls, a 4,950-foot cascade that is broken up into seven tiers; according to popular belief, the rock formation above the top level resembles the three-headed elephant Erawan of Hindu mythology. The park provides sanctuary to a considerable variety of wildlife, including eighty species of birds, gibbons, barking deer

> "The Japanese did not consider human life of any value when viewed in the light that the railway must be pushed on regardless of cost."
>
> C. A. McEachern, prisoner of war

and rhesus monkeys, as well as a profusion of luxuriant plant life; also within its boundaries are two impressive caves, Phrathat and Wang Badang, both adorned with huge stalactites and stalagmites. Bungalows and dormitories are available for visitors who want to stay overnight in the park.

THE DEATH RAILWAY

In June 1942, six months after the start of its triumphant conquest of Southeast Asia, Japan ordered the construction of a railway from Thailand to Burma as a substitute for the long sea route to Rangoon; it was intended to play a major role in the transportation of men and material for the planned invasion of British India. The engineering task was formidable, the track leading through dense malarial rain forest, over rocky mountains, and across swift rivers, finally crossing into Burma at the lofty Three Pagodas Pass. For labor, the Japanese deployed about 61,000 Allied prisoners-of-war captured in Malaya, Singapore and the Dutch East Indies, plus an estimated 270,000 conscripted Asian workers. Slowly, painfully, over the next three years, the almost impossible task was completed, but at a horrifying cost in human life: over 12,000 Allied prisoners and 240,000 Asians died during the ordeal – or 393 men for every mile of the eventually useless Death Railway, as it came to be called by survivors. The bodies of 6,982 victims lie in a tranquil Allied War Cemetery near Kanchanaburi, where the railway began, and a museum displays other grim reminders of what one writer has called a "supreme monument to folly."
The track itself was dismantled by the British after the war but a length still runs along the Kwai Yai River and several of the bridges have been rebuilt. Toward the end of November, an annual fair is held in Kanchanaburi under the auspices of the Tourism Authority of Thailand, featuring a sound and light show at the so-called *Bridge On The River Kwai* (based on the fictitious span made famous by the movie) and displays of prehistoric artifacts found in the region.

THREE PAGODAS PASS
The pass lies on the frontier between Thailand and Burma, and was the historic crossing point for Burmese armies who invaded Ayutthaya. It was also the place where the Death Railway led into Burma, though the tracks were dismantled by the British at the end of the war.

RIVER KWAI
Kanchanaburi gained its fame from the popular film *The Bridge on the River Kwai* – actually filmed in Sri Lanka – which in turn was based on the novel of the same name by Pierre Boulle. Local entrepreneurs cash in on this fame but the story is entirely fictional.

The owner of the Ancient City looks upon the project more as an act of philanthropy than as a tourist attraction. Apart from providing work for countless traditional artisans whose skills are no longer in wide demand, he has preserved many ancient buildings that would otherwise have been neglected or destroyed.

THE OLD ROAD TO PATTAYA

The old Sukhumwit Road, once the only route to Pattaya and other resorts on the eastern gulf coast, leads through Samut Prakarn Province and passes a number of popular tourist attractions before it joins a newer, more modern highway. **THE ANCIENT CITY.** Muang Boran, or the Ancient City, started by an art-loving millionaire in the early 1970's, contains numerous buildings and monuments – some replicas, others genuine – from Thailand's past, on a 200-acre site roughly shaped like the country itself. One enters from the far south, passing such attractions as the Phra Mahathat stupa of Nakhon Si Thammarat and another from the Srivijaya city of Chaiya ● *96*, and then moves upward to the north through the splendors of Ayutthaya and Sukhothai. The idea might sound contrived, but it is executed with considerable taste, and expert advice from various authorities – among them a former director of the National Museum – which have been consulted throughout to ensure authenticity of detail. The replicas are one-third the original size, but there are also many original buildings. The village stilt-houses around the

"floating market" and the so-called "Market of Yesteryear" were once Thai houses that have been completely dismantled and moved to the site and then refurbished with original antiques and objects of everyday use. Two northern buildings of significance, a Lanna-style temple from Chiang Rai ● *94* and the Shan-Burmese temple from Ngao, have been salvaged from destruction and carefully restored in the Ancient City.

ชาวพัทยายินดีต้อนรับ
WELCOME TO PATTAYA

THE CROCODILE FARM. A popular tourist attraction, the Crocodile Farm is believed to be the largest of its kind in the world, containing more than 30,000 crocodiles, both local and foreign species. The reptiles are bred not only for the amusement of visitors but also as a source of hides to be turned into belts, wallets, handbags, shoes and other items. (A brochure once wittily described the farm as "a happy compromise between wildlife conservation and commercial enterprise.") Starting daily at 9am, there is a show featuring fearless handlers who "tame" some of the larger and more fearsome-looking specimens. There is also a zoo at the farm where other animals are kept.

PATTAYA

The new expressway between Bangna and Chonburi means that Pattaya is only 90 minutes drive from Bangkok. It also means you can avoid part of the heavily congested road leading to Bang Saen, a seaside resort popular with Thai families. Beyond Laem Chabang, the region's main port, you turn off the expressway to Pattaya and its world-famous string of beaches. Pattaya began attracting visitors from Bangkok in the 1950's, thanks to the relative ease with which its long stretches of white-sand beach could be reached from the capital. The only form of accommodation in those days consisted of a few simple bungalow complexes, and the first hotel did not open until 1965. Development began to accelerate at a feverish pace during the Vietnam War, when thousands of American soldiers came there on leave, and by the mid-1970's it had become a major resort, with hotels, restaurants and nightclubs extending the entire length of the main beach. The environmental cost of such rapid expansion has been high and most, if not all, of Pattaya's natural charms are gone; similarly, the free-wheeling nightlife has come in for much criticism in foreign newspapers and magazines. Many visitors enjoy its rowdy, laid-back atmosphere, however, and continue to come in large numbers. Those who prefer a quieter atmosphere and more privacy, at least after nightfall, can go further down the coast to less developed beaches or to offshore islands such as Koh Larn. There are several good golf courses in the area, as well as shooting ranges and other land-based sports facilities.

CROCODILES
Thailand's rivers, swamps and coastal areas are home to both fresh- and salt-water crocodiles ■ 23. One large fresh-water specimen, nicknamed Ai Dang, was killed in Chanta-buri in the 1960's; preserved, it was a popular attraction at fairs all over the country, displayed with a set of false teeth found in its stomach.

TRANSIENT WIVES
"The Europeans that trade with Siam provide themselves as they will do in Pegou with transient wives and more or less on similar terms and no one would think it shameful to have as many transient husbands but on the contrary to be an honour to have been loved by so many different men."
Captain Hamilton, 17th century

"On the 4th of January, at 8 o'clock in the morning, we arrived in the city of Chantaboon. It is built along the river, six or seven miles away from the mountains. About one third of the population is composed of Christian Annamites. The rest is mostly composed of Chinese merchants, some pagan Annamites as well as Siamese. The latter are all fishermen of Annamese descent. Their ancestors sailed all the way from Cochin-China hoping to fish in the northern waters of the Gulf of Siam. Little by little they settled in Chantaboon." Henri Mouhot

CHANTABURI

Known in old travel accounts as Chantaboon, Chantaburi has been a famous center of gem-mining since the early 15th century. The two main stones found in the area are sapphires and rubies, mostly mined in privately owned pits in the surrounding countryside. Gem trading is concentrated in a few blocks of the downtown area, where nearly all the shops are devoted to the business, particularly on weekends when traders come from Bangkok to make their selections. Chantaburi – the name means "city of the moon" – is also noted for the high quality of its tropical fruits.

KOH CHANG

Koh Chang, the second largest Thai island after Phuket, lies off the coast of Trat Province, near the Cambodian border. Along with fifty other nearby islands, Koh Chang comprises a beautiful marine national park. It is linked by ferry to Laem Ngob on the mainland and also by air to Bangkok.

RAYONG

Rayong, about 133 miles southeast of Bangkok, is a busy fishing port known for the high-quality fish sauce, *nam pla*, which is produced in many small local factories and then sold throughout Thailand. Along the coast east of the town are several peaceful resorts. Boats from Rayong may be available for hire to visit the various scenic offshore islands.

RAYONG'S GREAT POET
Sunthorn Phu (1786–1856), one of Thailand's greatest poets, was a native of Rayong. He was a particular favorite of King Rama II, with whom he collaborated on a number of works, and wrote the still-popular romantic epic *Phra Apaimani*. A statue has been erected in his memory at Amphur Klaeng, his birthplace.

KOH SAMET

A long, narrow island, Koh Samet lies about 45 minutes by boat off the coast near Rayong. Since 1981, it has been part of a national park that also includes Khao Laem Ya on the mainland, a move that has limited the development of overly intrusive tourist facilities. Koh Samet is still a favorite weekend destination from Bangkok.

The South

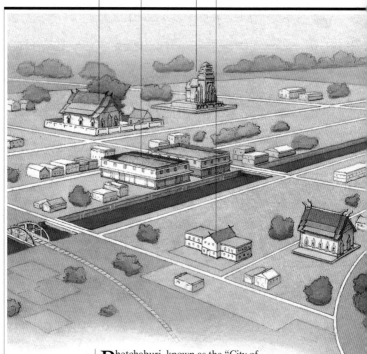

WAT YAI SUWANNARAM MARKET WAT KHAMPHAENG LAENG CITY HALL

A VIEW FROM KHAO WANG
Henri Mouhot, on the view from Khao Wang in 1858: "About 25 miles off stretches from north to south a chain of mountains called Deng...Beyond these rises a number of still higher peaks. On the low ground are forests, palm-trees, and rice-fields, the whole rich and varied in color. Lastly, to the south and east, and beyond another plain, lies the gulf, on whose waters...a few scattered sails are just distinguishable."

Phetchaburi, known as the "City of Diamonds," is an ancient settlement, with Khmer ruins that go back to the late 12th and early 13th centuries. It came under Thai rule during the Sukhothai period and later was an important post on the trade route that led from Mergui on the Andaman Sea to Ayutthaya. Numerous traditional Thai crafts flourished in the town, among them woodcarving, silk-weaving and ornamental work on gold and silver, some of which still survive today. More than most provincial Thai cities, modern Phetchaburi has preserved its old temples, several of which contain important mural paintings, as well as traditional wooden houses in the Central Plains Thai style.

KHAO WANG

Khao Wang, the "Mountain Palace," was built by King Rama IV in the middle of the 19th century as a place where he could escape the pressures of the capital and also spend more time on astronomy, one of his favorite hobbies. Consisting of several European-style buildings, an observatory, and a Buddhist chapel, the palace complex is located on one of the shoulders of a hill just outside Phetchaburi; other buildings are scattered around the hill at lower levels, and a stairway leading to the top is lined

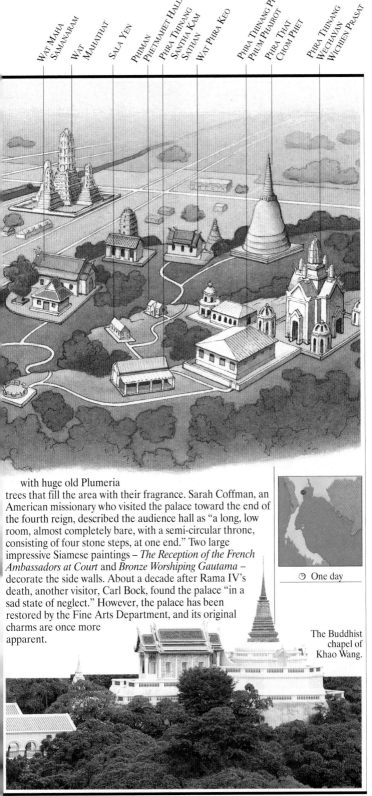

WAT MAHA
SAMANARAM

WAT
MAHATHAT

SALA YEN

PHIMAN
PHETMAHET HALLS

PHRA THINANG
SANTHA KAM
SATHAN

WAT PHRA KEO

PHRA THINANG PHET
PHUM PHAIROT

PHRA THAT
CHOM PHET

PHRA THINANG
WECHAYAN
WICHIEN PRASAT

with huge old Plumeria trees that fill the area with their fragrance. Sarah Coffman, an American missionary who visited the palace toward the end of the fourth reign, described the audience hall as "a long, low room, almost completely bare, with a semi-circular throne, consisting of four stone steps, at one end." Two large impressive Siamese paintings – *The Reception of the French Ambassadors at Court* and *Bronze Worshiping Gautama* – decorate the side walls. About a decade after Rama IV's death, another visitor, Carl Bock, found the palace "in a sad state of neglect." However, the palace has been restored by the Fine Arts Department, and its original charms are once more apparent.

🕘 One day

The Buddhist chapel of Khao Wang.

KHRUA IN KHONG
Khrua In Khong, one of King Rama IV's favorite painters, responded to the ruler's keen interest in Western culture by including European buildings and landscapes in his murals. At Wat Bowornivet in Bangkok, for example, he incorporated a building similar to that of Mount Vernon, George Washington's home, along with such contemporary subjects as an operation for cataracts.

WAT MAHA SAMANARAM

Located at the foot of the hill near the king's palace, Wat Maha Samanaram was built by King Rama IV. The chapel contains a beautiful Ayutthaya-style Buddha image and is decorated with murals by Khrua In Khong, a famous priest-painter of the fourth reign ● *106.* The main scene in the murals depicts the pilgrimage of the Buddhist followers to the Buddha's Footprint at Saraburi.

WAT YAI SUWANNARAM

Dating from the 17th century, Wat Yai Suwannaram is one of Phetchaburi's most beautiful temples. The interior walls of the bot are decorated with some of the oldest surviving mural paintings in Thailand, dating from the late 17th or early 18th century; these show two rows of celestial beings facing the principal Buddha image, a large bronze statue in Ayutthaya style. Within the compound are also several wooden buildings adorned with fine carvings that attest to the high quality of Phetchaburi artisans. The *sala* ● *88–9,* in front of the bot, has superbly carved doors, one of which has a gash supposedly made by Burmese invaders; inside are painted panels, one of which shows a rhinoceros, at that time found near the city. Except for this particular *sala* and the bot, the other buildings date from the reign of Rama V, who ardently supported the extensive renovations to the monastery.

WAT MAHATHAT

The most visible feature of Wat Mahathat is its towering central prang, surrounded by a cloister lined with Buddha images. Also noteworthy are the stucco decorations on one of the sanctuaries, which contains a number of Buddha images of the Ayutthaya period as well as several recently restored mural paintings.

> "Phetchaburi is a very pretty place…justly popular with Europeans resident at Bangkok as a summer resort for a change of air or a little bit of rustication."
>
> Frank Vincent

WAT KO KEO SUTHARAM ★

Wat Ko Keo Sutharam, popularly called Wat Ko, lies on the bank of the Phetchaburi River. Inside one of the chapels are some well-preserved murals dating from 1740; one of the figures depicted on the side walls is believed to be that of a Jesuit priest in the robes of a Buddhist monk, possibly recalling an earlier French mission that came through Phetchaburi in the reign of King Narai of Ayutthaya, while another panel shows the conversion of foreigners to Buddhism. The monastic buildings of the temple, raised on posts around a courtyard, have been little altered over the years; one of the buildings contains a small collection of items that have been donated to the monastery.

FOREIGNERS IN WAT KO KEO SUTHARAM Foreigners first began to appear in temple murals in the latter part of the Ayutthaya period. The earliest were Chinese, Persians and Indians, who came to trade in the capital; later, Europeans were seen, some obviously inspired by the French embassies who came to the court of King Narai in the late 17th century and others by various adventurers of the time.

WAT KHAMPHAENG LAENG

Wat Khamphaeng Laeng is a relatively modern temple that contains within its precincts a very important Khmer ruin dating from the 11th century. Remains of a massive stone wall (*khamphaeng laeng* in Thai), once encircled by moats, and a prang built in laterite can still be seen. The monument is of historical interest as it marks the southernmost point of expansion of the Khmer empire.

KHAO LUANG ★

This famous cave temple, in a hill just outside Phetchaburi, has long been one of the town's major attractions; it reminded Henri Mouhot, who arrived in 1860, of "the beautiful fairy scenes represented at Christmas in the London theaters." Light from a hole at the top of the main chamber dramatically illuminates a display of enormous stalactites along with numerous Buddha images that have been placed in the cave and that are presented with regular offerings. The late morning hours are the best time to view the effective natural lighting. Monkeys rush out from among the bushes to greet visitors to the cave.

HUA HIN

Credit for "discovering" the resort possibilities of Hua Hin, a scenic seaside village on the west coast of the gulf, 140 miles from Bangkok, usually goes to Prince Chakrabongse, a brother of King Rama VI, who in 1911 took a visiting group of European royalty there for a hunting holiday. The prince and his Russian wife built a bungalow by the sea, other members of the royal family soon built houses nearby and eventually a king's palace, which was called Klai Klangwan, "far from care." The entire court moved to Hua Hin for several months of the year, thus giving it a fashionable atmosphere still apparent in some of the spacious old bungalows visible from the beach. Completion of the southern railway line in the 1920's made Hua Hin easily accessible to the capital, leading to the Railway Hotel, a golf course, and other holiday homes owned by prominent Bangkok families. Even today, despite the addition of several large hotels and rows of condominiums, Hua Hin retains a sedate atmosphere, especially when compared with Pattaya, its boisterous competitor across the gulf. At Wat Khao Lao, the temple on top of the hill, visitors can enjoy charming views of the town.

FISHING PORT. One of the most colorful sights near Hua Hin town is the fishing port, where the daily catch from the Gulf of Thailand is brought in by fishermen in their trawlers in the early hours of the morning.

RAILWAY HOTEL. A rambling Victorian structure, built in 1923, with broad verandas and a garden of topiary shrubs, the old Railway Hotel fell on hard times when the mass tourist trade shifted to Pattaya in the early 1960's. It has been beautifully restored today by a French company without sacrificing its spacious, airy charm.

GOLF COURSE. The golf course at Hua Hin was the country's first, with "a stock of golf requisites and the loan of clubs" available through the Railway Hotel, according to a 1929 guide book. The 18-hole course overlooking the sea is still one of the most popular in the area, and the fact that it contains a temple and a topiary garden gives it a special Thai flavor.

A STAR PERFORMANCE The Railway Hotel played a prominent role in the award-winning film, *The Killing Fields*, about Cambodia's trials under Khmer Rouge rule. The producers used the picturesque old building in place of the Royal Hotel , where many journalists who covered the war stayed in Phnom Penh.

KHAO SAM ROI YOT NATIONAL PARK ★

Covering 39 square miles, Khao Sam Roi Yot – literally, "the mountain of three hundred peaks" – was established as a park in 1966. Conveniently situated just a few miles south of Hua Hin, the park boasts numerous picturesque limestone peaks, the highest rising to 1,997 feet, as well as caves, and unspoiled beaches fringed by casuarina trees. It was formerly famous for its marshes, waterfalls and wading birds. However, recent encroachment by private shrimp farmers has seriously affected the state of the natural habitat. Several scenes in *The Killing Fields* were filmed within the boundaries of the national park. Bird life is especially varied in this park, with more than 275 identified species, 60 of which – painted storks, grey herons, egrets and rare imperial eagles among them – are found mainly in the marsh areas. Monkeys and deer are particularly common. Other mammals include crab-eating macaques, Malayan porcupines, leopard cats and, in the offshore waters, Irrawaddy dolphins.

PHRAYA NAKHON CAVE. The largest cave in the park is Phraya Nakhon, named after a ruler of Nakhon Si Thammarat who discovered it two centuries ago when he came ashore in a violent storm; a pavilion in the cave was built for a visit by King Rama V in 1896.

PRACHUAB KHIRI KHAN

Prachuab Khiri Khan is approximately 54 miles south of Hua Hin. Off the main southern highway, it is a tiny port overlooked by Khao Chang Krachok ("mirror mountain"), on top of which sits a temple offering panoramic views of the sea. There are bungalows to rent and seafood restaurants down at the beach near the town.

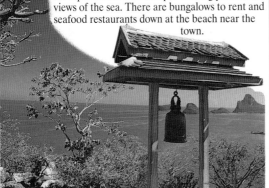

PINEAPPLES
A common sight around Hua Hin and along much of the southern peninsula are vast plantations of pineapples, which thrive in the sandy soil. Today, Thailand is one of the world's largest producers of canned and fresh pineapples for export, having long ago surpassed Hawaii. Southern pineapples are especially noted for their sweetness and succulence.

FAR FROM CARE
Although Klai Klangwan, the name of the royal palace at Hua Hin, means "far from care," it hardly proved so for King Rama VII. He was in residence there when he received word in June 1932 of the coup d'état that ended Thailand's absolute monarchy. Though he agreed to grant a constitution, he later abdicated in 1935 and died in England in 1941.

199

CHUMPHON

Despite the construction of a sizeable seaside hotel some years ago, Chumphon has never really found popularity as a resort. It is noted, however, for its relatively inexpensive supply of edible birds' nests ■ 28–9, gathered from the offshore island of Koh Lanka Chiu. The island can be visited by boat from the port of Paknam Chumphon.

KRA ISTHMUS

Just below Chumphon is the Kra Isthmus, only 15 miles wide and the narrowest point on peninsular Thailand, an area of rocky limestone precipices and breathtaking scenery. For many generations, this spot has been envisioned as the site of a Suez-type canal, which would cut nearly a thousand miles off shipping routes between ports on the Indian Ocean and the Gulf of Thailand. Several plans have been drawn up for such an undertaking – one proposer even suggested the use of nuclear weapons to ease the task – but thus far none has been successful, doubtless to the great relief of Singapore further south.

SRIVIJAYA
The Srivijaya kingdom ▲ 35, which originated in Sumatra, dominated the southern peninsula of Thailand between the 8th and 13th centuries. Though historians disagree over its extent, it was a Hindu culture that also practiced Mahayana Buddhism and produced some of Thailand's finest art in stone and bronze. This bronze Bodhisattva was found by Prince Damrong at Wat Mahathat, Chaiya, together with a number of other excellent pieces, and is now preserved in the National Museum in Bangkok ● 160.

RANONG

Ranong, located on a river of the same name that empties into the sea across from Victoria Point, the southernmost extremity of Burma, is a quiet provincial capital whose prosperity is mainly based on tin from nearby mines and a fishing fleet that sails far out into the Indian Ocean. The older houses, like those of Phuket and Songkhla further south, are built in the Sino-Portuguese style of Malacca and some of the downtown streets have covered arcades to shelter pedestrians from monsoon rains. The town is noted for a number of hot mineral-water springs, one of which supplies the Jansom Thara Hotel, picturesquely situated at the foot of a mountain just outside the town. Boat trips can be arranged from the port to visit off-shore islands, among them Koh Pa Yam where a company produces cultured pearls. (Entry into Burma, however, is not allowed at this point.) More hot springs – one of which produces 130 gallons of

"At low water immense tracts of mud and sand
are laid bare, for the edification of flocks of
pelicans, cormorants and herons."

H. Warrington Smyth

hot (158°F) water a minute – as well as tin
mines can be found at Hat Sompin,
about an hour away from Ranong
by car. Another sight is Nam
Tok Ngao, a waterfall on the
highway southward. It is at
its most impressive after a
heavy rain.

CHAIYA

An ancient town, Chaiya is
believed by some scholars to
have been the capital of the
great Srivijaya kingdom (8th–13th
century) ● 35, which ruled most of
peninsular Thailand from its base in Sumatra. The
only remaining traces of this former glory are the ruins of
several once-impressive temples. Wat Phra Boromathat is
surrounded by walls and contains a chedi restored by
King Rama V in 1901, but dating from the 8th century
and considered the best example of Srivijayan
architecture ● 96, while Wat Keo, which was
discovered in 1978, has a crumbled brick prang of the
Srivijaya period (below left). A small museum displays
antiquities found in the area, mostly within Wat
Phra Boromathat itself, with reproductions of
important pieces that are now displayed in the
National Museum in Bangkok.

WAT SUAN MOK

Wat Suan Mok is a modern temple popular
with Buddhists as a place for retreat and
study. It is renowned for teaching meditation to
foreigners and offers courses in English to
anyone ready to accept its extremely strict and
spartan rules. For others, its most notable
feature is a collection of colorful murals left
by visiting foreigners depicting a somewhat
bewildering variety of subjects, ranging
from Zen to compositions inspired by
Egypt.

SURAT THANI

Surat Thani is an important
southern railway and highway
center as well as a busy seaport.
Although it has a number of
excellent seafood restaurants
serving dishes and offers
attractive views along the water-
front, Surat Thani is of interest
to most travelers today
mainly as an embarkation
point from which ferries
leave for Koh Samui, and
the islands that lie beyond it.

TEN VOWS
A novice monk
takes these ten vows:
"I take the vow
not to destroy life."
"I take the vow
not to steal."
"I take the vow
to abstain from
impurity."
"I take the vow
not to lie."
"I take the vow
not to eat at
forbidden times."
"I take the vow to
abstain from dancing,
singing, music
and stage plays."
"I take the vow
not to use garlands,
scents, unguents,
or ornaments."
"I take the vow
not to use a broad
or high bed."
"I take the vow
not to receive gold
or silver."

BANG PO BAY

THONG SALA

MAENAM BEACH

CHOLOKLAM BAY

KOH PHANGAN

KHUAT BE

KOH TAEN

NATHON TOWN
FERRY PIER

KOH SAMUI

🕐 Two days

Thailand's third-largest island, about the size of Penang, Koh Samui is one of a group lying 18 miles off the coast of Surat Thani. Ferries from the mainland call at the port of Tong Yang, while express boats berth at Nathon, Koh Samui's administrative capital and only sizeable town. Covering 100 square miles, the hilly island has a thinly scattered population of about 35,000, most of whom traditionally derive a livelihood from huge inland plantations that produce some of the best coconuts in Thailand.

Koh Samui islanders
dry squid in the sun.

CHAWENG BEACH

LAMAI BEACH

HIN TA AND HIN YAI

Thousands of coconuts are sent to Bangkok and other parts of the country annually, and there is also a factory producing coconut fiber. Until the late 1970's the physical charms of Koh Samui were a closely guarded secret among a relatively small number of adventurous travelers – mostly budget-minded backpackers in search of accommodation at only a few dollars a night, long, virtually empty beaches, and a generally laid-back atmosphere. All that is now rapidly changing. A regular air service links the island with Bangkok, thus eliminating the time-consuming bus or train journey to Surat Thani for those in a hurry. New, more luxurious tourist facilities are springing up along the beaches, particularly on the east coast, with the result that Koh Samui is beginning to rival nearby Phuket as an international destination. Actually, the two island resorts complement each other in

KOH SAMUI SEASHELLS

Cassis cornuta is very solid and heavy and has a short spine with about seven whorls.

Casum ceramicum is also solid and heavy, with a high spine.

Spondylus regius is a striking thorny oyster with seven elevated ribs bearing pointed spines.

Mitra mitra This is the largest of the mitra family.

terms of weather, since Phuket's season of heaviest rain (July through September) runs concurrently with one of Koh Samui's sunniest times; the latter island's wettest months are toward the end of the year.

BUFFALO FIGHTING. One of the favorite pastimes of the islanders used to be buffalo fighting. To discourage gambling, the fights that were held every weekend are now restricted to festive occasions such as the Lunar New Year or the Thai New Year. A long ritual is performed before the fight. The brightly decorated buffaloes are splashed with holy water and kept apart by a curtain that is lifted at the very moment the two animals clash against each other. The fight ends when one of the buffaloes is pushed out of the arena.

NORTHERN BEACHES.

BIG BUDDHA
The Big Buddha of Wat Phra Yai towers above the shrine of Koh Fan and is dedicated to the Parinirvana (reclining) Buddha. At the entrance of the temple, a figure of Maitreya, the Buddha of the Future, welcomes monks and visitors before they ascend to the colossal hilltop figure.

BIG BUDDHA BEACH (HAT PHRA YAI). This beach derives its name from a 40-foot-high image of the meditating Buddha at a monastery on a small islet called Koh Fan, connected by a causeway. The beach boasts a smooth stretch of sand, calm waters and a generally restful atmosphere. A boat ferries passengers daily over to Hat Rin on Koh Phangan.

BOPHUT BEACH. East of Maenam is Ban Bophut, one of Samui's oldest settlements, with wooden shophouses lining the main street. The nearby beach is about a mile long, and the placid water, while not as clear as some others, is ideal for water-skiing. Boats ply the route from the village pier to Koh Phangan and a trip on one of these takes about 40 minutes.

MAENAM BEACH. This beach, near a village of the same name and with easy access to Nathon, is a 2½-mile stretch of white sand on a picturesque bay with a great view of Koh Phangan offshore. Bungalows are available at a wide range of prices and boats can be hired for excursions to other beaches.

BANG PO BAY. This beach is still relatively undeveloped, mainly because the rocks and corals break the surface during the low tide. It is, however, one of the best locations for snorkeling and scuba-diving.

WHEELS FOR RENT
In Nathon motorbikes and automobiles are easily available for rent to those who want to tour the island on their own.

NATHON TOWN

On the west coast of Koh Samui, near the jetty for ferries from Surat Thani, is the small town of Nathon. Apart from the grocery shops and basic essential services such as post and banking that serve the islanders, there are also several bars and souvenir shops catering mainly for tourists.

CHAWENG BEACH

The most developed of Koh Samui's beaches, Chaweng is a 4-mile crescent with white sand and clear water. Tourist facilities and nightlife are concentrated in the central section, which also overlooks the best part of the beach. Unlike other resorts in Thailand, bars, discotheques and restaurants are patronized mainly by foreigners traveling on a shoestring budget. As a result, local nightbirds do not flock here to earn the tourist dollar. Equipment for windsurfing, para-sailing and scuba-diving are available. Water scooters have also invaded the beaches, robbing Koh Samui of its little-island charm.

OVERLAP STONE
This stone is a popular Samui landmark, a huge boulder balanced on a promontory above Lower Lamai Beach, where there are a few bungalows for rent and a refreshment stall. Another mile further up is a point of land that affords impressive views of the island's interior scenery.

LAMAI BEACH

After Chaweng, Lamai is probably the most popular beach, appealing to a younger crowd of budget-conscious visitors. Besides the wide choice of accommodation, there is nightlife with numerous restaurants and discos. Lower Lamai offers good swimming even when the seas elsewhere are too rough.

COCONUT PLANTATIONS

Until the advent of tourism, and to a large extent even today, Koh Samui's economy has been based on the graceful coconut palms that cover most of the interior, even extending up the mountain sides; an average of two million coconuts are transported to Bangkok monthly, a sizeable part of the national production. The sweet juice of young coconuts is a favorite drink, while coconut cream plays a bigger role in the local cuisine than it does elsewhere in the south. Some growers have trained monkeys who scamper nimbly up the lofty trunks, select only those coconuts ready for picking, and drop them to the ground.

HIN TA AND HIN YAI
Hin Ta and Hin Yai, or "Grandfather Stone and Grandmother Stone," are a pair of much-photographed rock formations suggesting genitals at the tip of a headland that separates Central Lamai and Lower Lamai. Hin Ta points toward the sky, while his companion is a wave-splashed cleft about 132 feet away.

WATERFALLS

For those who enjoy waterfalls, the interior of Samui offers a number of scenic opportunities. The two most popular are Hin Lat, which spills over several levels and has a pool good for bathing, and Na Muang, which cascades for over 130 feet down a slab of yellow limestone.

KOH PHANGAN ★

Less developed than Koh Samui – at least for the time being – is Koh Phangan, the largest of its neighboring islands, 9 miles away. The island covers approximately 76 square miles and has a relatively small population of about 8,000, mostly concentrated in the main town of Thong Sala. Tourist accommodation is simple and the atmosphere appeals to the sort of backpack travelers who once flocked to Bali. There are dozens of beautiful, unspoiled beaches, among the most popular being Hat Rin, which has direct boat services to and from Samui; Hat Khuat ("Bottle Beach"), in a secluded cove on the northern coast; and Choloklam Bay, on which there are several stretches of sand. There are daily express boats from Nathon pier to Thong Sala, as well as boats from Bophut Pier and Big Buddha Beach to Hat Rin; all boat services are subject to weather conditions.

KOH TAO

Koh Tao, "Turtle Island," is so called because of its shape. A small island covering only 8½ square miles, it takes two hours to reach by express boat from Thong Sala on Koh Phangan, three to four hours by the regular ferry. Almost untouched by development, the island offers a tranquil ambience. Clear waters and extensive offshore coral reefs make it ideal for scuba diving and snorkeling, and there are a few simple bungalow facilities, the majority on the western and southern coasts of the island.

ANG THONG NATIONAL MARINE PARK ★

Lying 19 miles northwest of Koh Samui, Ang Thong National Marine Park includes some forty islands and is characterized by impressive limestone outcrops and blue lagoons. Koh Tao is one of the larger islands in the group; the others vary greatly in size and many have hidden coves with white-sand beaches. Koh Wua Ta Lap ("Isle of the Sleeping Cow") has bungalow facilities, while Koh Mae ("Mother Island") has a beautiful beach surrounded by towering cliffs. There is a daily boat to the park from Nathon, leaving in the morning and returning in the afternoon.

WATER BABIES
"Little children, long before they can walk, are thrown into the water by their mothers, who fasten under their arms a tin float that always keeps the head above water. The wee brown dots splash and splutter about in the luke-warm current of the river, involuntarily learning the correct action of the limbs in swimming, and gaining an acquaintance with this element that ever afterwards prevents any feeling of fear. In this way many children learn to swim almost as soon as, if not before, they can walk."
Ernest Young

HISTORY

One of the oldest settlements in Thailand, Nakhon Si Thammarat was known to ancient travelers as Ligor and was an important center during both the Srivijaya ▲ *200* and Dvaravati periods, over a thousand years ago. Many notable works of art – both Hindu and Buddhist – have been found in and around the city, testifying to the variety of cultures that influenced its development even before the Thais appeared on the scene. King Ramkhamhaeng of Sukhothai is popularly believed to have visited Nakhon Si Thammarat in the 13th century and to have been so impressed by the teachings of the city's Buddhist monks that he brought a group of them back to the first independent Thai capital.

The resplendent Viharn Luang of Wat Mahathat.

MUSEUM. The Nakhon Si Thammarat branch of the National Museum ▲ *158– 61* is the most important in the country after Bangkok's. Among the items on display is an impressive collection of early Hindu images and some of the earliest Buddhist sculpture. The Hindu figures, found at Takua Pa, include a beautiful Vishnu once wrapped in the roots of a tree. It was decapitated by vandals and when the roots were cut away to move the figure, the missing head was discovered to have been a fake; the original one, now restored to its proper place on the body, was buried beneath the statue.

WAT MAHATHAT. The most revered of Nakhon Si Thammarat's Buddhist monuments is Wat Mahathat, founded during the Srivijaya period (8th–13th century). The temple's dominant feature is a towering 254-foot-high chedi, the spire of which is covered with gold leaf and studded with precious stones. The chedi stands in an immense cloister covered with colored tiles and surrounding it is a gallery lined with numerous Buddha images. A standing Sukhothai-style Buddha image is enshrined in one of the temple's two chapels while on the altar of the other there are bas-reliefs that show Westerners among the various figures. Outside the cloister of Wat Mahathat is the Viharn Luang, with columns that lean inward in the Ayutthaya style and a richly decorated ceiling.

LAKAWN WALLS.

NIELLOWARE
One of Nakhon Si Thammarat's outstanding traditional arts is niello, which arrived before the 12th century, probably from India. An amalgam of dark metals is applied to etched portions of silver or gold to create intricate designs covering trays, boxes, vases and other objects. A 15th-century law in Ayutthaya decreed that high-ranking nobles could proclaim their position through the possession of a nielloware pedestal and tray, while in 1687, King Narai is recorded as having sent a nielloware bowl to King Louis XIV of France. Bangkok rulers have also traditionally presented the ware as gifts to foreign heads of state.

SONGKHLA

Songkhla, once known as Singora, is the only natural port on the lower Gulf of Thailand side of the southern isthmus and as such has long been an important center of trade, founded and largely developed by Chinese. Much of the trade, along with the money it brought, moved some years ago to Haadyai, more conveniently located at a railway junction, with the result that Songkhla has been able to retain some degree of its old atmosphere.

SAMILA BEACH. Koh Samui and Phuket have lured many of the foreign tourists away from the nearby Samila Beach, an attractive strand on the gulf lined with casuarina trees and stalls selling freshly cooked seafood, though visitors from Malaysia still come during the hot season. A hill behind the Samila Beach Hotel, surmounted by an ancient chedi, is the highest point in Songkhla and offers scenic views of the sea. Boats can be hired for side trips around an inland sea or Thale Sap, which empties into the gulf, or to nearby Muslim fishing villages.

WAT MACHI MAWAT. This temple boasts a collection of several interesting murals showing life around the port in the late 1800's and early 1900's.

SONGKHLA MUSEUM. A beautiful old Chinese mansion dating from the latter part of the 19th century, once the residence of a provincial governor, has been restored and is now open to the public as a museum (below). Chinese porcelains, statuary and objects from the excavations of nearby Sating Phra are displayed in its spacious rooms.

NANG TALUNG
A form of shadow play called *nang talung*, closely resembling the Indonesian *wayang kulit*, is frequently staged at festivals in the far south. The buffalo-hide figures have movable parts – arms, legs, or chin – and their concealed manipulators accompany their actions with songs and often ribald repartee. ● *68–9.*

THALE NOI BIRD SANCTUARY

Just a few miles north of Songkhla is an 11-square-mile region of freshwater and swamp ecosystem known as Thale Noi. Several canals flow through the area, making it accessible to nature-lovers and bird-watchers.

BIRD-WATCHING. Nearly 200 species of birds – including several rare ones such as the lesser adjutant stork, white ibis, spot-billed pelican and gray heron – have been recorded in this nature reserve. Egrets, cormorants, terns and jacanas are also common here. The best period to observe the birds is between January and April. Boats can be hired for a three-hour trip from the nature reserve headquarters to Sala Nang Riam on the other side of the lake. The fishing village offers visitors to Thale Noi a peek at life in this typical southern community.

> "It was with no small pleasure that we rattled down the
> anchor in Songkhla, and contemplated the beautiful
> hill-girdled harbor that lay before us."
>
> H. Warrington Smyth, 1898

HAADYAI

Strategically situated at the junction of major railways and roads, Haadyai has become one of the most prosperous southern cities in recent decades, of little architectural or cultural distinction but with a definite boom-town air of excitement. A large part of the money derived from such major industries as tin, rubber and seafood processing passes through Haadyai's bankers and businessmen as well as an even greater amount from tourism. Malaysians come in large numbers – around 600,000 a year, according to a recent estimate – across the border just 36 miles away, drawn by lower prices for luxury goods and by an uninhibited nightlife not available in their own country. Haadyai has more than 5,000 hotel rooms, most of them filled on weekends, plus hundreds of discos, bars and massage parlors.

FISHING BOATS
The fishing boats of southern Thailand have intricate colorful motifs similar to those of the northwestern coast of peninsular Malaysia – proof of the cultural link existing in this region. The decorations are to please the spirits and invoke them to bless the boats and protect the occupants from hazards at sea. When boats are launched a shaman is called to perform an ancient animistic ritual during which prayers are recited and offerings made to the spirits.

PATTANI AND ANCIENT MUSLIM KINGDOMS

Muslims comprise Thailand's largest religious minority, over two million in all, mostly Malay living in the southernmost provinces. Pattani and Pattalung have been in fact prosperous, independent kingdoms and active trading posts since the end of the first millennium. This wealth

ended when the Siamese invaded and destroyed Pattani, bringing the entire area under the rule of the Kingdom of Siam. Since then, there has always been friction between the Muslims and the Thai government, most evident during the 1960's and 1970's, when many Muslims fled to the jungles to join the communists. Since the end of 2003, after decades or relative calm, violence – often bloody and lethal – has again become an everyday feature in these southern provinces. But today it is difficult to tell whether the armed groups are genuine separatists or the agents of political manipulation. On April 28, 2004, thirty or so rebels entrenched in the historic mosque of Krue Se, in Pattani, were killed when it was stormed. The government is trying unsuccessfully to put a halt to this escalation of violence.

SARASIN BRIDGE

KATU VILLAGE

MONUMENT TO
PHUKET'S HEROINES

KOH NAKHA NOI

KOH NAKHA

MAI KHAO
BEACH

AIRPORT

BANG TAO
BEACH

PAN SEA
BAY

SURIN BEACH

PATONG BEACH

KARON NOI
BEACH

KARON
BEACH

KATA YAI BEACH

KATA NOI
BEACH

NAI HAN
BEACH

⏱ Three days

RAWAI BEACH

WAT CHALONG

PHUKET TOWN

SEA GYPSIES VILLAGE

CAPE PHANWA

Dazzling white-sand beaches, crystal-clear water, and limestone cliffs rising in fantastic shapes from the sea – these are the magical images most visitors carry back from a visit to Phuket in the Andaman Sea. But the island's modern tourist boom is only the latest development in a history that goes back hundreds of years.

HISTORY

To sailors of the 16th and 17th centuries, Phuket was known as "Junkceylon" or "Jonkcelaon"; only in relatively modern times did Thailand's largest offshore island acquire its present name, derived from the Malay word *bukit,* meaning "hill," referring to its mountainous terrain. The waters around Phuket were notorious hunting grounds for pirates, who hid in countless secret coves along the coast, but traders still came, for the island was rich in one of the ancient world's most prized commodities – tin, easily extracted from seemingly inexhaustible veins close to the surface. There were also other alluring treasures: ambergris, rhinoceros horn, rare corals and edible birds' nests, a delicacy that is much esteemed by Chinese gourmets ■ 28–9. As Thailand's trade with the outside world expanded in the 19th century, tin mining on Phuket enjoyed a boom that brought in thousands of Chinese workers, some of whom later became wealthy mine-owners themselves. The Chinese, indeed, soon comprised the larger part of the island's population while Sino-Thais still controlled its economy. In 1903, the first rubber trees began another major industry. Soon Phuket was the richest province in the country in terms of per capita income. Tourism arrived in the early 1970's, with the opening of the Sarasin Bridge linking Phuket with the mainland. Roads were cut through mountains to the beaches of the western shore and within a short time, the island had emerged as a leading travel destination. The area was badly damaged, with a huge loss of life, by the tsunami of December 2004.

PHUKET'S HEROINES
On the road from the airport leading toward Phuket Town stands a memorial to two Phuket heroines. In 1785, the brave pair rallied the residents of Thalang (then the island's main town) to defend it successfully against the Burmese invaders, in reward for which the two ladies were given noble titles by King Rama I of Bangkok.

OLD HOUSES
Adding considerably to the charm of Phuket Town are its surviving old Chinese houses (above), built in the Sino-Portuguese style also found in Malacca. Many of these houses belong to families whose ancestors first came to the island as laborers in the 19th-century tin mines.

MOVIE-MAKERS
The scenic beauties of Phuket and neighboring Phangnga Bay have attracted numerous movie-makers, foreign as well as Thai. Part of the movie *The Man with the Golden Gun* was filmed at Phangnga, while Phuket's interior was used in Brian De Palma's *Casualties of War* and the old District Office appeared as the French embassy in *The Killing Fields.*

TROPICAL FISH
Filled with much
marine life and
activity, the Andaman
Sea off Phuket
shelters a great
variety of fish.
Among the most
beautiful are:

the squirrel fish
(*Myripristis adustus*),
which usually hides
among the corals;

the sweetlips – such
as the striped grunt
(*P. diagrammus*),
which tastes as good
as it looks;

the snub-nosed
*Chaetodon
ephippium*, a butterfly
fish known for its
changing colors;

and the surgeon fish
(*Acanthurus
glaucopareius*) whose
body colors blend
with those of the
coral reefs.

PHUKET TOWN TODAY

Phuket Town, the bustling provincial capital, has a population
of around 50,000. A boom in real estate in recent years has
spurred developers to build countless shophouses, hotels and
condominiums, with an inevitable loss of atmosphere, though
many of the elegant old millionaires'
mansions remain, as well as the
stately building that once
housed the District
Office that served as the
French embassy in the
film *The Killing Fields*.
Particularly colorful is
the public market on
Rasada Street, just

across from the main minibus terminus, where all the local
seafood, fruits, vegetables and spices are piled in tempting
abundance amid busy vendors and price-haggling customers.
Close to the center of town is the hill known as Khao Rang,
on top of which are a landscaped "fitness park" and a
restaurant offering splendid views of the town itself, the
harbor and the sea and distant offshore islands.

PHUKET AQUARIUM

Overlooking the sea on Chalong Bay, not very far from
Phuket Town, the aquarium is part of the Marine Biology
Research Center and rears a variety of sea creatures from
local waters. It also serves as a hatchery for the eggs of huge
sea turtles that come ashore to lay between October and
February.

PHUKET PORT

A visit to Phuket's main port, east of the town, reveals the
importance of deep-sea fishing. About 350 industrially
equipped boats fish the waters around the island and all the
way to the Indian Ocean, hauling in about 40,000 tons of
seafood annually. The port scene is most
colorful when the boats return to unload
in the early morning.

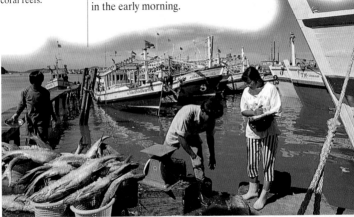

> "The strongest statement of Chinese culture evident in Phuket is probably the Vegetarian Festival."

CHINESE TEMPLES

Phuket's Chinese character is reflected in a number of temples. The principal ones are at Kathu, where the Vegetarian Festival originated in the 19th century, and Put Jaw Temple in town, both lavishly adorned with red and gold carvings and images of various gods and goddesses.

VEGETARIAN FESTIVAL. Held annually in October, this is another manifestation of the strong Chinese flavor that pervades the island. The festival was started by immigrants who flocked in large numbers from China and nearby Malaya to work in the tin mines, supposedly in response to a mysterious fever that was afflicting them. It now lasts for ten days and, in addition to abstinence from meat and rituals held at various Chinese temples, features gala processions that attract crowds of visitors as well as local believers. Many of the

participants go into deep trances, enabling them to endure a wide range of self-inflicted ordeals, from walking over beds of red-hot charcoal to piercing their cheeks with long metal skewers; such practices are not a part of traditional vegetarian festivals in China and were most probably assimilated over the years from India.

BUDDHIST TEMPLES

Although Phuket has a sizeable number of Muslim residents, about 60 percent of the population are Buddhists, who attend

one or another of the island's twenty-nine temples. The largest and best-known is Wat Chalong, which contains images of two revered monks who helped put down a rebellion of Chinese immigrants in 1876; the images are kept supplied with offerings of flowers and incense. Another important temple is Wat Phra Thong (above), on the airport road, where the main attraction is a large Buddha image supposedly made of gold, half buried in the earth; after its discovery by a farmer, the image was left as it was and the temple built to shelter it.

LAK MUANG. In most old Thai cities, a shrine, or the *lak muang*, was erected at the "central axis," usually around a wood or stone pillar that marked the center of the settlement and provided a home for the spirit who guarded it. In the case of Phuket, the pillar is near the monument to two heroines in the sleepy district of Tha Rua ▲ *211*, where the island's principal community once thrived.

A HEAVY SMOKER
In Phuket, at the end of the last century, a monk who was a heavy smoker became famous. An image was erected in Wat Chalong and ever since has been kept supplied with offerings. These offerings commonly take the form of lighted cigarettes, placed in the mouth. A gentle draft causes the cigarettes to continue to burn. The image of the monk, therefore appears to be smoking.

A LOCAL DELICACY
Prawns are skewered
and arranged
between lengths of
bamboo and left to
dry in the sun before
they are eaten.

SOUTHERN CUISINE
Southern food
has a reputation
for being the hottest
in Thailand. As well
as standard dishes
found in most parts
of the country – often
with lashings of extra
chillies – many local
restaurants also
offer Malay-style
fare that reflects
Indian influence
in its use of curry
powder and
turmeric.

PATONG BEACH

Stretching for 2½ miles around a bay, Patong was the first of
Phuket's beaches to be developed and is still
the only one to offer a really varied
Bangkok-style nightlife. Hotels
large and small, restaurants,
shops, bars, even a
towering new
condominium, line its
main street, overlooking a
turquoise sea that, so far at
least, remains remarkably
clean. All sorts of water sports
are available, from windsurfing to
para-sailing, and boats can be hired for trips to
less crowded swimming areas along the
coast. The seabed shelves gently and, with
usually calm waters and the natural
grandeur of the forested
backdrop, swimming and
other water activities are
very popular. Thanks to
the efforts of the Thai
people, scarcely any traces of
the disastrous tsunami of
December 2004 remain.

OTHER BEACHES

All of Phuket's best
beaches are located on
the western side of the
island, facing the Andaman Sea,
and range from strands several
miles long to smaller crescents.
There are thirteen major ones,
starting at Mai Khao near the

airport and extending down to Rawai at the southern tip, each with a distinctive character of its own. A narrow road connects the string of beaches and cuts down travel time along the coast considerably.

MAI KHAO AND NAI YANG. The northernmost of Phuket's west-coast beaches, Mai Khao and Nai Yang are still relatively undeveloped and therefore quiet. They stretch for more than 10 miles altogether. The water, however, is not as clear as at other beaches, especially at low tide.

KARON. This stretch actually consists of two beaches, one an idyllic little cove popularly known as Relax Bay and occupied by Le Méridien Hotel, and the other much longer and now lined with a variety of tourist accommodation large and small.

PAN SEA. Scenically, Pan Sea is one of the most enchanting beaches, with very good opportunities for snorkeling and swimming during the dry season. Its principal tourist facility, the Pan Sea Phuket Bay Resort, boasts attractive thatched-roof huts spilling down a hillside.

KATA. Like Karon, Kata is divided into Kata Yai (Big Kata) and Kata Noi (Little Kata). The former, a long stretch of fine beach, is the site of the Club Méditerranée and several smaller facilities; the latter is further south and has a hotel, the Kata Thani, and several bungalow complexes.

SURIN. A picturesque strand with steep hills that rise sharply at the back, this is especially popular with Thai day-trippers on weekends and holidays. The spectacular Thai-style Amanpuri Hotel overlooks one end of the beach.

NAI HAN ★. Site of the Phuket Yacht Club, Nai Han is an otherwise undeveloped beach with white sand, clear water and a scenic view of Phrom Thep at the southern tip of the island.

RAWAI. An attractive strand fringed by coconut palms, Rawai is located on a shallow, silty bay and therefore less popular with swimmers. Boats can be hired here for trips to the offshore islands.

LAEM PHROM THEP. This is an elevation at the far southern tip of Phuket, attracting tourists and many local people because of its panoramic views of the sea and often spectacular sunsets. As a result, traffic jams in the vicinity are a common sight. Among the picturesque islands offshore is Koh Keo, where there are meditation cells for Buddhist monks and a graceful chedi.

SEA GYPSIES
The Sea Gypsies or Chao Ley are probably Phuket's oldest inhabitants. While some still live on board their boats in other parts of the Andaman Sea, most have now settled in Phuket in small villages (such as those in Rawai) close to the sea, their favored element. The Sea Gypsies earn their living by fishing, diving for oysters and other shells, and harvesting edible birds' nests deposited on lofty limestone cliffs and in caves ■ 28–9, ▲ 223, 226.

BEAUTIFUL BEACHES
Kata, Nai Han and Laem Phrom Thep (below) are just three of the beautiful beaches that make up the main tourist attraction on Phuket.

215

RUBBER TREES
"Beyond the forest the level of the land was higher and there were more rubber plantations – nothing but rubber. Thousands and thousands of acres were planted with the dark, dull green heveas. The trees stood in straight rows, and by the side of each was a stick. On the top of each stick was a porcelain cup upside down. In some places the cup was attached to the tree by a bit of wire below the tin spout

through which the latex flowed when the tree was tapped. Coolies passed barefoot and soundlessly among the trees and turned the cups out into large zinc churns similar to European milk churns."

M.H. Lulofs

RUBBER PLANTATIONS

The first rubber trees, brought from Malaysia, were planted on Phuket in 1903, only a decade after they were first acclimatized to Southeast Asia at Singapore's Botanical Gardens. Thus began the vast plantations that are now scattered over the island, producing around 14,000 tons of dry latex annually. Thanks to these plantations and others on the mainland, Thailand is today a major exporter of rubber.

KHAO PHRA THAEO NATIONAL PARK

Located just off the airport road, Khao Phra Thaeo National Park contains the last remnants of the tropical rain forest that once covered Phuket. Near the entrance to the jungle is Tone Sai Waterfall, an attractive site popular with local day-trippers on weekends but virtually deserted at other times.

OFFSHORE ISLANDS

A number of Phuket's smaller offshore islands can be easily reached by boat on short trips. The most popular with visitors, especially snorkelers and scuba divers, is probably Koh Hi, also called Coral Island because of the extensive reefs that surround it, just east of the tip of Phuket. Koh Mai Thong, a little further, has fine beaches on the far side, while up the eastern coast are Koh Nakha Yai and Koh Nakha Noi. The latter has a cultured-pearl farm, where oysters are seeded and carefully tended for two years, the amount of time required for a pearl to form inside. Yet another attractive island is Koh Lawa Yai, located at the southern extremity of Phangnga Bay.

SHELLS
The waters around Phuket are a rich source of shells, both rare and common for sale in the numerous shops. Some of the more serious dealers employ divers to search for the rarest specimens at great depths and sell their finds to international collectors at high prices.

> "The lapping of the waves is all too often drowned
> out by the rumble of concrete mixers."
>
> Alistair Shearer

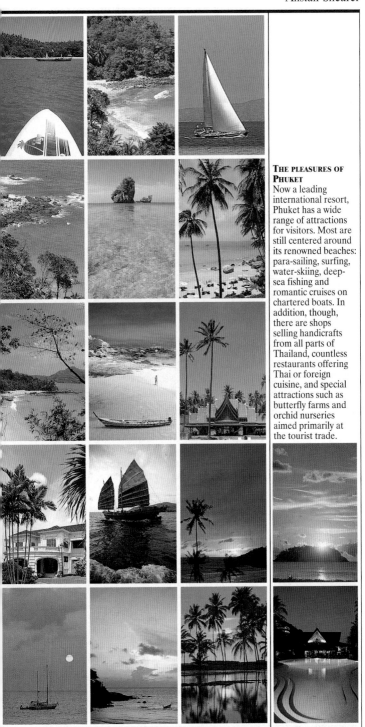

THE PLEASURES OF PHUKET

Now a leading international resort, Phuket has a wide range of attractions for visitors. Most are still centered around its renowned beaches: para-sailing, surfing, water-skiing, deep-sea fishing and romantic cruises on chartered boats. In addition, though, there are shops selling handicrafts from all parts of Thailand, countless restaurants offering Thai or foreign cuisine, and special attractions such as butterfly farms and orchid nurseries aimed primarily at the tourist trade.

▲ The South Phangnga Bay

MANGROVE SWAMPS

KOH HONG

LIGHTHOUSE

KOH PHING

KOH MAK

KOH YAO NOI

One day

**PHANG NGA BAY,
THE RECOVERY**
Phang Nga Bay was
one of the areas most
affected by the 2004
tsunami. One year
later, thanks to the
efforts of the Thai
people, scarcely any
traces of the disaster
remain.

Millenniums ago, Phangnga Bay was dry land with scattered limestone mountains; the sea invaded as glaciers melted, around 10,000 years before the beginning of the Christian era, leaving only a spectacular profusion of mountain peaks rising from the water to form one of the world's greatest natural attractions. The upheaval also led to the formation of several sea caves, some of which lie below sea level while others rise high above the rocks and remain mostly unexplored even to this day. Thirty-eight miles from Phuket by road, or about three hours by boat, the bay and surrounding areas it were declared a marine national park in 1981. More than forty islands are included, several reaching an altitude of 1,000 feet and shaped like animals, with dramatic sea caves and sheltered, pristine beaches. On the mainland around the bay are canals threading through dense

KOH PANNYI KOH KHIEN KOH NOM SAO PARK HEADQUARTERS MANGROVE SWAMPS PHANGNGA BAY RESORT HOTEL KOH TALU

LIMESTONE BEAUTIES
Much of the attraction of Phangnga's countless caves, both on the mainland and on many of the islands in the bay, lies in their limestone formations. Intricate stalactites and stalagmites and the atmospheric lighting from cave openings produce a theatrical effect.

mangrove swamps and caves. Wildlife in the national park includes dolphins, crab-eating macaques and huge fruit-eating bats (also known as flying foxes) and numerous species of birds, of which the most easily seen are kingfishers, sea eagles and white egrets. Mudskippers, that queer breed of fish that use their flapping fins to move about on land, thrive among the mangroves ■ *22–3*. Most visitors come on day trips from Phuket or Krabi, though excellent food and accommodation are provided by the Phangnga Bay Resort Hotel.

PHANGNGA NATIONAL PARK

The headquarters of Phangnga National Park are located on Highway 4144, near one of the estuaries leading to the bay. The Phangnga Bay Hotel is nearby and offers the best rooms in the area. This is also a good point from which to explore by boat the park's fascinating mangrove swamps. The trees have strange root systems that protrude from the water and provide shelter for such creatures as mudskippers, fiddler crabs, lizards and numerous colorful birds.

KOH KHIEN

Koh Khien ("Writing Island") has a large cave, on the walls of which are ancient paintings of men and such animals as sharks, dolphins and crocodiles. These paintings are believed to have been the work of people who inhabited the region 3,000–4,000 years ago and are visible from the sea.

KOH PANNYI

GLOSSARY OF MARINE TERMS
koh = island
khao = mountain
hat = beach
tham = cave
laem = cape
hin = stone
ao = bay
thale = sea

On Koh Pannyi, a picturesque little Muslim fishing village of about 400 people nestles in the shadow of an immense limestone slab that protects it from the

> "The uniqueness of ponga depends upon its limestone peaks, which stand in sharp points and steep precipices out of its waters, some more than 1,500 feet in height."
>
> H. Warrington Smyth

monsoons. The houses are built above the water on stout piles of mangrove wood obtained from the mainland and most of the people earn their living by fishing and making shrimp paste. Additional revenue comes from the many tourists who visit Phangnga Bay to photograph its quaint scenery and enjoy a sumptuous seafood lunch at one of the numerous restaurants.

KOH MAK

A flat round island with coconut palms, a Muslim village and beautiful beaches, Koh Mak makes an ideal picnic spot.

KOH HONG

"Hong" in Thai means "room," and this curiously shaped island – part of a group of the same name – contains an extraordinary enclosed waterway lit by an opening above and accessible to small boats. The chamber offers wonderful opportunities for swimming and photography.

THAM KEO

Tham Keo means "Glass Cave," and a shimmering grotto, hung with dazzling white stalactites, is the principal attraction of this island. Small boats enter the cave, which leads to an adjacent cavern with views of the sea below.

KOH PHING KAN

Consisting of two separate rock formations leaning one against another, Koh Phing Kan is also popularly known as James Bond Island, thanks to the fact that several scenes from the film *The Man with the Golden Gun* were shot there. The island has now become a tourist trap, its natural beauties obscured by boatloads of visitors and others trying to profit from them.

ORIGIN OF PHANGNGA
The name of Phangnga originates from a legend linked to a limestone mountain with dramatic slopes that loom over the provincial capital. Some farmers in remote times had attacked and killed by mistake an elephant god which at once turned into stone. The massive cliff in Phangnga Bay is said to be the petrified form of the pachyderm with its butchered tusks leaning on its flanks.

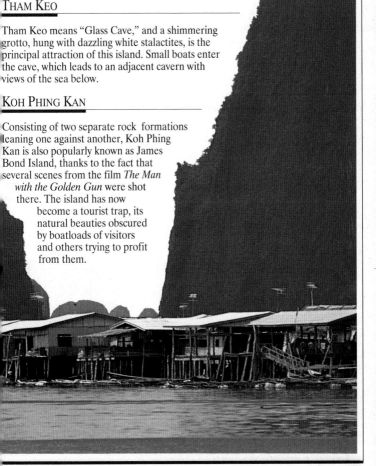

PHI PHI VILLAGE   YONGKASEM BAY   **KOH PHI PHI DON**   LODALAM BAY   TON SAI BAY   WANG BAY

LANAH BAY

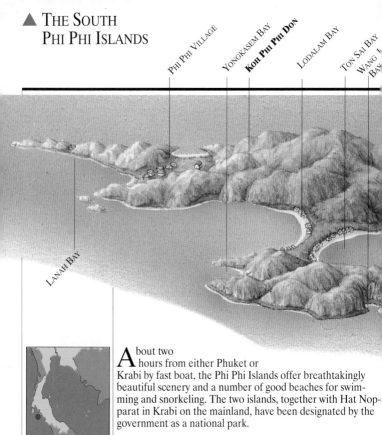

⏲ One day

About two hours from either Phuket or Krabi by fast boat, the Phi Phi Islands offer breathtakingly beautiful scenery and a number of good beaches for swimming and snorkeling. The two islands, together with Hat Nopparat in Krabi on the mainland, have been designated by the government as a national park.

KOH PHI PHI DON

The larger of the two islands, Koh Phi Phi Don is also the most developed in terms of tourism. Boats generally unload their passengers at a fishing village on Ton Sai Bay, protected by steep, jungled limestone cliffs on one side and by low hills on the other. Thanks to all the day-trippers, however, plus the numerous restaurants and other tourist facilities, the main beach there has lost much of its former tranquility and serious swimmers go to a series of quieter ones on the west side of the bay, culminating in Hat Yao, or Long Beach. Several other resorts have been built on serene beaches at the northern end of the island on the west coast, while across a narrow strip of

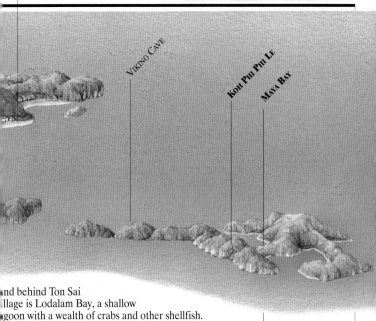

LONG BEACH

VIKING CAVE

KOH PHI PHI LE

MAYA BAY

...nd behind Ton Sai
...llage is Lodalam Bay, a shallow
...goon with a wealth of crabs and other shellfish.

KOH PHI PHI LE ★

...n terms of scenery, the smaller Koh Phi Phi Le is by far the
...ore spectacular, with limestone cliffs that plunge hundreds
...f feet down to the sea and numerous secret coves with small
...rescents of white sand and crystal-clear water; a particularly
...eautiful spot is Maya Bay, surrounded by soaring cliffs and
...arboring three largely unspoiled beaches with good snorkel-
...g to view exotic fish so used to visitors that they can be fed
...y hand. A popular tourist attraction on Phi Phi Le is an
...mmense, cathedral-like cave, festooned with stalactites and
...talagmites, where edible birds' nests are harvested ■ 28–9.
...he cavern is popularly known as Viking Cave because of
...ome ancient rock paintings that do vaguely resemble Viking
...oats, though their origin is unknown.

EDIBLE BIRDS' NESTS. The main ingredient of birds' nest
...oup is produced by a tiny, fork-tailed swift known as
Callocalia esculenta, which favors lofty caves and cliffs. The
...mall cup-shaped nests, about 1½ inches
...n diameter, are composed of a gluey
...ecretion discharged by the birds in long
...trands that harden after exposure to the
...ir. As they are harvested at specified
...mes – by Sea Gypsies ■ 215, who
...earlessly climb tall spindly bamboo
...dders (right), often in total darkness –
...he swiftlets may have to build the nests
...p to three times between February and
...uly. The birds' nests can be eaten raw or
...oached in soup, and are an expensive
...elicacy highly regarded for their
...utritional value by Chinese gourmets.

PHI PHI EXCURSIONS
Most excursions to
the Phi Phi Islands
are in large boats,
leaving Phuket
either from Chalong
or Rawai Beach
around 8am and
starting back around
3.30pm. When hiring
smaller fishing craft
be sure to check on
the weather since the
crossing can be rough
during the monsoon
season.

223

RAPID RECOVERY Since the 2004 tsunami, the fu[...] force of which struck the region of Krabi and th[...] islands causing thousands of casualties, most of th[...] infrastructure has been rebuilt thanks to great effor[...] on behalf of the Thai people, for whom tourisr[...] represents one of the most important industries[...]

If enthusiastic word-of-mouth reports and[...] increasingly frequent mention in travel literature are any indication, Krabi is definitely the southern Thai destination of the near future. Like Phuket an[...] Koh Samui in the early 1970's, it was accidentally "discovered" by intrepid backpackers and cruising yachts only a few years ago. There are already signs of a more affluent clientèle, appearing in the form of restaurants, shops and bungalow hotels. Krabi's popularity with escapist travelers is not difficult to understand. It has several beautiful beaches with clear water ideal for snorkeling and diving, towering limestone cliffs, a prehistoric shell cemetery, atmospheric caves, mangrove forests ■ 22–3, rubber plantations, a national park (Khao Phanom Bencha) full of interesting wildlife, and access by boat to more than eighty scenic offshore islands. Krabi has yet to encounter – though it is only a matter of time – the sort of rapid, uncontrolled development that has disfigured so many beaches on Phuket and other southern island resorts, and if the efforts of newly aware Thai environmentalists are successful, Krabi has more than a fair chance of escaping this unhappy fate.

OIL PALMS Extensive oil palm plantations can be seen on the mainland around Krabi, forming an important local industry. The palms, which yield an oil used in both cooking and food processing, originated in Africa and were first acclimatized to Southeast Asia by the Dutch during their rule of Indonesia.

BEACHES ★

Krabi's beaches, though less numerous than those of Phuket, are relatively unspoiled and exceptionally beautiful. The most easily accessible beach from Krabi town is Hat Nang, on a wide, shallow bay, where there are several bungalow-hotels and restaurants; the town can be reached either by road or, more quickly, by the local long-tail boat up the mangrove-lined river. About a mile further on is Nopparat Thara Beach, a casuarina-lined strand that is part of the national park including the Phi Phi Islands. Far more spectacular in terms of scenery, however, are several others that are only accessible by boat around the sheer limestone cliffs of Laem Nang. The first is Re Lai, framed by mammoth rocks on the north and south, with an extensive coral reef at the southern end of the sandy beach. Around another headland and past the lofty, picturesque island of Koh Nang is a long, palm-fringed strand that many visitors regard as the most

beautiful in the entire region; between the beach and Koh Nang is a coral reef excellent for activities such as snorkeling and diving.

CAVES

The limestone mountains around Krabi contain a large variety of caves, several of which are popular tourist attractions. Sua (Tiger) Cave, down a jungle trail about 2 miles from Krabi town, is a noted Buddhist monastery for meditation. Along Highway 4, leading to Ao Luk, is a small cavern called Tham Sadet, while two unspoiled caves, Tham Lot and Tham Phi Hua To, can be reached by boat from Tao Than village in Ao Luk. The so-called Princess Cave in the cliffside of Cape Phra Nang contains a shrine where fishermen leave offerings before going out to sea.

OFFSHORE ISLANDS

The many islands that lie off the coast of Krabi have superb beaches and beautiful coral reefs that can be quite easily visited by boat from the mainland. Alternatively, you can decide to stay on the islands with bungalows, for example Koh Poda, Koh Dam, Koh Jam and Koh Kai. Although much further

out, the Phi Phi group, made worldwide famous by the Alex Garland book and film of the same name, *The Beach* (2000), can also be reached from Krabi town where you can easily hire a boat and crew. Further south, the island of Koh Lanta has enjoyed a tourist boom in recent years.

SHELL CEMETERY BEACH
Hat Su San Hoi, or the Shell Cemetery Beach, is located in Ban Laem Pho, about 10 miles from Krabi town. Countless petrified shells, some of which are about 75 million years old, have formed immense slabs of rock along the beach. Japan and the United States are the only other countries where this phenomenon can be seen.

DISAPPEARING REEFS
The coral reefs that abound close to the beaches provide exciting underwater seascapes thriving with marine plants, sea anemones and reef fishes. However, easy access to these reefs and ongoing exploitation may well destroy the beautiful ecosystem within the next decade.

KOH SIMILAN NATIONAL PARK ★

Approximately 60 miles northwest of Phuket in the Andaman
Sea, the Similan group covers 51 square miles and consists of
nine small islands, the name being derived from the Malay
word *sembilan*, meaning "nine." Designated a national park in
1982, the islands have long been uninhabited except for Sea
Gypsies ■ *28* ▲ *215* who come to fish the rich coral reefs
surrounding them. Tour groups have been coming in large
numbers, attracted by the unspoiled beaches and the
remarkable variety of underwater life,
especially off Koh Miang. The Similans
have over two hundred species of hard
coral, hundreds of colorful fish and
other sea creatures such as huge sea
fans and barrel sponges, manta rays
and whale sharks. Sea turtles come
to lay their eggs on some of the
beaches ■ *30*, and wildlife on land ■
18–19 includes macaques, langurs, bats
and about thirty species of birds.

TARUTAO NATIONAL PARK

Established as Thailand's first national marine park in 1974,
Tarutao consists of fifty-one mountainous islands
in the Indian Ocean near Malaysia. The
largest of the group is Koh Tarutao, about 16
miles off the mainland and 3 miles from the
Malaysian island of Langkawi, while the most
beautiful is Koh Adang, which has fine
beaches, clear water and coral reefs.
Dolphins, sea turtles, and rare whales and
dugongs are occasionally spotted in the area. Government bungalows and tents are available on both Koh
Adang and Koh Tarutao. The best time to visit the park is
between December and March, when the sea is usually calm.

The Northeast

NAKHON RATCHASIMA GATE
Nakhon Ratchasima is the most populous town in the northeast of Thailand.

TOOLS OF THE TRADE
Traditional silk spinning wheel and implements (above).

"MUDMEE"
Mudmee is a kind of handwoven silk material (*ikat*) in which the threads are dyed before weaving. Popularized by Queen Sirikit, *mudmee* is now fashionable among Thai women.

The northeast – or Isan as it is called by most Thais – makes up a third of the country's total area, contains seven of its most populous provinces, and offers both varied scenery and numerous ancient sites of great interest. Nevertheless, it remains the least known of Thailand's major regions among tourists for a variety of reasons. One was its long isolation. Though a railway linked Bangkok with Nakhon Ratchasima (Korat), the region's commercial center in 1900, it was not extended to the large city of Ubon Ratchathani until 1926 and reached Nongkhai on the Mekong River only in 1955. Even as late as the 1950's, there were few all-weather roads in the region, and northeastern Thais did not receive a personal visit from their ruler until the mid-1950's, when the present king and queen made a pioneering tour of the area. Another probable reason was social prejudice. The northeast has long been Thailand's chronic "problem" region, afflicted with drought and hampered by infertile soil, its people often driven to seek a livelihood in Bangkok as taxi drivers, laborers or domestic servants. To other Thais, Isan hardly seemed a place to spend a pleasant holiday, nor were foreigners much encouraged to do so. Many of these obstacles have now been overcome. Sharing borders with Laos and Cambodia, the northeast suddenly assumed a strategic importance during the Indo-Chinese war and an excellent network of highways was built, while government concern has brought greater prosperity to its cities. Moreover, thanks to the region's increased accessibility, more outsiders are beginning to discover the region's natural and archeological attractions.

THAI SILK PRODUCTION

Silk is undoubtedly the most famous of northeastern handicrafts. Even in the early decades of the 20th century, when production declined in other regions due to competition from foreign textiles, the family loom remained a part of most Isan village households and thus kept the skill alive. The booming industry of today depends to a large extent on silk from the northeast, particularly in the area around Nakhon Ratchasima; at nearby Pakthongchai, for example, the Jim Thompson Company ▲

182–3 has the largest handwoven silk facility in the world. Other notable weaving centers are Surin and Roi Et.

BAN CHIANG

In the early 1960's, during the construction of a road, some extraordinary fragments of painted pottery were unearthed near a small hamlet called Ban Chiang in Udon Thani Province. Subsequent excavations led to the discovery of a major prehistoric culture going back to 4000 BC and numbering among its achievements not only the painted pots but also the art of bronze metallurgy, at a period far earlier than any scholars had previously believed. A museum at Ban Chiang displays some of the remarkable items that have made the name world famous among archeologists and one of the excavations has also been preserved to show the different levels at which they were found. The discoveries at Ban Chiang are still a controversial subject; on the other hand, the site has undeniably shaken the traditional view of Southeast Asia as a "cultural backwater" that received its influences entirely from outside sources like China and India.

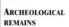

ARCHEOLOGICAL REMAINS
This vase was found at a dig in Ban Chiang, and is now on display in a Bangkok museum. Genuine pieces should not be confused with "discoveries" that are in fact manufactured in neighboring villages.

ELEPHANT ROUNDUP

Each year in November the provincial capital of Surin holds a gala elephant roundup in which up to 150 of the huge animals take part, demonstrating their ability to haul logs and serve as mounts in warfare ● *52–3*. The Tourism Authority of Thailand organizes special tours from Bangkok by train or bus for this popular event.

BEASTS OF BURDEN
Apart from spectacles promoted by Thailand's tourist authority, elephants are mostly used to work in the ricefields.

NAKHON RATCHASIMA   PRASAT PHANOM WAN   PHIMAI   PRASAT PHANOM RUNG   PRASAT MUANG T   BURI R

🕐 Four days

The Prasat Phanom Wan, viewed from the outside.

THE KHMER LEGACY

For almost 400 years, from the 9th century onward, much of the northeast was dominated by the Khmer civilization, which was centered around the famous temples of Angkor, in Cambodia. Khmer power extended much further at its peak during the 11th and 12th centuries, covering much of the Chao Phraya River valley and reaching down into the southern peninsula; not until the 13th century did it begin to wane and eventually give way to the rising Thais. The growth of the Khmer empire ● 35 began with the reign of King Jayavarman II (AD 802–50), who removed the capital to Angkor, but the great period of building in Thailand came under King Suriyavarman I (AD 1002–50), whose father had seized the throne of Lopburi from a Mon king and who himself captured the Cambodian throne at Angkor. Northeastern Thailand lay in the path of Khmer expansion and was thus regarded as a natural part of the empire, while the central region was an outlying province. Several monuments were built during this period in Nakhon Ratchasima, Surin and Buri

SURIN   SIKHORAPHUM   SISAKET   UBON RATCHATANI   KHAO PHRA VIHARN

Ram provinces, splendid earthly abodes in stone and brick, and laterite for Hindu deities; temples with rounded prangs that represented the thirty-three levels of heaven, the highest being occupied by the god Indra. Suriyavarman II (AD 1113–50), who built Angkor Wat, was also responsible for northeastern edifices, among them Phimai in Nakhon Ratchasima. By the late 12th century, Mahayana Buddhism had replaced Hinduism and the last great Khmer builder-king, Jayavarman VII (AD 1181–1218), adapted many of the older structures, including Phimai, to suit the new religion. After his death, the empire collapsed, leaving several temples still unfinished ● 35.

PRASAT PHANOM WAN
The interior of the 11th-century Prasat Phanom Wan, with several Buddha images still venerated by local people.

PRASAT PHANOM WAN

Built in the early 11th century during the reign of Suriya-varman I, Prasat Phanom Wan, near Nakhon Ratchasima, is a Hindu temple later converted for Buddhist use. A central prang dominates its rectangular courtyard, surrounded by four older ones. There also is a fine stone lintel above the north entrance to the main sanctuary, which contains a number of Buddha images.

PRASAT HIN PHIMAI

Located about 30 miles from Nakhon Ratchasima, off the road to Khon Kaen, Prasat Hin Phimai dates from the end of the 11th century and is one of the finest examples of early Angkorian art, which was later modified to suit the needs of Mahayana Buddhism. The temple has been restored by the Thai Fine Arts Department in cooperation with Bernard Groslier, who had previously been in charge of the restoration work at Angkor.

THE TEMPLE COMPLEX. The complex of buildings stands in a large quadrangle that once also included a town and was surrounded by a fortified wall. The complex was originally an artificial island, surrounded by the Mun River, two other natural waterways, and a man-made canal, the last trace of which has now disappeared.

GATEWAYS. The imposing southern gate, known as Pratu Chai, or Victory Gate, is a pavilion-like structure with walls of pink sandstone. It faces in the direction of Angkor, with which Phimai was linked by a straight road; traces remain of three other gateways at the other cardinal points.

ROYAL RESIDENCES. Among the notable structures within the walls are a group of royal residences added by Jayavarman VII; a laterite prang called Meru Baromathat (supposedly where the cremation of King Baromathat took place) that once enshrined a statue of Jayavarman VII, now in Bangkok's National Museum; the remains of a pink sandstone prang known as the Hin Daeng; and a central sanctuary, topped by a lotus-bud finial.

THE CENTRAL SANCTUARY. The sanctuary predates the construction of Angkor and was modified when Phimai was converted into a Buddhist structure in the 12th or 13th century. It is the best-preserved part of the complex.

JAYAVARMAN VII (AD 1181–1218), the last of the great Khmer builder-kings, adapted many Hindu temples in northeast Thailand built by earlier kings. Jaya-varman VII is considered the last great Khmer ruler of the Angkor period. In less than 15 years, the borders of the kingdom were extended further to the south and to the north into neigh-boring Malaya, Burma, Annam and Champa. Under his rule Mahayana Buddhism was declared the state religion, thus replacing Hinduism.

It stands on a square base and has four entrances, each guarded by five-headed *naga*, or sacred serpents; the main door, a major projection, is to the south. The lintels inside are particularly fine, and are richly carved with scenes from the Buddha's life and with Tantric deities that rank among the finest in Khmer art.

General floor plan of Prasat Hin Phimai (above) and east (side) elevation of the Inner Courtyard (top and left).

Khmer temples were built according to symbolic criteria: the moat represented the cosmic ocean, the surrounding walls the mountains, and the sanctuary tower Mount Meru, the mythological axis of the world, according to Hindu cosmology.

Prasat Phanom Rung ★

Scenically situated on a small hill in Buri Ram Province and facing the Dongrek Mountains that mark the frontier with Cambodia, Prasat Phanom Rung was built over a long period of time. Three of its brick prangs date from the early 10th century, while the main sanctuary was started in the 11th century but was never completed. The temple has since been restored by the Fine Arts Department with the help of several French experts, and with the same techniques as those used at Phimai. An impressive avenue built by Jayavarman VII, 600 feet long and 36 feet wide, leads to the main building atop a series of terraces, the lowest of which has a balustrade of *naga* (sacred serpents). Situated on an east-west axis, the main sanctuary consists of a prang on a square base with ante-chambers at the four compass points, the main entrance facing east. Beautifully carved lintels adorn the doorways, and there are friezes of very fine quality on the walls and columns.

Prasat Muang Tham ★

About 3 miles from Prasat Phanom Rung is Prasat Muang Tham (below right). Construction of the temple began in the second half of the 10th century and was completed by Jayavarman V. Consisting of an outer and an inner courtyard surrounded by a laterite wall, Prasat Muang Tham is notable for the well-preserved bas-reliefs on small prangs at the four corners of the outer courtyard and for a large variety of beautifully carved lintels, doorway decorations and stone mullions, all rich in Hindu deities. To the north of the temple is one of the reservoirs built during the period to provide a constant source of water.

Khao Phra Viharn ★

The imposing sanctuary of Khao Phra Viharn perches on a spur of the Dongrek mountain range, 1,800 feet above sea level. After a long dispute between Thailand and Cambodia over the ownership of the temple, international law in 1962 adjudged it to lie in Cambodian territory, even though it is quite easily accessible from the Thai side of the border. Khao Phra Viharn is expected to reopen soon to visitors, after being closed for nearly three decades. Built partly during the reign of Suriyavarman I in the early 11th century, then continued later by other Khmer rulers, the complex was built on four different levels, each connected by stairways and each containing the remains of numerous buildings as well as tanks for water storage. Walls and doorways are decorated with a profusion of carvings. However, from the architectural point of view, the structures at the summit are more impressive than those below.

PRASAT HIN SIKHORAPHUM

Prasat Hin Sikhoraphum (right), in Surin Province, dates from the late 11th century and is built in the Angkor Wat style. It consists of a central brick prang and four smaller prangs at the corners of a laterite platform; the lintels and pillars of the entrance to the main prang are intricately carved with guardians, *apsara* (female divinities) and scenes from Hindu mythology.

OTHER KHMER RUINS

Besides major Khmer ruins, such as those mentioned in these and preceding pages, the northeast has thirty other smaller sites. Among the most interesting are Prasat Hin Non Ku in Nakhon Ratchasima Province and Prasat Thamuen Thom in Surin, both in the Baphuon style of the late 10th and 11th centuries; Prasat Ban Phluang in Surin, on the road from Angkor to Phimai; and Prang Ku in Chaiya-phum, which boasts several carved lintels.

"There is no doubt that the Khmer art created in Thailand contains foreign elements beyond the style which evolved in the metropolitan area. However, the local differences are but variations upon a theme; the guiding analytic principle is that such provincial Khmer art was made with the standard technology and within the esthetic context of Khmer civilization."
Piriya Krairiksh

CHIANG KHONG

NAM NAO NATIONAL PARK
ERAWAN CAVE
VIENTIANE AIRPORT
NONGKHAI
UDON THANI
KHON KAEN

One week

MEKONG MOSAIC
Two scenes (right) of daily life by the Mekong in the 19th century and fishing boats (below) at the confluence of the Mekong and Mun rivers.

The world's twelfth-longest river, the great Mekong originates on the Tibetan plateau and winds its way across 2,500 miles, through six countries, before it empties into the South China Sea. It serves as the border between Thailand and Laos for more than 500 miles in both the north and the east before flowing on through Cambodia and Vietnam. The most fertile areas of the northeast lie along the banks of the Mekong, where the rich alluvial silt from the river nourishes mulberry and tobacco plantations, vegetable gardens and orchards. Its waters provide a steady supply of fish as well, including a gigantic variety of catfish called *pla duk* in Thai, which can weigh up to one ton. For nearly 20 years after the end of the Indo-Chinese War, the Laotian side of the Mekong was closed to most tourists. Recently, however, relations between Thailand and its neighbor have improved and traffic across the river is steadily increasing. There is already a bridge linking the two countries a Nongkhai and two more are under construction.

FROM NONGKHAI TO KHONG CHAM

A weathered road runs along the Mekong from Nongkhai, a bustling port that serves as the gateway to the Laotian capital

LAMPAO DAM

PHU PAN NATIONAL PARK
PADDY FIELDS
LAMPAO

SAKHON NAKHON

NAKHON PHANOM

THAT PHANOM

MUKDAHAN

UBON RATCHATHANI
WARIN CHAMRAP
SUWANNAKHET

KAENG TANA NATIONAL PARK

of Vientiane, to Mukdahan, across from Suwannakhet. Among the attractions that lie along this scenic route are the Phu Wua Wildlife Sanctuary, across from the Laotian town of Pakse, the riverside provincial capital of Nakhon Phanom, and That Phanom with its famous chedi. A small national park at Mukdahan contains some unusual rock formations and Buddhist sites. At Mukdahan, the main highway moves away from the river and leads to Ubon Ratchathani, where each year in July, on the eve of the three-month Buddhist Lent period, there is a procession of enormous carved candles and figures carried on floats through the city streets. A boat can be hired here for the short trip along the Mun River to Khong Cham, a picturesque confluence of waterways at the point where the Mekong curves and heads toward Cambodia and Vietnam on its journey to the sea.

WAT PHRA THAT PHANOM. Overlooking the Mekong, Wat Phra That Phanom is the most famous of all northeastern Buddhist temples. Its central chedi, originally built in the 9th century and containing a sacred relic, was modeled after the well-known That Luang in Vientiane. When the spire collapsed during a monsoon storm in 1975, it was regarded as a dire omen and was immediately reconstructed; the present one was inaugurated four years later by the Thai king.

THE MEKONG'S OTHER NAMES
The Mekong probably has as many names as the countries it passes through. Also called Lancang Jiang in the province of Yunnan, the river first flows into Burma at an altitude of 8,250 feet and continues through Thailand and into Laos (Kingdom of a Thousand Elephants). The river then meanders towards Thailand and Laos again, then into Cambodia and Vietnam, assuming the names Han Giang, Co Chien, Cua Dai and Bassal respectively.

237

▲ THE NORTHEAST NATIONAL PARKS

FOREST TYPES
In Khao Yai National Park some of the last remaining rain forests can still be observed ■ *18–19*. Most of the forests of the dry northeast, however, are deciduous, including teak trees and deciduous dipterocarps, so called because of their two-winged seeds. Found in both types of forest are more than 70 species of bamboo. The acidic soil of the northeast also supports pine trees at an altitude of between 1,980 feet and 4,620 feet. The Phu Kradung National Park is famous for its pine trees. Flowering trees thrive in the dry northeast and, after long spells of drought, spectacular blooms appear. Khao Yai's pride are the thousands of species of orchid ■ *20–21* that cling to the trees in the wetter parts of the forest.

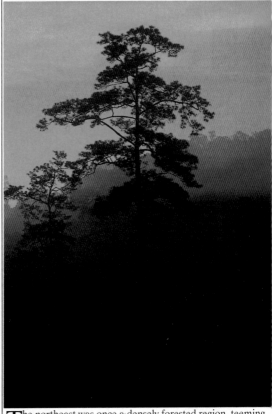

The northeast was once a densely forested region, teeming with wildlife. Logging, together with the demands of an expanding population, has denuded vast areas and its former natural wealth can be found mainly in those designated national parks.

KHAO YAI

Covering 869 square miles in four provinces – Nakhon Ratchasima, Saraburi, Nakhon Nayok and Prachinburi – Khao Yai was established in 1962 as the first of Thailand's national parks. It is also the most popular, thanks to its ease of accessibility from Bangkok, 120 miles away. Largely because of the number of visitors (700,000 in 1990), the government has recently decided to close a motor lodge and golf course run by the Tourism Authority of Thailand, as well as other bungalow facilities, although visitors with special permission will still be allowed to camp overnight in the park. There are picturesque trails through lush forests and a rich variety of wildlife ■ *16–19*, including a sizeable number of elephants, clouded leopards, gibbons, mouse deer, Malayan sun bears, and such birds as the great hornbill, the Siamese fireback pheasant, the silver pheasant and the brown needle-tail, allegedly the fastest bird in the world.

NAM NAO

Established as Thailand's fifth national park in 1972, Nam Nao covers 387 square miles of rolling hills and pine forests in Chaiyaphum and Petchabun. It was once a stronghold of communist insurgents but has been made safe for visitors

since the early 1980's. Thanks to the adjacent Phu Khieo Wildlife Sanctuary, the park is unusually rich in animal life ■ 16–19, including elephants, Asiatic black bears and clouded leopards. In 1979 rhinoceros tracks were found in the park. Over 200 species of birds have been confirmed. A popular attraction in the park is Yai Nam Nao Cave, home to hundreds of thousands of bats.

KAENG TANA

Located near Ubon Ratchathani, where the rivers Mekong and Mun meet, the Kaeng Tana National Park covers a sprawling 32-square-mile expanse of land. Although not ranked as one of the popular ones in Thailand's northeast, the scenic park boasts features such as giant sandstone slabs, a cave and a waterfall with rapids.

PHU KRADUNG ★

Phu Kradung is a bell-shaped mountain in Loei Province, crowned with a 24-square-mile plateau of exceptional natural beauty. The climb to the top involves a 5-mile trek, sometimes up steep areas, but there are benches and shelters along the way. Plant life on the cool plateau includes many temperate-zone specimens such as rhododendrons, pines and oaks, and among the existing wildlife are elephants, sambar deer, gibbons and 130 bird species. The park is closed from June to August to allow for environmental recovery from the damage caused by visitors.

BIRD-WATCHING
The majority of Thailand's wild mammals tend to be shy creatures and sightings are rare. Birds, on the other hand, are plentiful, and visitors to any of the national parks will easily spot several of the estimated 928 species that live in the country.

HORNBILLS
Easily spotted because of their size and their noisy flappings, hornbills are among the largest jungle birds, distinguished by a huge beak often surmounted by a casque. After laying her eggs the female immures herself inside a tree cavity.

GIBBONS
Gibbons are among the most endearing of Thailand's native wildlife, swinging like gymnasts from the upper heights of the trees and hooting mournfully at daybreak. They are the subject of continuing research at Khao Yai, where both the white-handed (or lar) and the pileated species live in considerable numbers.

> "Today, no large mammals survive
> outside the boundaries of national parks."
> National Research Institute of Thailand, 198

ENDANGERED SPECIES

The national parks of the northeast provide sanctuary for several once-common animals that are now regarded as endangered species. Around 200 wild elephants, for example, live within the boundaries of Khao Yai, the largest population of any park in the country. Some of Thailand's estimated 250 remaining tigers have also found their habitat there. Thailand has recently signed the international CITES treaty, and increasing attention and resources are dedicated to the country's natural heritage.

LEOPARDS. Though rare today, leopards and clouded leopards may still be sighted in Khao Yai and Nam Nao. Prized for their skin, these beasts have been the target of persistent poachers who flout wildlife preservation laws.

BEARS. The Malayan sun bear is a smallish jungle bear that eats mostly fallen fruit, fish and carrion. It has the misfortune of being highly regarded as a medicinal ingredient by certain groups like the Koreans, who come on special tours just to eat

grilled bear meat. The Asiatic black bear, still existing at Khao Yai and Nam Nao, is a much bigger animal, distinguished by its long hair and a wide V-mark from the upper breast to the shoulders.

THE KOUPREY. A recent discovery by Western zoologists, the kouprey is a bovine distinguished by huge lyre-shaped horns and a long dewlap drooping from the neck. Once commonly found along the Dangrek range near the Cambodian border, the beast was slaughtered for meat during the Cambodian conflict and is probably now an extinct species.

THE GAUR. This is a huge ox up to 10 feet long and 6 feet tall at the shoulder. Black with scimitar-like horns and white legs, they inhabit open forests in herds of six to 20, although one will see only their tracks. Nocturnal browsers, they feed in open spaces and are the prey of tigers, leopards and humans, who have reduced their numbers to under 500 and put them on the endangered species list.

FURS
Up to the early 1980's, tiger and leopard skins were openly sold at souvenir shops in Bangkok. Today, they are sold secretly in small border villages.

EXTINCT SPECIES
During the 19th century, Thailand exported about 8,000 rhinoceros horns a year to China, where they were much prized for their supposed medicinal qualities, including that of high male potency. The number of rhinoceros was so drastically reduced that by 1977 it was estimated that not more than ten Sumatran rhinos and perhaps only a few of the Javanese species remained in the country. Today, none are left; rhinoceros-horn powder, however, is still sold at exorbitant prices in the markets of Bangkok's Chinatown.

The Central Plains

WAT PHRA SI SANPHET
VIHARA PHRA MONGKOK BOPIT
WAT NA PHRA MERU
NATIONAL MUSEUM
WAT PHRA B

WAT CHAI WATTANARAM
WAT PHUKAOTHONG

TREASURES OF GOLD
In a crypt beneath Wat Raja Burana's central prang King Boromaraja II once hid a collection of gold objects in memory of his two dead brothers. They are now housed at the National Museum at Ayutthaya.

HISTORY

Founded in 1350 by King Ramathibodi I, Ayutthaya grew from a small town with fortified mud walls on an artificial island on the Chao Phraya River into one of the largest, most cosmopolitan cities in Southeast Asia. With only one interruption, when it fell to the Burmese in the mid-16th century, it was the center of Thai power for more than 400 years, its rule extending over the entire Central Plains as well as many areas of the far east and south. The 33 rulers of Ayutthaya adopted the Khmer concept of divine kingship, complete with Brahminic rituals, and built spectacular palaces as well as great Buddhist monuments; most of the major remains visitors see today were constructed in the city's first 150 years. The peak of opulence, however, came in the 17th century, when ships from all over the world sailed up the Chao Phraya to trade and Ayutthaya had a population of more than a million, among them Indians, Chinese, Japanese and assorted Europeans; during the reign of King Narai (1657–88), two French embassies came from the court of Louis XIV and a

Thai embassy was sent to Paris. Ayutthayan power began to decline after the death of Narai, and a series of wars ensued with Burma, Thailand's traditional enemy. In 1767, after a 15-month siege, the city fell to an invading army that wasted little time in burning almost every building. Under the leadership of the future King Taksin, the Thais rallied and managed to expel the enemy in a remarkably short time. Ayutthaya was too thoroughly destroyed for re-occupation and the capital was moved further downriver, first to Thonburi and later to Bangkok.

🕐 One day

THE RUINS OF AYUTTHAYA

WAT RAJA BURANA. The best known of Ayutthaya's monuments, Wat Raja Burana was constructed in 1424 by King Boromaraja II, on the site where two princes had killed one another in a duel on elephant-back. The king first built two chedis and later a far more imposing temple surrounded by a wall, with monumental gateways, a towering prang on a stepped platform and numerous smaller prangs and chedis ● 97.

Thailand's oldest paintings decorate the vault of the crypt of Wat Raja Burana.

243

An engraving of the ruins of Wat Phra Si Sanphet.

ISLAND CAPITAL
Ayutthaya, like Bangkok later, was conceived as an island fortress, formed by digging a canal at a point where the Lopburi River curved sharply. Later shunts were dug linking the city with the Chao Phraya and Pasak rivers and these in time became the main courses of the two rivers. Canals also provided avenues of communication within the walled city as well as out into the surrounding countryside. Huge water gates blocked the access to the city when necessary.

WAT PHRA SI SANPHET. Dating from 1491, Wat Phra Si Sanphet (left) was located inside the compound of the king's palace – the foundations of which are still visible – and served as the royal chapel, as Wat Phra Keo does in Bangkok. The three main chedis, although poorly restored, contain the ashes of three Ayutthaya kings, and the extent of the temple's ruins attests to its former splendor.

VIHARN PHRA MONGKOL BOPIT. Near Wat Phra Si Sanphet, this modern building houses huge seated Buddha image, dating from the 15th century and originally intended to stand in the open air. The image was restored several times and is the object of considerable veneration among Buddhist visitors to Ayutthaya.

WAT PHRA MAHATHAT is believed to be one of Ayutthaya's oldest temples, possibly built by King Boromaraja I (1370–88). Its central prang, of which only the base remains today, once rose to a height of 165 feet. Traces of the original stucco decorations can still be seen on some of the surrounding chedis.

WAT PHRA RAM. Though founded in 1369, the ruins of Wat Phra Ram (right) date mostly from its restoration in the 15th century. Its main feature is a well-proportioned prang that stands on a stepped terrace adorned with chedis. Some of the prang's stucco decorations, including walking and standing Buddhas, still remain.

WAT MAHEYONG. This temple is unique as its main feature is a chedi supported by a base with stucco elephants, similar in style to those seen in Sukhothai and Si Satchanalai.

NATIONAL MUSEUM

A branch of the National Museum, also known as Chao Sam Phraya Museum, is located on Rojana Road and is open daily except Mondays and Tuesdays. On display in the museum is a remarkable collection of Buddhist art, mostly Ayutthayan, as well as the treasure found in Wat Raja Burana, which, besides the famed gold objects, comprises a collection of small well-preserved Buddha images of exquisite workmanship. Worthy of mention also are a set of painted banners with religious subjects and a lacquered book cabinet decorated with a representation of the Buddhist cosmos.

> "The city of Ayutthaya, at the period of our visit, consisted of some six fisherman's huts and a betelnut vendor's stall."

Frederick A. Neale

TEMPLES ALONG THE RIVERSIDE

WAT CHAI WATTANARAM. Built in 1630 by King Prasat Thong, Wat Chai Wattanaram (left) was conceived as a replica of an Angkorian temple, with a huge prang surrounded by smaller ones, symbolizing Mount Meru, the abode of the heavenly gods. Now restored, the temple has lost much of its former charm.

WAT YAI CHAI MONGKOL. A lofty chedi dominates Wat Yai Chai Mongkol (right) on the opposite side of the river. It was given its name by King Naresuan to commemorate a battle fought against the Crown Prince of Burma in 1592. Naresuan's victory brought independence to Ayutthaya after 15 years as a Burmese vassal. In the complex is also a huge image of a reclining Buddha in brick and stucco ● 97.

WAT NA PHRA MERU. Located across the river north of the palace, this temple ● 91 has been restored a number of times but still has a finely proportioned bot and a viharn. The latter contains a large Dvaravati stone Buddha seated in European style, his hands on his knees, which some scholars think originated in Nakhon Pathom.

WAT PHANAN CHOENG. Overlooking the river on the opposite bank from the main city, Wat Phanan Choeng was founded shortly before the establishment of Ayutthaya as the capital. Its main building enshrines a huge, seated Buddha image, 57 feet tall, the object of particular devotion to Thais of Chinese origin. The temple is a popular stopover for riverboat cruises along the Chao Phraya.

ELEPHANT CORRAL

Off the road from Ayutthaya to Ang Thong is the Elephant Corral. Repaired by King Rama I of Bangkok and restored by several of his successors, it was once the place where wild elephants were rounded up, sorted, and eventually trained for work and use in warfare.

CHANTARAKASEM PALACE
AND MUSEUM

Originally built for King Naresuan (1590–1605) when he was Crown Prince, Chantarakasem Palace was reconstructed in the 19th century by King Rama IV of Bangkok, who used it as a summer retreat. Now overlooking a main street in the modern town, one of its elegant buildings contains a small but interesting collection of objects found in Ayutthaya.

MONUMENT PRESERVATION
The Fine Arts Department is gradually restoring all the monuments in Ayutthaya. However, the nature of the brick monuments is such that they cannot be stabilized without complete reconstruction. Buddhists generally frown upon damaged Buddha images, so statues found among the ruins are being replaced with replicas in cement, often made by unskilled craftsmen, while the original pieces have are treasured by discerning collectors.

ELEPHANT SHOWS
Although the Elephant Corral was not used for its original purpose after the destruction of Ayutthaya, later Bangkok kings staged spectacular roundups there as a form of entertainment for distinguished visitors from abroad. One of the last great shows was recorded by photographer Robert Lenz in 1890.

LIFE ALONG THE KLONGS

KLONGS
"The numberless canals that thread their way across the plains in every possible direction, have turned the lower portion of Siam into a veritable labyrinth of winding waterways. The klongs differ in age, appearance and size, as do the roads of more densely populated countries."
Ernest Young

Leading off the river in this area are numerous klongs, or canals, all dug centuries ago to facilitate communications. Cruising along these, one can catch glimpses of a lifestyle that has largely vanished in most other parts of the country: elegant wooden houses in the Central Plains style, raised above the ground on tall posts; huge hump-backed barges loaded with rice, being towed to the markets and warehouses of Bangkok; vendor boats supplying waterside houses with various necessities; the spires of Buddhist temples rising above feathery bamboo groves; and stretching away on either side, all the way to the horizon, the vast ricefields ■ *24–5* that have traditionally nourished and enriched the kingdom.

RICE FARMING. The majority of rural Thais are rice farmers, following an ancient cycle that begins with plowing the fields in April or May just before the rains; the young seedlings are then planted and carefully tended until harvest time, usually in late November or early December.

TRADITIONAL HOUSE PRODUCTION. In Ang Thong Province, a short drive from Ayutthaya, many skilled craftsmen earn their livelihood by prefabricating the components of traditional Thai-style houses: paneled walls, gables, roof beams, and the characteristic curving bargeboards. These are then transported elsewhere, mainly to Bangkok, and assembled on a framework of pillars in private compounds ● *86*.

BANG PA-IN

THE THAI HOUSE
The classic Central Plains house is raised off the ground on stout pillars, with a veranda in front where most family activities take place. The walls lean slightly inward and the roofs are steep; traditionally, it has bargeboards that curve gracefully at the end, adding to the general effect of lightness and airiness ● *86*.

A few miles down the Chao Phraya River from Ayutthaya is the Bang Pa-In Summer Palace. The site was first used by the royal court as a retreat from the hot weather in the 17th century but fell into ruin after the fall of Ayutthaya; it was restored by King Rama IV in the mid-19th century, though most of the buildings that exist today date from the reign of King Rama V, who regularly spent his summers there.

Typically of the fifth reign, the structures represent a variety of architectural styles, set in a large park around ponds and waterways. The only one of the royal residences open to the public is the Chinese-style Vehat Chamroon Palace, constructed entirely of materials imported from China. In addition, there is an Italian-style palace, a circular pavilion with steps leading down to a pool, the graceful Thai-style Aisawan Tippaya Asna pavilion in the middle of a lake, and, across one of the waterways, a Buddhist chapel in neo-Gothic style with stained-glass windows. Scattered around the extensive gardens are European statues as well as monuments erected by King Rama V in memory of members of his family, one of them to a much-loved Queen who was drowned in a boating accident.

RICE BARGES
For many centuries, the Chao Phraya has been the main highway for transporting rice and other produce to Bangkok and the outside world, usually in long processions of huge teakwood barges pulled by tugboats. Filled with heavy rice sacks, the round-bottomed barges appear to be almost submerged in the water.

WAT PHAI RONG RUA

Located on the river near Bang Pa-In, Wat Phai Rong Rua is worth visiting mainly as a curiosity, since its grounds are filled with large, rather garish statues depicting scenes from Buddhist hell and the grim fate that awaits those unlucky enough to go there.

BANG SAI

Bang Sai, also near Bang Pa-In, is a small riverside village established in 1982 by Queen Sirikit as a place where farmers are given the opportunity to learn the traditional crafts and thus acquire a supplementary source of income. There are regular demonstrations of basket making, cloth weaving, and leatherworking. A souvenir shop markets the finished products.

WAT PHAI LOM

Located on the riverbank below Bang Pa-In is Wat Phai Lom, famous as a bird sanctuary. Each December, thousands of rare open-billed storks fly over the temple from Bangladesh and head for their nests among the treetops to raise their young before departing in June.

The Aisawan Tippaya Asna pavilion at Bang Pa-In.

The fortifications of Lopburi were built with the help of the French engineer Monsieur de la Marre, who came to Siam with the mission of the Chevalier de Chaumont.

Once known as Louvo, Lopburi served as an important city during the Dvaravati period and also as an outpost of the Khmer empire. King Narai of Ayutthaya (1656–88) began using it as a summer retreat and eventually spent so much of his time there that it became virtually a second capital.

KING NARAI'S PALACE. Known as Phra Narai Raja-nivet, this palace was built by King Narai between 1665 and 1677 and was the scene of most of the important events during his reign. High crenellated walls with imposing gateways surround the large compound, which in turn was divided into separate areas for government offices, ceremonial buildings and the king's private residence. French architects assisted in the design of part of the palace, particularly the Dusit Sawan Thanya Maha Prasat, where the king regularly received foreign ambassadors. Here King Narai spent the winter months going out in search of wild elephants, often hoping to find an auspicious white one; walked through gardens described by Simon de la Loubère as "delightful," filled with

plants and cool fountains; discussed affairs of state with his chief minister, the shrewd Greek adventurer Constantine Phaulkon; and, in a hall said to have been ablaze with mirrors brought from France, met with the envoys of Louis XIV. It was here too, in the spring of 1688, that he fell ill and subsequently died. The palace was restored and used again as a residence by King Rama IV in the 19th century. The buildings from the latter period are now used to display the finds from excavations of prehistoric sites in the Central Plains as well as numerous memorabilia from King Rama IV's reign, including giant shadow puppets and various items of furniture. A collection of Lopburi-style Buddha images is displayed in the throne hall.

> "Louvo stands most pleasantly and in a most wholesome air; the compass of it is very large and it is become very populous since the king hath been pleased to live there."

Father Guy Tachard

PHAULKON'S RESIDENCE. "One of the most amazing of the adventurers who have made the east the scene of their exploits" is how Somerset Maugham described Constantine Phaulkon, and many other writers and historians have agreed. Born in 1647 on the island of Cephalonia, then under Greek rule, he came to Asia as a cabin boy on an English merchant ship and after a series of adventures turned up at King Narai's court in Ayutthaya. A natural talent for politics, together with a gift for languages and what must have been considerable charm, led him to the highest echelons of power; by 1685, he was in charge of Ayutthaya's foreign trade and was one of the king's closest confidants, with the royal title of Chao Phraya Wichayen. The remains of Phaulkon's Lopburi residence – he had another, much grander one in Ayutthaya – stand in a compound with those of a Catholic church and a house built for members of a French embassy that came in 1685, all in a blend of European and Thai styles. Though the French mission was regarded as a success, it increased opposition to Phaulkon among conservative elements at court. When King Narai fell mortally ill in 1688, one of them, Phra Petchara, took the opportunity to stage a revolt; Phaulkon was arrested, tortured for several days, and finally beheaded near a lake outside Lopburi.

FRENCH EMBASSIES
When King Narai reigned, two French embassies from the court of King Louis XIV were received by him in Ayutthaya (1685) and Lopburi, (1687); a Thai embassy bearing royal gifts returned with the first group and was received by the French king at Versailles in 1686. The French were encouraged by reports from Jesuit missionaries, who believed that Narai might be converted to Christianity; the king, however, was more interested in countering increased pressure from the Dutch and the British. After Narai's death, his conservative successor expelled nearly all foreigners from Ayutthaya
● *61, 100–101, 118.*

WAT PHRA SAM YOT. Built in the 13th century and located in the center of old Lopburi, Wat Phra Sam Yot (left) is a Khmer temple with three laterite prangs; two of the prangs contain partially ruined Buddha images. The laterite blocks were once covered with elaborate stucco decorations, of which only a few traces now remain.

WAT PHRA SI RATANA MAHATHAT. Lopburi's most important religious structure, Wat Phra Si Ratana Mahathat (right) dates from the period of Khmer rule but was restored and enlarged by King Narai. It contains a large laterite prang as well as a brick viharn, added by King Narai, which reflects foreign influences in its pointed arch windows.

PHRA PHUTTHABAT

Phra Phutthabat, more commonly known as the Temple of Buddha's Footprint, is a much-revered shrine about 17 miles from the town of Saraburi. The sacred footprint – measuring 5 feet long – was discovered during the Ayutthaya period, but the buildings that enshrine it today were built by King Rama I of Bangkok and his successors. Many hermits still live in caves in the surrounding hills.

K hamphaeng Phet, on the left bank of the Ping River, was one of the most important centers of the Sukhothai kingdom, although its principal monuments were built somewhat later than those of the other satellite city of Si Satchanalai. It was in Khamphaeng Phet that the last ruler of Sukhothai submitted to King Boramathat of Ayutthaya in 1378.

INSIDE THE "DIAMOND WALL"

A WESTERN VISITOR
In 1882, traveler Carl Bock spent a night in Khamphaeng Phet on his way to the far north. He dined with the governor of the province, an occasion he described as follows: "The menu was a good one, and the dinner was served in a style that would have done credit to a first-class hotel... Soon after I returned from the hospitable table of the governor, I was disturbed by the noise of drums and gongs, accompanied by the desultory discharge of firearms in all directions. Hastily getting up, I crossed over to a temple which stood opposite to my *sala*, where I found the priests assembled in full force, surrounded by an excited multitude of natives gazing at the great dragon swallowing the moon, and endeavoring by dreadful clamor to avert the calamity. In other words there was an eclipse of the moon."

Khamphaeng Phet ("Diamond Wall") was surrounded by massive ramparts of earth topped with laterite. The two principal temples are Wat Phra Keo (top and right), which has two large seated Buddha images, and Wat Phra That, which has a chedi surrounded by columns. Also of interest is the *lak muang*, the city's foundation stone pillar.

OUTSIDE THE WALLS OF KHAMPHAENG PHET

The finest of Khamphaeng Phet's ruins lie outside the city walls, where the surroundings were more conducive to prayer and meditation. Wat Phra Non enshrines the remains of a reclining Buddha, while Wat Phra Si Iriyabot (above left) has images of the Buddha in four attitudes – standing, walking, seated and reclining. Wat Chang Rob, "Temple Surrounded by Elephants," is notable for the remains of a large chedi surrounded by imposing elephant buttresses made of laterite covered with stucco, a decorative motif that originated from Sri Lanka.

TWO FORTS. At the southern and northern corners of Khamphaeng Phet's walls are the remains of two forts (above) :Phom Chao Indra and Phom Phet. The latter has been excavated, is well preserved and suggests the impressive scale of ancient fortifications.

SUKHOTHAI

Sukhothai was the northernmost citadel of the Khmer empire and had flourished for centuries before the Thais began emigrating from the north in increasing numbers. During the first half of the 13th century, when Khmer influence was waning, a Thai chieftain later known as King Intradit united various groups, overthrew their Khmer overlord, and founded the kingdom of Sukhothai, the Pali version of which means "Dawn of Happiness." Sukhothai's power lasted less than two centuries before it became a vassal of Ayutthaya in 1378, but it enjoyed a brilliant flowering in both politics and culture. Under its third and most famous ruler, King Ramkhamhaeng (1275–1317), direct or indirect rule was extended over much of present-day Thailand, and a Thai alphabet was devised. Most impressive of all were the remarkable achievements in art and architecture. Drawing from a variety of cultures – not only Khmer but also Mon, Indian and Sinhalese – Sukhothai artisans created superb temples, Buddha images and ceramics that were also distinctively Thai and are regarded as the finest examples of the country's cultural heritage ● 36.

One of Sukhothai's many chedis, photographed in 1910.

The Sitting Buddha at Wat Si Chum ▲ 255.

RESTORATION OF SUKHOTHAI

Declared a national historical park by the Thai government, Sukhothai has also received international attention in the form of aid from UNESCO. Over the past decade, many of the ancient capital's principal monuments have been carefully restored and villagers who had settled in the ruins were moved elsewhere. The original layout of the city was revealed and enhanced by dredging the moats and ponds, which had filled with silt over the centuries.

LOY KRATHONG
According to legend, the beautiful Loy Krathong festival held at the end of the rainy season to honor the water spirits originated at Sukhothai. The festival has been revived under the auspices of the Tourism Authority with a gala event that includes spectacular illuminations, colorful parades and thousands of lotus-shaped floats set adrift on ponds and waterways ● 73.

251

RAMKHAMHAENG NATIONAL MUSEUM · WAT MAHATHAT · WAT SRI SAWAI · STATUE OF RAMA KHAMHENG · WAT TRAPANG NGERN · WAT TRAPANG THONG LANG

WAT TRAPANG THONG · WAT CHETUPON · SAN THA PHA DAEN

RAMKHAMHAENG INSCRIPTION

"This Sukhothai is good. In the water there are fish. In the fields there is rice." Every Thai school-child learns these lines taken from a stone inscription dealing with life in the ancient capital, usually dated 1292 and attributed to King Ramkham-haeng. Of late, some scholars have questioned the authenticity of the inscription and even suggested that it might have been produced by King Rama IV in the mid-19th century.

RAMKHAMHAENG NATIONAL MUSEUM

The Ramkhamhaeng National Museum of Sukhothai, one of the richest in Thailand, is the best introduction to a visit to the ruins of the ancient capital. Located in a garden to the east of Wat Mahathat, the museum houses a large collection of Sukhothai Buddha images (among them a magnificent bronze Walking Buddha), Khmer statues, stucco decorations, ceramics, and a copy of the famous 1292 stone inscription attributed to King Ramkhamhaeng. In front of the museum, the Fine Arts Department has reconstructed an open Sukhothai-style viharn.

WAT MAHATHAT

Sukhothai's main Buddhist monastery, Wat Mahathat was adjacent to the former royal palace and covers a square measuring

① 1 day

60 feet each side.
Construction of the temple, started by King
ntradit, Sukhothai's founder, continued
nder several other rulers before its
ompletion by King Li Thai in 1345.

HE LOTUS CHEDI. The dominant
tructure is a central chedi, covering
n old Khmer tower, with a lotus-
ud finial, a distinctive feature of Sukhothai architecture. A
ine stucco frieze showing Buddhist disciples adorns the base
f the main chedi.

OTHER BUILDINGS. On two sides are towering standing
Buddha images enclosed in a *mondop* (open image-
ouse). There are also nearly 200 other chedis and the
emains of 10 viharns, among other structures, all axially
aligned with the rising and setting
sun. Noteworthy is a stepped
chedi that resembles the one
in Polonnaruwa, and which
acts as an important link
between Sri Lankan and
Thai art. Its unusual shape
as replicated in several northern Thai
emples, the most famous of which is at Wat
u Kut, Lamphun ▲ 275. Sukhothai was a
enter of influence for Sinhalese culture,
hich spread to the northern mountains in
hailand ● 90, 116.

**SUKHOTHAI
BUDDHA**
The Sukhothai
Buddha
image
(below),
particularly
when cast in bronze, is
regarded as the most
beautiful in all Thai
art ▲ 158–9. Depicted
in seated, standing,
reclining and
walking attitudes,
the images are
not meant to be
realistic. Rather,
they
emphasize
the
Buddha's
super-
natural
qualities.

253

Wat Sri Sawai. A Khmer-style temple southwest of Wat Mahathat, Wat Sri Sawai (left) was probably dedicated to the Hindu god Siva in pre-Thai times before it became a Buddhist shrine. Three well-restored prangs adorned with some of their original stucco decorations stand behind the remains of the principal sanctuary, which was added in the 15th century.

SUKHOTHAI KINGS
Between 1238 and 1488, Sukhothai was ruled by nine kings, the last three of whom served mainly under the control of Ayutthaya. The most famous was King Ramkhamhaeng, under whom the kingdom achieved its greatest power, though the scholarly King Li Thai (1347–74) is remembered as the author of the *Tribhumikatha* (the Three Worlds of Buddhism), the oldest Thai literary work.
● 36.

Wat Sa Sri. Picturesquely sited on an island in a pond northwest of Wat Mahathat, Wat Sa Sri (right) shows the refinement of Sukhothai architecture. Roofless columns rise from the base of the main sanctuary, which also contains a large stucco Buddha image; behind are two elegant chedis, one of them in rounded Sinhalese style.

Wat Trapang Thong Lang. This temple has some remarkable stucco decorations (left) on the outer wall of a square chapel. Perhaps the most famous is the southern panel, which shows the descent of the Buddha from heaven surrounded by celestial attendants and which is regarded as one of the masterpieces of Sukhothai art.

Wat Trapang Thong. Situated on an island set in a peaceful pond, this temple has an elegant bell-shaped chedi. Inside its *mondop* is a print of Buddha that is said to have been discovered by Li Thai at the top of Phra Baht Yai in 1359.

Wat Trapang Ngern. Located just behind Wat Mahathat, this temple comprises a number of buildings sited around a big pond. The main feature is an elegant lotus-bud chedi. Many visitors enjoy walking across the wooden bridge to the islet that once housed a viharn.

LOTUS CAPITAL
The lotus capital is one of Sukhothai's unique contributions to religious architecture. Though possibly inspired by finials from the Mon period at Pagan in Burma, it is original enough in design to be called Thai.
● 90–91.

San Tha Pha Daeng. East of Wat Sa Sri, inside the city wall, San Tha Pha Daeng is a Khmer laterite sanctuary consisting of a square cell and an antechamber. It is believed to be the the oldest building in the Sukhothai area, dating from the first half of the 12th century.

Wat Chetupon

Located south of Sukhothai's city walls, Wat Chetupon is notable for an interesting, partially ruined chedi with images of the Buddha in the four ritual attitudes in stucco bas-relief; the tall standing Buddha is particularly fine. A wall of gray stone surrounds the compound.

Wat Saphan Hin

Situated west of the city on a small hill, Wat Saphan Hin derives its name (Stone Bridge) from the stone stairway leading up to it. Within the columns that remain of the viharn is a 41-foot-tall standing Buddha built against a thick brick wall that provides support for the huge image. In the groves and on the surrounding hills there are ruins of monasteries once inhabited by forest-dwelling ascetic monks.

WAT SI CHUM

This temple, southwest of the walled city, is one of the most impressive religious monuments in the area ● 90. It is dominated by a huge structure, 50 feet tall, enclosing a seated Buddha of stucco-covered brick almost the same height and 37 feet wide at the lap; the image is referred to as Phra Achana in the 1292 stone inscription attributed to King Ramkhamhaeng. Within the wall is an enclosed stairway, the ceiling of which is lined with engraved slabs of stone. The reason for the construction of the stairway, which leads to the top of the structure, is not known. Some have suggested that it may be linked with a legend that the image could speak to supplicants below.

Each of the 100 engravings depicts a self-contained scene from the Jataka tales, moralistic stories dealing with the Buddha's previous lives. The slabs may have been made for Wat Mahathat and later moved to Wat Si Chum for safekeeping.

WAT PHRA PHAI LUANG

North of Sukhothai's walls and partially surrounded by ponds are the extensive ruins of Wat Phra Phai Luang (below), which rivaled Wat Mahathat in size and importance. Originally, three concentric moats surrounded the main religious complex, consisting of a group of buildings. The complex, besides the religious symbolism related to the representation of the Primordial Ocean, undoubtedly served a practical purpose, similar to the one in Angkor. It is thus evident that the original layout of the city of Sukhothai was set out by the Khmers according to their religious beliefs. The temple originally had three Khmer-style prangs, only one of which remained when it was converted into a Buddhist temple by the Thais. On the same terrace are the remains of a viharn and a chedi, decorated with Buddha images in stucco. A nearby structure enshrines the Buddha in walking, standing, sitting and reclining attitudes.

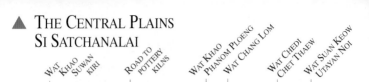

WAT KHAO SUWAN KIRI | ROAD TO POTTERY KILNS | WAT KHAO PHANOM PLOENG | WAT CHANG LOM | WAT CHEDI CHET THAEW | WAT SUAN KEOW UTAYAN NOI

⏱ Half a day

BAN KO NOI
EXCAVATIONS
Anyone interested in ceramics should visit an ancient kiln site at Ban Ko Noi, a few miles north of Si Satchanalai. Here a Thai-Australian project headed by Don Hein has uncovered more than 200 kilns and evidence of more, many of them predating those of Sukhothai by four centuries.

A bout 40 miles north of Sukhothai, on the west bank of the Yom River, Si Satchanalai was a satellite city usually governed by a son of the Sukhothai ruler. Though smaller than the capital, it was similar in plan and has a more picturesque location overlooking the river and rural scenery; the two cities were linked by the Phra Ruang Highway. A number of impressive Buddhist temples were built in Si Satchanalai, some as beautiful as those at Sukhothai, and a nearby district to the north became famous for kilns that produced superb ceramics known as Sawankhalok, the name given to the area during the early Ayutthaya period.

WAT CHANG LOM. Located in the center of the old city, Wat Chang Lom was built in the late 13th century. Its main feature is a large bell-shaped chedi that enshrines relics placed there by King Ramkhamhaeng; around the base of the chedi are several elephant buttresses, hence the name "Temple Surrounded by Elephants."

WAT CHEDI CHET THAEW. Covering a large area, this temple consists of a sanctuary and seven rows of chedis, which probably contain the ashes of Si Satchanalai rulers. Adorning one of the chedis is an impressive stucco image of a seated Buddha protected by the hood of a *naga*, or sacred serpent ● 96.

WAT KHAO PHANOM PLOENG. Wat Khao Phanom Ploeng, "Temple of the Mountain of Fire," is located on a hill within the city, accessible by a steep flight of steps. The laterite columns of the temple remain, along with a restored seated Buddha image and a tall chedi.

The labels at top:

CHALIENG VILLAGE

WAT PHRA SI RATANA MAHATHAT

SUSPENSION BRIDGE

The hilltop site affords sweeping views
of the old city and the countryside.

KILNS

The popular legend that the art of making ceramics came
to Sukhothai through Chinese potters brought back from a
mission during the reign of King Ramkhamhaeng has been
disproven. Nevertheless, ceramics were certainly a thriving
export of the kingdom since the early 14th century. The first
flask-shaped kilns were built in Sukhothai itself, outside the
city wall, but around 1350 the craft moved to three main sites
near Si Satchanalai, where superior clay was available. Water
jars, bowls, jarlets, covered boxes and numerous other items
were produced in bulk, mostly for export to the Philippines,
Indonesia and Borneo; the glazes were equally varied, ranging
from dark brown to sea-green celadon.

WAT PHRA SI RATANA MAHATHAT ★

Located just a mile from Si Satchanalai, in the village of
Chalieng, Wat Phra Si Ratana Mahathat is one of the most
remarkable Sukhothai-style temples, believed to
date from the 13th century but restored and altered
during the Ayutthaya period. The temple complex is
aligned on an east-west axis and consists of several
ruined buildings, a large Sinhalese-style chedi, and a
magnificent prang showing Khmer influence.
Among the images are a large seated Buddha and a
standing Buddha partially imbedded in the ground;
the walls of a sanctuary near the prang are decorated with very fine stucco reliefs that include a
beautiful walking Buddha.

FISH MOTIF
One of the
characteristic motifs
on bowls and dishes
produced during the
Sukhothai period is
that of a gracefully
curving fish, drawn in
profile. Sometimes
surrounded by flower
and leaf patterns, the
fish has an appealing
light-hearted quality,
appealing to the eyes.

257

A bout 35 miles away, Phitsanulok is often used as a meeting base for visitors to Sukhothai. It is an almost entirely new provincial capital, as much of the old town burned down in the 1970's.

PHRA BUDDHA CHINARAJ
Such is the fame of Wat Mahathat's Phra Buddha Chinaraj that many replicas have been made for other temples in the country. The most noted was enshrined by King Rama V at Wat Benchama-bopit (the Marble Temple), the last royal monastery to be built in Bangkok at the beginning of the present century ● 93.

FLOATING HOUSES

Along the Nan River that flows through Phitsanulok, there can still be seen many of the floating houses and shops that were once characteristic of all Thai towns on waterways, including Bangkok. Some of the floating houses have been converted by their enterprising owners into restaurants where visitors can enjoy their meals and watch life go by on the river ● 86.

WAT MAHATHAT

Wat Mahathat, more formally known as Wat Phra Si Ratana Mahathat, is the most important temple in Phitsanulok and well known throughout the country; thanks to its large compound, it escaped serious damage from the fire that destroyed many buildings nearby. Its dominant feature is a gilded, Khmer-style prang, built during the Ayutthaya period, and the doors of the main sanctuary are beautifully decorated with inlaid mother-of-pearl designs. Surrounding the prang is a cloister that also contains the main sanctuary flanked by two chapels. The principal Buddha image, a majestic seated bronze figure known as Phra Buddha Chinaraj and dating from the late Sukhothai period, is one of the most revered in Thailand. On either side of the altar where the majestic bronze image sits are numerous other Buddhas, while the wall behind is beautifully decorated with paintings of gilded angels and floral motifs.

The North

"The city of Zimmé, which lies 430 yards to the west of the river, is divided into two parts, the one embracing the other, like a letter L, on the south and east sides. The inner city faces the cardinal points, and is walled and moated all round. The inner city contains the palace of the head king, the residences of many of the nobility and wealthy men, and numerous religious buildings. In the outer city, which is peopled chiefly by the descendants of captives, the houses are packed closer together than in the inner one, the gardens are smaller, the religious buildings are fewer, and the population is more dense. The roads in both cities are laid out at right angles to each other; no rubbish is allowed to be placed outside the gardens of the houses, which are palisaded; water is led into the town from a stream flowing from Loi Soo Tayp (Doi Suthep); the floors of the houses are all raised six or eight feet from the ground; and the whole place has an air of trim neatness about it."

Holt S. Hallett,
A Thousand Miles on an Elephant,
1890.

Appealing in both culture and scenery, the Chiang Mai valley is one of the most popular Thai destinations. It may no longer be the remote Shangri-La described by early visitors – who had to journey for weeks by river and elephant to reach it – but it still possesses a beguiling blend of ancient ruins, local crafts and continuing traditions.

HISTORY

Once the cultural, religious and political center of a northern kingdom known as Lanna Thai, Chiang Mai (once known as Zimmé) was founded in 1297 by King Mengrai, who had previously established the city of Chiang Rai and also conquered the old Mon capital of Haripunchai (Lamphun today) ● *38–9*. A northern legend says Mengrai had the assistance of two allies, King Ramkhamhaeng of Sukhothai and King Ngam Muang of Phayao, and that the site was selected because an auspicious assembly of rare animals had been seen there: two white sambar deer, two white barking deer, and a white mouse with a family of five. Over 90,000 laborers were supposedly involved in the construction of the city. By the time of Mengrai's death in 1317, he had set up a well-organized kingdom that extended from the northern frontiers of Sukhothai to the southern provinces of China, as well as a dynasty which would rule the north for another 200 years. The original walled city of Chiang Mai, containing the royal palace, noble houses and several important temples, was modified often by subsequent rulers. Chiang Mai's golden age came in the reign of King Tilokaraja (1441–87), during which a major Buddhist conference was held there in 1455 and numerous splendid temples were built. A period of instability followed, marked by wars with Ayutthaya and Burma. By 1558 Chiang Mai had fallen to the King of Pegu, and most of Lanna Thai remained under Burmese control for the next two centuries. King Taksin of Thonburi ● *39*, who expelled the Burmese after the fall of Ayutthaya, recaptured Chiang Mai in 1776 but shortly afterward the impoverished city was abandoned for 20 years, its population being moved to Lampang. It was revived by King Rama I in 1796, with a son of the Prince of Lampang as ruler, and remained semi-autonomous until the late 19th century. The last Prince of Chiang Mai died in 1939, by which time the city was merely a provincial capital under control of the central government.

> "The woodwork of the temples is beautifully carved and gilded, and richly inlaid with glass and tinsel of various colours."
>
> Holt S. Hallett

THAI TEMPLE DÉCOR

Anyone who spends even a short time exploring Thailand's religious buildings ● *94–7* is struck by the Thai penchant for elaborate decoration. Nowhere has this fondness been more abundantly realized than in Chiang Mai, where it is supported by a wide variety of traditional skills that have been handed down through generations and that remain vividly alive today. Most temples, and private homes as well, are adorned by a profusion of splendid wood-carvings, large and small, on gables, lintels, doorways, windows, columns and roof eaves, often further embellished by bright gilding and colored-glass mosaics. In addition there are murals depicting both religious and secular subjects, intricate designs in gold-and-black lacquer, stucco decorations, and numerous figures of mythological creatures, from fierce guardian *naga,* or sacred serpents, to serene divinities. Techniques brought by Burmese artisans, such as gilded metal filigree and embossed lacquer panels, add to the overall sense of richness that distinguishes even lesser-known temples in the northern city. Relatively few are allowed to fall into disrepair; the desire to earn merit through donations and other forms of assistance ensures that most undergo frequent renovations, thus maintaining their splendid appearance.

THE OLD AND THE NEW
Chiang Mai in the 1940's (above), and the city today (right). If some of the main streets have lost their charm due to modern construction, many smaller ones still to recall a more leisurely past, with picturesque temples and bungalows set in shady compounds among fruit trees.

🕐 Five days

ROAD TRAFFIC
Dodge through the cars on a bicycle, a motorcycle or a tuk-tuk, which can all be hired by the day.

NAWARAT BRIDGE
The first bridge built across the Ping River in Chiang Mai was the Nawarat, which leads into Tapae Road. Originally a covered

structure made of wood, it was replaced by the present one in the 1950's. Five other bridges now span the river in the city area.

CHIANG MAI TODAY

Modern Chiang Mai, with a population of around only 1,500,000, is Thailand's fifth-largest city, after Bangkok and Khon Kaen. Its center, just east of the reconstructed Tapae Gate, is Tapae Road, especially around Charoen Prathet and Chang Klan roads, where many hotels, guest houses, and shops are located. The most fashionable residential area – as well as the site of several new hotels and Chiang Mai University – is along Huay Kaeo Road leading to Doi Suthep, the low mountain that overlooks the city. While progress has come in the form of unsightly high-rise buildings, traffic congestion and air pollution, numerous Buddhist temples and shady side streets offer ample opportunities to discover the city's fabled charms.

NIGHT BAZAAR. Originating as a cluster of stalls on Chang Klan Road and conveniently located near several hotels, the night bazaar now consists of a permanent structure but also has many sidewalk vendors who offer a variety of things for sale every evening from sundown until about 11pm. Most of the local specialties are here: woodcrafts, lacquerware, silverware, antiques, sausages, fruits, fancy clothes and garments.

WALLS AND MOATS. The original layout of Chiang Mai was altered by several of King Mengrai's successors. The walls and moat that can be seen today, for example, date only from the early 19th century; and the Ping River, which was once a considerable distance away, has changed its course and now flows through the middle of town.

264

> "There is an excellent path to Chiang Mai which elephants
> can follow, arriving there in nine marches."
>
> An Englishman's Siamese Journals, 1890–93

THE PING RIVER. Flowing through Chiang Mai, the Ping River is one of the four major northern waterways, and stretches for over 350 miles. Until the construction of the Bhumibol Dam across the Ping near the town of Tak in 1964, it was possible to go most of the way by boat from Chiang Mai to Nakhon Sawan and then on the Chao Phraya to Bangkok. The Bhumibol Dam is one of Thailand's largest and generates electricity for Bangkok and many of the country's provinces.

FESTIVALS

Chiang Mai not only celebrates more festivals than anywhere else in Thailand but does so with an enthusiasm that attracts tourists and native visitors from all over the country. Dates of the festivals may vary from year to year since some celebrations are based on the lunar calendar, so it is best to check beforehand when planning a trip. The Chiang Mai Flower Festival, replete with colorful parades of blossom-covered floats, takes place in February, while Songkran ● *73,* the traditional Thai New Year, is celebrated for a full three days beginning April 13 and blends solemn religious ceremonies with riotous throwing of water on passers-by. Late October or November brings Loy Krathong ● *49, 73,* the magical water festival, when by the light of a full moon thousands of little lotus-shaped boats are set adrift on the Ping River and all sorts of activities take place on land. The year ends with the Winter Fair, three days of shows, sports and competitions, and a popular beauty pageant to select Miss Chiang Mai. In addition to these major functions, innumerable smaller ones that are equally high-spirited are held in surrounding towns. In January, for instance, the little umbrella village of Bor Sang, which is approximately 3 miles from San Khamphaeng, stages a festive fair along its main street, while in August the annual harvest of longan – a highly prized lychee-like fruit known in Thai as *lamyai* – is celebrated by the people of Lamphun. The paper umbrellas made in Bor Sang are waxed and painted in vivid colors with flowers and scenes from folk tales. Beauty contests are an essential element of any northern Thai festival, large or small, resulting sometimes in such singularly colorful events as the selection of a Miss Garlic.

A restored section of the walls near Suan Prung Gate (top) and the banks of the Ping River (above).

The traditional way of entertaining guests in Chiang Mai is with a *khantoke* dinner – *khan* meaning "bowl" and *toke* being a low round table made of lacquer or rattan. Guests sit on the floor around the table and help themselves to various dishes, generally eaten with glutinous rice, a specialty of the northern region.

An aerial view of Wat Phra Singh in about 1930.

WAT PHRA SINGH

One of Chiang Mai's most important sanctuaries, Wat Phra Singh was founded in 1345 by King Pha Yu of the Mengrai Dynasty to enshrine the ashes of his father, King Kham Fu. The lofty main viharn, however, was built in 1925 and has recently been restored. Of greater interest is the older Viharn Laikam on the left, perhaps the finest building that survives in Chiang Mai, built in late Lanna style in 1806 or 1811 ● *94, 98*. This structure houses the famous Phra Buddha Singh, an early Lanna bronze image brought from Chiang Rai in 1400; the head of the original image was stolen in 1922 and the present one is a replica. The walls of the viharn are decorated with some fine murals painted in the late 19th century. Also notable in the compound is a wooden bot with beautiful stucco decorations and a graceful, elevated library adorned with carved wood and glass mosaics.

WAT PHRA SINGH PAINTINGS
The late-19th-century mural paintings at Wat Phra Singh, believed to be the work of a local artist named Jek Seng, are the best-preserved in Chiang Mai. In addition to scenes from Jataka stories, they vividly depict everyday northern life a century ago, from children's games to interior decoration ● *104–5.*

OTHER TEMPLES WITHIN THE WALLS

WAT CHEDI LUANG. Located on Phra Pokklao Road, Wat Chedi Luang is noted for its enormous ruined chedi. The structure was originally built in 1401, enlarged and raised to a height of 300 feet by King Tilokaraja, and destroyed by an earthquake in 1545. What remains has remnants of beautiful stucco figures flanking the steps and a seated Buddha in a niche. Also in the compound, to the left of the entrance, is an ancient gum tree, below which a small building shelters Chiang Mai's City Pillar; according to local legend, King Mengrai, founder of the city, was killed by a bolt of lightning near this spot in 1317.

WAT PAN TAO. Near Wat Chedi Luang on Phra Pokklao Road, Wat Pan Tao has one of the most beautiful Lanna-style viharns, with walls made wholly of wood panels and a roof resting entirely on wooden columns. The doors and windows of the viharn are decorated with exceptionally fine gilded stucco work.

MENGRAI SHRINE. Located across from Wat Pan Tao, at the corner of the Ratchadamnoen intersection, the Mengrai Shrine honors the founder of Chiang Mai and the dynasty that ruled the Lanna kingdom for 600 years. Local devotees regularly bring offerings to the shrine.

WAT PUAK HONG. Not far from Suan Prung Gate, on a lane off Samlan Road, Wat Puak Hong has an unusual chedi in the form of a round, stepped pyramid dating from the 16th or 17th century. Decorated niches on the chedi shelter images of meditating Buddhas.

The shape of the chedi of Wat Puak Hong is probably inspired by that of Chinese pagodas. Although unusual, it is not the only one in the north; a similar one can be seen at Wat Rampoeng, just outside Chiang Mai.

WAT CHIANG MAN. Located on Ratchaphanikai Road, in the northeastern corner of the old city, Wat Chiang Man is believed to be the first temple built by King Mengrai ● *38* ▲ *262* on the spot where he camped when Chiang Mai was being constructed. Most of its buildings, however, are of more recent date, the chedi itself probably being a 15th-century reconstruction of the first one ● *98*.

A 19th-century wooden bot contains an interesting collection of bronze images, while two more recent viharns enshrine a number of revered images, among them the tiny crystal Phra Buddha Setang Khamanai, which probably dates from the 7th century and is believed to have the power to bring rain.

TEMPLES ALONG TAPAE ROAD

WAT SAEN FANG. Just off Tapae Road, at the intersection with Kamphaengdin Road, a lane flanked with *naga* (sacred serpents) leads to Wat Saen Fang. Burmese influence is strong in its tall chedi, adorned with golden parasols, a large building where the monks reside, and a recently restored viharn resplendent in fresh red and gold paint.

MENGRAI IMAGE
Though a modern temple made entirely of cement, Wat Mengrai, off Ratchamanka Road, Lane 6, is of interest because of its ornate stuccoed entrance gate and a Buddha image cast during King Mengrai's reign and believed to resemble the first ruler.

WAT BUPPARAM Facing Wat Saen Fang on Tapae Road, Wat Bupparam is a blend of Burmese and Lanna styles. The facade of the main viharn, for example, has Burmese-style arches under a Lanna roof, while another small wooden viharn with stucco decorations is classic Lanna and enshrines three large Buddha images ▲ 161.

WAT MAHARAM. This temple contains a chedi and a viharn in Burmese style while the bot is Lanna. Of particular interest are the witty caricatured figurines of mythological beasts that stand on the wall facing the road.

WAT BUA KROK LUANG

Across the Ping River, on a side lane off the road to San Khamphaeng, Wat Bua Krok Luang has a viharn containing the second most important mural paintings in Chiang Mai, after those in Wat Phra Singh. These were painted more than a century ago and show the life of the Buddha and scenes from the Jataka tales.

WAT UMONG

Wat Umong, at the end of a long, winding lane off Suthep Road, contains underground cells for meditation and is one of Chiang Mai's oldest monasteries. Of the original stucco decorations, only a few fragments of *naga* and the guardian giants known as *yaksa* remain. The chedi, which rises above the old meditation cells, is a recently built monument, though the cells themselves contain faint traces of the oldest surviving paintings in early Lanna style, dating from the 15th century. The new monastery in the compound is popular with Western Buddhists, who are welcome to join in the retreat and meditation.

WAT CHED YOD

Also known as Wat Potharam Maha Viharn, Wat Ched Yod is located outside the city walls on the highway near the Chiang Mai branch of the National Museum. Its principal feature is a chedi unlike any other in the north, composed of seven chedis on a laterite base with a barrel-vaulted chamber inside. The shape was possibly inspired by the Indian Mahabodhi temple of Bodhgaya or by

Mon replicas in Burma. Most northerners are convinced of the former source and claim that it was built by King Tilokaraja in 1455 for a major Buddhist gathering. The fine stucco decorations on the walls represent 70 celestial deities.

WAT KUTAO

Wat Kutao's unusual chedi is probably the main reason for visiting the temple, which is not very far from the National Stadium. Showing Chinese influence ● *92*, it consists of a series of hemispheres superimposed in descending order of size. Wat Kutao was supposedly built in 1613 to hold the ashes of a Burmese ruler of Chiang Mai.

WAT SUAN DOK

About half a mile west of Suan Dok Gate is Wat Suan Dok, the "Flower Garden Temple," which was built on the site of a royal garden. The temple's huge, bell-shaped chedi, similar to those in Sukhothai, was erected at the end of the 14th century by King Ku Na in honor of a well-known monk named Maha Tera Sumana. The latter had come from Sri Lanka to teach in Chiang Mai and supposedly lived in the garden. Near the chedi is a complex of tombs and other structures containing the remains of Chiang Mai's royal family. Wat Suan Dok is the scene of a major religious ceremony during Songkran ● *73*, which is the traditional Thai New Year's celebration in mid-April.

BURMESE INFLUENCE
Many temples in Chiang Mai reflect traces of Burmese influence. This is due to the immigrant carpenters and craftsmen from Burma who, in the late 19th century, came to work for British timber firms and also took part in temple construction. The use of Burmese clothing in murals reflects a tradition of idealizing heroes and other noble characters by using the attire of rulers, who were Burmese at the time ● *98*.

A ROYAL CEMETERY
Behind Wat Suan Dok are the funeral chedis of the royal family of Chiang Mai.

The themes of traditional Thai woodcarving were more often than not religious. In the early 1980's a ban on the

export of religious Thai items was enforced. Wood-carvers turned to Burma as a source of inspiration, since Burmese religious items were not included in the official ban.

Partly because of skills handed down from generation to generation and partly because of its long relative isolation from the changing fashions of Bangkok, Chiang Mai has preserved its strong crafts tradition, with skills that have remained unchanged for centuries. These constitute an important aspect of its attraction for modern visitors as well as a profitable export industry for many local producers.

WOODCARVING

Considering the extensive forests of teak and other hardwoods that once covered the northern mountains, it is not surprising that woodcarving ranks high among the local skills, as can be clearly seen in the splendid gables, panels and roof supports that decorate almost every temple in the region. Though wood is scarcer today, craftsmen still produce a wide range of furniture, animal figures, trays and other wooden items. The largest concentration of dealers is at Bantawai, off the highway to Mae Hong Son.

POTTERY

Local potters make a handsome array of lightly glazed earthenware water jars and pots used in most households; according to northern tradition, jars of cool water were placed outside gates for the relief of thirsty strangers who passed by. Celadon pottery production – which moved to the northern town of San Khamphaeng after the collapse of Sukhothai and eventually died out there – has also been revived by several local companies whose handsome tableware, vases and lamp bases are being exported and sold throughout the world.

LACQUERWARE

CELADON WARE
Pale blue-green celadon is one of Chiang Mai's most popular crafts. The Mengrai Kilns, started by a former British consul who settled in the city, produce fine replicas of old designs, both Thai and Chinese, which are now being exported and sold in leading shops all over the world.

Lacquerware, which probably came to Thailand from Burma, is made by applying successive coats of translucent colored lacquer to a wood or bamboo base, then embellishing it with designs. The most popular decorations are gold-and-black lacquer paintings, either figures or traditional motifs. Many household objects, from simple bowls to large cabinets, are made by this ancient process, which can be observed at the cottage factories in the Chiang

Mai area, especially on the road to San Khamphaeng.

UMBRELLAS

The small village of Bor Sang ▲ 265, on the San Khamphaeng Road, is almost entirely devoted to the production of umbrellas. These are made of handmade paper stretched over a frame of bamboo, then lightly lacquered to make them relatively waterproof and adorned with colorful flower patterns by artists. The umbrellas come in varying sizes, from tiny to huge, and are popular as souvenirs or as sunshades on patios and terraces.

TEXTILES

Northern weavers are noted for the quality of their silks and cottons, as well as for their skill at embroidering them with bands of brocade and woven designs. These are traditionally produced in sarong-length pieces for women, the silk being reserved for special occasions and the cotton for everyday wear; a cotton sarong for men, called a *phakoma* ● 56, comes in plaid patterns. The villages of San Khamphaeng and Pasang, near Chiang Mai, are noted for their weaving, and a wide selection is also available at the night bazaar.

SILVERWARE

Even though silver is not mined in Thailand, silverware has long been a Chiang Mai specialty, particularly bowls with intricate *repoussée* designs that are used in numerous ceremonies. The main community of silversmiths is based at Wualai Road, near Chiang Mai Gate, where one of the characteristic sounds is the constant clangor of hammer on metal. In addition to the classic bowls, more contemporary items like trays, teapots and tableware are also produced. In former days, the silver was generally obtained by melting down old coins from British India and Burma. Some of the hill tribes still produce their distinctive silver jewelry by this method, but the Chiang Mai artisans now import their silver from abroad. The price of a silver item is based not so much on the workmanship as on the quality of the metal.

BETEL BOXES
A set of beautifully crafted betel-nut boxes was an accessory found in every aristocratic household and many ordinary ones as well, consisting of a lacquerware tray and assorted containers used in the once-universal ritual of betel chewing.

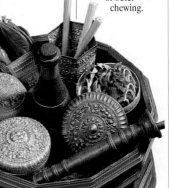

DOI SUTHEP

Overlooking Chiang Mai is the 5,283-foot mountain called Doi Suthep, which is part of the twin-peaked Doi Suthep–Doi Pui National Park. There was no proper road up the mountain until the mid-1930's, when a monk named Phra Khruba Srivijaya initiated the construction of one, mainly with volunteer labor, to help pilgrims who wanted to visit the famous Wat Phra That Doi Suthep near the summit. The winding road offers spectacular views of the city below and considerably lower temperatures even in the hottest months. The National Park headquarters are just beyond the temple car park.

WAT PHRA THAT DOI SUTHEP. According to legend, holy relics discovered during the reign of King Ku Na (1355–85) were placed in a howdah on the back of a white elephant, which carried them to Wat Suan Dok. The elephant was then set free to wander at will and it climbed Doi Suthep to the site of Wat Phra That, where it dropped dead. The present complex dates from the 16th century and was expanded or restored several times later. A flight of 290 steps, bordered by a *naga* balustrade, leads up from the parking area to the temple, which has beautifully decorated buildings and a Lanna-style chedi covered with engraved gold plates, flanked by four ornamental umbrellas.

PHUPING PALACE. Built in 1972, Phuping Palace is located about 2½ miles beyond Wat Phra That Doi Suthep and serves as the royal family's northern residence. The buildings are closed to the public, but when no members of the family are present the extensive gardens are open. January is the best month to see of the numerous temperate-zone plants and trees in flower.

GOLDEN CHEDI
The famous golden chedi of Wat Phra That Doi Suthep, 79 feet high and 39 feet across at its base, is covered with engraved gold plates; on the platform around it are four ornamental umbrellas, brightly gilded and adorned with beautiful filigree decorations, while the walls of the surrounding cloister are painted with murals from the life of the Buddha.

CHIANG MAI ZOOLOGICAL PARK

The Chiang Mai Zoological Park, near the foot of Doi Suthep, began as the private collection of Harold Young, an American working in Chiang Mai, and was taken over by the government in 1965 after his death. It has more than 500 animals in an attractively landscaped setting.

SAN KHAMPHAENG

The 8-mile road from Chiang Mai to the village of San Khamphaeng is lined for most of its length with shops selling and producing various handicrafts and also passes the Bor Sang umbrella village ▲ *271*. San Khamphaeng itself is famous for its handwoven silks and cottons, sold at many shops along the main street.

> "Fine fruit trees, and beautiful bamboo clumps in the gardens bordering the road, form a magnificent and shady avenue."
>
> Holt S. Hallett

HANDICRAFT VILLAGES

Several interesting villages devoted to handicraft production lie on or just off the Chiang Mai-Chom Thong highway. In Muang Kung the people make pottery for household use, while villagers at Hang Dong specialize at weaving bamboo into attractive baskets ● *74–5*. In the once-sleepy village of Bantawai, there are hundreds of woodcarvers, as well as modern facilities for packing and shipping their products all over the world.

WOODCRAFT
"Woodcarving is a favorite occupation, in which some technical artistic skill is displayed, and the native chiefs and some of the princes constantly employ men to make ornaments. Carved scroll work for doors, posts, household articles, is in much request."

Carl Bock

DOI INTHANON NATIONAL PARK

Covering an area of 193 square miles, this scenic park can be visited on day trips from Chiang Mai. The park includes the 8,465-foot Doi Inthanon, Thailand's highest mountain. At the top is a chedi containing the ashes of the last ruler of Chiang Mai. Pilgrims wishing to pay homage originally had to go up on foot or on ponies. During the 1970's, despite the protests of conservationists, the army built a 28-mile road to the summit, opening it to a greater number of visitors. However, the park still has many unspoiled trails, superb waterfalls (such as the Mae Ya falls in the southern part), beautiful mountain butterflies and 383 species of birds.

WAT SI CHOM THONG

Less than a mile beyond the turn-off to Doi Inthanon is Wat Si Chom Thong. It contains a Lanna-style chedi ● *98* dating from the 15th century and sheathed in brass plates, as well as a more recent Burmese-style chedi. The viharn, built in 1516 and restored in 1817, is beautifully decorated with intricate woodcarvings.

CATTLE MARKET
About a mile beyond the village of San Pa Thong on the Chiang Mai-Chom Thong highway, a colorful *kadwua*, or cattle market, is held on Saturday mornings, perhaps the largest of its kind in the north. Besides cattle and buffaloes, a wide range of other items are on sale, from exotic foods to herbal medicines.

WAT PHRA THAT HARIPUNCHAI
The compound was originally built to face the river, with the entrance at the back of the temple. There is a mixture of styles, as is often the case in Thailand.

A new expressway can now be used for the trip to Lamphun, 16 miles south of Chiang Mai, although the old road is still the more attractive of the two; some people, indeed, regard it as the most beautiful in the north, lined as it is with stately trees growing to 66 feet tall and meeting at the top to form a cool canopy. On the way, it passes large plantations of *lamyai*, a fruit much prized in the north, and the basket-weaving village of Saraphi.

HISTORY

SERENITY
The tranquil terracotta face (right) is on display in the museum opposite Wat Phra That Haripunchai.

Lamphun, now a quiet town on the Kwang River, was once an important cultural center. Founded in AD 660, it was the capital of the Mon kingdom of Haripunchai and remained independent until it was incorporated into the Lanna kingdom by King Mengrai in 1281. The walls and moat that can be seen today date only from the early 19th century, but a number of fine temples attest to the city's ancient glory ● *38–9*.

WORLD'S LARGEST GONG
One of the most popular attractions in Wat Phra That Haripunchai is an enormous bronze gong. Cast in 1860, this is supposedly the largest gong in the world ● *63*.

WAT PHRA THAT HARIPUNCHAI

One of the major temples in the north, both historically and architecturally, Wat Phra That Haripunchai, facing the Kwang River, was founded in 1044 by King Athitayaraj of Haripunchai on the site of a former royal palace. A modern viharn, built in 1925 to replace the original, houses the Phra Chao Thongthip, a Chiang Saen-style bronze Buddha image; to the right of the viharn is an enormous bronze gong, while to the left is a Lanna-style repository for religious scriptures built in the early 19th century. The most prominent feature of the temple complex – and the most sacred part – is a 165-foot-tall Lanna-style chedi built in 1467, sheathed in copper and adorned with a gold umbrella. Slightly behind this monument is the Suwanna Chedi, a stepped-pyramid form of chedi, dating from 1418 and a replica of one in Wat

Chamadevi, also in Lamphun. Elsewhere in the compound are a viharn enshrining a standing Buddha known as Phra Chao Tan Jai and a pavilion containing four Buddha footprints, one inside another.
MUSEUMS. Some of the many Buddha images presented to Wat Phra That Haripunchai have been been placed in a small museum within the temple grounds. Opposite Wat Phra That Haripunchai is a small branch of the National Museum. It contains a fine collection of bronze Buddha images, together with stucco and terracotta figures of the early Haripunchai period found during archeological excavations in the area.

WAT CHAMADEVI

Also known as Wat Ku Kut, Wat Chamadevi contains Lamphun's oldest monuments: two brick chedis decorated with stucco figures of the Buddha. According to the noted authority Jean Boisselier, these ruins date from 1218 and are among the last surviving examples of Dvaravati-period (7th–11th century) architecture. The larger chedi, Sat Mahal Pasada, is in the form of a stepped pyramid 69 feet high and 51 feet wide and was possibly inspired by a similar monument at Polonnaruwa in Sri Lanka; it served as the model for similar structures elsewhere in the region. The other small chedi is octagonal and dates from the same period.

WIANG KUNGAM

Wiang Kungam, which can be visited on an excursion to Lamphun, is a recently unearthed old city built by King Mengrai shortly before he founded Chiang Mai. He lived there for six years before he decided the site was inconvenient and moved across the river to a new one. Among the temples in the area, Wat Chedi Liem has a tall chedi – it is similar to the one at Wat Chamadevi – which was restored at the turn of this century with the addition of Burmese-style decorations. Wat Chan Kham has a spirit house where the soul of King Mengrai himself is believed to reside.

MCKEAN INSTITUTE

Not far from Wiang Kungam, on a small island in the Ping River, is the McKean Institute, where leprosy patients are treated. It was founded in 1908 by Dr James W. McKean, a Presbyterian missionary, and has become internationally recognized for its approach to the once-dreaded disease.

Amongst the ruins of Wiang Kungam, the shapes of some chedis can be seen.

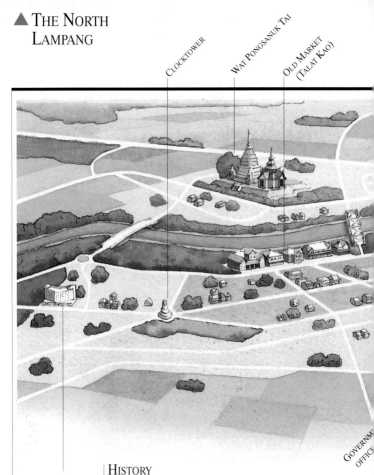

CLOCKTOWER

WAT PONGSANUK TAI

OLD MARKET
(TALAT KAO)

GOVERNMENT
OFFICE

TIP CHANG
HOTEL

HISTORY

Located in the valley of the Wang River, a tributary of the
Ping, Lampang is the second-largest town in northern
Thailand. Its long history goes back to the 7th century, when
it was supposedly founded by a son of the Haripunchai queen,
Chamadevi ▲ 275, who had established a
Mon kingdom in the north. Originally
known as Kelang Nakhon, it had
four outlying fortified satellite
settlements, of which only Wat
Phra That Lampang Luang still
exists ● 94. Lampang theoretically
became part of the Lanna kingdom
under Mengrai, though in many ways it

The
distinctive
style of Lanna
temples ▲ 94–5 is
captured in this old
engraving based on a
sketch by Carl Bock,
who visited the town
in the early 1880's.

was ruled autonomously; like Chiang Mai, it
was occupied by the Burmese for three centuries. The specific
location of Kelang Nakhon is unknown, but the town that
thrived in the Lanna period was on the opposite bank of the
river from the main part of today's city. At the beginning of
the 20th century, Lampang was
a center of the northern teak
industry, with a population of
more than 20,000 and some
4,000 working elephants; it was
also visited yearly by ten
caravans from the Shan states
of Burma, bringing goods that

Lampang women
during a local
festival.

⊕ Two days

...ranged from lacquerware to opium. Despite the less appealing cement constructions of recent years, this era is still reflected in a number of fine old teak mansions in the area of the old market along the river.

OLD MARKET

Lampang's old market, known as the *talat kao*, was located along the river and still preserves much of its former charm. The shophouses display a mixture of Chinese, Burmese and Western influences, and many are adorned with Victorian fretwork imported by Burmese carpenters.

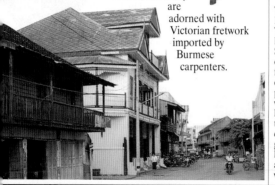

HORSE-DRAWN CARTS
The symbol of Lampang, at least to Thai visitors, is the horse-drawn cart. Such carts were originally imported from England in the early years of the present century and, while they are no longer as common as they once were, enough remain to give the town a leisurely ambience and offer a pleasant way to explore it.

MOSAIC CEILING
"The only note of incongruity," wrote Reginald Le May in 1926, "was a series of small gilt angel figures (of the Raphael type), pendent from the ceiling. How easily and only too well they learn from the West!" Such figures of cupids as well as horses and soldiers of Victorian inspiration had been widely used by Mandalay artists since the early days of the British occupation of Burma.

WIANG LUANG LAKON
Each year, usually in February, a festive parade called *Wiang Luang Lakon* is staged in Lampang. This celebrates the splendors of Queen Chamadevi's 7th-century court, with hundreds of participants in colorful period dress.

WAT PHRA KEO DON TAO

The most important temple in Lampang, Wat Phra Keo Don Tao supposedly once enshrined the famous Emerald Buddha, which is now housed at Wat Phra Keo in Bangkok ▲ *148, 170*. This image, according to legend, was being brought from its place of discovery in Chiang Rai to Chiang Mai in 1436 when the elephant bearing it stopped in Lampang and refused to proceed; it therefore remained in the town until 1468, when King Tilokaraja finally took it to Chiang Mai. The name of the temple, however, comes from another image, the Phra Keo Don Tao, which was housed there before it was moved to Wat Phra That Lampang Luang. The only original structure remaining in the temple is a 165-foot chedi, reputed to enshrine a hair of the Buddha, while the most interesting building is a Burmese-style structure built in 1909 as a donation by a Thai prince. The latter has a three-tier roof, elaborate mirror mosaics and superb woodcarvings. The principal viharn, Phra Chao Thong Tip, was constructed in 1930 by the venerated northern monk Khruba Srivijaya and contains a fine Buddha image. A small museum in the temple

> "This country of Lanna…makes the stranger feel that, if he must be exiled from his native shores, he could not find a land of greater charm and sympathy to spend his days."

Reginald Le May

compound displays a collection of Lanna-style furniture.

WAT SUCHADA. Adjacent to Wat Phra Keo Don Tao, Wat Suchada is regarded as part of the same monastery. Built by residents of Chiang Saen who were forcibly resettled after their hometown was destroyed at the beginning of the 19th century, it has a chedi and two viharns in late Lanna style; the main viharn houses a large brick and stucco Buddha and has some beautiful lacquer decorations.

OTHER OLD LANNA TEMPLES

WAT SENG MUANG MA ★. Also one of the Chiang Saen temples, Wat Seng Muang Ma is located on Thamma Oo Road. It contains a small but well-proportioned chedi, as well as a viharn that enshrines a large Buddha image and has some interesting paintings on wood panels dating from the turn of the century (above).

WAT HUA KUANG. Like Wat Suchada, this was built by resettled Chiang Saen people and has an interesting old viharn in late Lanna style, as well as Chiang Saen images and manuscripts on the art of casting bronze that the displaced people brought with them.

WAT PONGSANUK TAI ★. Located on Pongsanuk Road in Wiang Neua, the area occupied by the old Lanna town of Lampang, Wat Pongsanuk Tai is regarded by many as the most charming temple in the town. Within a tree-filled new monastery is an old one, almost intact, in Lanna style on a high platform that can be reached by flights of steps on each side. A Lanna chedi ● 95, 98 is covered with copper sheets and also on the platform is a splendid open-sided structure with a tiered roof and a mondop (right) in old Lanna style and a newer viharn containing a reclining Buddha image. All the buildings are gracefully proportioned and elegantly decorated.

KU YA SUDHA ★. "The Grotto of Grandmother Sudha" is the local name of the gatehouse of a now-destroyed monastery on Wiang Neua Road. Decorated with deities in stucco, it dates from the 15th century and is one of the oldest examples of Lanna art.

HO AMOK. The Octagonal Tower is one of the few parts of Lampang's ancient fortifications that remain today. Located in the modern part of the new town, on the west bank of the Wang river, it served as a lookout and is today a venue of a grand shamanistic ceremony in honor of the spirits of the town.

CHIANG SAEN REFUGEES
At the beginning of the 19th century, with the support of King Rama I of Bangkok, the Chiang Mai ruler, Kawila ● 39, launched a determined effort to increase the population of Lampang and Chiang Mai, depleted by so many years of war. In 1804, he destroyed Chiang Saen and resettled the inhabitants in Lampang. This group was responsible for the construction of a number of temples and the casting of major Buddha images in the city.

CEREMONIAL GATES
Monasteries in the north usually had very imposing ceremonial gates, richly adorned with stucco figures. With the disappearance of the wooden temple buildings over the years, these are the only structures that now survive ● 95.

279

WAT PRATU PONG ★ Not far from the Ho Amok and near a remaining part of the old city wall is Wat Pratu Pong, which, although slightly restored, is still one of the best examples of classic northern style. The gable is decorated with a fine woodcarving of a mythological creature with a serpent emerging from its mouth, while the doors of the temple are also exquisitely carved.

BURMESE TEMPLES

After the Burmese Occupation, many Burmese came to the north in the late 19th century to work in the timber trade and some became prosperous resident businessmen. The latter built or restored numerous temples ▲ 289, which partly accounts for the strong Burmese element in northern architecture ● 94–5, 98.

WAT PHA FANG Located opposite the office of Thai International Airways on Airport Road, Wat Pha Fang is one of several temples in Lampang that show a strong Burmese influence, even though it has been recently restored. Its chedi, for example, is typically Burmese, while each of the chapels surrounding the temple contains an image in Mandalay style. The bot, which is located near the chedi, is more elaborately decorated than the viharn.

WAT CHEDI SAO. Located a few miles to the left off the road to Jae Hom, Wat Chedi Sao – "Temple of the Twenty Chedis" in northern Thai – is a charming country monastery. The whitewashed chedis after which the temple is named are built in a blend of Thai and Burmese styles, and the compound also contains a remarkable collection of fanciful statues added by imaginative abbots in recent

EARLY TOURISTS IN LAMPANG
Unfortunately destroyed by fire early in 1991, Wat Sri Chum, one of Lampang's Burmese-style temples, contained some fine lacquered wall paintings. Among the subjects depicted were foreigners, shown traveling by automobile through the forest to visit the temple and pausing at a local refreshment stand.

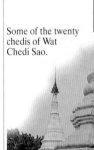

Some of the twenty chedis of Wat Chedi Sao.

years. These include the twelve animals associated cyclically with various years in the Chinese calendar as well as figures from Buddhist legends. The principal image in the viharn is a Lanna Buddha made of brick and stucco.

TEMPLES OF LAMPANG LUANG

Located just about 12 miles from Lampang in the Kokha district, Lampang Luang was once a *wiang* (citadel) established during the early Haripunchai period. Protected by three earthen ramparts separated by moats, the site was part of a group of satellite fortresses associated with the ancient city of Kelang Nakorn.

WAT LAI HIN ★. The first temple in the Kokha district, Wat Lai Hin ● *98*, is located on high ground overlooking a stream and ricefields. The main viharn, in old Lanna style, has elaborate stucco decorations on the gable and fine lacquer-work inside, both possibly 200 years old, while the gatehouse dates probably from the 15th or 16th century.

WAT PONG YANG KOK ★. Just past Wat Phra That Lampang Luang on the road to Hang Chat, Wat Pong Yang Kok has a beautiful open wooden viharn in the old Lanna style. Inside are some famous lacquer decorations featuring a motif of the bodhi tree repeated throughout.

THE PHRA KEO DON TAO
A small jasper image believed to have magical powers, the Phra Keo Don Tao, now housed at Wat Phrathat Lampang Luang, was much coveted by northern rulers of the 15th century.

WAT PHRA THAT LAMPANG LUANG ★

Many an enchanted traveler in northern Thailand has called Wat Phra That Lampang Luang the most beautiful temple in the country. Offering a spectacular display of Lanna religious architecture ● *94–5* and decorative skills, the temple was founded in early Haripunchai times, part of a group of satellite fortresses, and contains a 165-foot chedi believed to contain genuine relics of the Buddha. This and all the most important buildings are located within a porticoed enclosure, situated on top of a hillock; the main entrance is a monumental gatehouse adorned with stucco-work. Lions and *naga* (sacred serpents), also in stucco, guard the steps. The main viharn behind the gatehouse is an open-sided structure built in 1496 and restored several times. The painting on the wooden panels below the roof eaves date from the late 19th century, but the building was actually reconstructed by Phra Khruba Srivijaya in the 1930's. It enshrines a gilded *ku* ● *94* (pagoda-like structure inside the temple) containing the presiding Buddha image (right). Also in the enclosure are a bot, a *mondop* and three viharns. The Viharn Nam Tam, is worthy of attention, as it is probably the oldest surviving Lanna building, beautifully restored to its original form. Sixteenth-century paintings were revealed during the restoration.

Lampang Luang is the main surviving example of a fortified settlement, which was built around a citadel, or *wiang*. This type of stronghold was once very common in northern Thailand, and is quite similar to those found in Europe in the Middle Ages. The ancient settlement was used for military purposes until the 18th century, when it was occupied by the Burmese. In 1736, Lampang Luang became the scene of a famous duel between the Burmese general and the Thai hero, Tip Chang, who had cleverly sneaked inside the walls through a drain to confront the enemy. Today the farming community is still clustered around the temple, which was built on high ground, though its fortifications have been dismantled. Traces of three parallel earthen ramparts – separated by two moats filled with water – can still be seen in various parts of the village.

MAIN STRUCTURES OF WAT PHRA THAT LAMPANG LUANG
1. Phra That – a chedi containing relics of the Buddha
2. Principal viharn
3. Viharn – built in 1802
4. Viharn (contemporary)
5. Viharn Nam Tam (early 16th century)
6. Viharn – reconstructed in 1967
7. Bot – built in 1924
8. *Mondop* – housing Buddha's footprint
9. Ceremonial gate-house leading to the porticoed enclosure
10. Stairways flanked by *naga*
11. Bodhi tree

Wat Phumin (above) is undoubtedly the most famous wat in Nan.

Nan can be reached from Chiang Mai by road in around four hours or by air in 45 minutes. The road trip is worthwhile since it offers an opportunity to enjoy some pleasant rural scenery – forested hills and lush, fertile valleys – and also to visit some interesting attractions, such as Phrae and Phae Muang Phi, along the way.

PHRAE

Coal mining and, until recently, logging have traditionally been the sources of Phrae's prosperity, still evident in some fine old wooden mansions and a thriving local furniture industry. Burmese influences can be seen in Wat Chom Sawan, while the most famous temple is Wat Phra That Cho Hae, atop a teak-covered hill just outside the town.

HILL TRIBES
The Phi Thong Luang, "Spirits of the Yellow Leaves," who live in the Nan area, are among the most elusive of the hill tribe groups, still following a virtually prehistoric lifestyle ● 33. Only in the 1960's was their existence confirmed by an expedition that came across some of them in their jungle hiding place. In the Nan Valley are also several hundreds of Khamus, an Austro-Asiatic tribe that inhabited the region before the arrival of the Thais.

PHAE MUANG PHI

Phae Muang Phi, the "Ghost City," is located off Highway 101 on the way to Nan. This is actually not a town but a shallow depression where soil erosion has resulted in a number of strange rock-like formations that do indeed resemble the deserted dwellings of some mysterious race.

NAN TOWN ★

As late as the first decade of the present century, Nan was the capital of a semi-autonomous principality, founded in 1368. In its early period, until around 1450, the city had a close relationship with Sukhothai, and subsequently came under the indirect control of the Lanna kingdom. It was ruled by the Burmese from 1558 to 1788, when it pledged allegiance to Bangkok, but the local ruling dynasty retained considerable authority until the central government finally assumed full control in 1931. Spread out along the west bank of the Nan River, the modern town has a prosperous air suggested and many shops selling luxury goods.

TEMPLES

WAT PHUMIN. This temple is the leading landmark of Nan, established in 1596 by a ruler named Phra Chao Chetabutra Phromin and extensively renovated in 1867. The cruciform viharn has steps leading up to splendidly carved doors on each of the four sides, while the interior is dominated by four large Buddha images facing the cardinal points ● *95*. Of special interest are the murals that adorn the walls, probably painted at the turn of the

century by Tai Lue artists. These mainly depict the Khatta Kumara and Nimi Jataka tales and contain a wealth of detailed visual information about the dress, tattoos and hairstyles of the period.

WAT PHRA THAT CHAE HAENG. Located southeast of the town on the opposite bank of the Nan River, Wat Phra That Chae Haeng is notable for the enormous *naga* (serpent) stairway that leads to the entrance. Inside the courtyard is a 180-foot-high golden chedi with four smaller chedis, while the viharn is a beautiful structure showing Laotian influence.

WAT CHANG KHAM VORA VIHARN. This temple, directly opposite the local branch of the National Museum, dates from 1406 but has been restored several times; it once contained five Buddha images commissioned in 1426 by a Nan ruler, only one of which – a 5-foot walking Buddha in solid gold – is kept at the temple in the monks' residence.

WAT PHRAYA PHU. This houses two of the other images, both made of bronze in the Sukhothai style. Wat Suan Tan, on the western side of town, enshrines the important Buddha image known as Phra Chan Thong Thip, a fine example of Sukhothai style, while Wat Satharos on the northern outskirts has an unusual chedi mounted on a high square base.

NAN BOAT RACES
Held to celebrate the end of Buddhist Lent in late October or early November, the Nan boat races take place along a stretch of river near the Governor's residence. Over 40 *naga*-prowed boats, each with up to 50 oarsmen, participate in this colorful event, one of Thailand's most exciting festivals. Ernest Young wrote in his book, *The Kingdom of the Yellow Robe*, "In these races no consideration is paid to 'fouls.' The object of each crew is to reach the winning-post first, and any crew is allowed to prevent its opponents attaining that desirable end, by any means they care to employ. The consequence is that the first part of the race revolves itself into a series of 'ramming' manoeuvres. There is a fierce struggle between the rival crews who try to upset each other. The intense excitement prevails amongst the spectators as two boats near each other."

WAT DON JADEE

WAT PHRA THAT DOI KONG MU

WAT HUA WIANG

MARKET

WAT PANG LOR

ON THE WAY TO MAE HONG SON

The first metalled road from Chiang Mai to Mae Hong Son was opened in 1965 and has been extensively improved in recent years. It winds through some of Thailand's most beautiful scenery – misty mountains and forests of pine trees planted to replace those cut down by the hill tribes – with the view at its most spectacular as the road descends steeply into the valley of the Pai River where Mae Hong Son is located.

OB LUANG GORGE. A narrow defile with steep walls, the Ob Luang Gorge is one of Thailand's most celebrated beauty spots. Nearby is a nature park, where trails lead 650 feet down to the bottom of the gorge.

MAE SARIANG. A small town 62 miles from Hot on the road from Chiang Mai to Mae Hong

WAT PHRA NON   WAT KHAM KHO   JONGKHUM LAKE   WAT KRANG TUNG   WAT CHONG KAM

🕓 Four days

Son, Mae Sariang has wooden shophouses and a rickety bridge that spans the Yuam River and leads to the mountain range bordering Burma. Two local temples are worth visiting for their Burmese-style architecture ● 98. Wat Utthayarom, which dates from 1896, has three chedis, one of which has nine spires, while nearby Wat Boonruang is much more elaborately decorated and has the monks' quarters in a longhouse raised on stilts. A dirt track leads south from Mae Sariang along the Burmese border all the way to Tak, but as it is known to be unsafe, the route is seldom used by foreigners.

HISTORY

Though constituted as a city by the ruler of Chiang Mai in 1874 and as a province under the Ministry of Interior in 1893, Mae Hong Son is regarded as the back of beyond by most people in Thailand. It remained isolated from the rest of Thailand until 1965 when the metalled road was opened. Mae Hong Son is in fact so remote that it was a favored place of exile for government officials charged with serious offenses against the State. Today, however, a regular domestic air service links the city with Chiang Mai, thus opening up the valley to tourism.

SHANS
Shans, who belong to the same ethnic group as the Thais, began visiting the Mae Hong Son valley from northern Burma centuries ago, and worked seasonally in the forests. By the mid-19th century increasing numbers were settling permanently, and one group built an elephant-trapping corral on the site that eventually became Mae Hong Son. The Shans still constitute nearly 50 percent of the province's population.

MAE HONG SON TODAY ★

Nestled amid forested, mist-shrouded mountains, Mae Hong Son still has a tranquil feeling of remoteness, a leisurely ambience that comes as a welcome contrast to the bustle of most other modern northern towns. The liveliest time of day is between 6am and 8am, when a busy market springs up behind the Mae Tee Hotel, with stalls selling food, clothing and household goods, and colorful hill tribe people mingle with the local populace. Otherwise the chief charm of Mae Hong Son is strolling about scenic Jongkhum Lake, visiting various temples in the area, and enjoying its cool climate during the winter months.

Wat Chong Kam and Wat Chong Klang are situated beside a small lake (above).

WAT PHRA THAT DOI KONG MU ★

Doi Kong Mu is the name of the small hill that dominates Mae Hong Son, often covered with mist in the morning. A road leads to Wat Phra That Doi Kong Mu at the summit, where there are a number of Buddha images and two chedis – one built in 1860, the other in 1874. The mist

SHAN ORDINATION CEREMONY
Each year in early April the Shans of Mae Hong Son observe a colorful ritual known as Poi Sang Long. This marks the initiation of young boys into the monkhood ● 47 and involves a gala procession in which the novices are carried to the monastery with dances performed by participants dressed in animal costumes.

clears in the afternoon, giving visitors spectacular panoramic views of the valley and the surrounding mountains; the wonderful experience is enhanced by the tinkle of bells from the tops of the chedis, which are quite dramatically illuminated after dark.

LOY KRATHONG. The water festival ● 73 is celebrated in Burmese fashion in Mae Hong Son. Instead of being set adrift on rivers and ponds, as in the rest of the country, the lotus-shaped *krathong* are attached to paper lanterns and released into the air from the top of Doi Kong Mu overlooking the town.

OTHER TEMPLES

WAT HUA WIANG. Located near the morning market, Wat Hua Wiang is a dilapidated wooden temple that houses an exceptionally fine brass seated Buddha, a replica of the one in Mandalay. Sections of the image were cast in Burma, then transported overland and by river and assembled in Mae Hong Son.

WAT KHAM KHO. Across the road from Wat Phra Non, Wat Kham Kho was built in 1890; the covered walkway from the main gate and the viharn have elegant filigree work on the eaves. The viharn contains five principal Buddha images, the central one being Burmese in style. In front of the altar there is a beautiful 80-year-old peacock throne inlaid with colored glass.

WAT PHRA NON. Located at the foot of Doi Kong Mu is Wat Phra Non, a rebuilt temple that houses two large Buddha images made of plaster over brick. One, 40 feet long, is in the reclining position, and the other is seated; both have realistic, painted faces in the Burmese style. Just behind this temple are two huge stone lion statues carved in Burmese style. They guard the entrance to the old deserted footpath up Doi Kong Mu. A few steps further on is a row of six chedis built on an elevated platform – all that remains of Wat Muay Toh.

Deserted Wat Hua Wiang has an elaborately decorated corrugated-iron roof.

Detailed filigree work is a feature of Shan temples.

WAT CHONG KAM AND WAT CHONG KLANG ★. These are two Burmese-style temples in the same compound, picturesquely sited beside a small lake and surrounded by a palm grove. Of special interest is a collection of 33 wooden figures. These figures are kept in a small barred room just inside the entrance to the viharn of Wat Chong Klang. Representing figures from the Vessantara Jataka – one of a collection of stories dealing with the Buddha's previous lives – these were brought from Burma in 1857. Near Wat Chong Kam is Luang Pho To, which enshrines a revered 16-foot-tall brick and plaster Buddha image.

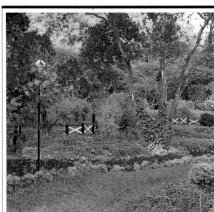

One of the most scenic drives in the Chiang Mai area is through the Mae Sa Valley, a recently developed area that begins with a left turn at Mae Rim, about 7 miles out of Chiang Mai on the road to Fang. Several resorts have appeared in the valley over the past few years, with terraces on the mountain slopes and neat, landscaped gardens of mostly temperate-zone plants. There are also rustic cottages that attract city-dwellers longing for a change of scene and a taste of country life without the usual discomforts. The winding road eventually slopes down to the Chiang Mai–Chom Thong Highway. The scenery, however, is most attractive along this least developed section.

"The road to Tatong lay through a somewhat open forest, with a high mountain-chain, running north and south, rising abruptly to the left. The trees were literally covered with orchids, which were just past their prime, the dry season being the time for flowering. Many other varieties of flowers, of most gorgeous colours and often of gigantic size, flourished in the open patches between the trees. I do not remember to have seen anywhere such a profusion of flowers as when travelling through Lao and in this particular district they seemed more abundant than ever."
Carl Bock

ORCHID FARMS

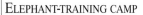

There are several orchid nurseries in the Mae Sa Valley, all open to visitors for a nominal entrance fee. In addition to dazzling displays of blooming plants ● *20–1*, both native and hybrid, most of the nurseries also have demonstrations of orchid propagation and shops selling such souvenirs as orchid blossoms coated with gold.
FA MUI ORCHID. One of the most beautiful of northern Thailand's indigenous orchids is *Vanda coerulea*, known in Thai as Fa Mui, the natural color of which is a heavenly blue that comes in a variety of subtle shades. This is prized by foreign orchid growers for hybridization and was used to produce the famous *Vanda rothschildiana* (right) ● *20*.

ELEPHANT-TRAINING CAMP

One of the most popular tourist stops along the Mae Sa Valley road is an elephant-training camp near the Mae Sa Waterfall. The animals and their trainers give a performance at around 9am every day. Elephant rides through the jungle to the Mae Sa Valley Resort can also be arranged.

CHIANG DAO CAVES

Doi Chiang Dao, at 7,540 feet Thailand's third-highest mountain, is 45 miles from Chiang Mai. Nestling at the foot of the mountain are the Chiang Dao Caves, accessible through a narrow entrance at the top of a covered stairway. They consist of several chambers (above), the first of which receives some light from an opening above and is the most impressive. Shan Buddhists have long venerated the caves and have placed a number of large Buddha images there. Further in, more steps flanked by a long *naga* lead down to a large reclining Buddha carved out of the limestone and a life-sized statue of one of the Buddha's disciples.

FANG

Founded by King Mengrai ● *38* in 1268 and once a prosperous, independent city, Fang was destroyed by the Burmese at the beginning of the 19th century and deserted until 1880. The present town is mainly of interest because of its proximity to Burma and the colorful tribal people who come to its market to sell their goods.

TO CHIANG RAI BY BOAT

Tha Thon is a small village on the bank of the Kok River, about 14 miles north of Fang. From a landing near Wat Tha Ton, long-tail boats leave at 12.30pm daily for a three-hour trip down the river to Chiang Rai, which offers exciting rapids and exceptionally beautiful natural scenery. A three-day trip can be made by bamboo raft. Booking for the trip should be made 10 days in advance.

PHI POB PEOPLE
Legend has it that the little town of Chiang Dao was once inhabited by people possessed by *phi pob*, spirits ● *51* who ate the entrails of their victims. Like lepers, such people were sent to live in remote communities far away from others.

FARMHOUSES
The Fang valley, is peppered with picturesque farming communities made up of simple native huts with thatched roofs, reflecting a timeless way of life in striking contrast to the bustling, modern ways of larger northern towns and cities.

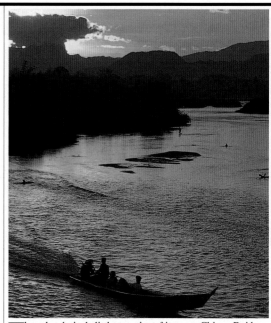

Treks into the northern mountains to enjoy the scenery and visit remote and exotic hill tribe villages became an important part of Chiang Mai's appeal about 15 years ago, especially with adventurous travelers. That area eventually became "overtrekked," at least among more dedicated enthusiasts, and the main center of operations has now shifted to Chiang Rai. Consequently, dozens of agencies have opened in the city offering everything from a two-day mini-excursion to one that lasts a week or more, with a wide range of prices and amenities available. Look for an agency that meets your particular requirements, keeping in mind a few basic considerations. The best time for trekking is the cool, dry season from November through the end of February; March through May can be hot and hazy, while during the rainy season the mountain trails are often muddy and slippery. Most of the villages provide a place to sleep, and food is generally part of the trek package, but bring along snacks to supplement the limited variety of food available there.

Though relatively little remains of its past, Chiang Rai has an ancient history, having been founded by King Mengrai in 1262 ● *38*, on a site protected by the Kok River and by three small hills. Its strategic location near the border made it an important trading center but also ensured that it would suffer during the frequent wars between Thailand and Burma; for a long period during the 19th century it was more or less abandoned, with only a few hundred families remaining within the old city walls. Prosperity returned slowly – as late as 1970, it had a population of only around 10,000 and has had a strong visible effect only in recent years.

CHIANG RAI TODAY. Modern Chiang Rai has little to offer in the way of physical beauty or exotic atmosphere, being for the most part a typical Thai provincial capital full of nondescript rows of cement shops and drab, dusty streets. Nevertheless, it has enjoyed a considerable boom over the past decade, thanks to its proximity to the fabled Golden Triangle and its convenience as a base for trekking expeditions into the nearby hills. New hotels, including a large one on an island in the Kok River, have risen almost everywhere, along with restaurants and shops catering to foreign tourists and numerous agencies that organize visits to tribal villages.

CHIANG RAI TEMPLES. Wat Phra Singh, on Singhakai Road, once enshrined the revered image known as Phra Buddha Si Hing, now at the temple of the same name in Chiang Mai; a replica is kept at the Chiang Rai temple. Wat Phra Keo, on Ruang Nakorn Road, contains an early bronze Chiang Saen image and a reconstructed chedi, where in 1436 the famous Emerald Buddha was discovered. Wat Ngam Muang has an ancient chedi with the remains of King Mengrai. Wat Doi Tong is on a hill that commands a fine view of the Kok River.

CITY WALLS. In the late 1980's, the municipality of Chiang Rai became aware that the city's claims to an ancient and glorious past are not supported by an adequate amount of archeological and architectural evidence, and tourist attractions are somewhat wanting in the town. It was then decided to build them and sponsors, historians and artists were called in to help to restore the glory of the city.

The first objective was the city walls. The original walls were pulled down in 1920 on the advice of Dr Briggs, an American missionary physician who argued that they were not only useless but were also a permanent source of all kinds of illnesses because they obstructed the flow of fresh air. Initially, it had been hoped that a complete city gate and a good part of the walls could be rebuilt, but no evidence whatsoever was found to help with the reconstruction except an engraving showing an elephant passing through a gate against the rays of the rising sun. The elephant was quickly taken as a yardstick, and assuming that its height may have been at least 8 feet, a stretch of cement wall covered with bricks was quickly built. It measured 330 feet long and 16 feet high, with an opening in the middle (no evidence upon which to reconstruct the gate was found). This "antiquity" now stands proudly in front of a shopping center.

CITY PILLAR. The second achievement was the construction of a city pillar, which Chiang Rai never had. This was erected on a hilltop – Doi Chomthong – on the outskirts of the town where a telephone exchange was about to be built. Pittaya Boonag, a lecturer from the Faculty of Architecture at the University of Chiang Mai, was called in to design a city pillar according to Thai cosmology, and he ended up with a complex of 108 granite pillars surrounding "the navel of the Universe," a larger column of phallic shape 5.5 feet high. The design represents major features of the universe as illustrated in various Thai murals in Bangkok, and therefore completely alien to the Lanna culture of old Chiang Rai. The complex was inaugurated on January 31, 1989 (six days after the date on the commemorative inscription), but has gone unnoticed since.

OPIUM
Source of heroin, opium is prepared from the juice of *Papaver somniferum*, one of the more than 250 species of poppy, which requires very specific climatic and geographical conditions for commercial cultivation. The plant grows best at altitudes of 3,000 to 7,000 feet and prefers a relatively dry climate; crop production can vary 300 percent from year to year depending on the weather. When the petals fall, the seed pod is sliced to release the juice, which is milk-white at first but dries to a gummy brown substance that can be stored for years without losing its potency ▲ *294–5.*

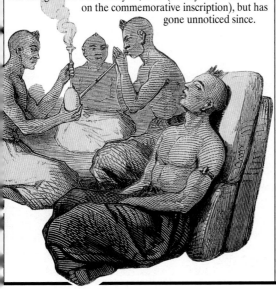

OPIUM EATER
"The vapors of opium fill up her empty head, Reclining her bust on the silky cushions; She follows in the ether the fanciful reverie, That phantasy unravels to her eyes."
Anonymous

**THE FIRST
HILL TRIBES**
The Lahus were the
first hill tribes to
migrate to northern
Thailand in the last
quarter of the
19th century.
The Akhas were
the last to arrive
and their first village
was erected in 1905.
The largest migration
took place in the
1960's and 1970's,
and by 1983 the total
population was
416,000.

The mountains of Thailand's far
north, along the borders of Burma
and Laos, are home to a number of
tribal groups, each with its own
distinctive culture and traditions. Only
one tribe, the Karens, has lived in the
region since ancient times; others began
migrating in the 19th century into what was
then rugged hills, left unpopulated by the Thais, who are
lowland farmers. Some have come only in relatively recent
years, driven by the wars in Indo-China and the unrest in
northern Burma. The total tribal population is estimated at
about half a million, divided into two general ethnic groups.
The Hmongs and the Miens (known to Thais as the Yao)
belong to the Sino-Tibetan group, while the Karens, Akhas,
Lisus and Lahus are members of the Tibeto-Burmese group.

HILL TRIBE SETTLEMENTS

The tribes ● 33 do not possess definite territories but live
interspersed in a number of settlements, each at a preferred
altitude. Traditionally all the tribes are semi-nomadic. They
will settle on the hills, clear the land by fire, and cultivate it
for a few years until the soil is impoverished.
They will then move on to another hill site. Slash-and-burn
cultivation has caused considerable damage and efforts are
being made to resettle them at lower altitudes where the land
can be irrigated. However, tribesmen find difficulty adapting
to the heat in the valleys and to new developments
in rural life.

OPIUM CULTIVATION

With the exception of the Karens, the hill tribes are mainly
opium cultivators. The practice of opium cultivation
was originally forced upon the Hmongs by
the French government in
Indo-China, which was
secretly selling

> "Wherever you go…may your feet not stumble,
> your arms not falter; may your words prove true, your
> hopes be fulfilled…and all you undertake flourish."
>
> Tribal blessing

opium to the Marseilles gangsters to finance the war against the communists. When the Hmongs migrated, they spread opium cultivation and trade in the region. Subsequently, the Americans, working through the CIA, encouraged opium cultivation to win the support of the Hmongs in the secret war against the Phratet Lao. Only when public opinion became concerned about drugs did the Western powers try to stop opium cultivation, forcing Third World countries to ban what had become a major source of income and a powerful political tool. While the military elites of many Indo-Chinese countries are still actively involved in the opium trade and drugs keep reaching the West, the big losers are the hill tribes, whose only source of income is being threatened. Once addicted to opium, most tribesmen now turn to heroin, and there are reported cases of children below school age being addicted to the drug. A scheme to eradicate opium cultivation has been initiated by the King of Thailand, who has sought to introduce new commercial crops to replace the opium poppy as well as to bring better medical treatment and social welfare to the tribal groups. Among the crops introduced successfully thus far are coffee, vegetables, strawberries, peaches, lychees and apples. As a result of such efforts, opium production has dropped drastically in the country, many hill tribe children are receiving a basic education in settled villages, and their elders are more often seen mingling with the majority Thais in lowland towns and cities.

Old postcards from the early 20th century depicting typical Akha attire (left) and Karen dress.

THE KARENS

Numbering about 250,000, the Karens are the largest hill tribe group. They are skilled farmers and have become sedentary, living on irrigated land. Karen women are noted for their skill in weaving cotton, commonly red or orange, which they embroider and decorate with seeds.

THE MIEN

"Hill tribes" is not an ideal term for these divers
peoples of Thailand. Though they each possess a
strong ethnic identity, their communities are
dispersed throughout northern Thailand, with no
unifying "tribal" organization. These groups do
share some characteristics that justify the name o
hill tribe, differentiating them from the other
ethnic groups of northern Thailand. One of thes
characteristics is a rich material culture. The Mie
or Yao peoples are among the most "Chinese" of the hill tribes,
probably originating from southern China about 2,000 years ago.
There are large numbers of Mien in China, Laos and Vietnam.
They first migrated to Thailand from Laos in the mid-19th centu
They use Chinese script, their social organization is patriarchal,
and their religion shows a strong Chinese influence. They share
with other groups great skill in textile-making, specializing in cros
stitch embroidery work.

MIEN TEXTILES

Homespun
cotton cloth,
dyed a deep
indigo is the
basic material
for most Mien
textiles. Today
that cloth is
purchased
from Thai
weavers of the
lowlands. The
patterns were
originally
embroidered with
naturally dyed
homespun silk,
the embroidery
stitches running
in parallel with
the warp or weft.
Today Mien
embroiderers
buy threads, in new
colors, and prefer the
cross-stitch, in which
the embroidered
thread runs
diagonally across the
warp and weft. The
turban, waistcloth and
pants of a traditional
woman's outfit are
embroidered; the
tunic with its red fur
collar is not as fully
adorned.

APPLIQUÉ
The appliqué technique allows women to adorn their textiles with shapes which are more organic than motifs on embroidered cloths. Though still symmetrical, the shapes are made of complex lobes and tendrils. The appliqué example shown above is from a saddlecloth, white braiding highlighting the appliqué shapes.

SILVER
Silver is a crucial part of hill tribe costume. These ornaments, to be suspended from a silver neck ring, are also decorated with cloisonné, enamel.

RELIGIOUS PAINTINGS
Mien religion draws its visual expression from archaic forms of Chinese folk religion. These paintings depict figures in a large hierarchical pantheon of gods and spirits.

ANCESTOR FIGURES
The Mien traditionally practice forms of ancestor worship that owe much to Chinese ritual. Ancestors' names are recorded in a special book, and recited when offerings are made. Ancestor figures such as this one symbolize the generalized presence of the ancestors, who are informed of births and weddings, and who provide protection to their descendants.

▲ CRAFTS OF THE HILL TRIBES
HMONG TEXTILES

Hmong women are particularly skilled in the production of textiles. Their traditional version of the backstrap loom is unique, equipped with foot treadles for shifting the warp threads. They are the only group in mainland Southeast Asia to use the batik resist-dyeing technique, producing designs in blue and white monochrome. These designs are often enhanced with a layer of embroidery. To a modern eye, the Hmongs' mastery of geometric designs is especially pleasing. Special clothes are worn by young women at New Year, but the Hmongs traditionally reserve their full repertoire of textile expression for ornate funerary costumes, as in this woman's set.

CHILDREN'S JACKETS
The Chinese-style asymmetrical front fastening is highlighted with fine embroidery in this child's jacket. The abstract embroidery motifs are particularly attractive and even the smallest clothes are richly adorned.

SPIRIT LOCKS
This silver ornament, one of many kinds favored by Hmong men and women, is said to represent a lock, binding the soul to the body. It hangs from a neck ring. The incised patterning seems to be derived from the embroidery patterns used in women's collars.

> "A tiny needle, strands of bright thread, and the genius of a hmong woman – these are the ingredients of some of the most exquisite needlework to be found anywhere."
>
> Paul and Elaine Lewis

NERARY ELEGANCE
ial clothes are made by wife for her husband herself. Made from emp cloth, apart from the pants or skirt, there are three or more upper richly embroidered garments.

COLLARS
These collar pieces (right), made by the women of the White Hmong subgroup, demonstrate a range of embroidery and appliqué techniques. Measuring around 5 by 6 inches, they hang from a flap down the back.

The Lahu, Akha and Lisu peoples are distinguishd from the other hill tribes by their languages, all in the Yi subgroup of the Tibeto-Burmese family. These hill tribes migrated to Thailand from the Shan states of Burma and from Yunnan, China in this century. Though all the peoples of the Golden Triangle use silver ornaments, arguably the most dramatic use of the precious metal is by these three Tibeto-Burmese speaking groups. Silver is plentiful in Yunnan and the upper Irrawaddy in Burma, and has been used in mainland Southeast Asia for centuries. But it became even more popular in the region thanks to the influence of the Europeans, who brought in relatively cheap New World silver to trade for Asian goods. Today, silver is still used for exchange and as a currency. Aluminum is now replacing silver for some uses.

BANGLES
Many of these dramatic twisted wire bracelets are made by Chinese silversmiths. They are hollow and some feature engraved designs. They are worn predominantly by the Akha people.

AKHA HEADGEAR
Adorned with silver coins and hollow silver balls, beads and buttons, Akha head-dresses show one of the most striking uses of silver by a hill tribe group. This piece (right), with a large trapezoidal silver plate at the back, is in the Loimi-Akha style, favored by recent migrants from Burma. It is worn by young girls in festive occasions.

PENDANTS
The fish is a favori motif in the penda worn by many hill groups. Such pend like the one shown above, can be worn around the neck in front or hanging fr a solid neck ring at back, over a jacket Elongated bell-shaped beads and a set of stylized grooming implements such as tweezer and ear cleaners, hangs below this fish.

NECK RINGS

Plain flat silver neck rings are particularly favored by Akha women. Often they serve as a kind of a base for the many silver ornaments that may be dangled from them, in front or at the back. They are often covered by the ornaments that hang from the headdress. The omega shape, with the scrolls at each end, is a popular form in much Southeast Asian jewelry, though this is a particularly vigorous expression of the basic form. These rings are flat, but others may be hollow, with a similar shape but rounded in profile. Neck rings like these are often copied in aluminium, to deter robbers.

PIPES

Apart from opium, the hill tribes also use the more respectable tobacco. The two pipes pictured here are solid silver, the bottom one exhibiting some cloisonné decoration as well. They could have been used by any of the three groups considered here, or indeed by the Miens or Hmongs as well.

CONTAINERS

Small silver containers like these are usually made by the Shan peoples who live mostly in Burma, and traded to the hill tribes. Used for betel nut paraphernalia and tobacco, they are collected as status objects, particularly by the Akhas.

FANG

AIRPORT CHIANG RAI WIANG CHAI

🕓 Two days

Wat Phra That
Chom Kitti.

HISTORY

The origins of Chiang Saen ● *38, 39* are
obscure. However, most historians
agree that a town of considerable
influence probably existed earlier on the
site before the city of Chiang Saen was
founded in 1328 by Phra Chao Saen Pu,
a grandson of King Mengrai ● *38*.
Chiang Saen became associated with
Chiang Mai and was ruled by Lanna
kings until 1558, when it was invaded by
the Burmese, who remained in control for more
than two centuries. In 1804, forces loyal to King
Rama I seized the city and burned it after which
the city was abandoned. Chao Inta, an offspring of
the Prince of Lamphun, brought back the
descendants of its former population and rebuilt
the town 70 years later.

CHIANG SAEN SIGHTS

Chiang Saen's former importance is underlined by
the fact that the Fine Arts Department lists 66
ruined monuments within its once-fortified walls
and 75 outside. Among these is Wat Pa Sak, the
city's oldest chedi, built in 1295 and adorned with
fine stucco decorations; the structure displays a
number of influences, in particular that of the early

MAE CHANAI · MAE SAI · WAT PA SAK · WAT PHRA THAT CHOM KITTI · MEKONG RIVER · CHIANG KHONG

KOK RIVER · CHIANG SAEN MUSEUM · CHIANG SAEN

Haripunchai period. About half a mile away, atop a hill accessible by 350 ancient steps, is Wat Phra That Chom Kitti, which contains an 82-foot-high chedi (left) on a rectangular base. At Wat Chedi Luang, an octagonal chedi rises 190 feet, supposedly constructed in 1331 and rebuilt in 1515. Nearby is the Chiang Saen Museum, which displays several Chiang Saen bronze images as well as objects unearthed during excavations at Wat Chedi Luang. Along the road leading to the old town are several other ruined chedis, most notable among them being Wat Mung Muang and Wat Phra Buat.

MAE SAI
Situated at the summit of the Golden Triangle, the atmosphere in this frontier town is more Burmese than Thai. For a few dollars you can cross the Burmese border and spend the day in its twin city, Takhilek, in Shan province.

THE GOLDEN TRIANGLE

The so-called Golden Triangle – a term coined by journalists and since then often used by novelists – is the area where Thailand's borders meet those of Burma and Laos. Its fame, or, more accurately, notoriety, stems from the fact that over 50 percent of the world's opium supply is produced there; converted into heroin by secret refineries, it eventually finds its way to the streets of major Western cities, bringing "gold" to a number of dealers

> "The mystery of old Chiang Saen still haunted me…long lines of women, priests, soldiers and princes kept passing before me, whispering their history from the depths of the jungles."

Reginald le May, 1926

who act as middlemen but not to the tribal people who actually grow the poppies. Thailand's share of the market has dropped dramatically in recent years, thanks to a royalty-sponsored program to introduce new, more profitable crops for the tribes; but sizeable quantities are still coming from beyond its borders. Although geographically inaccurate, a spot designated as the center of the triangle is located near Chiang Saen where the Kok River joins the Mekong, complete with a noticeboard and a picnic pavilion.

MAE SAI

Thailand's northernmost town, Mae Sai is located on the Mae Sai River, which forms the border with Burma. While foreigners are not allowed to cross the bridge linking the two countries, there are numerous shops and stalls on the Thai side of the border, some selling herbal medicines but most offering tourist souvenirs brought from Chiang Mai.

DOI MAE SALONG ★. A popular excursion from Mae Sai, this mountain is inhabited by the Akhas and the Miens. Most of the villages along the road set up street bazaars, which of course attract tourists. At the end of the road is the village of Santi Kiri, inhabited by the families of the former Kuomintang army. The village is now developing into a hill station with several hotels and guest houses, but the town still looks very much like a typical Chinese settlement. Most of the products in the market are imported over the mountains from China. Many families here are Chinese Muslims, originating from Yunnan.

RIVER TRIP TO CHIANG KHONG

From Chiang Saen visitors can hire a boat down the Mekong River to the small town of Chiang Khong. The trip takes about two hours and offers some scenic views, particularly of the less developed Laotian side. With Thai-Laotian relations improving, Chiang Khong may once more become an important point for crossing the river.

Practical information

Key

 Editor's choice   Quiet

Air conditioning   Swimming pool

Credit cards accepted   Telephone

Garden   Television

Hot water   Terrace

Live music   Town center

Parking   View

◆ GETTING THERE

ADDRESSES

→ ROYAL THAI EMBASSY

■ **United Kingdom**
29–30 Queen's Gate
London SW7 5JB
Tel. 020 7589 2944
http://thailand.embassy homepage.com

■ **United States**
1024 Wisconsin
Ave. NW, Suite 401
Washington, D.C.
20007
www.thaiembdc.org
Visa services:
Tel. (202) 298 4815
Consular services:
Tel. (202) 298 4814

◆ OTHER CONSULAR OFFICES:
– 611 North
Larchmont Blvd,
2nd floor,
Los Angeles,
CA 90004
Tel. (323) 962 9574
www.thai-la.net
– 700 North Rush St
Chicago, IL 60611
Tel. (312) 664 3129
www.thaichicago.net
– 351 East 52nd St
New York, NY 10022
Tel. (212) 754 1770
http://thaiconsul newyork.com

→ TOURISM AUTHORITY OF THAILAND (TAT)

www.tourismthailand. org

■ **In the UK and US**
◆ 3rd Floor,
Brook House,
98-99 Jermyn St
London SW1Y 6EE
Tel. 0207 925 2511
tatuk@tat.or.th
◆ 611 North
Larchmont Blvd, 1st
floor, Los Angeles,
CA 90004
Tel. (323) 461 9814
tatla@tat.or.th
◆ 61 Broadway, Suite
2018 New York,
NY 10006
Tel. (212) 269-2597
info@tatny.com

■ **In Thailand**
TAT Head Office
1600 New
Petchaburi Rd,
Makkasan,
Ratchthewi,
Bangkok 10400
Tel. +66 (0)2 250
5500
Email: center@tat.or.th
There are TAT offices
throughout
Thailand; see p. 310
for a complete list of
addresses.

→ OTHER WEBSITES

www.thaiwebsites. com
A useful web
directory for English-
language websites
about Thailand
www.thailand.com

FORMALITIES

→ PASSPORT

A passport still
valid for six months
at the time of entry
into Thailand is
required. EU
members and United
States citizens may
enter Thailand for a
period of 30 days
without a visa, as
long as they have a
valid ticket for their
return journey.
Leave of stay will
not be extended and
a fine of 100 Baht
per day exceeded
will be charged.

→ VISAS

A tourist visa of
60 days can be
obtained from the
Thai Embassies or
Consulates upon
presentation of
a passport valid for
at least six months
after the planned
date of return and
two passport
photographs. Tourist
visa fee: £10.50/$15.
For extensions of
tourist visas once in
Thailand, contact:
■ **Immigration
Division**
Soi Suan Phlu,
Sathon Tai Rd,
Bangkok 10120
Tel. 02 287 31 01

HEALTH

No vaccination is
required for visitors.
Preventive
innoculation against
typhoid, tetanus,
hepatitis A (caused
by unhygenic
conditions and
contaminated
water) and hepatitis
B is recommended.
Preventive
treatment of
malaria prophylaxis
and Japanese
encephalitis B is only
recommended if you
intend trekking
along the borders
and in the jungle
(allow enough time
to arrange this with
your doctor before
departure).
◆ Avian flu has been
rife in Thailand for
some time – avoid
contact with poultry
or pigs.
◆ Caution: the HIV
virus can not only be
transmitted through
blood and sexual
contact, but also by
contaminated
equipment such as
acupuncture and
tattoo needles, etc.
■ **Information**
Call MASTA (Medical
Advisory Services for
Travellers Abroad)
Tel. 0845 600 2236
or browse websites
such as:
– *www.traveldoctor. co.uk*
– *www.travelhealth. co.uk*
– *www.nathnac.org*
◆ BANGKOK NURSING HOME
Tel. 02 632 05 50

INSURANCE

You are advised
to purchase
comprehensive
personal insurance
covering theft, loss
of property and
medical treatment
before departure.
Ask your travel
agent to make the
necessary
arrangements, or
check whether
insurance is included
in the services
offered by your
credit card company.
Be sure to mention
specific-risk activities
such as scuba diving
or trekking.

MONEY

→ CREDIT CARDS

Bahts can be
purchased with Visa
and MasterCard
from international
bureaux de change.
Visa can be used at
the Thai Farmers
Bank and
MasterCard at the
Bangkok Bank and
Siam Commercial
Bank. These cards
are also accepted by
autotellers and most
stores, hotels and
restaurants – but
beware of charges!

→ EXCHANGE

The Thai monetary
unit is somewhat
unstable.
£1 = 70 Baht
US$1 = 37 Baht
100 Baht = US$2.65
(at time of printing)
The best rates for
cash can be obtained
in Bangkok.
Exchange rates for
traveler's checks are
fixed, but the service
charges are lower
than those for cash.

→ TRAVELER'S CHECKS

(In US$) are
accepted by most
banks and official
exchange bureaux.

TIME DIFFERENCE

GMT+ 7. When it is
noon in Bangkok,
it is 6am in London
and 1am in New
York in summer and
5am/midnight
respectively in
winter.

TELEPHONE

■ **Calling Thailand
from the UK/US**
Dial 00 (from the
UK) or 011 (from the
US) + 66 (Thailand) +
area code + number.
■ **Area codes**

Ayutthaya	035
Bangkok	02
Chiang Mai	053
Chiang Rai	053
Hua Hin	032
Kanchanaburi	034
Koh Phi Phi	076
Koh Samui	077
Krabi	075
Mae Hong Son	053
Nakhon Ratchasima	044
Nakhon Si Thammarat	075

Pattaya	038
Phang Nga	076
Phitsanulok	055
Phuket	076
Sukhothai	055
Surat Thani	077

Omit the 0 before the area code when calling within Thailand.
■ International directory enquiries: 3212

TOUR OPERATORS
Numerous hotels in Thailand negotiate preferential rates with tour operators in Bangkok and abroad. This means that savings of up to 50 percent off the normal rates can be made. However, allow for seasonal variations: in the high season (from November to April) reservations are essential, especially around Christmas and New Year when prices are at their highest. In the low season, it is much easier to get favorable rates. You are advised to check the exact location of your hotel before booking; the heavy traffic in Bangkok can mean that a taxi or bus ride which should only take 15 minutes can turn into a two-hour nightmare!

TRAVEL BY AIR
→ **FROM THE US**
There are regular direct flights from New York and Los Angeles to Bangkok. Roundtrip prices start from US$650 from LA and US$850 from New York.
■ **Thai Airways International**
Tel. 1 800 426 5204
www.thaiairways.com
■ **Japan Air**
Tel. 1 800 525 3663
www.japanair.com
■ **Singapore Airlines**
Tel. 1 800 742 3333
www.singaporeair.com

→ **FROM THE UK**
There are regular flights from London direct to Bangkok. Prices start from about £500 return.
■ **British Airways**
Tel. 0870 850 9850
www.ba.com
■ **Thai Airways**
Tel. 020 7491 7953
www.thaiairways.co.uk
■ **Quantas Airways**
Tel. 020 8875 9191

→ **TRANSFER FROM BANGKOK AIRPORT**
■ **Don Muang International Airport**
Vibhavadi Rangsit
Tel. 02 535 1111
Departure information:
Tel. 02 535 1254
Arrival information:
Tel. 02 535 13 01
Avoid traveling to the airport in the morning or late afternoon, when the traffic is at its most congested.
■ **Don Muang–center**
♦ AIRPORT BUS:
This bus runs on the freeway and serves the main centers in Bangkok: 70 Baht per person.
♦ LIMOUSINE WITH DRIVER: 1,000 Baht
♦ TAXIS: go to the "Public taxi" counter rather than the "Airport taxi" counter, which is more expensive. The fare is set according to the journey: 200–300 Baht payable in advance, no tipping. Choose official taxis (yellow registration plate and "taxi" sign on the roof), rather than unofficial ones, which are often cheaper but are not authorized to pick up passengers.
♦ BUSES: lines nos. 29, 59 and 95 (no air conditioning) or lines nos. 4, 10, 13 and 29 (with air conditioning,100 Baht). A list of buses and hotel stops is available from the

airport TAT office.
♦ TRAINS: Don Muang–Bangkok (journey time: 45 mins), 10–100 Baht according to the type of train.

TRAVEL BY BOAT
Some cargo boats with passenger cabins travel from Europe and the US to Bangkok. Cruise liners stop at Pattaya while some charter boats depart from ports on the Malaysian coast.

TRAVEL BY TRAIN
Trains run between Singapore, Malaysia and Thailand.

WHAT TO PACK
Sunglasses, total sunblock cream and insect repellent are essential. Take light shoes that can be easily removed before entering temples and houses. For a holiday by the beach, snorkeling equipment and plastic sandals to protect against corals are useful.

WHEN TO GO
Nov.–April and July–Aug. are the high tourist seasons. The best time to visit Thailand is Nov.–March when the rains are not too heavy and the heat is bearable. Temperatures ae milder in the south between April–June. Visiting the north is ideal between mid-Nov. and mid-Dec. and in Feb. Avoid Bangkok in April as it is very hot, and in October because of the heavy rains.

→ **SEASONS**
Thailand is a tropical country with only three seasons: the hot and dry season (March–May), the rainy but also sunny period (June–Oct.),

and the cool season (Nov.–Feb.). The average annual temperature is 80°F. In Bangkok, it ranges from 62°F in December to almost 100°F in April/May.

→ **THE MONSOON**
The monsoon season brings five months of unpredictable weather: some days you are caught by sudden storms, followed on others by brilliant sunshine

→ **TEMPERATURES**
At night in the north from November to February temperatures can fall to 40°F so you will have to take warm clothes with you during the cool season. From June to October, the rain falls 15–20 days every month. The humidity level remains close to 80 percent in most of the country.

COST OF LIVING
■ A bus ticket
3.50–16 Baht
■ Taxi fare 200 Baht
■ Admission to a monument
20 to 100 Baht
■ A traditional dance show 350 to 1,000 Baht
■ A meal
30 to 1,000 Baht
■ A beer
35 to 50 Baht
■ A bag of fruit
5 Baht

TEMPERATURES IN °F		
In Bangkok-Chiang Mai-Phuket		
Jan.	77	68	79
Feb.	79	70	81
Mar.	82	75	82
Apr.	84	79	82
May	84	82	82
June	84	82	82
Jul.	82	81	82
Aug.	82	81	82
Sep.	82	81	82
Oct.	79	77	81
Nov.	77	75	81
Dec.	77	74	81

◆ GETTING AROUND FROM A TO Z

AIR TRAVEL
→ **AIRPORT**
■ **Don Muang Domestic airport** (domestic flights)
Tel. 02 535 2081
♦ DEPARTURES
Tel. 02 523 1192 or 02 535 1277
♦ ARRIVALS
Tel. 02 535 1253 or 02 535 1305

→ **AIRLINES**
Domestic flights are now operated by quite a few companies and prices are subsequently getting lower:
■ **Air Asia**
Tel. 02 515 9999
www.thaiair.com
■ **Nok Air**
Tel. 1318 (freephone)
www.thaiair.com
■ **Thai Airways International**
89 Vibhavadi Rangsit Road
Tel. 02 280 0060
www.thaiair.com
■ **Bangkok Airways**
Queen Sirikit National Convention Centre, New Ratchadaphisek Rd Khlong Toey
Tel. 02 265 56 78 or 02 265 55 55
www.bangkokair.com

FINDING YOUR WAY
Along the *thanon* (avenues or major roads) and the *soi* (minor roads), blue road signs are in Thai and often English.

BANGKOK METRO
The first two lines of the 'Skytrain BTS' suspended metro were opened in December 1999. They were followed by the opening of the first underground line in August 2004. The government plans to extend the network with more than 56 miles of track by the year 2010. Although limited, the existing network makes it much easier for visitors to get around as it already links most of the city-center districts. Tickets: 10 to 40 Baht.

BOATS IN BANGKOK
→ **"LONG-TAIL" BOATS**
Passenger and motor boats are available if you want to slice along the *klong* (board at the Oriental Hotel or under Memorial Bridge). Set rides around 50 Baht.

BANGKOK METRO

→ **OMNIBUS LAUNCHES**
The Chao Phraya Express omnibus launches run every day from 6am to 6pm.

→ **PASSING BOATS**
For the modest sum of 2 Baht, passing boats will take you across the river from under any of the five bridges.

BICYCLES
Very convenient means of transport in Thailand, except in Bangkok. There are many places around the country that rent bicycles. Information in Bangkok:
■ **Thailand Cycling Club**
Tel. 02 612 47 47 or 02 612 55 10

BUSES
→ **STATE BUSES**
With around 100 itineraries, the national bus company, the Baw Khaw Saw, offers regular services between towns.
■ **Regular buses**
Painted orange, these buses are cheap but slow, with frequent stops by request.
■ **Air-conditioned buses**
These blue buses are air-conditioned. They are cheap and somewhat faster than regular buses but rather infrequent.

■ **VIP buses**
Air-conditioned buses, with a smaller number of seats that are reclinable.

→ **PRIVATE BUSES**
These buses, run by private companies ("tour buses"), are more comfortable but also more expensive.

→ **IN BANGKOK**
Regular (3.5–5 Baht) or air-conditioned (8–16 Baht) buses will take you everywhere. However, you have to change buses quite often and need a good sense of orientation as this can be confusing. The *songteos* and green minibuses (3 Baht) follow the bus routes and stop at your request as long as you can make yourself understood!
AC buses, which are faster than taxis during the rush hour, are also cheaper (8 to 16 Baht).

→ **BANGKOK BUS TERMINALS**
■ **North bus terminal (Morchit Mai)**
Behind the Weekend Market.
Tel. 02 936 3509 or 02 527 8055
Departures for Ayutthaya–Pattaya every 30 mins. Fare: from 50 Baht.
Departures for Chiang Mai every hour. Fare: around 600 Baht.
■ **South bus terminal (Sai tai mai)**
On the Pinklao–Nakhon Chaisri Road
Tel. 02 435 1199 or 02 884 6191/2, or 02 435 12 00
Departures for Phuket at 5.30pm, 6pm and 6.30pm. Fare: from 700 Baht.
Departures for Hua-Hin every 40 mins, from 4.20am to 10.20pm. Fare: around 150 Baht.
■ **East bus terminal (Ekhamai)**
Sukhumvit Road Opposite Soi 63
Tel. 02 391 25 04
Departures for Pattaya every 30 mins, from 6.30am to 8pm. Fare: from 80 Baht.

DRIVING
→ **DRIVING CODE**
The Thais drive on the left, in a very haphazard manner!

→ **TRAFFIC JAMS**
The increasing number of expressways and major roads as well as the recently created metro have improved traffic conditions. However, Bangkok

is still choked by the sheer number of cars that fill its streets and thoroughfares. It is best to avoid major roads at peak times.

CAR
→ RENTING A CAR
Driving is no doubt one of the most pleasant ways to explore a region, especially northern Thailand. Car rental, with or without a driver, is common in Thailand. To drive you will need an international driving license. Cars can be rented from such companies as Avis and Hertz. Rates include insurance, but a hefty deposit is required. You can also rent a car from a cheaper local agency; however insurance is limited and your passport must be left as guarantee.

→ CAR RENTAL COMPANIES IN BANGKOK
A comprehensive list of car rental companies is available from tourist offices.
■ **Avis**
2/12 Wireless Road
Tel. 02 255 53 00
Open 7.30am–7pm
Avis cars can usually be rented from major hotels in Bangkok.
■ **Budget Car Rental**
19/23 Building A
Royal City Avenue
Tel. 02 203 92 00
Fax 02 203 02 49

LOCAL TRANSPORT
→ MOTOR-TAXIS
Motor-taxis can be quite a hair-raising experience, even for those who like big thrills. You are advised not to use this form of transport at night.

→ SAMLOS
Although motorized *tuk-tuks* seem to be increasingly common, *samlos* (rickshaws powered by motorcycle or bicycle) are still to be found.

→ SONGTEOS
These are canvas-covered vans with seats at the back. For long trips, fares should be negotiated before setting off. Ride: around 5 Baht.

→ TAXIS
Only Bangkok and other major towns have good bus and taxi networks. Choose taxis with "Taxi-meter" on the roof, as they have meters. As a rule, whatever form of transport you decide to use, be sure to negotiate a price before starting your journey. Bargaining upon arrival could result in an unpleasant confrontation with the driver.

→ TUK-TUKS
For short distances, there's the famous *tuk-tuk*, a sort of three-wheeled motor scooter that is noisy and cheap (40 Baht for a short ride). Not recommended for the fainthearted!

MOTORCYCLE
Especially popular in the northern part of the country, they can be rented in many places. In Chiang Mai, for example, you can hire a motorcycle for 300 Baht per day plus a deposit (you must also leave your identity card or passport as guaranty). Insurance should be included in the rental price.

TOUR OPERATORS
Bangkok is full of travel agents and tour operators. Those listed below are among the most reputable, offering reliable services and good prices. You will find more at the following address
www.thaiwebsites.com /travelagents.asp
■ **Asia Voyages**
Siam Exclusive Tours
Building 1,
Wireless Road
Tel. 02 256 71 68/9
Fax 02 256 71 72
This French tour operator is renowned in Bangkok for its cruises aboard the *Mekhala*, a barge formerly used to carry rice, now converted into a cruiser that goes up the River of the Bangkok Kings to Ayutthaya. Asia Voyages offers personalized trips and exclusive services which include attractive cruises, lodges and eco-tourism. It is also recommended for trips to Indo-China from Thailand.
■ **Diethelm Travel**
Kian Gwan,
Building 2
140/1 Wireless Road
Tel. 02 255 91 51/70
Fax 02 256 02 48
www.diethelm-travel.com
Certainly the largest tour operator in Thailand, offering a wide range of services that include guided tours in English. Very professional.
■ **STA Travel Co Ltd**
Wall Street Tower
Room 1406
14th floor
33 Surawongse Road
Bangrak
Bangkok 10500
Tel. 02 233 25 82
Fax 02 237 60 05
Open Mon.–Fri.,
9am–6pm,
Sat. 9am–noon
Closed Sunday

The largest tour operator in the world (120 branches) specializing in student travel (under 26s). There are also special prices for non-students.

TRAINS
→ CLASSES AND CATEGORIES
The state railway (SRT) trains are reliable, comfortable (1st and 2nd class) and reasonably priced, but tend to be crowded. There are three types of trains (international express, express and standard trains) and three classes. Choose express rather than standard trains, which often stop to let other trains by. Reserve well in advance to be sure of a seat on the day you want to travel. Timetables can be obtained from the main station in Bangkok:
■ **Hualamphong station**
Krung Kasaem Road
Tel. 02 223 37 62
or 02 225 69 64
or 02 224 77 88

→ SPECIAL FARES AND RAIL PASSES
There are special fares for day outings on Saturdays, Sundays and public holidays. An SRT Rail Pass allows you to travel (unlimited travel) during 20 days in 1st class for 2,000 Baht and in 2nd class for 1,100 Baht. Information:
■ **Advance booking office**
Hua Lamphong station, Bangkok.

→ LEFT-LUGGAGE OFFICE
There are left-luggage offices in most stations.

ACCOMMODATION
Thailand has a first-rate hotel system, with accommodation ranging from very simple guesthouses to luxurious five-star establishments. Fluctuating exchange rates make it impossible to provide accurate prices here. In Bangkok most hotels are located within easy reach of the tourist districts. Rooms are usually air-conditioned, with a double room plus breakfast costing a minimum of £15/$21.50 in Bangkok, and £10/$14.50 outside the capital.

ANTIQUES
→ **IN BANGKOK**
Bangkok is a paradise for antique collectors: porcelain, Chinese furniture, sculpture, carpets and other desirable items are to be found in profusion. Many stores can arrange for goods to be shipped almost anywhere in the world.

→ **EXPORT**
Be aware that the export of certain objects of an artistic or religious nature (images of Buddha in particular) is subject to strict control. Some pieces may require an export license, but any reputable dealer will be able to advise on restrictions and necessary documentation.

BANKS
→ **OPENING TIMES AND SERVICES**
Thai and foreign banks are open Mon.–Fri. 9.30am–3pm. Some larger banks have a bureau de change that is open until 8pm and an autoteller either inside or outside the bank. Major credit cards are accepted throughout Thailand, but always check beforehand and oversee any transaction.

CALENDAR
Although Thailand officially follows the Western calendar, Thais still count the years according to the

WOODCARVER

Buddhist era, which began in 543 BC.

CRAFTS
Arts and crafts can be bought all over Thailand, but Chiang Mai and the Weekend Market in Bangkok offer the greatest choice: fabrics, jewelry, statuettes, dolls in traditional costumes, musical instruments, masks, painted parasols and silk are among the items most likely to tempt visitors. Handwoven Thai silk, plain or printed with monochrome patterns, is sold by the yard; it is renowned as being the best in the world.

■ **The handicraft route**
The road linking Chiang Mai to San Kampheng is lined with an uninterrupted succession of boutiques and specialist workshops.

→ **SILVER**
■ **Chiang Mai**
The silversmiths of Chiang Man Gate, among others, still work this precious metal in the traditional way.

→ **BAMBOO**
■ **Sisakhet**
High-quality objects made of bamboo.

→ **LACQUERWARE**
■ **Ban Tharam** (road to Mae Hong Son)
You can watch the delicate and complex workmanship involved in producing lacquerware.

→ **UMBRELLAS**
■ **Bor Sang**
The umbrellas of Bor Sang (6 miles from Chiang Mai) consist of a wooden frame and bamboo ribs over which cotton, silk or brown paper made from the bark of local mulberry trees is stretched.

→ **GEMS**
■ **Chantaburi**
Surrounded by rich sapphire and ruby mines, Chantaburi specializes mainly in the gem trade.
■ **Chiang Rai**
Chiang Rai is the center of a flourishing trade in semiprecious and precious stones (diamonds, rubies and sapphires). The town is also well known for the gold and silver that is worked by the skilled and artistic hill tribes of the Golden Triangle.
■ **Mae Hong Son**
This large gem-trading center is also famous for its woodcarvings and *shan* cotton garments.

→ **CERAMICS**
■ **Ban Muang Kung**
The type of earthenware traditionally used by villagers for storing water has been made in Ban Muang Kung (Hang Dong district) for centuries.
■ **Ban Sakom**
Traditional glazed pots, water jars and cups for domestic use are still produced in the kilns of Ban Sakom.
■ **Chiang Mai**
The celadon ware produced in Chiang Mai has long been among the most renowned hand-crafted goods in northern Thailand.
■ **Lampang**
Pottery is Lampang's specialty, and there

are hundreds of workshops around the town.

→ WOODCARVING

■ **Ban Tawai and chiang Mai**
The woodcarvers of Ban Tawai, to the south of Chiang Mai, and in numerous other regions of Thailand, are highly skilled and produce outstandingly intricate work. Lovers of antiques will delight in the sculptured panels from ox carts, which, before the arrival of tractors and cars, were used for transporting people, animals and merchandise. Panels from Chang Mai, sometimes painted in bright colors, are often decorated with elephant motifs. Old or reproduction lamps can also be found, and, more rarely, sugar cane presses and coconut graters.

→ SILK AND COTTON

■ **Ban Si Than**
It is in Ban Si Than that the famous triangular *mon khit* cushions are made.

■ **Chonabot**
The incomparable *mudmee* silk is still produced in the village of Chinabot, 34 miles from Khon Khaen. There you can observe all the various stages of the production process, from the raising of the silkworms and the mulberry trees to silk-weaving.

■ **Kalasin**
Like **Surin, Roi Et, Chayaphum** and **Sakhon Nakhon**, Kalasin owes its reputation to the outstanding quality of the silk woven in its workshops.

■ **Khon Kaen**
Thailand's true silk capital is still Khon Kaen, on the road to Laos.

■ **Pak Thon Chai**
(17 miles south of Nakhorn Ratchasima) A major silk-weaving center.

■ **San Kamphaeng**
San Kamphaeng and **Passang**, south of Chiang Mai, also produce silk and cotton fabrics.

■ **Sukhotai**

BO SANG UMBRELLAS

POTTER

Sukhothai and **Ban Hat Sio** produce handmade silk garments.

■ **Udon Thani**
Udon Thani and the neighboring village of **Na Kha** produce traditional cotton fabrics.

→ BASKETRY

■ **Nakhon Si Thammarat**
Nakhon Si Thammarat is still the home of an original craft tradition, which is encouraged by Queen Sirikit. The art of basketry, *yan lipao* (in the form of bags and purses made of a liana that grows only in the region), is one notable aspect of this tradition. Another is the shadow puppets that are cut out of buffalo hide and of enameled silver.

ETIQUETTE

■ Remember to take your shoes off when entering a temple or private dwelling.

■ Buddhist monks must be treated with respect. Women are not allowed into their quarters and must not pass anything to them by hand.

■ Almost every Thai garden contains a miniature house where the spirit of that place lives. The human inhabitants leave offerings of food, fresh flowers and incense sticks there.

FESTIVALS AND CELEBRATIONS

Constantly in search of some *sanuk* (fun), the Thais seize every opportunity to organize celebrations. The Thai calendar is punctuated with numerous holidays, festivals and sporting events, as well as many religious ceremonies.

→ CALENDAR

Some Thai holidays are also linked to the lunar calendar, which is why the Tourism Authority of Thailand publishes annually a revised list of festivals celebrated throughout the country called *Major Events and Festivals*.

■ **Magha puja**
(FEBRUARY FULL MOON) During this festival Thais perform deeds that earn them merit (such as making offerings to Buddhist monks, freeing caged birds, etc.). Thousands of devotees bearing candles and flowers come along to attend temple sermons and follow the rituals conducted by priests.

■ **Songkran Festival**
(MID APRIL: THAI NEW YEAR) Mainly a celebration of water and purification. Especially joyful at Chiang Mai, where the local people splash each other and tourists with water in the street.

■ **Rocket festival**
(SECOND WEEK IN MAY) Held in Yasothon (northeast), before the monsoon. Giant rockets are made and launched to encourage an abundant harvest for the farmers.

■ **Queen's Birthday**
(AUGUST 12) Celebrations include

◆ STAYING IN THAILAND FROM A TO Z
Food, Health, Historic sites, International bookstores, Internet

the illumination of major national monuments.

■ **Ok Phansa and Thot Kathin**
(OCTOBER)
End of the Buddhist fasting period and start of Kathin. The faithful offer robes, alms and other essentials to Buddhist monks.

■ **Canoe races**
(OCTOBER)
The most famous take place at Nan, 490 miles north of Bangkok.

■ **Loi Krathong**
(NOVEMBER)
The most beautiful celebration of the year. Thais release small lotus-shaped rafts onto streams and rivers. The rafts carry flowers, incense sticks and lit candles in honor of the water spirits and symbolizing the purification of sins committed during the previous year.

■ **King's birthday**
(DECEMBER 5)
Illumination of major national monuments and of major thoroughfares.

FOOD
A typical Thai meal consists of four or five dishes (beef, chicken, shrimp, fish soup, etc.) served with rice, followed by a dessert or fruit. The Thais love sweet things and coconut milk forms the basis of most desserts. A good way of getting an introduction to Thai food is by joining a cookery class.

■ **Blue Elephant**
233 South Sathorn Rd Bangkok
Tel. 02 673 93 53
www.blueelephant. com/bangkok

■ **Hotel Oriental**
Soi Oriental, Th Charoen Krung Bangkok
Tel. 02 236 04 00/39
www.mandarin-oriental.com

HEALTH
The medical system in Bangkok has a very good reputation not only in Thailand but throughout Southeast Asia. Language is usually not a problem as most doctors will be fluent in English. However many hospitals ask for a deposit (20,000 Baht) before admission or treatment; most of them will take major credit cards. The cost of medical treatment outside the hospital system may vary and can be exorbitant.

Make sure you have medical insurance.

■ **Bangkok Adventist Hospital**
430 Phitsanukol Rd
Tel. 02 281 14 22 or 281 11 00

■ **Bangkok Christian Hospital**
124 Silom Rd
Tel. 02 233 69 81
Famous for its pediatric unit.

■ **Bangkok General Hospital**
2 Soi Soonvichai 7 Petchaburi Rd
Tel. 02 318 00 66, or 02 318 15 49/52
Famous for its cardiology unit. Prices for consultations are very reasonable.

■ **Bangkok Nursing Home**
9 Convent Rd, North Sathorn (Nua) Rd
Tel. 02 632 0550 or 02 632 0560
Has foreign medics on its staff and offers a 24-hour ambulance service.

■ **Bumrungrad General Hospital**
33 Soi 3 Sukhumvit Rd
Tel. 02 667 10 00
Foreigner oriented general hospital. Prices can be high but this is probably one of the best hospitals in the region.

■ **Siriraj University Hospital**
Prannock Rd, Thonburi
Tel. 02 411 02 41, 02 411 31 92
Numerous out-patient clinics. Very reasonable fees.

■ **PSE Clinic**
1 Nares Rd
Tel. 02 236 13 89 or 02 236 14 89
Runs an international service which boasts a network of doctors from all over the world.

■ **Dental Hospital**
49 Sukhumvit Soi
Tel. 02 260 5000/15
www.dentalhospital bangkok.com

→ **WATER**
You can't drink the tap water in Bangkok. The safest option is to stick to bottled mineral water.

HISTORIC SITES
Seven archeological sites, corresponding to the former capitals of Thailand, have been designated "historical parks" by the Thai government: Ayutthaya, Chiang Mai, Kamphaeng Phet, Lopburi, Si Satchanalai and Sukhothai. Isaan, in northeastern Thailand, includes Khmer and Laotian temples.

■ **Admission**
Varies according to the sites and monuments.

INTERNATIONAL BOOKSTORES
The country's two major bookstores (Asia and DK) have several outlets in Bangkok. There is also an important secondhand book fair which takes place in Chatuchak.

■ **Asia Books**
(head office)
221 Sukhumvit Rd
(between Soi 15 and 17)
Tel. 02 252 72 77

■ **DK Books House**
Soi 2, Siam Square
Tel. 251 63 35/6

INTERNET
Thailand is one of the most advanced countries in South-East Asia. E-mail and access to the Internet are available at a growing number of establishments (guesthouses, hotels, cafés, bars, etc.), especially in Bangkok, Chiang Mai, Koh Samui, and Phuket.
Rates: from 3 Baht per minute.

FESTIVALS AND CELEBRATIONS	
Magha Puja	February
Flower Festival	February
Pattaya Festival	April
Songkran Festival	April 13–15
Labor Day	May
Rocket Festival	May
Visakha Puja	May
Her Majesty the Queen's Birthday	August 12
Ok Phansa and Thot Kathin	October
Canoe Race	October
Loi Krathong	November
Elephant Rally in Surin	November
Bridge on the River Kwai Week	November
His Majesty the King's Birthday	December 5

ISLANDS AND BEACHES

→ EASTERN COAST

■ **From Bangkok to the east**

◆ PATTAYA
The most famous seaside resort in Thailand, 93 miles from Bangkok, Pattaya is today a large town, but despite the increasing number of tourists, the beach here is still remarkably clean.

◆ BANG SAEN
More family-oriented and closer to Bangkok (65 miles).

◆ RAYONG
A 2–3 hour drive from Bangkok (133 miles) but much quieter than Pattaya. Do not miss Rayong's jewel, Koh Samet, a 30-minute journey by boat from Ban Phe.

■ **From Bangkok to the south**

◆ CHA AM
Well-equipped resort 112 miles from Bangkok.

◆ HUA HIN
Also well equipped with hotels, Hua Hin, 140 miles from Bangkok, is the oldest Thai beach resort. It's also a firm favorite with the Thai Royal Family so it's become a very hip destination. Beyond Hua Hin and as far as Surat Thani, there is a long stretch of deserted beaches.

◆ PRACHUAB
180 miles from Bangkok. It has a strange "mountain mirror".

◆ CHUMPHON
With a circle of uninhabited islands, it is located 292 miles from Bangkok.

◆ SONGKHLA
Coastal and lagoon resort 596 miles from Bangkok with a charming old-world atmosphere.

TON SAI BAY, KOH PHI PHI DON

PHANG NGA BAY

PATONG BEACH, PHUKET

KOH SIMILAN NATIONAL PARK

ISLANDS OFF KRABI

→ THE ISLANDS IN THE SOUTH CHINA SEA

■ **How to get there**
Boats make the trip from the mainland to the islands in two hours. Transfer from Surat Thani (station or airport) is well organized. Flights from Bangkok also serve Samui (422 miles away).

■ **The islands**

◆ KOH SAMUI
White sand, palm trees and a turquoise sea – easy to understand why it's so popular.

◆ KOH PHANGAN
Samui's neighboring island is more rustic. You can reach it in 40 minutes from Nathon or Bophut (ports on Samui) and rent an idyllically simple bungalow.

◆ KOH TAO
To get away from it all, go to Koh Tao (about 30 miles further north), a divers' paradise, which can also be reached by boat to Chumphon (regular 6-hour crossing).
www.awesomekohtao.com

→ THE ANDAMAN SEA

http://andaman-island-hopping.com/

■ **Phuket**
The best way to get to Phuket (420 miles from Bangkok) is by air. The island is a world in itself, and from there you can branch out and visit the surrounding islands. Many interesting excursions are available.

◆ PHANGNGA
If your time is limited, visit Phangnga, which is surrounded by a strange rock formation. Excursions are arranged by hotels (take the boat to Phangnga and return by road).

◆ PHI PHI ISLANDS
www.kohphi-phi.com/home.htm
Equally spectacular are the two Phi Phi Islands: one, Phi Phi Le, has dark caves full of birds' nests (you cannot stay overnight on the island). The other, Phi Phi Don (featured in the movie *The Beach*, starring Leonardo di Caprio), is a luxurious destination with two beaches divided by a coconut grove. The trip can be made in a single day, and there are charming hotels for overnight accommodation in this small paradise.

MARKETS

→ CHIANG MAI MARKETS

■ **Night Bazaar**
Chang Klan Road (between Suriwong Rd and Thapae Rd) Most of Thailand's artisans make and sell their products in Chiang Mai. There are good bargains to be had over a wide range of goods, but only if you are prepared to haggle.

■ **Ton Lamyai and Warorot markets**
Excellent fruit and flower markets.

→ BANGKOK MARKETS

■ **Weekend Market**
Chatuchak Park, Phaholyothin Rd Alight at the Mo–Chit 'BTS' metro station.
Open 8am–5pm Sat. and Sun. Enormous market offering a wide variety of goods ranging from fruit and vegetables to clothes, handicrafts and antiques.
Get there as early as possible to avoid the crowds and the heat. Don't hesitate to haggle.

■ **Klong Toey Market**
Rama IV Rd.
Open from 5am.
Cheap food market.

■ **Patpong Market**
Patpong Rd.
Open daily 7pm–midnight. Watches, souvenirs, T-shirts, costume jewelry and clothes.

■ **Pratunam Market**
At the corner of Petchaburi and Ratchaprarop roads Open from noon until late.
All sorts of clothes.

FLOATING MARKET, BANGKOK

FLOWER MARKET, BANGKOK

→ FLOATING MARKETS
The canal networks and floating markets of Bangkok have earned the city its name of the Venice of the East. There are numerous flower sellers and stalls offering exotic fruit, but the authorities are now filling in the canals, or *klong*, and turning them into streets. True floating markets are now restricted to the periphery of the towns.

■ **In Bangkok**
On the canal
Open 4–7.30am.

From Tha Chang Pier, near Wat Phra Kaeo, is a line of rowing boats loaded with goods. The most interesting section is that at Khlong Bang Khu Wiang, at Thonburi.

■ **Damnoen Saduak Floating Market**
65 miles southwest of Bangkok
Daily until 10am.
Bus no. 78 from South bus terminal every 15 mins.
The most colorful and the best-stocked floating market in Thailand.

MASSAGE

→ IN BANGKOK
Wat Pho Traditional Massage School
Tel. 02 221 36 86
One of the best-known addresses for traditional therapeutic massage.
250 Baht per hour.

→ IN CHIANG MAI

■ **D.K. Traditional Massage**
277/5 Chang Klan Rd
Tel. 053 274 919
Open
10am–midnight

Excellent traditional massage, with free transport provided by request.
200 Baht per hour. Special prices for longer sessions.

■ **Old Medecine Hospital**
78/1 Soi Moh Shivaga Komarapaj Wualai Rd
Tel. 053 275 085
Intensive courses in traditional Thai massage.

MONEY
The Thai monetary unit is the Baht, which is divided into 100 satang. There are two copper coins (25 satang and 50 satang), two silver coins (1 Baht and 5 Baht) and a 10-Baht piece which is silver around the edge and copper in the center. Notes come in six denominations:
10 Baht (brown), 20 Baht (green), 50 Baht (blue), 100 Baht (red), 500 Baht (lilac) and 1,000 Baht (beige).
See p. 306 for exchange rates.

→ LOSS OR THEFT OF CREDIT CARDS

■ **American Express**
No toll-free number in Thailand.
Call the US collect: (336) 393 1111

■ **MasterCard**
001 800 11 887 0663

■ **Visa**
001 800 11 535-0660

NATIONAL PARKS
Thailand has 79 national parks, including 18 marine parks, managed by the National Parks Division (Pahol Yothin Rd in Bangkok). Most have reception facilities. Among them are Doi Inthanon (Chiang Mai), which boasts the highest point in the country; Kaeng Krachan

(Phetchaburi), the largest; Khao Sok (Surat Thani); Khao Yai (Nakhon Ratchasima), the oldest; Nam Nao (Chaiyaphum); Phu Kradung (Loei); Similan Islands (Andaman Sea and Thaleh Ban (Satun).

Warning:
For safety reasons it is advisable to choose a suitable time to visit a park, according to the season and the characteristics of the park.

■ **Information**
On site or at the tourist offices (TAT).
■ **Admission fee**
Usually around 30 Baht.

→ **REAL NATURE**
For a breath of fresh air well away from civilization, choose a mountain park such as **Phu Kradung** (382 miles northeast of Bangkok) or the 31 miles of marked paths of **Khao Yai** (120 miles from Bangkok). The latter is the oldest nature reserve in the country; it also has an 18-hole golf course and a hotel that is the complete opposite of the simple hiker's lodge.

→ **MARINE PARKS**
Thailand also offers spectacularly beautiful, unspoilt seashore and coastline experiences. Do not miss the national marine parks, islands and archipelagos circled by coral reefs.
■ **Gulf of Siam**
In the Gulf of Siam, **Koh Samet** is easily reached from Rayong and you can stay overnight. Even more spectacular is the national park of **Ang Thong**, in the Samui archipelago;

its 37 uninhabited islands make it quite unique. You can take a day trip (from Samui or Ban Don, on the mainland), or stay overnight in the tiny lodge at Wua La Tap.
■ **In the sea of Andaman**
On the Andaman side, the parks of **Koh Similan** and **Koh Tarutao** can be explored by boat. Individual and group cruises can be arranged from Phuket.

→ **ACCOMMODATION**
■ **Bungalows**
Most national parks have bungalows that can be hired. Rates: 500 to 1,500 Baht per night for 10 people. Out of season you can get a room for 100 Baht per person.
■ **Camping**
Camping is permitted in most of the national parks. Rates: from 5 Baht per person per night.

→ **RESERVATIONS**
It is advisable to reserve in advance, especially for weekends and public holidays. Reservations in Bangkok:
■ **Forestry Department National Park Bureau** Th Phahonyothin, Bangkhen Tel. 02 579 48 42 or 02 579 05 29

NEWSPAPERS
The two main English-language newspapers are the *Bangkok Post* and *The Nation*. The *International Herald Tribune* is also available, as are other major international newspapers. A free English-language weekly called

Where is distributed to hotels.

NIGHTLIFE
Most top-class and middle-category hotels in Bangkok have their own nightclub and discotheque. The big hotels put on classical concerts and supper-theater evenings. Nightlife in Bangkok is primarily concentrated around Patpong, in the Silom and Sukhumvit districts.

OPENING HOURS
→ **ADMINISTRATION BUILDINGS**
Mon.–Fri., 8.30am–noon and 1–4.30pm

→ **BANKS**
All banks throughout the country are open Mon.–Fri. 9.30am–3pm, except on public holidays.

→ **DEPARTMENT STORES**
Open at 10am and close at 9pm and later.

→ **POST OFFICES**
■ **Main Post Office in Bangkok**
Mon.–Fri. 8am–8pm, and weekends and public holidays 8am–1pm
■ **Outside the capital**
Mon.–Fri, 8.30am–4.30pm, and Sat. 9am–noon

POLICE
Bangkok may have a reputation as "the city of angels", but visitors should still be cautious when walking alone in isolated places or when using public transport. Members of the Tourist Police speak English and there are

always officers stationed in busy tourist areas. The central police station is located between Rama IV and Rajadamri roads.
■ **Tourist police**
Tel. 11 55, ext. 1
■ **In case of emergency**
Tel. 16 99
or 02 221 62 06/10
■ **Stolen/ lost credit cards**
See under 'Money'.

POST OFFICE
→ **OPENING TIMES**
The main post office in Bangkok is located on New Rd, and is open Mon.–Fri.7.30am–4.30pm, and 9am–noon at weekends and on public holidays. Outside the capital post offices close at 4pm.
■ **Bangkok Central Post Office**
1160 Charoen Krung Rd
Tel. 02 234 95 30
There are 13 main post offices and 22 sub-post offices in Bangkok.
→ **POSTE RESTANTE**
There is a *poste restante* service at the central post office in Bangkok (1 Baht per letter). Most hotels also have excellent postal facilities.

→ **POSTAL RATES**
■ Airmail letters less than 10 g:
Asia: 14 Baht
Europe, Africa, Australia and New Zealand: 17 Baht
North and South America: 19 Baht
■ Postcard: 12–15 Baht

SCUBA DIVING
→ **PATTAYA**
■ **Dave's Divers Den**
190/11 Moo 9
Central Pattaya
Good venue for diving enthusiasts. Minimum fee of 2,000 Baht for basic training and one

deep-sea diving expedition.

■ **The Scuba Professionals**
Dusit Resort Hotel, 240 Beach Rd
Tel. 038 429 901/3
Deep-sea diving school with a good reputation.
Minimum cost 2,000 Baht.

■ **Mermaid's Dive School**
Soi Mermaid, Jomtien Beach
Tel. 038 420 411
Professional diving school. Deep-sea diving trips at reasonable prices.2 dives: 800 Baht.

→ **KOH SAMUI**
■ **Swiss International Diving School**
Tel. 077 421 538
The school has centers on Great Buddha Beach, Central Bay Resort and Coral Cove Resort and on the island of Koh Tao. It provides coaching for all levels of experience, and instruction is given in English or in German. Accommodation is included.

→ **PHUKET**
■ **Phuket Aquatic Safari**
62/9 Rasada Rd
Tel. 076 216 562
Diving and equipment rental.
■ **Phuket Divers**
31/1 Phun Phon Rd
Tel. 076 215 738
Diving and equipment rental.
■ **Phuket International Diving Center**
Coral Beach Hotel Patong Beach
Tel. 076 321 106

STREET HAWKERS
The hawkers who set up stalls along the pavement offer a wide range of *khanom* (sweet disges) and other foods, which they

prepare at the stall. They use very simple equipment (a charcoal burner and downsized pots and pans).
Warning:
Thai cuisine can be extremely spicy.

TELEPHONE
→ **OVERSEAS TELEPHONE SERVICES**
You can telephone from hotels or private booths, but it is easier and less expensive to use the Overseas Telephone Services at post offices. It is cheaper to call 5–7am and 9pm–midnight.
■ **In Bangkok**
The Overseas Telephone Services is located opposite the central post office in Charoen Krung Rd and is open 24 hours a day. You can make calls as well as send faxes, telexes and telegrams.

→ **CALLS AND CODES**
For local calls, dial the area code ◆ *307*; for international calls, dial 001, followed by the country code, area code and the number.

→ **TELEGRAMS**
Numerous post offices offer telex, telegram and fax services. You can also send telexes and faxes from major hotels.

TEMPLES
There is a Buddhist temple, or *wàt*, in nearly every Thai village. Proper dress is expected of visitors (arms and legs must be covered). Do not forget to take off your shoes before going in. Icons and representations of the Buddha

must be treated with respect (this includes not having one's photograph taken with them, or pointing one's feet in their direction when sitting).
A small admission fee is sometimes charged; if not, it is customary to leave a few coins in the collection boxes provided, or on the floor near the Buddha or near the entrance if there are no boxes.

USEFUL ADDRESSES
→ **EMBASSIES IN BANGKOK**
■ **British Embassy**
1031 Wireless Rd, Lumpini Pathumwan, Bangkok 10330
Tel. 02 305 83 33
www.britishemb.or.th
■ **US Embassy**
American Citizens Service, 95 Wireless Rd, Bangkok 10330
Tel. 02 205 40 49
Embassy operator
Tel. 02 205 40 00
www.usa.or.th/ embassy

→ **CONSULATES IN CHIANG MAI**
■ **British Honorary Consulate**
198 Bumrungraj Rd, Muang, Chiang Mai 50000
Tel. 053 263 015
Fax 053 263 016
ukconsul@ loxinfo.co.th
■ **US Consulate General**
387 Witchayanond Rd, Chiang Mai 50300
Tel. 053 252 629 (ext. 2104 or 2138)
Fax 053 252 633

→ **TOURIST OFFICES**
(Tourist Authority of Thailand offices)
www.tourismthailand. org
■ **Ayutthaya**
108/22, Moo 4
Tambon Phratoochai
Tel. 035 246 076/7
■ **Bangkok**

4 Ratchadamnoen Nok Avenue
Bangkok 10100
Tel. 02 504 2701
■ **Chiang Mai**
105/1 Chiang Mai-Lamphun Rd
Tel. 053 248 604/7
tatchmai@tat.or.th
■ **Chiang Rai**
448/16 Singhaklai Rd
Amphoe Muang
Tel. 053 717 433
or 053 744 674/5
tatchrai@tat.or.th
■ **Hua Hin**
500/51
Phetkasem Rd
Amphoe Cha-am
Tel. 032 471 005/6
■ **Kanchanaburi**
Saeng Chuto Rd
Amphoe Muang
Tel. 034 577 200
■ **Nakhon Ratchasima (Khorat)**
2102–2104, Mittaphap Rd
Amphoe Muang
Tel. 044 213 666
or 044 213 030
tatsima@tat.or.th
■ **Nakhon Si Thammarat**
1180 Bovorn Bazaar, Ratchadamoen Rd
Tel. 075 346 515/6
tatnksir@tat.or.th
■ **Pattaya**
246/1 Chahat Rd, Amphoe Bang Lamung
Tel. 038 428 750
or 038 427 667
■ **Phitsanulok**
209/7–8
Boromtrilokanat Rd
Tel. 055 231 063
tatphlok@tat.or.th
■ **Phuket**
73–75 Phuket Rd, Amphoe Muang
Tel. 076 212 213
or 076 211 036
tatphket@tat.or.th
■ **Surat Thani**
5 Talat Mai Rd, Ban Don
Amphoe Muang
Tel. 077 288818/9
tatsurat@tat.or.th
■ **Tak**
193 Taksin Rd, Amphoe Muang
Tel. 055 514 341
tattak@tat.or.th
■ **Udon Thani**
16/5 Mukmontri Rd
Tel. 042 325 406/7
tatudon@tat.or.th

m.: a man says
w.: a woman says

PRONUNCIATION
Note: Thai is a tonal language and is spoken syllable by syllable. The five tones are :
unaccented monotone,
\ : low,
^ : falling,
/ : high,
v : rising.
The accents used here do not relate to conventional European accents.

SHOPPING
Go shopping: pai soéu khov ng
Too expensive: phe n g mǎk koeun pai
Bigger: yav ǐ kwà
Smaller: nov ǐ kwà, laík kwà
This one: ahne ní
That one: ahne nône
How much is it? thaów rai?
Color: Siv
Do you have another color? khun mi siv hoeùn mav i?

FOOD
Beef: noeúa
Pork: mov u
Chicken: kai
Duck: paìt
Fish: pla
Crab: pou
Shrimp: koûng
Shrimp and lemon grass soup: thòme yam koûng
Cuttlefish: pla moeùk
Egg: khài
Spicy soup: thome yam
Noodles: pà mì
Rice noodles (fine): sen láik
Fried rice: khaów phàt
Fried noodles: phàt thai
Bread (cake-bread): kànov m pàn
Banana: khoùei
Pineapple: sapparót
Orange: pou
Papaya: máláko
Rambboutans: ngnów
Mango: má mǔang
Sugar: nám than

DRINKS
Water: nám
Coffee: kafaidam
Iced coffee: o-liéng
Beer: biya
Orange juice: nám sôm
Alcohol: laôw
Tea: nám tcha

CALENDAR
Monday: wane djan
Tuesday: wane ang kane
Wednesday: wane phoút
Thursday: wan pároeuhàt
Friday: wan soúk
Saturday: wane saov w
Sunday: wane ha thít
Today: wane ní
Yesterday: moeuv a wane ní
Tomorrow: phroung ní
Week: sàpda
Month: dœuene

NUMBERS
Zero: sov un
One: nùng
Two: sov ng
Three: sav m
Four: sì
Five: hâ
Six: hòk
Seven: djèt
Eight: pèt
Nine: kaov w
Ten: sìp
Eleven: sìp aìt
Twelve: sìp sov ng
Twenty: yî sìp
Thirty: sav m sìp
Forty: sì sìp
Fifty: hâ sìp
Sixty: hòk sìp
Seventy: djèt sìp
Eighty: pèt sìp
Ninety: kaôw sìp
One hundred: rói, nùng rói
Two hundred: sov ng rói
One thousand: phane
Ten thousand: moeùan
One million: láne

FINDING ONE'S WAY
Where? thî nav i
When: meûarai
Go (to): pai.
I want to go to...: yàak dja pai...
Come (to): maa
Airport: sànav m bine
Hotel: rong raime
Bus terminal: sàthani rótmai
Station: sàthani rótfai
Street: thà nov ne
Small street: soi
Bridge: sà phav ne
Stop (to): yoùt
Turn (to): liaów
To the left: sái
To the right: kwav
Straight on: trong pai
Go by boat: pai rouea

FAMILY
Greet (to): waî
Brother or sister,
– elder: phî,

– younger: nóng
Woman: phoù yivng
Man: phoù tchai
Mother: maî
Father: phov
Daughter: loùk saov w
Son: loùk tchai
Age: a-yoú
How old are you? khun a-you thaôwrai?
I am ... years old: di-chav n/phov m a-you... pi
How many children...? dèk ki khone?
Play (to): laîne

USUAL EXPRESSIONS
Excuse me: khov w thôde
It doesn't matter: Maî pen rai
Yes: tchai
No: Mai tchai
I don't speak Thai, (m.): Phov m phoûd pha sav thai mai dai, (w.):** di-chav n phouv d pha sav thai maî daî
I speak a little Thai, (m.): Phov m phoûd pha sav thai nít nói, (w.):** di-chav n phoûd pha sav thai nít nói
What do you call ... in Thai? Nî khov w khaov w rîak arai pha sav thai?
What's your name? khun tchôeu à-rai?
My name is..., (m.): phov m tchôeu..., (w.):** di-chav n tchôeu...
Where do you live? khun yoù thî nav i?
I am English/American:
(m.):** phom pen khone Ankrit/Amerikan-sèt,
(w.):** dí-chan pen khone Ankrit/Amerikan-sèt.
I don't understand: Maî kaôw djai
Do you understand me? Kâo djai mav i?
Where are the toilets? Hông nám yoù thî nav i?
Smoke cigarettes (to): soùp bouli

FOOD
Eat (to): ráprathan, fam.:** kin
I'd like to eat: than
Drink: doeùm
I don't want any: maî than, mâi aow
Eat rice (to): kin khaôw
Be thirsty (to): hiov u nám
Hunger: heo kao
Food: a-hav ne

Is it good? a-ròi mav i?
Salty: khaim
Salt: kloeu
Side dishes (served with rice): kàb khâow
Spicy/Hot: phaít
Not spicy/hot: maî phaít
Hot: rónne
Cold: yen
Sour: priaów
Sweet: wuv.an
Restaurant: ráne à-hav nne
The bill, please! (m.): Gep taang khráp, (w.):** Gep taang khav
Chopsticks: ta kiàp

GREETINGS
Hello (m.): Sà wàt dii khráp, (w.):** Sà wàt dii khâ
How are you? (m.): khun sa bai di roe v u khráp?, (w.):** khun sa bai di roe v u khâ?
Well, thank you ! (m.) sa bai di, khòp khun khráp, (w.)** sa bai di, khòp khun khâ
Thank you very much: khòp khun mâk

EMERGENCIES
I'm not feeling well (m.): phov m maî sà bai, (w.):** dì-chav n maî sà bai
I need a doctor: tông kan môw ma reów
Telephone (to): khov
May I use the phone? Kor chai tho rá sàp dai mav i?
Police station: sàthani tamruat
Hospital: rongpháyabane
Post office: praisàniv
Embassy: sàthav n thoûde

SIGHTSEEING
House: bâne
Town: nakhorn
Village: mou bâne
Garden: suav n
Temple: wát
Go to the temple (to): pai wát
Beach: haàt
Island: kò
Mountain: phoù khaov w, doi
Market: ta-làt
Floating market: talàtnám
Canal: khlong
River: maî nám
Country: muang
Royal: luav ng
Lotus: bua

◆ USEFUL ADDRESSES
Ayutthaya, Bangkok

Towns are in alphabetical order. The ▲ symbol refers to the "Itineraries" section; the letter and number (e.g. A1) are grid references to the map on the front and back endpapers. A list of symbols can be found on page 305.

HOTELS
· < 1 000 Baht
1 000 to 2 500 Baht
2 500 to 5 000 Baht
> 5 000 Baht

AYUTTHAYA

▲ 242 E5

RESTAURANT

Pae Krung Kao
U-Thong Rd
Tel. 035 241 555
Floating restaurant moored on the Pa Sak River, with large and pleasantly decorated dining areas on terraces. The Pae Krung Kao, famous in Ayutthaya for its giant freshwater prawns, offers a delightful view of the continuous traffic of barges up and down the river. Boat excursions around the city can also be arranged by the restaurant.

ACCOMMODATION

Krung Si River Hotel
27/2 Rojchana Rd
Tel. 035 244 333
The most comfortable hotel in town, built on the banks of the Pa Sak River. Its boat, the Krung Si Princess, runs cruises on all the rivers in the region. There are many leisure activities available, such as bowling, billiards, fitness center, etc.

U-Thong Inn
Rojchana Road
Tel. 035 242 236
Fax 035 242 235
Open daily
A comfortable, middle-category hotel offering good value for money. Located on the edge of the town, just beyond the intersection leading to the railway station. Try and get one of the rooms in the new wing as they have a small sitting room. What better way to relax after a visit to the

ruins of Ayutthaya than to enjoy a dip in the pool, a sauna or massage. Up to 50 percent reductions during the low season (May–Oct).

BANGKOK

▲ 138 D5-E5

RESTAURANTS

Baan Klang Nam 2
76/77 Chatuchak
Rama 3 Rd
Open daily
A small 'chatuchak' or mini 'weekend market' has opened on Rama 3 Road which runs along the Chao Phraya river. Behind the stalls, on the banks of the river, is a vast paved esplanade where people come to enjoy an evening stroll and admire the sunset. The recently opened Baan Klang Nam 2 occupies a large wooden building on the esplanade, with a terrace overlooking the river. It still relatively unknown on the major tourist routes and offers a wide range of delicious regional dishes, especially fish and seafood. But since the restaurant has a predominantly Thai clientele, many of the dishes are very spicy, so choose carefully. Excellent value for money.

Ban Khanitha
Sukhumvit Soi 23
Tel. 02 258 41 81
Open 11am–2pm
and 6–11pm
If you appreciate traditional Thai food, you will enjoy the local specialties that are served here. The décor of silk paintings and carved teak furniture make for a peaceful ambience.

Cabbages & Condoms
10 Sukhumvit Soi 12
Tel. 02 229 46 10
Open 11am–10pm
The unusual name and décor of this restaurant may surprise the visitor. It is owned by the Thai Family Planning Association next door, and its profits go to various charities. Good Thai food served on two levels. Terrace open in the evening.

Café de Laos
16, Soi Silom, 19
Bangrak
Tel. 02 653 23 38/9
Open daily
This former private house has been attractively renovated. Discover Lao and Issan cuisine, popular throughout Thailand but especially in the northeast. A delightful interior and terrace, and a peaceful atmosphere in the heart of Bangkok. Prices are very reasonable.

Lemon Grass
5/1 Soi 24,
Sukhumvit Road
Tel. 02 258 86 37
This small, pleasant restaurant is particularly popular with the expatriate community. It serves delicious Thai cuisine that is not too spicy. Try the excellent grapefruit salad (Yam Somho).

Mango Tree
37, Soi Tantawan
Suriwongs Rd
Tel. 02 236 28 20
Open daily
Enjoy carefully presented Thai cuisine in a romantic and exotic atmosphere, against a background of

traditional live music. Only a few minutes from the busy commercial district of the Silom Road, it is open at noon and in the evening. A wide range of green and red curries.

Sala Rim Naam
Oriental Hotel
New Rd
Charoen Krung
Tel. 02 437 29 18
Buffet at noon
and from 7pm
The 'Waterside Pavilion' is one of six restaurants belonging to the Oriental Hotel on the opposite bank of the Chao Phraya River. Built and decorated in classic Thai style it serves traditional Thai cuisine (another one, the Normandie, specializes in French cuisine). From 8.30pm there are Sukhothai dance performances that are as appealing as the food. Exceptional setting.

Sea Food Market Restaurant
89 Sukhumvit Soi 24
Tel. 02 261 20 71
This is a rather unusual restaurant; you go round the market with a trolley selecting your food yourself, pay for it at the checkout counter then decide how you want it to be prepared. Large choice of ultra-fresh fish and exotic seafood. Cantine-style décor.

ACCOMMODATION

Amari Watergate
847 Petchburi Rd
Tel. 02 653 90 00
Fax 02 653 90 45
At the heart of the commercial district

RESTAURANTS

◻ < 500 Baht
◻ 500 to 1 000 Baht
◻ > 1 000 Baht

*Dialing codes: Ayutthaya: 035
Bangkok: 02*

of Pratunam, this modern 34-storey hotel is practical and charming. It has a 3,000-square-foot, top-quality sports center. Groups are welcome on a special floor with separate access.

◻◻◻◻◻◻◻

✿ Four Seasons
155 Ratchadamri Rd
Tel. 02 251 61 27
Fax 02 253 53 90
The main attraction of this beautiful, first-class hotel is its exquisite interior decoration. Hand-painted silk tapestries hang in every room, and those displayed in the entrance hall might actually make you dizzy. Craftsmen who painted the main piece that hangs above the central staircase took two years to complete their work. The Spice Market, the hotel restaurant, is also exceptional as it is set up as a former spice market where a wide range of exotic products are available for purchase. Famous for its impeccable service and exceptional level of comfort, The Four Seasons is considered to be one of the best hotels in South East Asia.

◻◻◻◻◻◻◻◻

Grand Hyatt Erawan
494 Ratchadamri Rd
Tel. 02 254 12 34
Fax 02 253 63 08
With huge marble columns and elephants, this hotel's imposing architecture may at first be rather over-whelming, but the spacious hall and its lovely greenery soon win over the visitor. The hotel is located at the heart of the

business district, and it houses an impressive collection of contemporary art. The Italian restaurant, the Spasso, becomes a trendy discotheque at night, with live performances by American artists.

◻◻◻◻◻◻◻

✿ Oriental
48 Oriental Avenue
Tel. 02 236 04 00/20
www.mandarin-oriental.com/bangkok
One of the oldest and most prestigious establishments

THE ORIENTAL, BANGKOK

in Bangkok. Built in 1876, the first wing of this hotel has kept its colonial style and has magnificent suites that were once occupied by W. Somerset Maugham and other famous writers. The new wing, erected in 1976, is also very comfortable and luxurious. The majestic teak chandeliers in the great hall are particularly

impressive. The Oriental's six restaurants (see previous page) contribute to its excellent reputation. So does its excellent spa.

◻◻◻◻◻◻◻◻

Rembrandt
Sukhumvit Soi 18
Tel. 02 261 71 00/4
Fax 02 261 70 17
A luxurious and charming hotel with extremely reasonable prices for an establishment of this category. The Rang Mahal,

one of the restaurants within the hotel complex, serves some of the best Indian cuisine in Bangkok. For a more informal atmosphere, head for the Señor Pico, a friendly Mexican eating place with a live South American band.

◻◻◻◻◻◻◻◻

Shanti Lodge
37 Sri Ayutthaya Rd
Tel. 02 281 24 97
Away from the

tourist areas but still easily accessible, the Shanti Lodge is a quiet and attractive guesthouse. The rooms are plain but quite charming. Friendly staff and family atmosphere. Vegetarian specialties.

◻

Silom Serene
7, Soi Pipat (Silom Soi 3) Bangrak
Tel. 02 636 65 94
Fax 02 636 65 90
Open daily
Only a stone's throw from the suspended metro station of Sala Daeng, the Silom Serene is a haven of tranquillity in the heart of the business district. Eighty-six tastefully decorated rooms, meticulous service and peace and quiet guaranteed. Ideally located for discovering Bangkok by metro – that way you don't waste precious time in traffic jams.

◻◻◻◻◻◻
◻◻◻◻

Sofitel
188, Silom Rd
Bangrak
Tel. 02 238 19 91
Fax 02 238 19 88
H3616@accor.com
Formerly the Monarch Lee Garden, this 38-story tower is centrally located on the Silom Road. Its 454 luxury rooms have all been recently renovated. The hotel offers meticulous service and has several prestigious restaurants, for example the V9 where you can enjoy wine tastings and a magnificent view of the lights of the 'City of Angels'. French management and a predominantly French clientele.

◻◻◻◻◻◻◻

◆ USEFUL ADDRESSES
Chiang Mai

Dialing code: Chiang Mai: 053

Swiss Lodge
3 Convent Rd
Tel. 02 233 53 45
Fax 02 236 94 25
This hotel, a few minutes' walk from the busy Silom area, offers a more personal service than most of the large hotels. Prices are very reasonable and the degree of comfort high. No groups.
▣◨▣✻▣➔▣▦

Viengtai
42 Tanee Road
Tel. 02 280 54 54
Fax 02 281 81 53
This establishment is located in a small, quiet street of Banglumpoo, an area that boasts many small hotels and guesthouses. It offers good value for money and is clean and comfortable, but is somewhat lacking in charm.
▣◨▣▥➔▣

◼ NIGHTLIFE

Bamboo Bar
Oriental Hotel
New Rd
Tel. 02 659 90 00
A bit overly-chic but a very romantic bar. Excellent music, jazz in particular, every day from 11am to midnight.
🎵

Hard Rock Café
424/3–6 Siam Square
Soi 11
Tel. 02 251 07 92/4
Daily 11am–2am
The famous chain has opened a Hard Rock Café in Bangkok. Rock music and American food attracts a young trendy crowd.
🎵

Irish Xchange
1/5 Convent Rd
Tel. 02 266 71 60/1
Daily until 2am
If you find yourself missing dark beer
and Irish music, this is the perfect place for you.
🎵

Met Bar
Metropolitan Hotel
27 South Sathorn Rd
Tel. 02 625 3333
One of the bars of the ultra-chic newly opened Metropolitan, sister to the no less hip London hotel.
🎵

Saxophone
3/8, Phayathai Rd
Victory Monument
Tel. 02 246 54 72
Open daily
A pub which has enjoyed a good reputation for a number of years. The Saxophone invites you to spend an evening in its extremely relaxed atmosphere among a local and international clientele. You can listen to live music – two groups per evening playing jazz, blues, funk or reggae – sitting near the band or upstairs, on cushions. Very affordable prices and only a stone's throw from the Victory Monument metro station.

Spasso's
Grand Hyatt Erawan Hotel
494, Ratchadamri Rd
Pathumwan
Tel. 02 254 12 34
Open Mon.–Sat.
10pm–1am
Easily accessible, which is very useful for getting back to your hotel in the early hours. The Art-Deco dance floor is tiny but exquisite.

◼ CHIANG MAI
▲ 260 D2

◼ RESTAURANTS

Antique House
71 Charoen
Prathet Rd
Tel. 053 275 125
Daily 11am–midnight
This old house, built over 125 years ago, in the time of Rama V, was at first an antique shop. It was declared an official Thai Cultural Heritage Center, and a few years ago part of it was turned into a restaurant, where northern Thai cuisine and specialties from various regions are on offer. Live band every night.
▣◨▣✖

Le Coq d'Or
68/1 Koh Klang Rd
Tel. 053 282 024
Created twenty years ago and set in a magnificent villa in south Chiang Mai, this is one of the most famous French restaurants in the city. Fine food in cosy surroundings.
◨▣▥▣✿

**Riverside
Bar and Restaurant**
9–11 Charoen
Rat Rd
Tel. 053 243 239
Warm and romantic, the Riverside is very popular and often packed. You can enjoy a candlelit dinner on the terrace, which looks out onto the banks of the Ping River, or inside, at the bar or in the more lively dining room where a quality band plays. Good coffee and cappucino. Thai and Western cuisine.
▨◨▣▣✖

✪ Tha Nam
43/3 Changklan Rd
Tel. 053 275 125
Set in an old wooden building, on the banks of the Ping River, the Tha Nam serves northern specialties, such as the famous Chiang Mai hors-d'œuvres or Pla-choum,
poached fish in a delicious hot sauce. There is a superb terrace decorated with a mass of plants and a hall where traditional music is performed every evening from 7pm until 10pm. Some rooms are also available. The owner is a painter who exhibits his works in a room near the entrance. Pleasantly furnished and decorated in rustic style, this restaurant has a very relaxing and soothing atmosphere.
▨◨▣

◼ ACCOMMODATION

Belle Villa
Amphoe Hangdong
Tel. 053 365 318/2
Reservations in Bangkok:
Tel. 02 693 28 95
www.bellevillachiang mai.com/
The Belle Villa is located some 18 miles from Chiang Mai, on the Hangdong to Samoeng mountain road. It consists of red-brick chalets set in a magnificent park surrounded by forests. Do not be surprised by the stone fireplaces in the chalets; during the winter the temperature can drop down to as low as 40°F. In the high season campfires are lit. A friendly atmosphere, and a place where fresh air and tranquility are guaranteed.
▣◨✻▣▥➔▦

Galare Guest House
7 Charoen
Prathet Rd
Tel. 053 818 887
Fax 053 279 088
www.galare.com
Situated on the banks of the Ping River, this large,

RESTAURANTS
- ◘ < 500 Baht
- ◘ 500 to 1 000 Baht
- ◘ > 1 000 Baht

fairly recently constructed house is built in the Lanna style of architecture. The rooms, set around a garden, are small but clean and, at moderate prices, offer all the comforts associated with a middle-category hotel.
◘◘☒▤▥◪◆➔◙

Joy's House
114, Moo 9
Sampeesrue Village
Tel. 053 854 213
Fax 053 248 960
Open daily
Thailand, a tourist destination with a remarkable hotel infrastructure to suit every pocket, doesn't offer 'bed and breakfast', an option widespread and popular in all English-language countries. So Joy, the owner, knew what she was doing when she opened this family hotel in the heart of Chiang Mai. Nine comfortable, spacious rooms and plenty of peace and quiet, with the opportunity to meet Joy's family. A warm welcome and friendly service awaits those who want to leave the beaten tourist track for a while.
▤▥◘▥▥◪ ◙◙◙

Regent Resort Chiang Mai
Mae Rim Samoeng Old Rd
Tel. 053 298 181
www.fourseasons.com/chiangmai
Reservations in Bangkok:
Tel. 02 251 61 27
This building is the most striking example of Lanna architecture and style of decoration. Opened in 1995, the Regent is surrounded by hillside paddy fields and consists of

pavilions which include several rooms and a terrace with comfortable teak furniture. It also has a renowned cookery school and an excellent spa. Impeccable service throughout.
☒◘◪☒▤▥◪◙

River Ping Palace
385/2 Charoen Prathet Rd
Tel. 053 274 932
Fax 053 204 281
A one-hundred-year-old house with original furniture and decor run by an Italian who has given it an intimate, friendly atmosphere. The restaurant, on the banks of the Ping, serves local specialties adapted to suit Western tastes. Reserve well in advance as this hotel only has ten rooms and is often fully booked.
☒◪▤▥◪➔◙

Rydges Tapae
22, Calyapoom Rd
Tel. 053 251 531
Fax 053 251 465
www.rydges-chiangmai.com
Opened in 2002, this is Chiang Mai's most recent and certainly its most modern hotel. It stands on the edge of the town, near the Tapae Gate, only 10 minutes from the airport and 15 minutes from the city center. All mod cons and reasonably priced.
▤▥◪☒◙◙ ◙

Tamarind Village
50/1 Ratdamnern Rd
Tel. 053 418 896/9
Fax 053 418 900
Open daily
Tamarind Village has 40 luxury rooms, a great deal of charm, and peaceful and serene atmosphere where you can relax and unwind.

A tasteful rustic decor, landscaped tropical garden and impeccable service make this one of the city's best hotels in this category.
◘◪▥◪◆▥☒◙◙

Crystal Cave
Empress Hotel
199 Chang Klan Rd
Tel. 053 270 240
Fax 053 272 467
The most popular discotheque in the Chiang Mai.

The Pub
189 Huay Kaew Rd
Tel. 053 211 550
Open 11am–2pm, 5pm–1am (midnight on Mon.
Located in a fascinating traditional house. Considered one of the best bars in the country, albeit a little expensive.

Riverside Bar & Restaurant
9/11 Charoenrajd Rd
Tel. 053 243 329
Open 10am–1am
Popular meeting place. Good music in the evenings. Friendly staff and management.

▲ 292 D1

Sabun Nga
226/50
Sunkhongnoi Rd
Tel. 053 712 290
or 053 716 440
Open 8am–1am
A perfect place to watch performances of the traditional folk dances of northern Thailand (every evening from 7.30pm), while enjoying a Khantoke meal on the first floor. On the ground floor, where a more international band performs, good Thai cuisine is served.
▤▥◙

Chiang Rai Inn
661, Uttarakit Rd
Tel. 053 711 483
or 053 712 673
Hotel built in the traditional architectural style and consisting of several buildings on three levels, set around a garden. The hotel has comfortable, spacious rooms and is quiet despite its central location.
◘▥◪▤▥◪◙➔◙

Golden Triangle Inn
590 Paholyothin Rd
Tel. 053 71 13 39
Fax 053 713 963
Charming hotel surrounded by greenery, with each room looking out onto the garden. Its restaurant is famous for its Thai and Western cuisine as well as for the traditional music shows that take place there on weekend evenings. The hotel also organizes high-class treks.
▥◪▤▥◪➔◙

Phu Chasai Mountain Resort and Spa
388, Moo 4
Baan Salong Nai
Mae Chan
Tel. 053 918 636/7
Fax 053 918 333
Open daily
A romantic resort in a magnificent mountain setting to the northeast of Chiang Rai. The hillside bungalows are designed to blend perfectly with the landscape. Enjoy a real retreat in the cool mountain air but, be warned, temperatures can drop below 50°F in December and January. There's a natural spa where guests can relax and unwind in the peace and tranquillity of this magical setting.
▥◪◪☒◆▥▥◙

◆ USEFUL ADDRESSES
Chiang Saen

Dialing codes: Hua Hun: 032
Chiang Saen: 054

CHIANG SAEN
▲ 302 D1

RESTAURANTS

Rimkhong
Golden Triangle Rd
Tel. 053 650 459
Open 8am–8pm
If you have never tasted pla-beuk, the largest freshwater fish in the world, be sure to try it at the Rimkhong. This restaurant, which is located on the banks of the Mekong River between Chiang Saen and the Golden Triangle, is popular for its range of specialties based on several varietes of fish. An added attraction is the pleasant view and generous dishes at reasonable prices.

ACCOMMODATION

✪ **Anantara Resort and Spa**
Golden Triangle
229, Moo 1
Tel. 053 784 084
Fax 053 784 090
www.anantara.com
Open daily
A magnificent example of the purest Lanna style, the Anantara overlooks the Golden Triangle and has a great deal of charm. It combines ultramodern luxurious comfort with a traditional architecture that blends perfectly with this splendid site. The two wings of the hotel have finely decorated rooms, all with an exceptional view. This is much more than a standard holiday resort; not only does it offer all the sports and leisure activities that are usually expected of such a high-class establishment, but is also an excellent departure point for exploring the cultural wealth of the region. The incredible variety of tropical fruit that is grown in the park is served to guests in generous quantities. Excellent value for money, considering the category of this hotel. The hotel offers a 3-night package that includes the activity of your choice – spa (superb), golf or polo on elephants!

Gin's Guest House
Golden Triangle Rd
Tel. 053 650 847
This guesthouse, tastefully decorated in a traditional rustic style, is located on the road leading out of Chiang Saen. It consists of bungalows set around a garden, some of which have attractive views out over the river. Modest and well-run establishment with a friendly welcome. In the high season, a small restaurant is open to those staying in the guesthouse.

HUA HIN
▲ 198 D6

ACCOMMODATION

Chiva-Som International Health Resort
73/4 Petchkasem Rd
Tel. 032 536 536
Fax 032 511 154
www.chivasom.com
The Chiva-Som is a health-spa center, with a dedicated team of health specialists at the service of guests. Personalized treatment includes beauty therapy, relaxation, hydrotherapy and massage, all in sumptuous surroundings. This is just the place for easing away stress, restoring energy, and finding a lasting sense of "inner peace, contentment and fulfillment". It comes at a price though.

Evason
9 Paknampran Beach
Pranburi
Tel. 032 632 111
Fax 032 632 112
www.sixsenses.com/ evason-huahin
Located a few miles south of Hua Hin, on Paknampran Beach, the Evason is one of a new generation of hotels that combines luxury and comfort with a traditional decor and architecture. Set in a magnificent park, it has an excellent spa and a magnificent pool overlooking the sea. Impeccable service, of course.

Royal Garden Village
41/1 Petchkasem Beach Rd
Tel. 032 520 250
Fax 032 520 259
Beautiful traditional Thai houses set in 25 acres of tropical gardens and with all modern amenities. Thai cookery classes are also available.

✪ **Sofitel Central Hua-Hin**
1 Damnernkasem Rd
Tel. 032 512 021
Fax 032 511 014
Reservations in Bangkok:
Tel. 02 233 09 80
Formerly known as the Railway Hotel, this jewel of colonial hotel architecture was built in 1923 and was later bought and restored by the French group Accor. This luxurious establishment is surrounded by 40 acres of gardens overlooking the Gulf of Siam. Its pre-1940s charm has attracted many movie makers. The Sofitel Central Hua-Hin is a good departure point for the many excursions that can be made to the nearby jungle waterfalls and caves. It also houses a library containing more than 2,000 works written in different languages.

KANCHANABURI
▲ 188 D5

ACCOMMODATION

Consaed River Kwai Resort
18/9, Moo 5, Ladya
Tel. 034 631 443/9
Located in the center of a superb park, the Consaed is the perfect place to stay in Kanchanaburi if you don't want to be too isolated in the heart of the jungle. All mod cons.

Floatel
Paksang, Tha Sao Saiyoke
Reservations in Bankok:
Tel. 02 247 53 73
Open daily
An hotel with a difference. The Floatel winds its way through the jungle like a 'train' of delightful floating bungalows built on rafts. Ideal if you like something out of the ordinary.

River Kwai Jungle Rafts
Reservations in Bangkok:
Tel. 02 243 30 69
Fax 02 246 56 79
For a complete

RESTAURANTS
- ▣ < 500 Baht
- ▣ 500 to 1 000 Baht
- ▣ > 1 000 Baht

change, go to Kanchanaburi and enjoy nature at its purest in the heart of the jungle. Very basic accommodation in boatels (bungalow-rafts) moored along the river. Basic comfort with a very authentic flavor.
▣ ▣

KOH CHANG
▲ *192* F6

ACCOMMODATION

Aiyapura Resort and Spa
29, Moo 3
Tel. 039 555 111/5
Fax 039 555 118
Open daily
A recently built and certainly the island's most luxurious hotel. The Aiyapura has all the ingredients for an 'exotic holiday' cocktail – a fine sandy beach, palm trees, transparent sea and luxury. Rather expensive.
▣ ▣ ▣ ▣ ▣ ▣
▣ ▣ ▣ ▣

KOH SAMET
▲ *192* E6

ACCOMMODATION

Ao Prao Resort
Ao Prao Beach
Reservations in Bangkok:
Tel. 02 438 97 71/2
Fax 02 439 03 52
www.aopraoresort.com
Only two hours' drive from Bangkok, Koh Samet is an ideal destination for visitors in search of tranquillity but with limited time. The Ao Prao is a luxury hotel with a private beach, tastefully decorated hillside bungalows and plenty of peace and quiet. It also offers the best value for money on the island.

KOH SAMUI
▲ *202* D8

RESTAURANTS

Le Bateau
Bophut Beach
Tel. 077 425 297
Closed Tue.
Thai cuisine based on fish as well as unusual French dishes are prepared by Christian, a Belgian who has been living in Koh Samui for fifteen years. Don't miss the swordfish in mustard sauce! The chef also organizes sea outings in his own boat.
▣

ACCOMMODATION

✪ Boat House
Choeng Mon Beach
Tel. 077 425 041
www.imperialhotels.com/boathouse
Reservations in Bangkok:
Tel. 02 261 90 00
The accommodation here is original and the bungalows themselves rather unusual. They are teak barges that were brought from Ratchaburi and Phitsanulok, then restored and luxuriously furnished. The boats, which are actually like small apartments, are rustic yet perfectly comfortable. You will feel as if you are sailing the high seas, albeit without the rocking and rolling motion. The swimming pool is also in the shape of a ship's hull. The Boat House is located in one of the quietest areas of the island, and faces an islet that can be reached on foot at low tide.
▣ ▣ ▣ ▣ ▣ ▣ ▣ ▣

Laem Set Inn
Laem Set
Ao Na Khai
Tel. 077 424 393

www.laemset.com
Renowned as the most elegant of the small hotels in Samui, the Laem Set Inn brings together the genuine architectural styles of traditional dwellings from different parts of Thailand. It stands in isolation on one side of a cove on the southern tip of the island; the location offers the opportunity to enjoy one of the last pieces of unspoilt paradise that are left in the world.
▣ ▣ ▣ ▣ ▣ ▣ ▣

✪ Le Royal Meridien Baan Taling Ngam
295 Moo 3
Baan Taling Ngam
Tel. 077 423 019
Fax: 077 423 220
www.meridien.kosamui.com
Perched on a hillside over a spectacular beach, Le Royal Meridien offers luxurious Thai-style beachside or cliff villas, deluxe rooms and suites. Managed by the Mandarin Oriental Group.
67 rooms
▣ ▣ ▣ ▣

Muang Kulaypan Hotel
Chawen Beach
Tel. 077 422 305
www.samui-hotels.com/kulaypan
Reservations in Bangkok:
Tel. 02 713 06 68
This hotel's 300-foot-long facade provides guests with an exceptional view over the sea and the nearby islets. At the Muang Kulaypan Hotel the Thai style of decoration is combined with all modern amenities and a touch of contemporary art. Most of the rooms have a view and those on the ground

floor have access to a small private garden.
▣ ▣ ▣ ▣ ▣ ▣ ▣ ▣

Baan Hin Sai
5/5, Moo 3
Bo Phud Beach
Tel. 077 422 624/7
www.samui-hotels.com/baanhinsai
The Baan Hin Sai, which means 'house of stone and sand', is built on the rocks overlooking the sea. Its pretty hillside bungalows are surrounded by lush vegetation and, although it doesn't have direct access to the beach, it offers good value for money. A terraced pool offers a splendid view of the sea.
▣ ▣ ▣ ▣ ▣ ▣ ▣ ▣
▣ ▣ ▣

KRABI
▲ *224* C9

RESTAURANT

Podaphranang Kitchen
Ao Nang Beach
Tel. 075 637 130/3
Fax 075 637 134/5
In a breathtaking setting at the foot of the famous Ao Nang cliffs, this restaurant, built on a circular plan, opens out onto the beach. Built of wood, it blends perfectly with its natural surroundings. The clientele consists mostly of tourists, yet the Thai cuisine on offer is varied, authentic and refined. A delightful locally produced white wine goes down a treat with the seafood dishes. Refined service. Behind the restaurant is a hotel, the Phra Nang Inn, which offers comfortable rooms decorated with seashells.
▣ ▣ ▣

Dialing codes: Krabi: 075
Lampang: 054

HOTELS
- < 1 000 Baht
- 1 000 to 2 500 Baht
- 2 500 to 5 000 Baht
- > 5 000 Baht

ACCOMMODATION

Krabi Resort
Ao Nang Beach
Tel. 075 637 030
Fax 075 637 051
Enticingly luxurious palm-roofed bungalows in a beautiful parkland setting. The resort's location, slightly away from the main road, is by the sea and is sheltered from the wind by a hill. The Krabi Resort offers good value for money and there is a choice of accommodation: either one of 63 comfortable and well-appointed bungalows with a veranda or one of 40 rooms with a balcony looking out onto the swimming pool.

Pakasai Resort
88, Moo 3
Ao Nang
Tel. 075 637 777
Fax 075 637 637
You can see the limestone cliffs of Ao Nang from your bath tub at the Pakasai resort. In fact, the hotel's palm-roofed bungalows are built on a hillside overlooking the sea and the bay, and surrounded by a carefully maintained tropical park. The height of luxury.

✪ Rayavadee
Ao Phranang Cape
Tel. 075 620 704
Fax 075 620 630
www.rayavadee.com
Only accessible by boat, this top-class hotel is set in natural parkland on the Ao Phranang Cape and is dominated by breathtaking cliffs. Its 100 circular pavilions with rounded roofs have

been constructed like private villas, and the restaurants that are part of the complex serve both Thai and Western cuisine. The Rayavadee also offers the tourist a wide range of watersports and other activities. Not for travelers on a tight budget!

LAMPANG

▲ 276 D2

RESTAURANT

Riverside Lampang
328 Tipchang Rd
Tel. 054 221 861
Similar to the Riverside in Chiang Mai, the Riverside Lampang is set in a charming location on the banks of the Wang River. Built of wood, in a rustic style, it serves good Thai and European cuisine, including pizzas (not so surprising, perhaps, as the restaurant is run by an Italian). A live band plays every evening from 7.30pm.

ACCOMMODATION

Ban Fai
Chiang Rai rd
Tel. 054 224 602
Ban Fai is a small family guesthouse with just seven rooms. Guests sleep on mattresses laid out on the floor. The building is a well-kept teak wood house. In Thai 'ban-fai' means 'cotton house', and indeed very pretty cotton artifacts, as well as pottery, are produced here. Also known for its restaurant, this friendly place is popular with local people, which is always a good sign.

Lampang River Lodge
229, Boonyawat Rd
Tel. 054 336 640/1
Fax 054 250 052
Open daily
A comfortable, rustic hotel on the banks of the River Wang, with 60 or so bungalows on stilts surrounded by a luxuriant park. Less than 4 miles from the town center.

MAE HONG SON

▲ 286 C1

ACCOMMODATION

Little Eden Guest House
Soppong (about 43 miles from Mae Hong Son)
Tel. 053 617 054
Fax 053 617 053
http://littleeden-guesthouse.com
Formerly the T-Rex House, this guest house at Soppong has nine bungalows with toilets and hot water, a definite plus in the dry season when temperatures can drop below 50°F. It stands in a pleasant setting with its own pool, and offers excellent value for money in this category. A good base from which to discover the villages in the area.

✪ Piya Guest House
1/1 Soi Khunlun Praphat Rd
Tel. 053 611 260
Fairly recently built guesthouse on the small Jonc Khan lake. It consists of basic but modest and well-kept rooms set around a small garden, and some bungalows. Bar and restaurant, with billiard table, available to guests, in front of the house. Excellent value for money so often fully booked.

Tara Mae Hong Son
Tambol Pangmoo
Tel. 053 611 021
Fax 053 611 252
Reservations in Bangkok:
Tel. 02 261 90 00
First-class hotel located on the outskirts of town and consisting of small buildings not much higher than the trees of the surrounding teak forest. Spacious and pleasant rooms. Comprehensive sports facilities.

MAE SAI

▲ 304 D1

ACCOMMODATION

Wangthong
299 Paholyothin Rd
Tel. 053 733 388/55
Fax 053 733 399
www.wangthong.com
Reservations in Bangkok:
Tel. 02 225 92 98/99
The luxurious Wangthong is without doubt the most comfortable hotel in Mae Sai, the northernmost town in Thailand. The hotel is less than a hundred yards from the border with Burma, which is marked by the Mae Sai River; from the ninth floor you can see the riverbank on the Burmese side. Small discotheque.

MUKDAHAN

▲ 236 G3

ACCOMMODATION

Mukdahan Grand Hotel
78 Songnangsatid Rd
Tel. 042 612 020
Fax 042 612 021
Reservations in Bangkok:
Tel. 02 931 04 55
This is the most modern and comfortable hotel

RESTAURANTS

- < 500 Baht
- 500 to 1 000 Baht
- > 1 000 Baht

Dialing codes: Mae Hon Son: 053; Mae Sai: 053; Mukdahan: 042; Nakhon Ratchasima: 044; Nong Khai: 042; Pattaya: 038

in the Mukdahan region. Across from Mukdahan, on the other side of the Mekong River, is Savannaket, the second-largest city in Laos. Barges cross the river several times a day, and it is possible to go over to the Laotian side as long as you have obtained a visa in Bangkok beforehand. Wat Phra That Phanom, about 30 miles from the hotel, is the most famous temple in northeastern Thailand and is open to visitors. Substantial discount for rooms reserved from Bangkok.

NAKHON PATHOM

▲ *186* D5

ACCOMMODATION

Rose Garden
Km 32,
Petchkasem Rd
Tel. 034 322 544
Fax 034 322 775
Located about 50 miles from Bangkok, the Rose Garden is set in extensive parkland on the banks of the Nakhon Chaisri River. This peaceful place is more than a hotel, and it figures in many excursions from the capital. A wide variety of cultural events are organized, ranging from traditional dances to elephant training. With its golf course, horse-riding center and tennis courts, the hotel is a luxurious holiday center no more than one hour away from Bangkok.

NAKHON RATCHASIMA (KHORAT)

▲ *230* E4

ACCOMMODATION

Chomsurang
2701/2 Mahat
Thai Rd
Tel. 044 257 088
Fx. 044 252 897
www.chomsurang.
com
The Chomsurang is good value for money in this rapidly expanding industrial city, which sees few tourists. Nakhon Ratchasima is an ideal departure point for a visit to the historic site of Phimai, a Khmer temple dating from the Angkor period, some 30 miles away. The hotel itself is well run and is as comfortable as any of the provincial hotels you may come across.

Khao Yai Park Resort
Thanarat Rd
Amphoe Pakchong
Tel. 044 297 297
Fax 044 297 279
Reservations
in Bangkok:
Tel. 02 613 72 73
A comfortable hotel set in a stunningly picturesque clearing in Khao Yai National Park, the largest national park in the country, which stretches across several provinces. The backdrop is luxuriant mountain landscape, with stunning waterfalls and flourishing plant and animal life, which can all be seen and explored. You can also enjoy the spring-water swimming pool, and take one of the canoe trips or four-wheel-drive excursions that the hotel organizes.

NONG KHAI

▲ *236* F2

ACCOMMODATION

Mekong Royal Nongkhai
22, Jomanee Beach
Amphoe Muang
Tel. 042 420 024
Fax 042 421 280
Reservations
in Bangkok:
Tel. 02 272 00 87
Luxurious hotel located on the banks of the Mekong River, near the bridge recently built between Nongkhai and Vientiane (capital of Laos) to celebrate Thai-Laotian friendship. It has spacious rooms and several bars and restaurants, as well as sports facilities.

Nongkhai Grand Hotel
589 Moo 5,
Nongkhai-
Poanpisai Rd,
Amphoe Muang
Tel. 044 420 033
Fax 044 412 026
www.nongkhaigrand.
com
Comfortable and convenient with a pool, bars and restaurants.

Sawasdee Guesthouse
402 Meechai Rd
Tel. 042 412 502
This is an unassuming little guesthouse in an old restored building opposite the Wat Sri Khun Muang, in the city center. Only four of the rooms have air conditioning and bathrooms with hot water; the rest are more basic but well maintained. The decoration is an intriguing mix of traditional Thai and western knickknacks!

PATTAYA

▲ *191* E6

ACCOMMODATION

Central Wongamat
Naklua Amphoe
Bang Lamung
Tel. 038 426 990
Fax 038 428 599
Reservations
in Bangkok:
Tel. 02 541 10 71
Chalets and bungalows set in tropical gardens extending over 25 acres overlook a superb private beach. The hotel resort includes several restaurants, and a famous barbecue for up to 350 people.

Garden Lodge
Naklua Rd
Tel. 038 429 109
Although this hotel does not directly overlook the beach, it offers total comfort and friendly service at very reasonable prices. During the dry season, breakfast (85 Baht) is served as an open-air buffet.

Rabbit Resort
Dongtan Beach
Jomtien
Tel. 038 303 303
www.rabbitresort.
com
Open daily Pattaya, which enjoyed a major tourist boom a few years ago, has an extensive hotel infrastructure of predominantly large and unprepossessing buildings. The Rabbit Resort offers attractive bungalows built in classic Thai style, in a tropical garden setting. The hotel has two pools and is less than 100 yards from the beach.

◆ USEFUL ADDRESSES
Phitsanulok

Dialing codes: Phitsanulok: 055
Phuket: 076

HOTELS
- ⬚ < 1 000 Baht
- ⬚ 1 000 to 2 500 Baht
- ⬚ 2 500 to 5 000 Baht
- ⬚ > 5 000 Baht

PHITSANULOK
▲ *258* D3

ACCOMMODATION

Rain Forest Resort
42 MU. 9
Amphoe
Wangthong
Tel. 055 293 085
Fax 055 293 086
www.rainforestthailand
.com
Built in a natural forest with rocky formations in the Phitsanulok region, this hotels consists of small stone houses which blend perfectly with the landscape. You can go for long walks in still unspoilt surroundings, or visit the Thung Salang Luang and Phu Hin Rongkla national parks, as well as the magnificent Kangsong and Kangsopa waterfalls nearby. You will enjoy the comfort and the tasteful decoration of this discreet and relaxing place. The restaurant serves excellent Thai and Western cuisine.
⬚⬚⬚⬚⬚⬚⬚

Youth Hostel
38 Sanambin Rd
Tel. 055 242 060
www.tyha.org
www.hostels.com/en/
th
One of the most charming youth hostels in the country. Its location on the road to the airport, away from the dusty center of this rapidly expanding town, is a distinct advantage. Large rooms furnished in pre-1940s style in a comfortable building dating from the 1950s. Also a pleasant garden and an open-air restaurant.
⬚⬚⬚

PHUKET
▲ *210* C9

RESTAURANTS

❂ **The Boathouse Wine and Grill**
2/2 Patak Rd
Kata Beach
Tel. 076 330 015
This hotel is situated above a magnificent beach and islet. It enjoys a high reputation thanks to its excellent wine list and the cuisine it offers, a combination of both Thai and European specialties. Intimate surroundings and comfortable armchairs in which you can watch the sun go down on the Andaman Sea every evening. Special introduction to Thai food by the chef at the weekend. The Boathouse also has 33 well-equipped rooms and 3 suites. This establishment is well worth a visit.
⬚⬚⬚

Kan Aeng
Chao Fa Rd
Chalong Bay
Tel. 076 381 212
Open
10am–10.30pm
Kan Aeng is in fact two restaurants standing a few hundred yards from one another along a cove used by local fishermen. Both places offer dishes based on various types of seafood. Do not miss the plamong-prao, a delicious local fish cooked on a grill.
⬚⬚

Old Siam
Karon Beach Rd
Tel. 076 65 52
The traditional Thai roofs that are a conspicuous sight along the coastal road above Karon Beach are not those of a wat but of a restaurant set in what was once
a Siamese house. Refined Thai food is served outisde on the terrace or in the dining room inside. Muffled atmosphere and xylophone music. Buffet-dinner every Wed. and Sun, 295 Baht.
⬚⬚⬚

Thai Naan, Srivichai
16 Wichitsongkhram Rd
Tel. 076 226 164
Former palace converted into a restaurant. Dinner-show every evening (classical Thai dance and music played on traditional instruments such as the ranat-ek). Sitting on cushions, you will enjoy both the food and the performance by the graceful Ramakien artists. The menu offers a variety of regional specialties.
⬚⬚⬚⬚

ACCOMMODATION

❂ **Amanpuri**
Pansea Beach
P.O. Box 196
Tel. 076 324 333
Fax 076 324 100
www.amanresorts.com
40 rooms
Set in a coconut plantation, this piece of paradise has 40 grand luxe, exquisite Thai-style pavilions and 30 private villas with spectacular views connected by elevated walkways to the main buildings. Perfect service, gourmet restaurants serving Thai and Italian food, and all watersports can be expected at this idyllic resort.
⬚⬚⬚⬚⬚⬚

❂ **The Banyan Tree Resort and Spa**
33 Moo 4
Srisoonthorn Rd
Cherngtalay
Amphur Talang
Tel. 076 324 374
Fax 076 324 375
www.banyantree.phuket.com
On Bang Tao Bay on the northwestern coast of Phuket, The Banyan Tree has 98 private villas, each with their own pools, jacuzzis, and walled gardens. The sophisticated restaurants vary from seafood to spa cuisine.
⬚⬚⬚⬚⬚⬚⬚

Cape Panwa Hotel
Cap de Panwa
Tel. 076 391 123/5
Fax 076 391 177
www.capepanwa.com
Reservations
in Bangkok:
Tel. 02 233 89 89
or 02 233 89 98
The southern extremity of Phuket, which is sheltered from the monsoon winds, is one of the few places on the island where it is possible to go swimming right through the year. The luxurious hotel and its restaurants overlook a superb beach served by a small funicular. There are some top-class villas on the hillside, and, on the paradisial beach, an old Chinese-Portuguese house containing the owner's private collection of objets d'art and Burmese furniture. Residents of the Cape Panwa can dine in this charming colonial setting or stroll around it during the day. The hotel also has a boat that guests may use.
⬚⬚⬚⬚⬚⬚⬚⬚

❂ **Chedi Phuket**
Pansea Beach
Tel. 076 324 017/20
Fax 076 324 252
www.phuket.com/chedi/
A maze of wooden walkways link a

RESTAURANTS
- ▣ < 500 Baht
- ▣ 500 to 1 000 Baht
- ▣ > 1 000 Baht

Dialing codes: Sukhotai: 055
Udon Thani: 042

group of bungalows built on stilts. Although made of woven rushes, the bungalows offer every luxury and modern comfort. Because of its location away from Phuket's main roads, and its setting amid luxuriant tropical vegetation, the Chedi gives an unusual feeling of tranquility. The main building, which has impressive columns and spacious halls, looks over peaceful Pansea Beach.

▩▢△▨▤▥⌂➔⊞

Marina Cottage
Karon Beach
Tel. 076 330 625
Fax 076 330 516
www.marinaphuket.
com
Luxury bungalows with verandas, tucked away under tropical trees at the far end of Karon and Kata, on a promontory overlooking the sea. Its special location between the two villages gives Marina Cottage a special place among Phuket's top-class establishments.

▩▢△▨▤▥⌂➔⊞

Pearl Village
Na Yang Beach and National Park
Tel. 076 327 377/83
Fax 076 311 304
www.pearlvillage.co.
th
Reservations
in Bangkok:
Tel. 02 260 10 22/6
Fax 02 260 10 27
Situated between Na Yang park and the beach of the same name, Pearl Village offers everything one could dream of for a peaceful and relaxed stay. Very beautiful beaches. Ideal for children.

▢△▨➔➔⊡

Serene Resort
Tel. 076 330 148/50
Fax 076 330 564
Open daily
Although the hotel doesn't have direct access to the beach, it's an excellent place to stay, especially if you have children. It has three pools, including a toddlers' pool, a jacuzzi, sauna, massage parlor and very comfortable rooms. Very good value for money for Phuket.

▢△▨▤▥⌂➔⊞

▲ 252 D3

RESTAURANT

Feung Fa
107 Kuhasawan Rd
Tel. 055 610 763
Small, centrally located family restaurant on the banks of the Yom River, across from Wat Ratchatanee. Warm welcome. Specialties based on freshwater fish, such as plakrao tôt katyam, a delicious fish fried in garlic.

▩◖▢

ACCOMMODATION

Im-Aim Resort
On the rd to the airport
Tel. 055 613 075/6
Fax 055 611 505
Reservations
in Bangkok:
Tel. 02 651 02 44/5
With its peaceful, green surroundings, this recently opened hotel is perfect for anyone with a longing for clean air and tranquility. The spacious and comfortable bungalows are set around a small lake in a well-kept park that is surrounded by paddy fields. The restaurant serves excellent Thai dishes. There is an open-air bar during

the dry season.

▢△▢▥⌂➔⊡

❂ **Lotus Village**
170 Ratchatanee St
Tel. 055 621 484
www.lotus-
village.com
Tan, originally from Sukhothai, was once an Air France executive. With the help of her husband Michel, who was formerly in charge of the French cultural center in Bangkok, she has converted her childhood home into a charming hotel. Visitors will enjoy the warm welcome and appreciate the small, neat Thai teak houses built on stilts and set in a tropical garden. The ponds, full of fish and lotus flowers, are a delight to the eye, and breakfast, with real coffee and homemade mango jam, is not to be missed. A convenient shuttle service runs between the hotel and the airport, as well as to and from the historical site of Sukhothai and the various other places of interest in the vicinity.

◖△⌂➔⊡

Paylin
Jarodvithitong Rd
Tel. 055 613 310
Fax 055 613 317
About 2½ miles from the historical park of Sukhothai, a World Heritage Site, the Paylin offers comfort and facilities on a par with a medium-category hotel. Set on four levels in a small garden, the building has two restaurants and a small discotheque. Lunchtime buffet 80 Baht.

▢▨▤▥⌂➔⊡

UDON RATCHATHANI
▲ 237 G4

ACCOMMODATION

Tohsang Khongjiam Resort
Tel. 045 351 174/6
Open daily
This charming luxury hotel, on the banks of the Mekong River, invites you to relax and unwind in the peaceful atmosphere of this little-known region. Enjoy the open-air spa at sunset and/or one of the hotel's organized mountain-bike or canoe excursions. Very reasonably priced.

UDON THANI
▲ 236 F3

ACCOMMODATION

Charoensi Grand Royal
277/1 Prachak Rd
Tel. 042 343 555
Fax 042 343 550
Situated about 30 miles from the archeological site of Ban Chiang and part of an enormous complex that includes a commercial center, movie theaters and restaurants. This hotel is definitely the most luxurious and comfortable in the rapidly expanding city. The restaurants serve Thai, Japanese and European cuisine.

◖▢▨▤▥➔⊡

Napalai
572 Pracharaksa Rd
Tel. 042 347 420
Fax 042 347 447
This comfortable provincial hotel is especially popular with local businessmen. It offers good value for money, compared to the mediocre quality of the other hotels in Napalai.

▢▨▤▥➔⊡

◆ PLACES TO VISIT

Towns are listed in alphabetical order. The ▲ symbol refers to the Itineraries section; the letter and number (e.g. E 5) are grid references to the map on the front and back endpapers. Opening times and admission fees are subject to change.

AYUTTHAYA		E 5
BANG PA-IN SUMMER PALACE	*Open daily 8.30am–3.40pm. Boat trips from Ayutthaya or tour included in the excursions organized by hotels. Entrance: 50 Baht.*	▲ 246
CHANTARAKASEM PALACE AND MUSEUM Northeast of the town, beside the Pasak	*Open 9am–noon, 1–4pm. Closed Mon. and Tue. Reliable town guide available for 25 Baht. Admission fee: 10 Baht.*	▲ 245
NATIONAL MUSEUM (Chao Sam Phraya Museum) At the intersection of Rojana Road and Si Samphet Road	*Open 9am–noon, 1–4pm. Closed Mon. and Tue. Admission fee: 10 Baht.*	▲ 244
BANGKOK		D 5-E 5
DUSIT ZOO Khao Din Between Chitrlada Palace and the National Assembly Tel. 281 20 00	*Open daily 9am–6pm. Good food available at reasonable prices. Buses nos. 10, 18 and 28. Admission fee: 30 Baht (adults), 5 Baht (children).*	
GRAND PALACE AND WAT PHRA KAEO Napralan Road Tel. 222 81 81	*Open 8.30–11.30am, 1–4.30pm. Guided tours in several languages. Suitable dress required (trousers can be hired opposite the entrance). Admission fee: 200 Baht.*	▲ 144
JIM THOMPSON'S HOUSE Soi Kasem San 2 Rama I Road Tel. 215 01 22	*Open 9am–5pm. Closed Sun. Houses masterpieces from all over Thailand along with an Asiatic art collection. Admission fee: 100 Baht (profits are donated to charities for the blind).*	▲ 182
KAMTHIENG HOUSE 131 Soi Asoke Sukhumvit 21	*Open Tue.–Sat. 9am–noon and 1–5pm. Houses the Library of the Siam Society, where numerous works on the history of Thailand can be consulted. Admission fee: 25 Baht.*	▲ 183
LUMPINI STADIUM Rama IV Road Near Sathorn Tai Road Tel. 251 43 03	*Open from 6pm Tue., Fri. and Sat.*	▲ 181
NATIONAL ART GALLERY Chao Fa Road (opposite the National Theater) Tel. 282 26 40	*Open 9am–noon, 1–4pm. Closed Mon., Tue. and public hols. Exhibition of classic and contemporary Thai paintings. Admission fee:10 Baht.*	
NATIONAL MUSEUM Sur Na Phra That Road Opposite the Grand Palace, on the other side of Sanam Luang, near Thammasat University Tel. 224 13 96	*Open Wed.–Sun. 9am–noon and 1–4pm. The Buddhist chapel contains the Phra Phut Sihing, one of the most important representations of Buddha in Thailand. Guided tours in English (Tue.: Thai religion, art and culture; Wed.: Buddhism). Admission fee: 40 Baht.*	▲ 156
NATIONAL THEATER 1 Rachinee Road Next to the National Museum Tel. 221 48 85, 221 98 38 or 221 01 71	*See the daily newspapers for current program.*	▲ 163
RATCHADAMNOEN STADIUM Ratchadamnoen Nok Road Near the tourist office Tel. 281 42 05	*Open from 6pm Mon., Wed., Thur. and Sun. Thai boxing matches. Seats: 300 Baht–1,000 Baht.*	
ROYAL BARGE MUSEUM Klong Bangkok Noi Near Phra Pinklao Bridge Tel. 424 00 04	*Open 9am–5pm. The collection includes the Suphanahong, the magnificent royal barge. To reach the museum, take a water taxi (5 Baht per person). Admission fee: 30 Baht.*	▲ 174
SAOVABHA INSTITUTE (PASTEUR) AND SERPENTARIUM Corner of Henri Dunant Road and Rama IV Road Tel. 252 01 61 or 252 01 64	*Open 8.30am–4pm. Closed Sat. afternoon and public holidays. Research institute with a large collection of poisonous snakes. Interesting demonstration of venom extraction: Mon.–Fri. 10.30am and 2pm, weekends and public holidays 10.30am. Admission fee: 70 Baht.*	

SUAN PAKKARD PALACE Wang Suan Phakkat 353, Si Ayuthaya Road At the corner of Phayathai Road and Ratchaprarop Road Tel. 245 49 34	*Open 9am–4pm. Closed Sun.* *Includes the exquisite Lacquer Pavilion,* *commissioned by Princess Chumbor of Nagara* *Svarga.* *Admission fee: 100 Baht.*	▲ 182
WAT ARUN Temple of the Dawn West bank of the Chao Phraya On the same side as Thonburi	*Open daily 8am–5pm.* *Access via Arun Amarin Rd (parking is difficult),* *by boat from Tha Tien jetty on Thai Wang Road),* *or by "long-tail" boat.* *One-way boat fare: 1 Baht.* *Admission fee: 10 Baht.*	▲ 170
WAT BENCHAMABOPIT Marble Temple Corner of Si Ayutthaya Road and Rama V Road Next to Chitrlada Palace Tel. 281 25 01	*Open daily 8am–4.30pm.* *Contains local and international representations* *of the Buddha.* *Bus no. 2.* *Admission fee: 10 Baht.*	▲ 179
WAT BOWORNIVET Phra Athit Road Banglampoo Near the Democracy Monument	*Open 8.30am–5pm.* *Buses nos. 15, 49, 50 and 67.*	▲ 165
WAT MAHATHAT Temple of the Great Relic Naphrathat Road Opposite Wat Phra Kaeo, Near Thammasat University	*Open 9am–5pm.* *Houses the Mahathat Rajavidyalaya university, a* *Buddhist meditation center. At weekends an* *amulet and antique market is held nearby.* *Buses nos. 8 and 12.*	▲ 162
WAT PO Wat Phra Chetuphon: Temple of the Reclining Buddha Chetuphon Street Opposite the Grand Palace Tel. 222 09 33	*Open daily 8am–5pm.* *The largest temple in Bangkok, one of the main* *centers for traditional Thai medicine and the best* *massage school in the country.* *Buses nos. 6 and 8.* *Admission fee: 20 Baht.*	▲ 152
WAT SAKET Phu Khao Thong Temple of the Golden Mount Rajadamnoen Avenue. Near the Democracy Monument	*Open daily.* *Admission to the temple is free but visitors must* *pay 5 Baht to climb the Golden Mount to view the* *relics of the Buddha.* *Buses nos. 11 and 12.*	▲ 164
WAT SUTHAT Bamrung Muang Road Between Ti Thong Road and Ban Din So Road	*Open daily 9am–5pm.* *Major ceremonies take place here, such as* *the Royal Labor ceremony in October, led by* *the Brahmans.*	▲ 166
WAT TRAIMIT Temple of the Golden Buddha Traimit Road At the end of Yaowaraj Road, near Hualamphong Station	*Open 9am–5pm.* *Admission fee: 10 Baht.*	▲ 177

AROUND BANGKOK

CROCODILE FARM Old road to Sukhumvit, 30 miles from Bangkok Tel. 703 48 91/5 or 703 51 44/8 Fax 387 00 60	*Open daily 8am–5pm.* *Shows are held every half hour, 9–11.30am* *and 1–3pm.* *Admission fee: 300 Baht (adults), 250 Baht* *(children).*	▲ 191
DAMNOEN SADUAK **FLOATING MARKET** 65 miles southwest of Bangkok	*Open daily until 10am.* *The most colorful and the best-stocked floating* *market in Thailand.* *Take bus no. 78 from the South bus terminal* *(every 15 mins.).*	▲ 186

CHIANG MAI D 2

DOI SUTHEP Approximately 10 miles northwest of Chiang Mai	*Accessible by songteo from the north gate of* *the city (Chiang Puak gate).* *Wat Phra That Doi Suthep stands at the top of* *the mountain.*	▲ 272

INSTITUTE FOR TRIBAL RESEARCH Chiang Mai University 239 Huay Kaeo Road Tel. 22 19 33 Fax 22 24 94	Open 8.30am–4.30pm. Closed Sat. and Sun. Houses a small museum. Bus no. 1.	
NATIONAL MUSEUM Chiang Mai-Lampang Highway 11 Near Wat Ched Yod Tel. 22 13 08	Open 9am–4pm. Closed Mon. and Tue. Pottery exhibits and numerous representations of the Buddha. Bus no. 6. Admission fee: 10 Baht.	▲ 268
KAMPHAENG PHET		D 3
NATIONAL MUSEUM Opposite Wat Phra That	Open 8.30am–4pm. Closed Mon. and Tue. The classic museum houses collections showing the evolution of Thai art, as well as exhibitions of the artifacts found in the region, in particular at Ayutthaya and Sukhothai.	
OLD TOWN	Historic park housing Wat Phra Kaeo. Impressive ramparts of the old town nearby. Admission fee: 20 Baht.	▲ 250
KANCHANABURI		D 5
ERAWAN NATIONAL PARK	From Bangkok's South bus terminal take bus no. 8170 to Kanchanaburi. Departures every 50 mins. 8am–4pm. The journey takes 2 hours. See the park's stunning waterfalls, reputed to be the most beautiful in Thailand.	▲ 188
JEATH WAR MUSEUM Wisuttharangsi Road Near Wat Chaichumphon	Open daily 8.30am–4.30pm. Replicas of the barracks of the prisoners of war who built the "Death Railway" in 1942–1943 and the famous bridge over the River Kwai . Admission fee: 20 Baht.	▲ 189
LAMPHUN		D 2
NATIONAL MUSEUM Inthayongyot Road (Opposite Wat Phra That Hariphunchai)	Open 8.30am–4.30pm. Closed Mon. and Tue. Collection of regional art. Admission fee: 10 Baht.	▲ 275
LOPBURI		E 4
KING NARAI'S PALACE Sorasak Road Entrance opposite Asia Lopburi Hotel	Open 9am–noon and 1–4pm. Closed Mon. and Tue. This magnificent palace, also the headquarters of the National Museum, contains Khmer and Western artifacts. It is best to use a guide for visits to Lopburi monuments. Admission fee: 10 Baht.	▲ 248
PHAULKON'S RESIDENCE Wichayen Road Opposite Wat Sao Thong Thong	Open 9am–noon and 1–4pm. Constantin Phaulkon, a Greek, was attached to the court of King Narai. The residence was built to receive and entertain foreign dignitaries. Admission fee: 20 Baht.	▲ 249
WAT PHRA SI RATANA MAHATHAT Na Kala Road Opposite the station	Open 9am–4pm. An impressive 12th-century Khmer temple. Admission fee: 20 Baht.	▲ 249
NAKHON PATHOM		D 5
PHRA PATHOM CHEDI (57 miles west of Bangkok)	Open 9am–noon and 1–4pm. Closed Mon. and Tue. Buses from the South bus terminal every 15 mins from 6am. The highest Buddhist chedi in the world (417 feet high). Also visit the museum opposite the botanical garden (Dvaravati period). Admission fee: 25 Baht.	▲ 186
NAKHON SI THAMMARAT		D 8
NATIONAL MUSEUM Ratchadamnoen Road	Open 9am–4pm. To get to the museum, take a southbound bus or a songteo.	▲ 207

PETCHABURI		D 5-D 6
West of the town	*A tram takes you to the top of the hill where the view is magnificent (5 Baht).* *Admission fee: 20 Baht (for the National Museum of Phra Nakhon Khiri).*	▲ 194

PHITSANULOK		D 3
DR THAWI FOLKLORE MUSEUM 26/43 Wisut Kasat Road Opposite the foundry	*Open 9am–4pm.* *Personal collection of handicrafts belonging to Dr Thawi. Fascinating stop for art-lovers.*	

SONGKHLA		D 9
NATIONAL MUSEUM Between Rong Muang Road and Jana Road	*Open 9am–4pm.* *Admission fee: 10 Baht.*	▲ 208
THALE NOI BIRD SANCTUARY Follow Highway N 4107 for 78 miles (exit 126) then turn off to the village of Khu Khut	*Canoes can be rented: an ideal way to explore the nature reserve.*	▲ 208

SUKHOTHAI		D 3
OLD TOWN Si Satchanalai and Chaliang	*The "city of potters" and second city in the Sukhothai kingdom. Take an elephant ride or bicycle ride around the immense national park (100 Baht). Light, comfortable shoes are advisable for exploring the park on foot.* *Admission fee: 20 Baht (for an entry permit to each of the five areas of the park).*	▲ 256
RAMKHAMHAENG NATIONAL MUSEUM Close to the main entrance to the city	*Open 9am–4pm. Closed Mon. and Tue.* *Excellent introduction to the ruins of Sukhothai.* *Admission fee: 20 Baht.*	▲ 252

◆ BIBLIOGRAPHY

ESSENTIAL READING

◆ COOPER (Robert and Nanthapa): *Culture Shock! Thailand* (Kuperard Ltd, London, 1982)
◆ CUMMINGS (Joe): *Bangkok* (Lonely Planet, 1992)
◆ PAULUS (Conrad L): *Fodor's Thailand* (Fodor's Travel Publications, 1993)
◆ VAN BEET (Steve): *Chiang Mai* (APA Publications, Hong Kong, 1992)
◆ WINTERTON (Bradley): *Insider's Guide to Thailand* (Moorland Publishing, 1991)

NATURE

◆ BONSONG (Lekagul) and CRONIN (Edward W.): *Bird Guide of Thailand* (Ladprao Press, Bangkok, 1991)
◆ BONSONG (Lekagul) and McNEELY (Jeffrey): *Mammals of Thailand* (Ladprao Press, Bangkok, 1991)
◆ GRAY (Denis), PIPRELL (Collin) and GRAHAM (Mark): *National Parks of Thailand* (Communications Resources Thailand Ltd, Bangkok,1991)
◆ THAILAND DEVELOPMENT RESOURCE INSTITUTE: *Thailand: Natural Resources Profile* (1987)

ETHNOLOGY

◆ FREEMAN (Michael): *Hill Tribes of Thailand* (Asia Books, Bangkok, 1989)
◆ GRUNFELD (Frederic): *Wayfarers of the Thai Forest* (Time Life Books, London, 1982)
◆ JUMSAI (Sumet): *Naga: Cultural Origins in Siam*

and the West Pacific (Oxford University Press, Singapore, 1988)
◆ LEWIS (Paul and Elaine): *Peoples of the Golden Triangle* (Thames and Hudson, London, 1984)
◆ SEIDENFADEN (Erik): *The Thai People* (Bangkok: Siam Society, 1967)
◆ SKINNER (G. William): *Chinese Society in Thailand* (Cornell University Press, Ithaca, New York, 1957)

HISTORY

◆ AIRES (Cristovão): *Fernão Mendez Pinto, Subsidios Para A Sua Biografia* (Lisbon, 1904)
◆ ALBUQUERQUE (Afonso Bras de): *Comentarios do Grande Afonso de Albuquerque* (Coimbra, 1923)
◆ BARROS (Joao de): *Decadas da Asia* (Lisbon, 1777)
◆ BEAUVOIR (Ludovic, Marquis de): *Java-Siam-Canton*, Paris,1869 (reproduced in *Voyage autour du Monde*, Paris, 1872)
◆ BOCK (Carl): *Temples and Elephants*, London, 1883 (Oxford University Press, 1986)
◆ BOUCAUD (André and Louis): *Burma's Golden Triangle: On the Trail of the Opium Warlords* (Asia Books, Bangkok; Asia 2000, Hong Kong, 1989)
◆ BOWRING (Sir John): *The Kingdom and People of Siam*, London, 1857 (Oxford University Press, Singapore, 1987)
◆ CHAKRABONGSE (Prince Chula): *Lords of Life* (Alvin Redman, London, 1960)

◆ CHOISY (Abbé de): *Journal du Voyage de Siam* (London/ Paris, 1687)
◆ CLARKE (Hugh V.): *A Life for Every Sleeper* (Allen & Unwin, 1986)
◆ COEDES (George): *The Indianized States of Southeast Asia* (translated by Susan Brown Cousing), Editor Walter F. Vella, East-West Center Press, Honolulu, 1968)
◆ COLLIS (Maurice): *Siamese White* (Faber, London, 1965)
◆ CORTESÃO (Armando): *A Suma Oriental of Tomes Pires* (Hakluyt Society, London, 1944)
◆ CRAWFURD (John): *Journal of an Embassy from the Governor-General of India to the Courts of Siam and Cochin-China*, London, 1828 (Oxford University Press, 1971)
◆ EARL (George Windsor): *The Eastern Seas*, London, 1837 (Oxford University Press, Singapore, 1971)
◆ FINLAYSON (George): *The Mission to Siam and Hué: the Capital of Cochin-China, in the Years 1821–1822*, London, 1826 (Oxford University Press, Singapore, 1987)
◆ GERVAISE (Nicolas): *The Natural and Political History of the Kingdom of Siam* (London, 1688)
◆ HALL (D.G.E.): *A History of South-east Asia* (Macmillan, London, 1968)
◆ HALLETT (Holt): *A Thousand Miles on an Elephant in the Shan States*, London, 1890

(White Lotus, Bangkok, 1988)
◆ HERBERT (Thomas): *Some Years Travel Into Diverse Parts of Asia and Afrique* (London, 1638)
◆ LA LOUBÈRE (Simon de): *Du Royaume de Siam*, Paris, 1691 (Modern edition *Étude Historique et Critique du Livre de Simon de la Loubère*, Editions Recherche sur les Civilisations, Paris, 1987)
◆ LE MAY (Reginald): *An Asian Arcady* (White Lotus, Bangkok, 1986)
◆ LEONOWENS (Anna): *The English Governess at the Siamese Court*, 1870 (Oxford University Press, Singapore, 1988)
◆ McCOY (Alfred W.): *The Politics of Heroin in Southeast Asia* (Harper and Row, New York, 1972)
◆ MOUHOT (Henri): *Travels in Siam, Cambodia and Laos 1858-60*, London, 1862 (Oxford University Press, Singapore, 1989)
◆ NEALE (F.A.): *Narrative of a Residence at the Capital of the Kingdom of Siam* (London, 1852)
◆ PALLEGOIX (Mgr J-B): *Description du Royaume Thai ou Siam* (Paris, 1854)
◆ PURCHAS (Samuel): *Pilgrimage, or Relations of the World and the Religions Observed in All Ages and Places Discovered From the Creation Unto the Present* (London, 1617)
◆ SMYTH (H. Warrington): *Five Years in Siam, from 1891-96* (London, 1898)

◆ TACHARD (Father Guy): *Second Voyage du Père Tachard et des Jésuites envoyés par le Roi au Royaume de Siam* (Paris, 1869)

◆ TACHARD (Father Guy): *Voyage de Siam des Pères Jésuites envoyés par le Roi aux Indes et à la Chine* (Paris, 1686)

◆ VINCENT (Frank): *The Land of the White Elephant*, New York, 1874 (Oxford University Press, Singapore, 1987)

◆ WHITE (Joyce): *Discovery of a Lost Bronze Age: Ban Chiang* (University of Pennsylvania and Smithsonian Institution, 1982)

◆ WYATT (David K.): *Thailand: A Short History* (Yale University Press, New Haven, and London, 1982)

ART

◆ APINAN (Poshyananda): *Modern Art in Thailand* (Oxford University Press, 1992)

◆ AUBOYER (Jeannine), BEURDELEY (Michel), BOISSELIER (Jean), ROUSSET (Huguette) and MASSONAUD (Chantal): *Oriental Art, A Handbook of Styles and Forms* (Faber, London, 1979)

◆ BOISSELIER (Jean): *The Heritage of Thai Sculpture* (New York, 1975)

◆ BOISSELIER (Jean): *La Peinture en Thailande* (Office du Livre, Fribourg, 1976)

◆ CHEESEMAN (Patricia) and SONGSAK (Prangwat-thanakun): *Lanna Textiles* (Suriwong's Book Centre, Chiang Mai, 1987)

◆ HOSKIN (John): *Ten Contemporary Thai Artists* (Graphis, Bangkok, 1984)

◆ LE MAY (Reginald): *A Concise History of Buddhist Art in Siam* (Tokyo, 1963)

◆ LYONS (Elizabeth): *Thai Traditional Painting* (Bangkok, 1973)

◆ LYONS (Elizabeth): *The Tosachat in Thai Painting* (Bangkok, 1971)

◆ PAWLIN (Alfred): *Dhamma Vision* (Visual Dhamma, Bangkok, 1984)

◆ PIRIYA (Krairiksh): *Art Styles in Thailand* (Bangkok, 1977)

◆ PIRIYA (Krairiksh): *Art in Peninsular Thailand Prior to the 14th Century* (Fine Arts Department, Bangkok, 1980)

◆ PIRIYA (Krairiksh): *The Sacred Image: Sculptures from Thailand* (Museum of Oriental Art, Cologne, 1979)

◆ PIRIYA (Krairiksh): *Sculptures from Thailand* (Hong Kong, 1982)

◆ STRATTON (Carol) and SCOTT (Miriam McNair): *The Art of Sukhothai* (Oxford University Press, Kuala Lumpur, 1981)

◆ SUBHADRADIS (Diskul M.C.): *Art in Thailand: A Brief History* (D.K. Books, Bangkok, 1976)

◆ SUBHADRADIS (Diskul M.C.): *The Art of Srivijaya* (Oxford University Press, Kuala Lumpur, 1980)

◆ SUBHADRADIS (Diskul M.C.): *Sukhothai Art* (D.K. Books, Bangkok, 1978)

◆ VAN BEEK (Steve) and TETTONI (Luca Invernizzi): *The Arts of Thailand* (Thames and Hudson, London, 1991)

◆ WARREN (William): *The House on the Klong* (Weatherhill, Tokyo, 1968)

◆ WENK (Klaus): *The Art of Mother of Pearl in Thailand* (Zurich, 1980)

◆ WIYADA (Thongmitr): *Khrua In Khong's Westernised School of Thai Painting* (Thai Cultural Data Centre, Bangkok, 1979)

◆ WRAY (Joe and Elizabeth), ROSEN-FELD (Clare) and BAILEY (Dorothy): *Ten Lives of the Buddha; Siamese Temple Paintings and Jataka Tales* (Weatherhill, Tokyo, 1974)

RELIGION

◆ BUNNAG (Jane): *Buddhist Monk, Buddhist Layman* (Cambridge University Press, Cambridge, 1973)

◆ NIVAT (Prince Dhani): *A History of Buddhism in Siam* (Bangkok Siam Society, 1965)

LITERATURE (GENERAL)

◆ BURUMA (Ian): *God's Dust* (Vintage, London, 1989)

◆ CONRAD (Joseph): *The Shadow-Line* (Penguin Classics, London, 1986)

◆ COOPER (Robert and Nanthapa): *Culture Shock: Thailand* (Times Books, Singapore, 1982)

◆ HO (Minfong): *Rice Without Rain* (Times Books International, 1986)

◆ HOLLINGER (Carol): *Mai pen rai Means Never Mind* (Houghton Mifflin, Boston)

◆ IYER (Pico): *Video Night in Kathmandu* (Vintage Books, New York, 1988)

◆ LULOFS (Madelon H.): *Rubber*, London, 1933

(Oxford University Press, Singapore, 1987)

◆ MAUGHAM (Somerset): *The Gentleman in the Parlour*, London, 1930 (Penguin, London)

◆ MISHIMA (Yukio): *The Temple of Dawn* (Alfred Knopf, New York, 1973)

◆ PHU (Sunthorn): *Nirat Phra Prathom* (translated by Montri Umarijari, The Amarin Press, Bangkok, 1986)

◆ REYNOLDS (Jack): *A Woman of Bangkok*, London, 1956, (D.K. Books, Bangkok, 1985)

◆ SAUL (John Ralston): *The Paradise Eater* (Grafton Books, London, 1989)

◆ SEGALLER (Dennis): *Thai Ways* (Post Publishing, Bangkok, 1985)

◆ SHEARER (Alistair): *The Lotus Kingdom* (John Murray, London, 1989)

◆ THEROUX (Paul): *The Great Railway Bazaar* (Penguin Books, London, 1977)

◆ WARREN (William): *The Legendary American* (Houghton Mifflin, Boston, 1970)

◆ GLOSSARY

A

ao: bay.
Apsara: female divinity.
Avalokitesvara: compassionate *bodhisattva* in Mahayana Buddhism.

B

bai-sri: traditional Thai flower arrangement.
ban: village.
baray: Khmer artificial lake surrounded by earth levees and fed by diverted river water. Their prime function was originally to irrigate ricefields, but they also symbolized the primordial ocean that, in Buddhist cosmology, surrounds the earth.
bodhisattvas: enlightened human or celestial beings who voluntarily delayed *Nirvana* to devote themselves to the salvation of all humans on earth.
Bodhi tree: the tree under which the Buddha reached the state of enlightenment.
bot (or *ubosot*): main building in a temple complex where novice monks are ordained.
Brahma: The creator god and, with Siva and Vishnu, one of the three main Hindu deities. Depicted with four heads, each facing one of the four directions of the universe.
Brahmanism: original form of Hinduism.
bun bang fai: north-eastern village festival at which homemade skyrockets are fired into the air.

C

chakhay: guitar-like instrument usually played in a large orchestra.
chakra: in Hinduism, a solar wheel and weapon given by Vishnu. To Buddhists it symbolizes the completeness of the law (*dharma chakra*).
Chakri: name of the present Thai dynasty, founded in 1737 by Rama I. *Chakri* is also

an honorific title that can be conferred on a high-ranking civilian or a religious or military leader. It means "he who carries the *chakra* or Wheel of the Law".
chedi (or *stupa*): monument where relics of the Buddha and ashes of prominent people are enshrined.
ching lek (or *ching yai*): set of small cymbals.
chula: star-shaped male kite.

D

dharma: Buddhist teaching or law.
Dharmacakra: the Wheel of Law.

E

Erawan: three-headed elephant, mythical mount of Brahma.

F

Farang: term derived from *farangse*, a phonetic translation of *français* (French), the first Europeans received by the Siamese court. By extension, *farang* today refers to any Westerner.
floating house: Thai shophouse on a river.

G

Gajasingha: mythical beast with the head of an elephant and the body of a lion.
Ganesha: Siva and Pavarti's son; elephant god of wisdom. In Thailand, considered the protector of artists and students.
Garuda: half human half bird, the legendary steed of the Hindu god Vishnu; appears as royal insignia among the wall decorations in the Grand Palace compound.
Guanyin: goddess of mercy, one of the main Mahayana bodhisattvas.

H

hat: beach.
hin: stone.
Hinayana (*Lesser Vehicle*): a form of

Buddhism that originated in Sri Lanka and incorporates elements of Hinduism and local beliefs. Predominates in Thailand, Burma, Laos and Cambodia.
ho trai: library built in the middle of a pond or on a raised platform to keep away termites.
hong: mythological swan-like creature.
hong yao: long-tailed boat, a common form of river transport along the klongs of Thonburi.
howdah: palanquin mounted on an elephant saddle.
huai: waterfall.
hun: small carved marionettes for enacting classical tales.
hun krabok: limbless puppets with detailed wooden heads and costumes that conceal a central rod.
hun lek: small marionettes similar to hun krabok.

J

jad paan (or *poom*): flower arrangement in the shape of a bowl.
Jataka: collection of stories dealing with Buddha's previous lives.
jongkrabane: women's garment consisting of a length of cloth wrapped round the waist then pulled through the legs and secured at the back.

K

Kadwua: local village cattle market near Chiang Mai.
kalae: v-shaped protrusion (like a pair of buffalo horns) at the end of a rooftop, common on northern Thai houses.
kao: mountain.
khanom: sweet.
khanom krok: popular delicacy made from a mixture of thick coconut milk, rice flour, eggs and sugar, and cooked in a special clay mold.
khantoke: traditional dinner where guests and hosts sit on the floor round a low table and help themselves to a

variety of dishes, usually eaten with glutinous rice.
khao niaow: glutinous rice.
khoi: book, with pages folded concertina-fashion, containing illustrations on subjects such as religion, anatomy and warfare. Old Thai manuscripts were written on khoi paper, made from the bark of local trees.
khon: traditional masked dance drama performed at the royal court.
khong wong lek and **khong wong yai:** circular series of small or large gongs suspended on a rattan frame.
kinnon and **kinnari:** mythological male and female bird-human creatures.
klawng yao: huge drum played at festivals.
klong: canal.
klong tad thapon: double-ended drum.
koh: island.
krabung: rice basket.
krathong: colorful miniature boat of paper, flowers and candles, with either a banana-leaf or styrofoam as its base; an array of krathong can be seen on waterways during the Loy Krathong festival.
Krung Thep: (City of Angels): abbreviated version of the name given to Bangkok by Rama I in the 18th century; for full name see page 141.
ku: gilded brick structure housing the image of the Buddha inside a temple.

L

laem: cape.
lakhon: theatrical performance, derivation of the khon performed in public.
lamyai: lychee-like fruit grown in northern Thailand, mainly in Lamphun
likay: popular satirical pantomime.
lingam: sacred standing stone in the form of a phallus symbolizing the Hindu god Siva.
look choop: ornamental fruit

GLOSSARY ◆

mixture made from mung bean paste and sugar.
Loy Krathong: probably the loveliest of Thai festivals, held in late October/early November in honor of the water spirits, with the launch of several small *krathong*.

M

mah (or *timah*): water basket.
Mahayana (*Greater Vehicle*): northern Buddhism practiced in China, Korea and Japan, stressing the importance of mercy.
Maitrey: a future Buddha in Mahayana Buddhism.
malai: garland.
mandala: meditation pattern in the form of a labyrinth representing cosmic order, and tracing the various stages in the Buddha's life. The best-known mandala is the Borobadur temple in Java.
mandapa: cube-like roofless structure that houses an object of worship, such as an image of the Buddha or a sacred footprint.
Manora a lakhon: romantic drama of Javanese origin.
mondop: cube-like building housing an object of worship, such as an image of the Buddha.
mudmee: handwoven silk fabric popular among Thai women.
Mara: in Buddhism an evil spirit that represents earthly temptation.
menam: river.
mor hom: cotton shirt worn by Thai farmers
mudra: gesture of the hand in Buddhist iconography.

N

naga: serpent.
nak: novice about to enter monkhood.
nakhon: town.
nam pla: condiment, sauce made from fermented fish.
nandi: Siva's sacred bull.
nang: shadow play. Nang yai and nang talung are variations of nang.

ngao: roof gable of Khmer origin.
Nirvana: absolute truth, "extinction of passion", the end of the cycle of rebirth and, therefore, liberation from suffering.

P

pannung: men's garment, counterpart of the jongkrabane
Paranirvana: "complete extinction", as when the Buddha was about to attain Nirvana
pasin: women's sarong, characteristic of northern Thailand
pha lai-yang: silk or cotton fabric with Thai motifs.
phakoma: multi-purpose cotton piece used as a sarong, headband or wash cloth.
phi: guardian spirit, which must be placated through offerings.
phi pob: legendary spirits that eat the entrails of their victims.
phipat: small musical ensemble.
Phra: honorific title meaning "sacred".
phrachedi: old term for a *chedi*.
pinai: oboe-like musical instrument that sounds like a bagpipe.
pla duk: catfish.
prang: Thai temple tower; older form of religious monument adapted from Hindu architecture.
prasat: Khmer temple tower and, by extension, temple at Khmer sites. The term *prasat hin*, "stone castle" is also frequently used.
prik: Thai for chilli.
pukpao: diamond-shaped "female" kite.

R

Ramakien: Thai version of the Indian epic *Ramayana*.
ranad: Thai musical instrument similar to a xylophone.
Rattanakosin: 18th-century name of Bangkok (for full name see page 141)
rishi: generic term for prophets and poets to whom the Vedic hymns were

first revealed.
rua chai: gunboats manned by 60 oarsmen, dating from the Ayutthaya period.
rua duang and **rua saeng:** small attendant boats in a royal barge procession of the 19th century.

S

sabai: long piece of cloth about 1 foot wide, usually worn diagonally above the waist and draped over the shoulder.
sai: trap for small fish and prawns.
sala: open pavilion mainly for rest and relaxation.
sala kanprien: meeting hall.
sangha: Buddhist priesthood.
sanuk: fun, leisure pursuit.
sarb: 3-foot-long fish trap characteristic of northeastern Thailand.
sarong: term of Indonesian origin meaning a fabric used as clothing, wrapped around the body.
saw sam sai: fiddle consisting of a coconut shell, an ivory neck and three silk strings.
sing: guardian lion (statue).
soi: lane.
Songkran: two-day celebration in mid-April of the solar New Year, a blend of ritual and riotous festival with parades, beauty contests and buckets of water thrown in fun at passers-by.
spirit house: miniature house where the *phi* is believed to dwell; usually supported on a pole outside the residence.
sutra: sacred texts containing sermons attributed to the Buddha.

T

taiji (or *tai chi*): Oriental form of martial art, mainly for relaxation and light exercise.
takraw: hardcourt game in which a light rattan ball is volleyed between two teams of three players on each side of a net.

talat: market.
Tamnak Daeng (*Red House*): a royal house with decorative features built by Rama II, now in the compound of the National Museum in Bangkok.
tantima: mythological bird.
Thai boxing: sport in which any part of the body other than the head can be used against the opponent in the ring; the foot is the most effective offensive weapon in this sport.
thale: sea.
tham: cave.
Theravada: southern Buddhism, the only surviving school of the Hinayana (Lesser Vehicle) system, which originated in Sri Lanka.
Thod kathin: ceremony in which groups of Buddhist devotees visit monasteries and offer alms to resident monks.
thong sampao: the 'hull of a ship'; a concave curved base feature of the *viharn* or *bot* of the Ayutthaya period.
Tonsure Ceremony: a complex ritual held in the Grand Palace to mark the coming-of-age of children in the Inner Palace.
tuk-tuk: three-wheeled and open-ended taxis that ply city streets.

V

Vedas: the four sacred books of Hinduism, revealed by Brahma.
viharn (or *vihara*): assembly hall for sermons, originally a meditation hall.

W

wai: traditional Thai greeting.
wang luang lakon: festival in Lampang celebrating the 7th-century reign of Queen Chamadevi; colorful parade of participants in period costumes.
wat: temple.
wiang: citadel.

Y

yaksa: demon.

LIST OF ILLUSTRATIONS ◆

◆ LIST OF ILLUSTRATIONS

LIST OF ILLUSTRATIONS ◆

We have not been able to trace the heirs or publishers of certain documents. An account is being held open for them at our offices.

◆ NOTES

◆ INDEX

◆ INDEX

◆ INDEX